Gullah Days

GULLAH DAYS

Hilton Head Islanders before the Bridge, 1861–1956

THOMAS C. BARNWELL, JR. | EMORY SHAW CAMPBELL | CAROLYN GRANT

with CHRISTENA BLEDSOE

Printed in South Korea

Cover design by Hannah Lee
Interior design by April Leidig

Blair is an imprint of Carolina Wren Press.

*The mission of Blair / Carolina Wren Press is to seek out, nurture,
and promote literary work by new and underrepresented writers.*

We gratefully acknowledge the ongoing support of general operations by the Durham Arts Council's Annual Arts Fund and
the N.C. Arts Council, a division of the Department of Natural
& Cultural Resources, and from Furthermore: a program of the
J. M. Kaplan Fund.

ISBN: 978-1-94946-707-9

Library of Congress Control Number: 2 019941193

FRONTIS: Young women with horse and wagon, boy looks on,
Hilton Head, SC, 1904. *American Museum of Natural History,
Library: Julian Dimock Collection*

ABOUT THE COVER PHOTO

Hilton Head Island Gullah Islanders Perry and Rosa Williams
Enjoying the Summer Breeze, Circa 1960

Photo courtesy of their grandchildren

As they sat on their porch one summer afternoon in the 1960s, a
curious passerby caught a glimpse of Perry and Rosa Williams,
Gullah residents of Hilton Head Island and the maternal grandfather and grandmother of book author Emory Campbell. With
their permission, the passerby took a picture of the Williamses
sitting on the porch of their home off of Bryant Road in Spanish
Wells, one of the many Gullah communities on the island. As
homes at that time didn't have air-conditioning, the Williamses
were relaxing on their porch to catch the fresh air circulated by
the summer breeze. A few years earlier in 1956, the bridge had
opened connecting Hilton Head Island to the mainland. Many
people had arrived on the island. They took pictures, explored
the island for artifacts, and offered to buy marsh tacky horses
and wares from Gullah islanders who would be willing to sell
them. Home on vacation after having migrated north, Emory
stopped by to visit his grandparents. They showed him the
picture and told him a "buckra" (a term Gullah people used to
describe Caucasian persons) woman had stopped by their home
and took the picture of them. In the Gullah community it was
rare for people to have their pictures taken, and if they did, they
wanted to be well dressed. Emory was surprised his grandparents allowed a stranger to take their picture, especially since
they didn't know what she was going to do with the picture. He
expressed his dismay. Despite that, the picture is treasured by
Emory and his family as it is the only photo they have of their
grandparents sitting together.

With great pride and love, we dedicate this book to our families and the Gullah families of Hilton Head Island, South Carolina. Thank you for your love, support, and patience.

Thomas C. Barnwell, Jr.

Emory Shaw Campbell

Carolyn Grant

Emory Campbell's paternal grandparents, Perry and Rosa Williams. Picture taken on the veranda of their home in the Spanish Wells neighborhood, Hilton Head Island, in the 1960s. Perry was a WWI veteran, retired U.S. Corps of Engineers dredge hand, and fish net knitter; Rosa was an expert fisher and homemaker. *Collection of Emory S. Campbell*

Contents

PART I. GULLAH HISTORY BEFORE THE BRIDGE

Drayton Plantation house, which was used as Union headquarters during the Civil War. Photo by Henry Moore, 1862. *Library of Congress*

(*Overleaf*) Planting watermelons, Hilton Head, 1904. *American Museum of Natural History, Library: Julian Dimock Collection*

Chapter One

FREEDOM'S DOOR

NO CLOUDS DARKENED THE SKY, no winds whipped the sea, yet thunder shook Hilton Head Island on November 7, 1861. Or so it seemed.

On nearby Lady's Island, a young boy listened in wonder to what sounded like rolling thunder on a calm day.

"Son, dat ain't no t'under," his mother told him in her lilting African speech, "dat yankee come to gib you Freedom."[1]

The "Day of the Big Gun Shoot" had begun.

The roar of heavy guns resounded throughout the low-lying Sea Islands of South Carolina, carrying as far south as Fernandina, Florida, seventy miles away. To the young boy and thousands of other enslaved people within earshot, the gun roar heralded freedom. It was as if Moses had leapt straight from the pages of the Bible to part the Red Sea again — this time to lead the children of Africa out of bondage.

Seven months earlier, in April, Confederate batteries fired on Fort Sumter in the Charleston Harbor, triggering the Civil War. Within three days, President Abraham Lincoln ordered an extensive blockade of the southern coast in order to cut off Confederate commerce and thus much of the Confederacy's wealth.

In July, planters on Hilton Head and neighboring islands sent their slaves to build two earthwork forts to guard the entrance to Port Royal Sound: Fort Walker on Hilton Head and Fort Beauregard at Bay Point on Phillips Island, located directly across from Hilton Head. As enslaved people built steep earth banks, cut palmetto logs for ramparts, erected powder magazines, and constructed gun emplacements, excitement seized them. Anticipating the end of slavery and slave rations, they made up a rhythmic work song:

No more peck of corn for me, no mo', no mo'
No more pint of salt, no mo', no mo'
No more drivers lash, no mo', no mo'
No more mistress call, no mo', no mo'.[2]

With each drive of an axe into a palmetto log or shove of a log into the earthwork embankment, the men sang in unison: "*no mo*'" (no more).

It was an upbeat song. They were hopeful.

Masters and slaves on Hilton Head and other islands had been on constant alert ever since those hot summer days. Masters feared the Union might invade. Slaves *knew* if the Union soldiers came, they would come to free them.

The day before the battle, headlines in the *New York Times* announced that South Carolina's Port Royal Sound appeared to be the likely site of a major battle.

For three weeks Northern readers had followed avidly news reports of a great Union fleet sailing south to wage war at an undisclosed location. When the colossal joint navy–army expedition reached, and passed, Charleston—"the birthplace of secession," the *Times* intoned—Port Royal Sound, with its splendid harbor, became the obvious destination.

After seizing Port Royal Sound, the Union intended, in a one-two punch, to set up a blockading station from which navy ships could patrol the East Atlantic and land an army to press the war inland. Hilton Head, at the mouth of the Sound, offered both the finest deep-water harbor on the lower southeastern coast and a valuable inland passage along South Carolina's Sea Islands. Strategically located between Savannah and Charleston, Hilton Head made an ideal choice.

"Our troops will find themselves lodged in the richest district in the State—yielding some fifty million pounds of rice annually, and thirteen thousand bales of the finest quality of cotton, the famous long-staple sea island [*sic*] cotton, the very kind Europe most wants," the *Times* correspondent effused.

"The Beaufort District, at the head of Port Royal harbor, contains 38,805 inhabitants, of whom 32,279 [81 percent] are slaves. . . . It is at this spot that the shaded maps of [N]egro distribution show the nightliest shade. We shall thus literally carry the war into Africa!"[3]

His words rang with prophecy.

Enslaved people living on the Sea Islands of South Carolina, and along the coasts of Georgia and the northern part of Florida, had kept more of their African ways

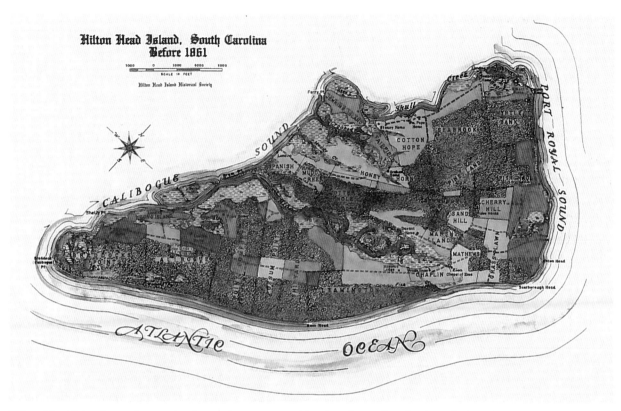

Hilton Head Island map from 1861, shows plantations and landmarks on the island just before the Union forces took over the island. *Courtesy of the Hilton Head Heritage Library*

than others on the North American continent. Sheer isolation enabled African traditions and ways to thrive.

Each island was its own world, surrounded by salt water, with no way to cross the waters except by boat. The overwhelmingly black population included recent African arrivals and men, women, and children just one or two generations removed from Africa. Africa lived in their memories.

Then too, their white owners often were absent. The harsh, subtropical climate and the threat of malaria and yellow fever, both mosquito-borne diseases that came on slave ships from Africa, drove white planters away in the dangerous warm-weather months.

The planters primarily lived on the islands during the crucial planting and harvest seasons and at other times as they chose. They kept island homes, but they kept finer homes elsewhere, on the mainland, or in the nearby town of Beaufort, or in Savannah and Charleston. Of thirteen major planters on Hilton Head, only one planter and three white overseers listed the island as their main residence.[4]

With the planters gone, Hilton Head, as did many other islands, resembled a West African homeland.

"Gola Negroes," some called black people of the Sea Islands. The term likely grew from the large number of enslaved Angolans imported to the Sea Islands or from the Gola tribe of West Africa, and became the forerunner of the word "Gullah."

But wave after wave of the slave trade brought far more than Angolans. It brought Africans from such locations as Senegal, Sierra Leona, Liberia, Ivory Coast, Ghana, Guinea, Togo, Benin (Dahomey), Nigeria, Cameroon, Niger, Congo, and Zaire.

Faced with the need to communicate with each other and with white planters and overseers, the Africans and their descendants cobbled together a common tongue. The quick, abrupt Gullah way of talking was based on English, but punctuated with African words, grammar, structure, and flair.

They also wove together differing spiritual beliefs, stories, and music; shared a fondness for foods they had known in Africa such as rice, yams, okra, cowpeas, watermelon, and "benne seed," or sesame; and based their way of life around a high regard for kinship bonds and respect for their elders.

The resulting Gullah culture owed much to West and Central Africa yet was unlike any single culture on the African continent.

Now, the North was about to come face-to-face with African traditions, customs, and language patterns that nothing in their experience had prepared them to understand.

At 8:00 in the morning, sailors ran the signal up the *Wabash*, the flagship of the Union fleet, to weigh anchor.

Surveying the long line of Union frigates, sloops of war, and gunboats from a bluff on Hilton Head, Confederate General Thomas F. Drayton, astride his horse, observed, "not a ripple upon the broad expanse of water to disturb the accuracy of fire from the broad decks of that magnificent armada."[5]

Drayton, a Hilton Head planter and West Point graduate charged with defending the Sea Islands, likely saw at once that the Union held the winning cards this day. The Confederacy had fewer soldiers, heavy guns, ammunition, and boats. He whirled away and went to his post.

Shortly after 9:00 a.m., Fort Walker on Hilton Head fired the first shot.[6]

Fort Beauregard fired next; then the Union opened up, firing broadside after broadside as its ships passed in an ellipse between Fort Walker and Fort Beauregard. The air grew gray with smoke and at the peak of battle, a *Harper's Weekly* correspondent counted no less than forty shells bursting at one time.

By 12:30, Confederate ammunition ran low.

Fort Beauregard fired its last shot by 1:00 p.m. Fort Walker fell silent at 2:00 p.m. The Union fired one last shot at Fort Walker, with no response. The *Wabash* signaled the Union fleet to cease fire.

At 2:45 p.m., a Union officer went ashore in a longboat under a flag of truce. Disappearing into the wreckage of the fort, he emerged atop a nearby plantation and drew the Union flag out of his pocket.

At 3:00, the Stars and Stripes flew once more over South Carolina soil.[7]

More than one hundred surf boats prepared to ferry ashore the expeditionary force of 12,653 soldiers and marines onto Hilton Head. With them came ambulances, wagons, horses, lumber tents, and other goods needed to build a small city for the duration of the war.

One hour later, at 4:00 p.m., a Union officer met the body-servant of General Drayton. The servant informed the officer that boats on Skull Creek, on the western side of the island, were ferrying Confederate troops off the island. The officer decided his men could not catch up in time to prevent the rebels from escaping. The Union would not pursue.

Fort Walker sat on the 803-acre plantation of Coggins Point, on the northeastern end of the island. At daybreak this day, General Drayton had used Coggins Point as his headquarters, along with Fish Haul Plantation, a short walking distance away.

Both plantations lay along the sound and were owned by the Pope family, the largest landowners on the island with five plantations on Hilton Head to the family's name. Drayton's late wife was a Pope; Fish Haul was part of her estate. He had managed Fish Haul on behalf of their minor children. With his ties to the Popes, Drayton had ready access to the two plantations—a fact that no longer concerned the Union command. Its generals were about to turn both plantations into Union headquarters.

To their surprise, they faced no opposition.

The late-day sun shone on nearby fields. Cotton bolls gleamed like the "white gold" cotton was said to be. The harvest season was under way, but where were the planters? Cotton was the basis of the planters' wealth. They, their families, and overseers always supervised the highly important cotton harvest.

Union generals were startled to find not a single white planter or overseer on the island. When the Union had invaded elsewhere, white property owners had stayed put.

Drayton Plantation house, which was used as Union headquarters during the Civil War. Photo by Henry Moore, 1862. *Library of Congress*

Only enslaved people remained on Hilton Head.

A Saint Helena rector had told his congregation to start packing. A Confederate general had advised white citizens to evacuate Beaufort. Hilton Head landowners had joined Beaufort and Saint Helena planters who fled en masse.

At Coggins Point, total silence reigned. The plantation was "resting," its soil overworked. Farm tools and slaves had been moved two years before to a plantation on Lady's Island.[8] The deserted slave cabins, filled with Confederate army commissary stores, now fell to the Union.[9]

Union soldiers began pitching tents where Confederate soldiers had awakened nine hours before.

Afternoon faded to dusk.

Blue-coated soldiers used bayonets to dig sweet potatoes from the fields to roast over campfires. Others prepared to stand evening sentry along the sound in case enemy fire resumed during the night. Still others prepared to bury the dead: eight Union soldiers who died this day and the bodies of fifteen Confederate soldiers the Union had found, *Harper's Weekly* would report. In later reports, the Confederate death toll would reach at least fifty-nine.[10] The rattling roll of the drum and measured notes of the trumpet sounded forth, paying homage to the dead of both armies.

As the somber tones carried across the land, heads poked out to listen. Black men and women stepped forth —some excited, some wary, all curious—to see what manner of men "Mr. Linkum" had sent to free them.

With the bright-eyed curiosity of youth, sixteen-year-old James likely joined those emerging from the slave quarters at Fish Haul.

Born here on an August day, James had the dark skin, black hair, and brown eyes typical of Gullah people. At five feet three inches, he was on the short side but was still growing. The average height of Gullah men was five feet seven inches, with the tallest coming from Senegambia and Gambia. Angolans usually were the shortest, averaging five feet five.[11]

James lived with his father, Simon; his sister, Julia; and his brothers, George and Morris, in one of Fish Haul's twelve slave cabins, set six to a row, with a wide avenue running between them.

Whites usually identified slaves by their owner's last name—for instance, a "Drayton slave." Since Thomas Drayton had long managed Fish Haul, many of those enslaved at Fish Haul believed him to be their legal owner.

James, however, remembered the late Mary B. Pope, Drayton's mother-in-law. He knew that she had been his owner, rather than Drayton. Perhaps it was a point of pride to him that he was not born a slave of General Drayton. He later would say—although his words, and those of other former slaves on the island, were recorded by whites in a manner that caught their meaning but did not reflect their Gullah speech—"I was a slave of Mary B. Pope, who lived when I was born . . . my father's master was mine."

His actual way of talking would have sounded more like, "I bina Mary Pope slave. She bina lib wen I bin bone [born]."

Adam, another young man at Fish Haul, thought of himself as a Jenkins. Even in slavery, some Sea Island blacks used, and often passed down within their families, "titles" they considered to be their last name.[12] The titles did not bestow legal right but gave enslaved blacks a sense of lineage. Often other blacks, and possibly some whites, acknowledged a slave's title. Frequently, the title was the surname of an earlier owner.

Photo of people enslaved at Drayton Plantation and soldier in 1862. *Library of Congress*

"My father Charles was bought from a man named Jenkins and that was how he came by the name. My mother got her name from my father. I think she was owned by Jenkins too. I never knew myself by any name other than Jenkins."[13]

While Adam did not say so, using a different last name from that of his current master may have helped him endure slavery a little better.

Venus, the mother of Adam, lived at Fish Haul too, along with her two daughters, Margaret and Hagar, as well as Adam's twin brother Jacob.[14]

The names of Fish Haul bondsmen and -women roll

on and on: July, Harriett, Daniel, Jane, Sophy, Sally Ann, Kate, Joshua, "Old" Hagar (as distinguished from Venus's daughter, "Young" Hagar), Judith, Tom, Jack, Paul, Caesar, Tenah, Martha, Sylla, Clara, Primus, Polydoice, "Mama," Paul, George, Primus, two men called Minus. There was a four-year-old girl, Nancy, who would grow up to become an important midwife on Hilton Head, and Mary Ann, a young woman on whom James may have already had his eye.

When the sun rose this day, fifty-two enslaved people were at Fish Haul.[15]

Night fell, and as it did, the pace of the bondsmen and -women pouring forth from nearby plantations quick-ened like the beat of long-suppressed African drums. Fearing the power of drums to signal revolt, South Carolina planters had forbidden them since the mid-1700s.

As black men in worn, homespun, coarse cloth known as "Negro cloth" and black women in high-necked bodices, long, full skirts, and African-style headdresses[16] peeked at the soldiers, a new beat reverberated in the air, if not on the drum — Freedom.

"Many dark objects were visible, and the cry is still they come," the correspondent for *Harper's Weekly* declared. "Their delight is unbounded at the prospect of future freedom."[17]

View of Skull Creek from Fort Walker. *Photo by Will Warasila*

Chapter Two

THE BOOT-SHAPED ISLAND

MAPMAKERS AGREED that Hilton Head Island resembled the shape of a boot. The type of boot they had in mind was low-cut, and the island could just as readily be compared to a work shoe.

The heel of the boot faces north, along the Port Royal Sound. Skull Creek, on the western side of Hilton Head, then runs from the boot's ankle to the top of the tongue.

As the boot begins its downward slope, slightly below the spot where shoelaces begin to be tied, a small island known as Jenkins Island lies so close to Hilton Head that the two islands are almost one. Then Calibogue Sound, a deep-water channel separating Hilton Head from Daufuskie Island, kicks in and rushes along a downward sloop until reaching the toe of the boot.

The tip of the toe points south and marks the merger of Calibogue Sound and the Atlantic Ocean. The sole of the boot faces the huge Atlantic Ocean. Miles of white-sand beaches line the eastern length of the island.

In addition to being surrounded by water, interior creeks abound on Hilton Head. Among these are Fish Haul Creek, Crooked Creek, and Muddy Creek, but Broad Creek is by far the largest body of water. Broad Creek cuts off of Calibogue Sound and snakes inland two-thirds of the way across the island to the eastern shore.

Captain William Hilton sailed into Port Royal Sound in 1663 on behalf of British planters in Barbados seeking land for new plantations in the Carolinas.

Hilton sailed on to what would become Charles Towne, but not before he named a high bluff for himself—the headland marking a safe entrance to Port Royal Sound from the Atlantic Ocean. By naming the island Hilton Head, he ensured lasting fame. Thereafter, the island was called Hilton Head.[1]

He was not the first explorer to be smitten by the island's deep-water harbor. French explorer Jean Ribault named the Port Royal Sound "Port Royale" in 1562. Spanish explorers, up from Saint Augustine, Florida, staked a claim to Hilton Head in 1520.

The British were not the first to spot the island, but they persisted longer. The first English settler on the island arrived in 1622, and the first English planter acquired seven hundred acres on Hilton Head in 1717.[2]

Soon, more planters arrived, and slavery became an institution.

As of this November day in 1861, the Union possessed the island. Much would change.

General Drayton had mobilized all the boats and barges on the island to rush the Confederate infantry, and survivors of the carnage inside the Fort Walker garrison, off the island.[3]

Some three-to-five-hundred Confederate soldiers waited on the western side of the island for boats to get them off the island, "a terrible panic" on them to get away. They feared Union attack at any moment, either by

The carte de visite of Brigadier General Thomas Fenwick Drayton (1808–1891), C.S.A. *Mt. Sterling Library Association Photographic Collection*

sea or land. In their haste, rebel troops scattered knapsacks, haversacks, canteens, and cartridge-boxes along the road. A few shed their muskets and bayonets.[4] Roughly a thousand Confederate soldiers who had been stationed across the sound were boated away from Bay Point.

Twenty-four plantations ringed the island and lined the interior. The plantations stood empty, but the plantation houses bespoke their past, and enslaved men and women on the plantations had their own stories to tell.

Myrtle Bank Plantation stood near the beach running along Port Royal Sound and Skull Creek, on the northwestern end of the island. The plantation's name came from the waxy-leaved myrtles lining its banks. But the thousand-acre plantation's fame grew from its starring role in South Carolina's love affair with Sea Island cotton.

Here, seventy-one years earlier, William Elliott II grew South Carolina's first commercial crop of Sea Island cotton, fueling a frenzy to plant the fine, long-stapled variety of cotton along the South Carolina coast. The frenzy spurred the state to reopen legal slave trade with Africa. "Fresh" Africans, sold into slavery and stripped of their liberty, were shipped to the Sea Islands to grow cotton for planters who sought riches through their forced labor.

The Elliott family became among the wealthiest of the Sea Island planters with a residence on the main street in the town of Beaufort, three plantations on Port Royal Island, one on Edisto Island, and others elsewhere, in addition to Myrtle Bank.

The luxurious Sea Island cotton built riches for other planters as well while their slaves had to depend on the basic humanity of their owners to provide two sets of clothes a year plus rations of corn and salt, and not to sell away their husbands, wives, or children.

Myrtle Bank was owned now by William Elliott III, former state senator, writer, sportsman, and holder of an MA from Cambridge and an honorary degree from Harvard.[5] His son, Thomas, had served as an aid to General Drayton.

The deserted Elliott home stood on its massive foundations of tabby, a building material made of shells, lime, and sand. Its tall sentry-like chimneys stared out into the night. The planter and his family abandoned Myrtle Bank before the Union arrived. The Elliotts took some slaves with them and left behind forty other slaves at Myrtle Bank.[6]

The enslaved people at Myrtle Bank had heard the guns roar, seen dark clouds of smoke hanging over the sound, and heard Confederate troops moving on the road along Port Royal Sound at midday.

Enslaved men, women, and children may have holed up in their cabins or hidden in the woods, staying out of sight of disgruntled rebels, waiting to make sure that the last Confederate soldiers had come and gone; waiting for the moment when freedom arrived.

Past the Elliott home, bounded by Myrtle Bank and

Seabrook Plantation, a sixteen-hundred-acre plantation bordered Skull Creek. This plantation was owned by James Seabrook.

A Union soldier dismissed the Seabrook plantation house as "a miserable white-washed concern set up on piles."[7] The house, like most on the island, had been built as a farmhouse rather than as a mansion since its owner did not live in it year-round.

James's second cousin, William Seabrook, had established the plantation out of parcels of land from three older plantation sites. A well-known Edisto planter and one of the best-known members of the elite Sea Island cotton planters, William Seabrook once entertained the Marquis de Lafayette.

In addition to farming, he had started a steam packet line that carried mail and then expanded it to reach Hilton Head before his death in the 1830s. He also built the wharf there that General Drayton had begun rebuilding to meet the Confederate needs.[8]

Up to eighty-nine men, women, and children in the Seabrook slave cabins waited anxiously for the soldiers to depart.

From Seabrook, one could enter the grounds of the next plantation. Here, the finest house on Hilton Head sat "in a large grove of live oak trees, with ample grounds neatly fenced." This was Cotton Hope Plantation, the island seat of Squire William Pope, patriarch of the Pope family. The fragrance from orange trees filled the night air.

"Two large libraries in the house were filled with books. Heavy plate glass mirrors and fine oil paintings adorned the walls. Rich furniture added to a scene of contentment and wealth," a Union soldier would write, without pausing to reflect that the "contentment and wealth" he saw was based on the labor of Squire Pope's slaves.

Polido and Martha, husband and wife, were among the enslaved people living in the slave quarters here. A little over five feet tall, Polido had black hair and brown eyes. His skin coloring was not as dark as that of most Gullah people, but he did not show any white blood, a friend noted. Martha was eight or nine years his junior.

Both Polido and Martha had been born on Hilton Head. "He and I," she would say years after slavery had ended, "both belonged to Squire William Pope. . . . We were married according to slave custom in my master's house," she said, a reference, apparently, to the old custom of jumping the broom used on many plantations. While these marriages carried no legal status, they were recognized unions.

To their master, the couple was Pope "property." He addressed them simply as "Polido" and "Martha." But, like Adam Jenkins at Fish Haul and many other enslaved people on Hilton Head, neither Polido nor Martha thought of themselves by their master's last name. Martha held onto an identity her father, Solomon, had passed on to her. Polido also kept the identity that his father, Peter, had passed to him.

"I was called Martha Joiner up to my marriage. My husband's name, from the time of his marriage on, was Polido Fields," Martha said.

Polido and Martha likely did not stray from their cabin this night. They had seven children to protect, including two young daughters.[9]

Cotton Hope was one of the largest, if not the largest plantation on the island. Squire Pope's estate would claim the loss of two hundred and one slaves.[10] His claim, however, would include at least one additional plantation on Hilton Head, Point Comfort, and one on the mainland at Bluffton. The number of slaves was not noted by location.

Perhaps fifty or more enslaved people at Cotton Hope prayed this night that the big guns had ended their bondage.

Inward from Cotton Hope, a road led to the plantation house of the Stoney family. The largest landowners on the island after the American Revolution, the family had since sold most of its Hilton Head holdings. This plantation, sometimes called Stoney, sometimes called Fairfield, was now the Stoney family's island seat. Wild blackberries abounded here in the spring, and Rose of Sharon, tall as trees, grew during the warm months.

Stoney was its own universe. The tiny cabins in the slave quarters sat a fourth of a mile from the house. Matthew, a dark-complexioned youth, was among the enslaved people here. "I was born on Stoney plantation," he later said.[11]

About sixteen years of age, Matthew was a minor who "belonged" to a minor. His master was George Stoney, whose property was held in trust for him until he came of age. Young George had eight slaves, including Matthew's parents.[12]

Unlike most slaves, Matthew never planted, hoed, or picked cotton or any other crop. He worked in the house and the dairy. "I grew up in the white folks' house and waited on them," Matthew said.

His lot was physically less harsh, but he did not control his destiny any more than a field worker. He remained at a master's beck and call.

Perhaps about forty enslaved people at Stoney kept a lookout in case stray Confederates were still on the island and headed for Ferry Point on Jenkins Island, a short distance from Stoney.

Below Ferry Point, where Calibogue Sound washes along the western shore, Spanish Wells, Muddy Creek, and Otter Hole cut inland. Spanish Wells Plantation sat on a bluff overlooking Calibogue Sound. Muddy Creek Plantation lay below Spanish Wells, with Otter Hole a little farther inland.

The name Spanish Wells came from fresh-water springs along its bluff. Spanish sailors had filled their ship casks with "sweet" water from these springs back before England won possession of the coast. That memory lived on in the plantation's name. Muddy Creek Plantation took its name from nearby Muddy Creek.

The Baynard family had owned Spanish Wells and Muddy Creek plantations since the late 1700s. Otter Hole, once owned by the Stoney family, now belonged to Middleton Stuart (sometimes spelled Stewart), who had married a Stoney.[13]

Simon, a friend of Matthew's, lived at Otter Hole. At five feet nine inches, Simon was taller than Matthew. He also was older and a newcomer on the island. He had been born at a Stuart plantation on Port Royal Island.

"I was born the slave of Mary M. Stuart and fell to Milton [Middleton] Stuart when I was sixteen, and came with him to Hilton Head and lived here with him until freedom," he later said.

His mother, Diana Simmons, had belonged to his owner. Her last name—or title—had come from her father, William Simmons. But bondsmen and -women often did not live on the same plantation. Simon's father had belonged to a different owner. He was known as Caesar Wallace. "I don't know where my father got his name," Simon said. Rather than take either parent's last name, Simon decided to pick his own.

"I titled myself Grant. I never was titled after my father or mother. Of course, some white people who [knew] that I belonged to Stuart called me Simon Stuart."[14]

Simon had lived on Hilton Head for six years; long enough to take a fancy to a young woman on the plantation, Maria Bryan, the daughter of Fottiemo Bryan, whose first name bespoke her African heritage.[15] Simon and Maria had married the previous year. They married at the praise house—a small wooden structure on several plantations where slaves met to "hold prays" on Sundays and weekdays led by black elders.

"The leader" married them.

Simon was perhaps twenty-two. Maria was about seventeen. With their life together just beginning, they may have swelled with joy as the big guns roared.

Calibogue Sound continues its way along the western shore of Hilton Head until reaching the southern tip of the island. Braddock's Point Plantation sat here at the juncture of Calibogue Sound and the Atlantic Ocean.

A half-built Confederate battery, with three 24-pounder guns and one 10-inch columbiad and a little ammunition, sat along the beach. General Drayton had ordered the battery abandoned after realizing the Union would not attack from the sea. He reassigned its commander, Captain Middleton Stuart—Simon's owner—to help defend Fort Beauregard.[16]

The old two-story Braddock's Point Plantation house sat slightly inland from the water. While modest in size at forty by forty-six feet, the mansion was the only plantation house on Hilton Head built entirely of tabby.

A fenced enclosure surrounded the main house and the domestic slave quarters. The main slave quarters sat off at a distance.

The Baynard family owned Braddock's Point Plantation, in addition to Spanish Wells and Muddy Creek.

Ruins of the main Baynard/Stoney house in the Braddock Point Plantation. *Photo by Will Warasila*

Ephraim Baynard either owned or managed all three on behalf of his family. One hundred and twenty-three enslaved men and women lived on the three plantations.

Prince and Mary lived either at Braddock's Point or at one of the other two Baynard plantations. Prince was a small, ginger-colored man approaching forty. He had been born on Hilton Head. Mary, his wife, was considerably younger. She had been born in Savannah, where her father and mother lived in the rear of the house of their master on East Broad Street.

Tabby foundation for house used by enslaved people at the Braddock Point Plantation. *Photo by Will Warasila*

"When I was about thirteen years of age, my father and four of us children were sold by Harry Hashin to Mr. Baynard of Hilton Head," Mary would say. She did not say what had become of her mother, who had not come to the island with them.

Mary bore the last name of her first master until arriving on Hilton Head. She then was known as a Baynard "up to the time of my marriage to Prince."

Most enslaved men and women on the island were married under old slave customs, as were Polido and Martha, or by a praise-house leader, as were Simon and Maria. But Mary remembered being married by "a white preacher named Richards, who used to travel about and preach."

The marriage of Prince and Mary took place "in front of Squire Pope's residence [at Cotton Hope] . . . near the water, where we colored people had met to be baptized," Mary said.[17] Mary and Prince already lived together and had for some time under slave practices. Richards likely regarded their union as pagan. He insisted on putting them on the "true path" of Christianity.

"This preacher refused to baptize us unless we should first be married, and then he read the marriage service to us and pronounced Prince Brown and I husband and wife, after which he baptized us."

Five years had passed. Prince and Mary Brown had two children. They and their children, along with Andrew Baynard, Mary's thirty-four-year-old brother, were among one hundred and twenty-nine Baynard slaves. They likely wondered if their master, who fought for the Confederates this day, had left for good.

Four miles inland, but still on the narrow South End, the Lawton plantation house sat near a road that ran the length of the island. The 1,820-acre plantation, often called Calibogue, had a wide, boxy shape. Fifty-six enslaved men and women lived here.[18]

At first glance the plantation seemed an idyllic village, complete with a manor house of six rooms and kitchen and outbuildings, around which the life of the plantation revolved: a corn house, a stable, a gin house with a new gin, a servants' house, a store room, a smoke house, a boathouse, two good barns, two old barns, a blacksmith shop, and sixteen cabins. The slave quarters belied the idyllic nature of the scene.

Enslaved people at Lawton Plantation had begun picking the year's cotton crop but had not yet finished. Winter provisions had been put aside: 1,400 bushels of corn, 300 bushels of peas, and 1,000 bushels of potatoes. Meat hung in the smokehouse.

The stable and grounds together held seven horses, six mules and twelve oxen, one hundred and forty head of cows, eighty head of sheep, and forty-six head of hogs, as well as poultry.

Two wagons, one old buggy, two tilt carts, one timber cart, and three ox carts stood ready for use. All manner of plantation implements abounded: new running gear, harnesses, saddles, bridles, medicines, carpenters' tools and smiths' tools. A cypress work flat, a fourteen-oar boat, eight-oar boat, four-oar boat, and a sailboat also were at ready. At their master's command, slaves had rowed members of the Lawton family off-island on both business and pleasure outings.

On the northern side of Lawton, three long, narrow plantations ran from the Atlantic to Broad Creek: Point Comfort, owned by Squire William Pope; Possum Point, owned until the past decade by the Fickling family; and Shipyard, where ships came in. A dark-skinned youth of sixteen years named Renty—an Ebo name popular in the Sea Islands[19]—lived on one of these plantations.

"I was born a slave to Francis Fickling who lived on

Hilton Head and Gillinsonville," he said, referring to the district's seat of government. "Thomas Miller was my father and Mr. Pope was his master."

Thomas, a brown-complexioned man, carried the last name of his father, and Renty, the first-born son of Thomas, bore his grandfather's first and last name: Renty Miller.[20]

North of Shipyard, the plantation of Leamington stretched three miles along the Atlantic coast. Joseph Pope, Sr., a relative of Squire Pope, owned Leamington. He had moved his forty-six slaves to another island before the Union fleet reached Hilton Head.

When slaves had risen this morning, they had worn a price on their heads. At Fish Haul, which General Drayton had administered, Venus Jenkins had a value of $500 on the plantation's "list of chattel."[21]

Her twin sons, Adam and Jacob, wore values of $900 and $700 each. Young Hagar had a value of $700, and her sister, Margaret, $300. Altogether, the family's value equaled $3,200.

Simon, the father of James, was valued at $1,000. James's brother George carried a value of $900, his brother, Morris, $400; and his sister, Julia, $200. James did not appear with his family on the list of chattel, although another son did: Button. He was valued at $500.

Button most likely was a "basket name." It was an African tradition for parents to give a young child a name to mark something significant about the birth of their child, such as the day of the week or the month in which a child was born, or a child's appearance. Perhaps to his parents, James had been cute as a button.

The moon set. Union soldiers camped near Fort Walker basked in their victory. "It was quite a pretty sight in the evening when the moon had gone down," a soldier wrote in his diary, "to see over a hundred fires burning in every direction and groups of soldiers [a]round them talking, smoking, and joking as if safe at home."[22]

The island now lay quiet under the light of millions of stars and the great Milky Way, a wave-flicked speck of land on the edge of the Atlantic Ocean, which flowed all the way to Africa and had brought African people here in the holds of slave ships.

The same moon and the same stars shone this night as had the night before, and the night before, and for the past one hundred and fifty years or more since slavery began on Hilton Head. The air still carried the smell of salt water from tidal creeks. Night birds still rose on startled wings. People still whispered in Gullah tongue. But nothing else would remain the same.

Slavery had been demolished in a single day, though the Union did not know it. The joint naval-military expedition had come to wage war, not abolish slavery. President Abraham Lincoln had not ordered the slaves freed.

Cannon at Fort Walker, which was occupied by Union soldiers in 1861. *Photo by Will Warasila*

Officially, enslaved people were "contrabands of war," a decree that made them spoils of war, but also meant that escaping slaves reaching Union lines would not be returned to their owners. Yet enslaved people were convinced they stood at freedom's door.

Within two days men, women, and children would begin arriving from the mainland and nearby islands in search of that freedom.

Hilton Head was "the first place," the contrabands would say. The first place behind Confederate lines where the white masters fled en masse and former slaves could live free.

Portrait of teacher Laura M. Towne, a founder of the Penn School, with students Dick, Maria, and Amoretta. *Schomburg Center for Research in Black Culture, Photos and Prints Division, the New York Public Library Digital Collections*

Chapter Three

THE PORT ROYAL EXPERIMENT

THE FIRST GLIMMER of light appeared in the sky. It was the time enslaved people called dayclean, when night began to fade and dawn had not yet come and the world was being reborn.

At Cotton Hope, Polido and Martha may have pinched themselves to see if they were free. At Stoney, Matthew likely rose to tend the dairy. Union invasion or not, the cows needed milking. At Fish Haul, James and his father, Simon, soon would hear soldiers emerging from their tents.

On the day after the big gun shoot, Hilton Head Island was indeed about to be remade. A Union bastion would rise: a twelve-mile stretch of free soil be-hind Confederate lines. As slaves awoke, their joy grew brighter than the growing light.

But out on the water, between the mainland and Hilton Head, the age-old mystery of dayclean brought fear to George and Lucinda Greaves, their daughter, Sylvia, and their frail sixteen-year-old son, Renty, who as a child had fallen into a big pot of plantation soup and been badly scalded. The family was fleeing its master and rowing to Hilton Head in a small wooden boat.

If caught, the Greaveses could be whipped, branded, or their family broken up and sold on the slave market.

"Against insubordination alone, we are severe," William Elliott of Myrtle Bank once wrote.[1]

Confederate patrols and sharpshooters were out attempting to block the rush of slaves seeking to reach Hilton Head. Like other slaves fleeing the mainland and the islands surrounding the Port Royal Sound, the Greaveses may have rowed down tidal creeks and inlets during the night, muffling their oars to keep their passage quiet. If so, before the water turned blue again and the first blue heron squawked to greet the day, the Greaveses had to hunker down and hide themselves and their boat.

On Hilton Head, soldiers and sailors and employees of the quartermaster's department began unloading vessels and preparing to erect a small town.

The commanding general of the Port Royal Expedition shared the last name of a more famous Union general: Sherman. General Thomas W. Sherman, however, was neither kin to General William Tecumseh Sherman nor as ruthless in waging war.

In his headquarters on Hilton Head, Sherman sat down to compose a message to all white residents of the Sea Islands. They had no reason to evacuate their lands, he wrote. The Union would not interfere with "social and local institutions." In short, the Union would let the institution of slavery stand. If contrabands made it to Union soil, they could remain, but the army did not intend to march forth and free the slaves.

Sherman's wording reflected what Congress had passed in July. But the general wasted his time. White residents of the Sea Islands did not heed his message. Both a Confederate general and a prominent minister had told them to leave.

Chaos descended on the Sea Islands. White planters who had not left when the cannons boomed the day before packed in haste, intent on moving inland and carrying away as many valued slaves with them as they could. Many slaves ran into the woods or marshes to hide. Others refused to leave, even as masters warned that the Yankees would sell them to Cuba, an island notorious for appalling slave conditions. Most slaves knew their masters were lying.

Some masters and overseers leveled guns and shot at slaves to attempt to force their slaves to go with them. At least a few hot-headed men shot point-blank and killed slaves who refused. Commodore DuPont received reports he deemed credible of slaves who burned to death in cotton houses.[2] Whether or not they were hiding in the cotton houses before the cotton was set on fire was unknown.

The entire white population of the Sea Islands surrounding the Port Royal Sound soon deserted the region.

For nights to come, the coastal sky would turn orange with burning cotton. Planters would steal back to burn their cotton rather than let it fall to the Union, which could gain money from its sale. But their second most valuable asset, nearly ten thousand Negroes, was left behind on the islands.

Two days after the big gun shoot, the Greaveses hauled their boat ashore onto Hilton Head. The family had won its gamble, won the prize of freedom.[3]

They had liberated themselves, and in this they were not alone.

"Contraband [N]egroes are coming in in great numbers. In two days one hundred fifty mostly able-bodied men have arrived," Rufus Saxton, assistant quartermaster, reported.

The contrabands were taken to a dilapidated building where they were questioned and signed in. Each man was asked where he was born and the last name of his owner. It made no difference that many of the contrabands, including the Greaves family, identified with another last name.

The quartermaster's department knew that President Abraham Lincoln had not ordered emancipation. If Lincoln did not do so in the future, or if the Union lost the war, the names of "rightful" owners of those who had been enslaved would be needed. Legally, the contrabands were still property.

George Greaves's turn came. He told the man registering him that his owner was Nathaniel P. Crowell, who lived on a plantation near Bluffton on the mainland.

The Northerner could not understand Greaves's speech. He wrote down what his ear heard—"Cruel"—a name that better described chattel bondage than a family of contrabands. The entire family would be known by that name throughout the war.

George "Cruel" likely joined other able-bodied contrabands put to work unloading union ships. His name would show up on the quartermaster's list of employees for November.[4] Renty "Cruel" likely did not work alongside his father. His father saw him as ill-fitted for hard work. Nothing about him signaled that one day he would be an important man, except that his full name was impressive: Renty Franklin Greaves.

New contrabands, including the family now listed as the Cruels, were assigned to tents. Their new life began.

Shortly after the Greaveses arrived, soldiers from at least four regiments ran amuck on Hilton Head, plundering everything in sight. From the road, soldiers could be seen pilfering pigs, poultry, and sheep. Everywhere Lieutenant H. S. Tafft went, ball cartridges whizzed over his head to such an extent he found it dangerous to travel about.

At Cotton Hope, Polido and Martha Fields must have watched in shock as men ran "shooting poultry and plundering the [N]egro houses of everything of value." The Fieldses' few hard-owned possessions likely were taken, along with any chickens they had and perhaps a pig or two. Most enslaved people raised both. They often sold the pigs to their master to get a little money for coffee, molasses, or pipe tobacco.

At Seabrook Plantation, a steamer was at the landing, loaded with forty-one bags of corn, likely the entire amount of corn on the plantation. "The [N]egroes had been collected near the wharf for the purpose of going on board. . . . They had collected as much of their clothing as time allowed them . . . but leaving everything in confusion."

As soon as the slaves left their cabins, the officer in charge allowed his men to shoot and plunder about the plantation. Tafft asked the officer if he had orders to take the slaves aboard the steamer. The lieutenant waffled, saying he had only verbal orders and he "hardly knew" who those were from. Tafft ordered the slaves back into their houses and charged the lieutenant "to prevent all plundering and arrest all persons disobeying this order."

Had Tafft not arrived on the scene, the contrabands at Seabrook would have been shipped off-island. The contrabands standing in line for the steamer had little choice but to follow the orders of soldiers with guns. But a single fear must have grabbed every former slave in the line: Were they to be sent to Cuba and sold?

Appalled by the soldiers' pillaging, Sherman ordered that "such depravations" must immediately cease and the culprits be brought to justice. But as word of the pilfering and the Seabrook incident spread across the island, it surely made contrabands wary. It may have been their first inkling that they could not trust all Union soldiers.

A week passed. Two docks and a plank road had been built to use in unloading the cargos of the military vessels. The cargo now filled new storehouses. Everything needed to run an army was in place, including new entrenchments, a commissary, a post office, and camp police.

"A thousand men at a time might be seen at the work along the shore, constructing wharves, driving horses through the water and along the sand, receiving cargoes, rolling barrels, guarding property," a correspondent for the *New York Times* recalled, "while three or four miles off, another thousand was engaged in digging trenches, moving guns, and preparing the new fort cannons which are to render the place impregnable. Besides these, four or five hundred men a day were frequently sent off on reconnaissance."

The contrabands were one of the most interesting parts of the scene, he noted. Some worked on shore. Others worked as oarsmen or as scouts and guides, while officers with money hired black men to serve them as waiters and black women to wash their clothes.

Though impressed with the contrabands, the correspondent did not understand them as a people. After listening to a prayer meeting one night, he wrote of the leader's "ardent ejaculations of thanksgiving for the favorable chance God had given to 'my colored brudden.' The jargon was absurd," he said, "but it was earnest; the singing was out of tune and time, but fervent."

He did not know that he was hearing an African-based creole and music with an African beat and cadence.

A second journalist would write, "I find it impossible to understand all they said . . . they have a curious accent, something like that of a Frenchman speaking English poorly, but, in addition, they have numerous contractions, inversions of form, and cant [peculiar tonal] phrases, which make the unaccustomed listener's task more difficult."

He came close to the mark, however, when he added, "The jargon of old people . . . gave me, unconsciously, sometimes the feeling that I was speaking with foreigners."[5]

Cotton had been the leading export of the United States before the war started. Demand was constant in England and cotton prices were at their highest point in forty-two years. Despite efforts of coastal planters to burn their cotton, much remained in cotton houses and in the fields. To the Union, the cotton was abandoned property that could help finance the war.

Salmon P. Chase, secretary of the treasury, sent an agent to collect the cotton. As the contrabands were abandoned property, he sent a representative to report on them too. Chase was then the most antislavery member of Lincoln's cabinet. To the contrabands' good fortune, the man Chase sent shared his views.

Edward L. Pierce had been present at the birth of the contraband policy at Fortress Monroe in Virginia, not long after Fort Sumter fell.

Three escaping slaves made it to the Union camp there. The men had worked on Confederate fortifications. General Benjamin Butler, a lawyer before the war, debated what to do. If he sent the escaping slaves back to their owners, the Confederates would use them against him.

Butler pronounced the escaped men "contraband of war" and declined to hand them over to their owners. From then on, escaping slaves who reached Union lines became contrabands. Pierce had supervised the work of the Virginia contrabands.

Chase sent Pierce with a specific instruction. The contrabands must be made ready "for self-support by their own industry hereafter." Chase privately believed they could never be returned to slavery.[6]

Pierce arrived in the Sea Islands in January of 1862, approximately two months after the Union captured Hilton Head. In a two-week tour, he checked on the contrabands throughout the islands, observing their conditions and abilities. He sent back a report designed to mold the opinions of Chase, the rest of Lincoln's cabinet, and the general public. He took pains to address concerns about the contrabands that he knew people in power would have.[7]

On each plantation he visited, including those on Hilton Head, he spoke with laborers and the buggy driver. Pierce found the drivers intelligent. He gathered that they had been the actual plantation superintendents (although there also had been three white overseers). But drivers were charged to inflict corporal punishment when needed, which made them unpopular with the field hands.

Pierce thought on the whole, though, that the drivers' knowledge of the plantation and the laborers, "when properly advised and controlled," might make the plantations productive and work to the good of the laborers.

He found others on the plantations he considered more intelligent than the average. These included the carpenter, the plowman, and religious leaders. Pierce reported that these men "if properly approached by us" may be expected to have "a beneficial influence on the more ignorant."

He recognized those men as leaders, but he may have underestimated the intelligence of many field hands. The contrabands he considered more intelligent were accustomed to speaking with white overseers or owners. Their English came closer to Standard English. Most field hands had a deeper African dialect. That dialect, combined with their pure African blood and features,

caused Northerners to often wrongly assume they were less intelligent.

When Pierce met contrabands who were wary of the Union, he told them that where he came from everyone was free, whether white or black. He assured them that the Union would not sell their children or separate man and wife. He further said that if they were to be free, they would have to work.

The laborers replied, "Yes, massa, we must work to live; that's the law."

Pierce wrote in his report, "[W]e wanted them to stay on the plantation and raise cotton, and if they behaved well, they should have wages—small, perhaps at first, and they should have better food . . . That their children should be taught to read and write . . . and we would stand by them against their master ever coming back to take them."

Pierce used the president's name with the contrabands, feeling it more likely to "impress them than the abstract idea of government." He told them that Mr. Lincoln was thinking about what he could do for them, but "the great trouble about doing anything for them was that their masters had always told us and had made many people believe that they were lazy and would not work unless whipped."

One day he spoke to a crowd of two hundred contrabands on Hilton Head. "[A] good-looking man who had escaped from the southern part of Barnwell District rose and said, with much feeling, that he and many others should do all they could by good conduct to prove what their masters said against them to be false, and to make Mr. Lincoln think better things of them.

"After the meeting closed, he desired to know if Mr. Lincoln was coming down here to see them, and he wanted me to give Mr. Lincoln his compliments with his name, assuring the President that he would do all he could for him."

Pierce sent Chase a sweeping outline of what would become known as the Port Royal Experiment as it would affect Hilton Head, which Sherman had renamed Port Royal for the duration of the war. He recommended a superintendent be appointed for each large plantation and a single superintendent handle groups of two or three smaller plantations. The superintendents should be as carefully chosen as if they were the guardians of one's own children. The contrabands would need paternal discipline for the time being, but it must be humane discipline, he wrote. Whipping must not be allowed.

A director-general or governor should be named who had authority to protect the contrabands, Pierce reported. Teachers and missionaries were needed, but they could be supported by benevolent societies in the North. In conclusion, he wrote that the contrabands were not yet ready for the privileges of full citizenship, but that everything should be managed in reference to preparing them for this.

Piece then boarded a steamer, arrived in Washington to make his report, then headed to New York to begin recruiting men and women of good moral character to take on benevolent work in the Sea Islands.

Whenever the army sent out contraband spies, they brought back women, children, and elderly family members. The contrabands wanted their families with them. "Useless mouths," General Sherman grumbled. He wanted only able-bodied men. As the number of escapees increased, Sherman began to see the contrabands as a burden.

His concern had some basis. Winter had set in. By tradition, planters gave their slaves two sets of cheaply made clothes each year. The Union had invaded before the slaves received their new sets of clothes. With their old clothes in tatters, contrabands dressed in rags, pieces of cut-up carpet from their masters' homes, or anything else they could find. Some were nearly naked.

Plantation food stores were running low. The army had confiscated the cattle. The corn had been used as forage. On Hilton Head, the plundering of cabins and grounds had lessened the contrabands' ability to feed themselves. More than one thousand five hundred old and new contrabands on the island faced destitution. Sherman feared they would starve to death.

Within days after a Boston printer published Pierce's report to Chase, making it available to the public,

Sherman appealed to the "highly-favored and philanthropic people" of the North for emergency relief for the contrabands.[8] From Philadelphia, the newly formed Port Royal Relief Committee sent shipments of food, including bacon, fish, molasses, buckwheat, and several cases of clothing, boots, shoes, soap, earthenware, combs, brushes, and notions. Other Northern societies pitched in also. Enough aid reached Hilton Head and surrounding islands to stave off starvation.

March brought forth the yellow jessamine on Hilton Head and the arrival of Pierce's first band of "Gideonites." The fifty-three young, idealistic abolitionist men and women from Boston, New York, and Massachusetts accepted the zealous nickname with pride. The group included graduates of Harvard, Yale, and Brown, as well as others from established divinity schools. Twelve women were in the group. Pierce assured the "Gideonites" that the work of any colony had never been so important, not even the *Mayflower*.

More women arrived, including Laura Towne and Ellen Murray — who would found the Penn School, the first permanent school for freedmen — and Charlotte Forten, a fourth-generation free black and a friend of the poet John Greenleaf Whittier.

The Gideonites reached Hilton Head aboard the steamer *Atlantic*. Most would go on to Beaufort and then be assigned to plantations on Port Royal Island,

Portrait of teacher Laura M. Towne, a founder of the Penn School, with students Dick, Maria, and Amoretta. *Schomburg Center for Research in Black Culture, Photos and Prints Division, the New York Public Library Digital Collections*

Saint Helena, and other locations. Seven men would be assigned to Hilton Head; some of these would become cotton superintendents.

The Reverend Charles Dwight Howard of Massachusetts would teach on Hilton Head. He moved into Stoney, the plantation where the house servant Matthew lived and where two officers of a Pennsylvania regiment were staying.

Pierce advised Howard that the contrabands "were to receive their first instruction in the responsibilities they were to assume." He had found on his earlier trip that the contrabands fervently desired the chance for their children, and themselves, to learn to read and write.

Pierce made it clear to Howard that his work would set a powerful example that could assist enslaved people elsewhere in the South when freedom at last came to them.

Howard set to work setting up schools. Like other teachers, he taught in praise houses or any available spot he could find. He opened schools at Cotton Hope, Graham (Honey Horn), and Stuart (Otter Hole).

Cotton Hope was his biggest school. Howard's young students sat in Squire William Pope's parlor, a sight that would have astonished him. Teaching slaves to read had long been illegal in South Carolina. Squire Pope's slaves had dusted the books in his libraries but were not allowed to open them. Now, children, such as those of Polido and Martha Fields, were able to learn their ABCs.

Charlotte Forten Grimke. *Schomburg Center for Research in Black Culture, Photos and Prints Division, the New York Public Library. "Lottie Grimke." New York Public Library Digital Collections*

On other islands, Laura Towne, Charlotte Forten, and others were finding their black students as able to learn as any white students they knew. It was an early sign to the teachers and the North that the Port Royal Experiment could help transform newly emerged slaves into emancipated citizens.

The Port Royal Experiment would become the largest and best-known forerunner for reconstruction in the South. It was a unique situation, made possible by the total absence of white planters and the influx of philanthropic Northerners. If the experiment worked, Pierce believed it could be duplicated anywhere in the South.

In his next missive sent to the North, Pierce put forth two questions he said must be answered with a resounding yes if the contrabands were to gain the rights of complete citizenship:

Will the people of African descent work for a living?

Will they fight for their freedom?

On Hilton Head, contrabands who had worked the fields as slaves returned to cotton fields again. The whip had been banished and they were proving they could work without it. They were becoming wage earners.

As to whether the contrabands would fight, that remained to be seen. Neither Lincoln, nor Congress, nor the Union army wanted black soldiers—yet.

Chapter Four

EMANCIPATION

FLOWERS SCENTED the April air as a *New York Times* correspondent rode forth to the navy's coaling station at Seabrook on Skull Creek. A Union officer had told him that the contrabands employed to coal the navy vessels were "lazy and insubordinate." He decided to see for himself.

The government supervisor told him that to the contrary, the contrabands were "industrious, civil and obedient." He had twenty-six contrabands and wanted as many more as the government could give him. The supervisor acknowledged that for about two months during the winter the men had been "discontented" when they did not receive their pay. Now that they were "paid and fed, all complaint has ceased," the correspondent reported.

They had not, however, received their back pay. The workers told the correspondent that they wanted to buy clothes for their families. They "seem to begin to feel the responsibility of self-support," the correspondent opined.[1] They were working as free laborers.

At Fish Haul, he rode through an avenue of trees to the rear of the plantation house. The house faced the water and a circular road ran down to the beach. A privet hedge ran between the house and the beach.

The plantation house and grounds showed a lack of care, as the Drayton family had not lived there regularly for some time, but the contrabands who lived on the plantation grounds were working.

The engineer of the cotton gin was a black man. The cotton on the plantation had all been ginned. The money from the sale of the cotton at Fish Haul and all Sea Island plantations would go into a cotton fund set up by the Treasury Department to support the Port Royal Experiment.

As the correspondent discovered, though, contrabands working the cotton fields for the next crop also were not getting their pay on time. Washington did not send money quickly enough, and some cotton superintendents were unduly slow in their efforts to get workers paid.

The Graham plantation, or Honey Horn, as it became known, lay on Skull Creek. The plantation was new. It was still under construction when the Union invaded. The dwelling house was unfinished, but an overseer's house, twelve slave cabins, barns, a gin house, and other buildings required to run the plantation had been built.[2]

Pierce's band of Gideonites had not included enough cotton superintendents to supervise all the plantations they had begun working on Hilton Head. As a result, without uniform standards, some plantations were better supervised than others.

To the *Times* correspondent, the Graham plantation showed poor supervision and the difficulties the contrabands faced.

"They are getting no food, but are obliged to fish for a living; evenings and mornings. . . . How long," he asked, "would white laborers endure such treatment?" The superintendent was at that moment trying to get their rations, but the correspondent considered the man's efforts "reprehensibly tardy."

Upon reaching the Elliott plantation, Myrtle Bank, he saw a fine plantation with beautiful live oaks and a large beach. But he came across an incident of callous abuse by a soldier. Union soldiers had been stationed in the fields as guards, presumably to prevent rebel attacks.

The superintendent, a Mr. Blake, said that the contrabands "had not been able to get their rations from the Government." As a result, one worker had been "impudent and disobedient."

"When Mr. Blake ordered a soldier to enforce obedience, the latter had fixed his bayonet and run it through the [N]egro's side, narrowly missing a vital part." The soldier also wanted to fire on him too but Blake "physically restrained him."[3]

It was small wonder that the glow enslaved people felt on the day of the big gun shoot was fading. Many began wondering what their futures held.

The North clamored for victories. After the capture of Hilton Head, many had expected Union troops to advance through the southern coast, defeating the Confederates in battle after battle. This had not occurred. Secretary of War Edwin Stanton removed General Sherman. He brought in a more aggressive man.

General David Hunter took command of what now was called the Department of the South on March 31, 1862. The department covered South Carolina, Georgia, and Florida.

Hunter was so known for his abolitionist views that some in the North called him "Black Dave." He once proclaimed: "I would advance south, proclaiming the [N]egro free and arming him as I go. The Great God of the universe has determined that this is the only way in which this war is to be ended."[4]

Hunter acted quickly upon reaching Hilton Head.

He had about seventeen thousand men under his command, but they were "scattered from Saint Augustine, Florida, to North Edisto Inlet, South Carolina." He lacked enough soldiers at any one place to strike strong blows.[5]

On his fourth day of command, Hunter fired off a telegram to Stanton requesting fifty thousand muskets and two hundred rounds of ammunition, and that each "be sent me at once with authority to arm such loyal men" as he could find in the region.

As few white southerners held allegiance to the Union, "loyal men" meant black men. Hunter thus put Stanton on notice that he intended to raise colored troops.

Major General David Hunter, between 1860 and 1862. *Library of Congress*

Hunter also requested fifty thousand pairs of scarlet pantaloons so that he could "distinguish" his men from any the Confederacy might put on the battlefield.[6]

He then sent for Abraham Murchison, an energetic, tall, copper-skinned man of great sway among Hilton Head contrabands. Murchison, an escaped slave preacher from Savannah, preached in the contraband camp and worked for the quartermaster's department as chief mess cook. General Hunter put his question before Murchison: Were the contrabands willing to fight for the Union?

Murchison agreed to call a meeting of black men and ask them. He left his meeting with Hunter excited about the prospect of black men earning their freedom by becoming soldiers, and impressed with the dark-haired general with a large moustache. A vigorous fifty-seven-year-old man, Hunter kept a gun by his side and held target practice every morning on the beach. "That's a fighting man," Murchison said with admiration.[7]

The meeting took place on the evening of April 7, just days after he met with Hunter. Secrecy surrounded the meeting. Guards stood at the door to exclude those whose presence was not desired and to prevent eavesdropping.[8]

Murchison spoke to the men clearly, explaining the benefits of freedom the men would reap by fighting, but also telling them of the labors, hardships, and dangers of soldier life, the *New York Times* reported. His language

"rose to eloquence" at times. The men listened "with breathless interest."

When Murchison asked all who were willing to take up arms to defend the Union to rise, "Every man sprang to his feet in an instant."[9]

After weeding out men too old to fight or too young, one hundred and five Hilton Head contrabands had signed up. Within days, their ranks rose to one hundred and fifty. Some were Hilton Head natives; others had fled to Hilton Head to find freedom.

In doing so, the contrabands on Hilton Head took a step toward the formation of a colored regiment in the Civil War.[10]

Hunter's regiment, however, would be short-lived.

Hunter sent out a black recruiter, possibly the first in the South, to nearby islands. But fewer men signed up than had on Hilton Head.[11] Hunter lacked allies on the other islands as convincing as Murchison.

While waiting for more recruits to come forward, Hunter clamped martial law on all the territory under the Department of the South. Next, he issued General Order No. 11, which declared martial law and slavery incompatible in a free country, and therefore proclaimed all persons held as slaves in South Carolina, Georgia, and Florida "forever free."[12]

For two days missionaries, teachers, and other aboli-

tionists on the Sea Islands rejoiced that Hunter would emancipate slaves within the Department of the South and hoped that President Lincoln would follow.

Anger and fear erupted on the third day.

Hunter's officers had promised the contrabands that they would be volunteers, not coerced. But Hunter had grown weary of waiting for more recruits for his colored regiment. Acting on his orders, Union soldiers swept onto Saint Helena, Lady's Island, and other Sea Islands, seizing "every able bodied [N]egro between the ages of eighteen and forty-five, capable of bearing arms."[13] The soldiers rushed five hundred men to Hilton Head.

"They were taken from the fields without being allowed to go to their houses even to get a jacket," treasury agent Edward Piece wrote in anger. "On some plantations the wailing and screaming were loud, and the women threw themselves in despair on the ground." On other plantations, "people took to the woods and were hunted up by the soldiers. . . . This mode of [enlistment of] violent seizure and transportation . . . spreading dismay and fright, is repugnant."[14]

In the end, Hunter had the men trained in army life and drilled them for several weeks, and then released those who wanted to return home. Others stayed on.

Meanwhile, in Washington, conservatives in Congress raised a ruckus about Hunter's unauthorized colored troops.

Earlier in the war, in August of 1861 — a month after Hilton Head planters sent enslaved men to build Fort Walker — General John Fremont, head of the Department of the West, had declared martial law in Missouri with the intention of confiscating the property of Missouri slaveholders and freeing their slaves.

Lincoln had revoked Fremont's order, concerned it would prompt the slave-holding border states to secede. Now, Lincoln revoked Hunter's order.

"No commanding general shall do such a thing upon my responsibility without consulting me," Lincoln declared.[15] The president was not ready to tie emancipation to the war effort.

Lincoln, however, stopped short of ordering Hunter to disband his regiment.

Hunter's regiment numbered several hundred men in June. The *Times* reported, "They are progressing finely, and show an aptitude for military maneuvers that one would hardly expect to see."

Hunter soon was told to send seven thousand of his troops to General George B. McClellan. Then, in early August, Hunter found himself forced to dismiss his black regiment. Because his unit had never received official recognition, he could not get money to pay the men.

One company stayed on without pay. The men, contrabands from Georgia, went to Saint Simons Island to help garrison the island. Proud to be the last soldiers in Hunter's regiment, they hunted invading rebels in dense palmetto thickets.

"If you wish to know hell before your time," a Confederate officer wrote, "go to Saint Simons Island and be hunted for ten days" by colored troops.[16]

Hunter's dream of raising an entire army of black men ended. He took personal leave and left Hilton Head and the Department of the South.[17]

Rufus Saxton took up Hunter's quest to organize colored troops. Saxton early on had served as assistant quartermaster on Hilton Head. After rising to chief quartermaster, he left the Port Royal Experiment. He returned as Military General in charge of the abandoned lands of the Sea Islands and the contrabands, responsible only to the federal War Department and the commanding general of the Department of the South.

General Rufus Saxton. *Library of Congress*

Saxton asked Stanton for permission to enlist five thousand black men in the quartermaster's department, to be "uniformed, armed, and officered" by men detailed by the army.

His timing was good. The Union faced a shortage of soldiers and Congress had now granted Lincoln the authority to enlist colored soldiers. Also, as Saxton noted, it helped that the men in Hunter's Regiment had performed well.

In late August, Stanton authorized Saxton "to arm, equip, and receive into the service of the United States such volunteers of African descent as you may deem expedient, not exceeding five thousand." The men who volunteered would join the first *authorized* black regiments in the Union.[18]

The scope of the Port Royal Experiment widened now.

In early November Saxton sent the few men left from Hunter's regiment on a raid along the Georgia and Florida coasts. They destroyed Confederate salt works and brought back new recruits. Two weeks later, on another raid, about thirty black men proved their mettle by fighting their way out of a Confederate ambush.[19]

Colonel Thomas Wentworth Higginson arrived the same month. A Massachusetts abolitionist, he thought himself the luckiest man in the world. Saxton had asked him to command the first official colored regiment, the First South Carolina Volunteers.

The pace of events had quickened. In late July Lin-

Colonel Thomas Wentworth Higginson, commander of the 1st SC Volunteers, the first African-American regiment. *Library of Congress, Prints and Photos Division, Alfred Bendiner Memorial Collection*

coln privately had told his cabinet that he planned to emancipate slaves in Confederate territory. Not yet, his cabinet advised. The Union was losing battle after battle and could lose the war. Issuing a proclamation of emancipation would appear a desperate move. Lincoln needed a victory first.

The Union won a meager victory at Antietam, near Sharpsburg, Maryland, in September. On September 22, 1862, Lincoln issued his preliminary Emancipation Proclamation. He warned the seceded states that if they did not cease rebelling by January 1, 1863, he would declare "all persons held as slaves within any State or designated part of a State, the people whereof shall then be in rebellion against the United States, shall be, thenceforth . . . forever free."

December came. The Confederate States fought on.

January 1, 1863, arrived. Lincoln was to sign the Emancipation Proclamation on this day.

Contrabands on Hilton Head and other Sea Islands behind Union lines grew giddy with excitement that they would gain their freedom this day. Abolitionists fervently hoped that the president would indeed sign the document.

General Rufus Saxon sent steamships to Hilton Head and other islands to transport contrabands, missionaries, teachers, cotton superintendents, officers, and cavalry to hear the Emancipation Proclamation read out loud. He expected five thousand people to attend.

The ceremony took place on the grounds of the former Smith Plantation, near Beaufort, within the sight of the campgrounds of the First South Carolina Volunteers.

Higginson did not expect much of the day. He

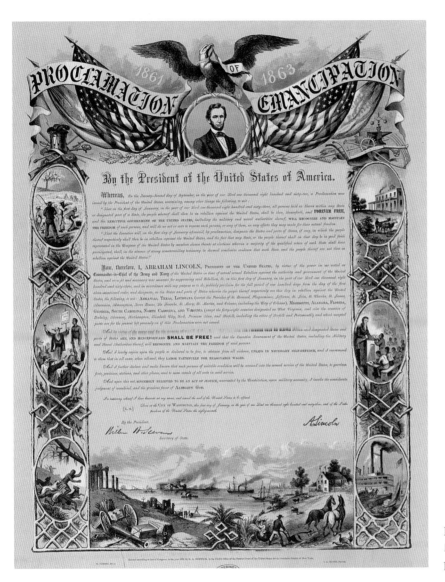

Broadside of the Emancipation Proclamation from C. A. Alvord printers. *Library of Congress*

reasoned that the contrabands had, for all practical purpose, been free ever since the Union invasion nearly fourteen months before. He failed to take into account two hundred years or more of longing for this day.

Watching the colored people arrive, he noted in particular, "a sprinkling of men, with that peculiarly respectable look which these people always have on Sundays and holidays."[20]

Charlotte Forten stepped off a boat from Saint Helena to see an "eager, wondering crowd of the freed people in their holiday attire, with the gayest of head-handkerchiefs, the whitest of aprons, and the happiest of faces. The band was playing, the flags streaming. Some companies of the First South Carolina Volunteers were drawn up in a line, near the landing, to receive us. A fine, soldierly-looking set of men," she said.

Aaron Christopher, a soldier born and raised on Hilton Head, was among the greeters. If not, he would march in the dress parade of the first colored regiment mustered into the service of the United States. The parade would follow the main ceremony. At five-foot-seven with dark eyes, hair, and complexion, Christopher must have cut a dashing figure in his regimental blue coat and red pantaloons.

Dignitaries and a military band sat on a platform erected under ancient live oaks with long, gray moss. The trees had grown in slave soil. From this day on, their acorns would bring forth trees in liberty.

The men of the First South Carolina Volunteers sur-rounded the platform. Throngs of contrabands waiting to hear Lincoln's words filled the spacious oak grove. Beyond them, visitors mounted on horseback stood.

The regimental chaplain kicked off the ceremonies with an opening prayer. A white Sea Islander, Dr. W. H. Brisbane, who had freed his slaves, read the president's proclamation. The Reverend Mansfield French, well-regarded among the missionaries, presented Higginson with a regimental flag for the First South Carolina Volunteers.

"Just as I took and waved the flag," Higginson said, "which now for the first time meant anything to these poor people, there suddenly arose, close to the platform, a strong male voice, but cracked and elderly, into which two women's voices instantly blended, singing,

My country, 'tis of thee,
Sweet land of liberty,
Of thee I sing."

Other freedmen and freedwomen joined in.

Higginson had never heard "anything so electric." It seemed "the choked voice of a race, at last unloosed."[21]

Lincoln signed the document at 4:00 p.m. He thought it both the right thing to do and the best thing he had ever done.

Aboard a boat back to Saint Helena, Forten regretted leaving. The moonlight and water seemed more beautiful than ever and she hated missing the grand shouts and general jubilee the soldiers would hold this night. "Our hearts," she said, "were filled with an exceeding great gladness; for although the Government had left much undone, we knew that Freedom was surely born in our land that day."

Lincoln had created a rallying cry. The purpose of the war was no longer just to preserve the Union, but also to free the slaves.

In the Sea Islands, Lincoln's proclamation freed nearly ten thousand people. But the paper Lincoln signed could not immediately free more than three million enslaved men, women, and children living behind Confederate lines. They would be freed if, and only if, the Union won the war.

Southerners scoffed at Lincoln's audacity to promise freedom to the slaves.

Black men and women on the South Carolina mainland, which the Union did not command, were among those who remained enslaved. The proclamation could not free them, and they chafed at their bonds. Hilton Head and freedom beckoned: so close, so tantalizing, and still a perilous journey.

Caesar Jones could not wait. Angry that he had not been freed, he decided to free himself. He drove a carriage for his master, Dr. John Kirk. The Kirks were among the elite white planter class. John Kirk had a plantation near Bluffton, on the mainland. The Kirk family also had been plantation owners on Hilton Head, possibly as late as the Union invasion.

On a carriage trip for his master, Kirk managed to escape.

Out on the water, Caesar; Mariah, his wife; Katie, a daughter; and a young baby named Ammie sat huddled in a small boat. Other slaves from the same plantation accompanied them in separate boats.

They stole across the May River, separating the mainland from Hilton Head, making every effort to keep quiet, as sound carried on the water.

The baby began squalling.

"T'row the baby overboard," a voice whispered.

"T'row de baby overboard," the man whispered again. "I aim to make me a get away."

Mariah grasped her baby. She wrapped her arms around her daughter and held her tight, trying to silence the crying infant.[22]

Caesar Jones, Mariah, the infant, and another daughter would make it to Hilton Head and would go on to be important figures on Hilton Head.

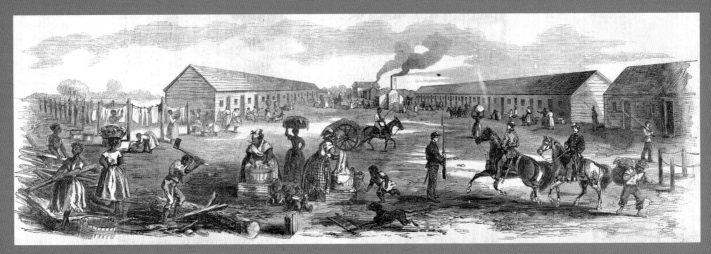

Sketch from *Leslie's Illustrated* depicting daily life in the military-style barracks set up for "contrabands" who left plantations or came from the mainland. *Library of Congress*

Chapter Five

MITCHELVILLE RISES

THE BILLOWING TENTS that had served as housing for families such as the Greaves family had disappeared long ago. Much had happened since the first contrabands reached Hilton Head back in November of 1861.

What to do with the contrabands had become "a large elephant-sized problem," a *New York Daily Tribune* correspondent opined in late 1861. The army decided to resolve the housing problem by building military-style barracks.

"[T]wo rows of commodious barracks" had opened by February 1862, Edward Pierce announced at that time in the northern press.[1]

About six hundred black men, women, and children moved into the barracks immediately. Most had come from the mainland, although men from Hilton Head plantations, such as Andrew Baynard, who had begun working for the quartermaster's department, likely moved into the barracks too. In all, four hundred and seventy of the contrabands who lived in the "camp," or barracks, worked for the quartermaster's department.

During the first summer the yard in front of the barracks bustled with activity. Black women in long full skirts scrubbed clothes in an iron pot over a fire in a scene from *Frank Leslie's Illustrated Newspaper*, while others poured out of the barracks with baskets of laundry on their heads or hung clothes on a line to dry. Children played nearby. A black man chopped wood for the fire. A woman with a long-handled hoe worked a garden, a basket of produce by her feet. A uniformed soldier stood at guard, rifle hoisted straight up, as two soldiers on horses rode up.[2]

By fall, the once-commodious barracks had grown so overcrowded that admiration turned to dismay.

A news correspondent dismissed the barracks as "a long row of partitions into which are crowded young and old, male and female, without respect either to quality or quantity."[3]

"The older people slept in bunks, the younger on the floor," Laura Towne of the Penn School wrote of similar barracks for contrabands at Beaufort. "The cooking utensils usually consisted of a single pot: the food was hominy or peas and salt pork. Long oyster shells were used for spoons." Furthermore, Towne said, "Large cracks [between wallboards] let in the bitter winter cold." The risk of disease sweeping the barracks posed a constant danger.

The close presence of so many soldiers without wives on the post also posed a serious problem. General Saxton noted that the black women "were held as the legitimate prey of lust, and as they had been taught it was a crime to resist a white man they had not learned to dare to defend their chastity. Licentiousness was widespread; the morals of old plantation life seemed revived in the Army of occupation."[4]

The army needed a better solution.

Changes occurred with the arrival of General O. M. Mitchel of Ohio. A dark-haired man with bushy eyebrows and a resolute brow, Mitchel had been raised in the slave state of Kentucky and come to believe that God intended all people to be free. He saw the war as "the battle of human liberty, not for this country alone, but for the whole world" and knew that the contrabands could play a key role.

During his time as commander of the Union forces occupying north Alabama, contrabands had been invaluable to him in relaying information in rebel territory. In two instances, he said, "I owe my own safety to their faithfulness."[5]

Mitchel arrived on Hilton Head on September 15, 1862, to fill in for General Hunter. After inspecting the troops, Mitchel pronounced them "highly satisfactory," but he found a bias against the contrabands that disturbed him.

Five days after his arrival, the new commander of the Department of the South advised Secretary of War Stanton, "I find a feeling prevailing among the officers and soldiers of prejudice against the blacks, founded upon the opinion that in some way the negroes have been more favored by the Government, and more privileges granted to them than to the volunteer soldier."[6]

The feeling lacked foundation, Mitchel told Stanton, but "was fraught with the most injurious consequences."

Before Hunter went on leave, he had authorized the construction of a church on Hilton Head, in order that all contrabands on the island could gain instruction in their Christian duties.

The new church was to be for and led by the contrabands—a radical departure from their past lives when slave masters usually forbid such freedom of assembly in fear it would ferment revolt.

The initial membership of the First African Baptist Church consisted of approximately one hundred and twenty contrabands. Of these, nearly seventy, according to the *New South*, a weekly newspaper published on the post, "were professing Christians under the rule of their late masters, while the others [about fifty] have been . . . baptized since our advent among them."

Abraham Murchison, who had gathered a flock he preached to while still in the old barracks, was duly installed as pastor during the organizational meeting.[7] He also worked for the quartermaster's department as chief mess cook.

The energetic reverend would prove equal to the task of inspiring the congregation.

The contrabands were moving forward. They would not be deterred by prejudice against them. Neither would General Mitchel who, as commander of the department, felt the contrabands were under his protection and guidance.

The *New South* soon reported:

Gen. O. M. Mitchell, USA, approximately 1861. *Civil war photographs, 1861–1865, Library of Congress*

Some wholesome changes are contemplated by the new regime, not the least of which is the removal of the Negro quarters beyond the stockade. It is widely determined to put them by themselves where they can at once have more comfort and freedom for improvement, for it is designed as soon as possible to educate them to self-respecting independence and habits of self-reliance. Accordingly, a spot has been selected near the Drayton plantation [Fish Haul Plantation] for a Negro Village. They are to build their own houses, and will probably be encouraged to establish their own police under supervision of their Superintendent. A teacher, Ashbell Landon, has been appointed to be paid from the quartermaster's department.[8]

Inside the plain wooden church, during its formal dedication on Sunday, October 12, contrabands could look around and sense freedom coming. Here was proof they could touch and see, and now General Mitchel was addressing them. He had come to them.

The congregation listened with rapt attention as the general told them that what the *New South* said was right. They would have their own village with houses of their own, and each of them would have a "patch of ground which you can call your own, to raise your own garden truck . . . and you are to have a school for your children."

He did not know for certain what would happen, but it seemed to him "that there is a new time coming for you colored people, a better day is dawning for you oppressed and downtrodden blacks. . . . I hope the day is being opened for your deliverance. And now, how deeply you should ponder these words. If now you are unwilling to help yourselves, nobody will be willing to help you."[9]

He admonished the men to labor with vigilance and zeal, serve God, and do all they can for their families. He advised the women to be careful of their children, "teach them to be clean, obedient and dutiful at all times," keep their house "neat and tidy, and speak kindly to their husbands."

"The whole North, all the people in the Free States, are looking at you, and the experiment now being tried in your behalf with the deepest interest. This experiment is to give you freedom, position, home and your own families—wives, property, your own soil. You shall till and cultivate your own crops; you shall gather and sell the products of your industry for your own benefit; you shall own your own earnings, and you shall be able to feel that God is prospering you from day to day, and from year to year, and raising you to a higher level of goodness, religion and nobler life. . . .

"If you fail, what a dreadful responsibility it will be when you come to die to feel that the only great opportunity you had for serving yourselves and your op-

Image of family with Union solder. Family is identified as a Mitchelville family by several sources. Photo title from photographer Henry Moore: "Drayton's negro quarters, Hilton Head, S.C., 1862."
Library of Congress

pressed race was allowed to slip . . . but if you are successful, this plan will go all through the country. . . .

"Upon your work depends whether this mighty result shall be worked out, and the day of jubilee come to God's ransomed people."

Nods of assent and approval swept the church.[10]

The general did not live to see the village he envisioned.

He had arrived during the season, the hot weather months when mosquito-borne diseases struck. In his first dispatch as commander, Mitchel notified General

Halleck in Washington of yellow fever on the post. It had begun with the illness of an officer returning from Key West on the steamer *Delaware*. Eight people had died. The medical director reported no new cases.[11] But the fever had not run its course.

An aide-de-camp to Mitchel died. A colonel seen conferring with the general a few days earlier died, and then General Mitchel died on October 30. He had been on Hilton Head just six weeks.

Thirteen-minute guns fired in salute. The flag flew at half-mast. Officers put on badges of mourning. The man who called himself a friend of enslaved people was gone.

The village soon bore the name Mitchelville, in honor of the late general. It was an all-black village of contrabands, and a self-governing town with streets laid out. With a mayor, councilmen, treasurer, and other officers, the town government eventually would oversee every aspect of village life from sanitary regulations to settling town disputes.

Mitchelville later would establish the first compulsory education law in South Carolina. Recognizing the importance of education, the law would require "every child, between the ages of six and fifteen years" to attend school.

Created, in part, by the Department of the South, it was the most visible experiment in what the *New South* had labeled "the department of experiments."

The village rose upon two hundred acres of former cotton fields on Fish Haul Plantation. It lay close enough to Port Royal Sound to see the waves lapping against the shore and catch the sea breeze. A mile and a half to two miles away from the army post, it was near enough to glance across broad, sandy fields and see the main fort.

Horse-powered government sawmills ripped out the pine lumber the contrabands used to build their homes. Men set about building simple, one-board-thick frame houses.

Each house in Mitchelville sat on a quarter-acre lot, on a regularly laid out street, divided into squares. The houses stood on two-foot wooden piers. Most were no more than ten feet by twelve feet square—smaller than a plantation cabin. This kept much of each lot free for growing food crops and other family activities.

Some houses had glass windows, a wonder to the former slaves. Others had wooden shutters that closed to cover window holes. Chimneys constructed of bricks salvaged on the island poked out from an occasional rooftop, although most houses had simple stovepipes vents. The front doors of some houses sported ceramic door knobs.

The village was a small step, but a huge one for people emerging from slavery. Contrabands had a home of their own in which to live and raise a family, and a big enough area outside to plant a few crops.

The northern press came to see.

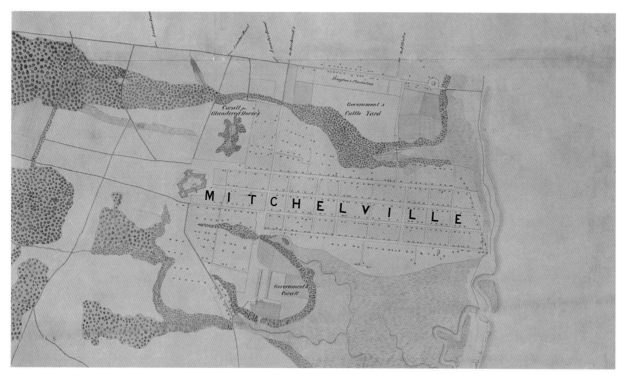

Map of Mitchelville on Hilton Head Island, First Freedmen's Village in the United States. *Records of the Office of the Chief of Engineers, 1789–1999, National Archives*

Outside of the army post, "General Mitchell caused a village to be laid out, where there are now upwards of a hundred houses; and on General Drayton's place another is growing up from the same demand," Charles Nordhoff wrote for the *Atlantic Monthly*.[12]

"General Mitchel's village was unfortunately laid out on too contracted a scale. The plot of ground assigned to each cottage is not large enough to furnish support to the owners, as is desirable, for the present. . . . However, the people are contented and industrious; I saw the women and children in every 'lot,' planting sweet potatoes, and preparing the ground for corn. I observed that wood ashes are used as manure."

At the time of his visit Nordhoff reported that "about one thousand able-bodied blacks are employed" in the military or as laborers "by the Quartermaster's Department for $4.00 a month plus military rations."

The figure represented a double-fold increase in the number of contrabands who worked over the previous year, explaining the need for additional housing on the grounds of the former Fish Haul Plantation. Most of the residents of Mitchelville worked for the quartermaster or the military, though some were engaged in business or trade.

That same March, forty-eight contrabands led by their plantation driver escaped from their master's fields on a plantation on the mainland near Grahamville.

Mitchelville gained forty-eight more residents that day.

A second news correspondent visited Mitchelville at about the same time as Nordhoff and found the houses crude to his taste.

Charles Carleton Coffin of Boston estimated that at the time of his visit "there were about 70 houses — or cabins rather — of the rudest description, built of logs, chinked with clay brought up from the beach, roofs of long split shingles, board floors, windows with shutters, plain board blinds without sash or glass. . . . There was no paint or lime, not even whitewash." Coffin failed to mention that few of the army's buildings were painted or whitewashed either.

In one cabin, no more than twelve feet square, Coffin could "see through the chinking in a hundred places. At the coping of the roof where it should have joined the walls, there was a wide opening all around, which allowed all the warmth to escape."

Some of the early houses in Mitchelville may have been built under the direction of the superintendent of contrabands on Hilton Head. During General Mitchel's address at the church dedication two weeks before his death, he had said, "I am told by your Superintendent [of Contrabands] that a gang of fifty men are building your houses at the rate of six a week."[13]

The general's comment seemed to conflict with *New South*'s statement that "the [N]egroes are to build their own houses," so it may be that the first houses were built by contrabands who were employed as carpenters by the quartermaster's department. Or it could be that after General Mitchel's death the responsibility for home-building fell to each family. The houses did not display a standard, military-style design or precision. They showed so much variety in materials and skill that many were apt to have been built by village residents.

A cabin Coffin entered may have been a hastily built shelter.

Inside the cabin, Coffin met an old man by the name of Jacob sitting before a fire trying to get warm. Jacob had escaped from a Florida plantation fifty miles inland, made his way to Fernandina, reached the lines of the Union army, and returned with the army to Hilton Head.

Tables, chairs, and a mahogany washbasin furnished the room, all of which Coffin judged to have come from a planter's home. A Dutch oven sat on the hearth. Other than those items, Jacob, dressed in old trousers and the "tattered cast-off blouse of a Union soldier," had an assortment of "pots, kettles, baskets, and bags, and a pile of rags and old blankets."

For the past five months Jacob had unloaded vessels at Hilton Head for the Union. So far he was yet to receive his pay, a not uncommon situation on the island. He was given his rations and a few clothes only, which left him in great need.

Seeing him in his present circumstance, Coffin questioned Jacob's ability to manage as a free man.

"Do you think you can take care of yourself?" Coffin asked.

" 'Jes let gubberment pay me, boss, and see if I can't,' Jacob replied with great earnestness." He was, after all, a man who had eluded would-be captors on a fifty-mile trek to freedom.

If Coffin was underwhelmed by the village in which others took pride, he was impressed with the symbolic heart of the community—the church.

"There were two rows of benches, a plain pine pul-

pit, a ventilated ceiling from which three or four glass lamps were suspended—all being very much like the rude churches to be found in the thinly-settled prairies of Illinois," he recorded.

As he entered the church, the congregation was singing "Roll Jordan," led by a young, energetic man "whose zeal was bounded only by the capacity of his lungs."

The women sat on one side of the house, the men on the opposite, Coffin observed, with "perfect decorum and solemnity. All heads were bowed when the preacher addressed the Throne of God. It was a prayer full of supplication and thanksgiving, expressed in fitting words."

After the sermon, a case of discipline was heard against the sexton.

Rev. Murchison called the sexton to the front and began.

"John, my son, you are arraigned for not doing as you have agreed and covenanted to do. We pay you one hundred and twenty dollars a year for lighting these very beautiful lamps which the church has generously provided, and sir, you have been remiss in your duties. On Thursday night, when we were assembled for holy prayer, we were in darkness. You did wrong. You broke your obligations. You must be punished. What say you? Brethren, we will hear what he has to say."

"I lighted the lamps, sah, but they went out. De oil was bad I reckon," said the sexton.

The pastor asked one of the deacons to take the chair so that he could stand among the congregation and express his point of view. The new chair was a middle-aged, bald-headed deacon wearing pants and a coat made of old sailcloth.

"Brother cheerman," Murchison began, "Our brother was presumptuous and should be punished. He said he light de lamps and dey go out. How does he know dey go out? He ought to stay and see dey don't go out. He was presumptions and should be punished. I move, sir, dat our brother be set side from comin to de Lord's table till he make satisfaction."

The question was put to the deacons.

The deacons voted unanimously to bar the sexton from the privileges of the church until he had made compensation.[14]

Coffin called the meeting more orderly than a legislative body he knew back East.

While set off from the post, the residents of Mitchelville still suffered intrusions from marauding white soldiers, some of whom came to houses on the pretense of enlisting blacks into the army.

A Mitchelville man came running to Murchison's house one night saying that three soldiers were "trublin'" his wife.[15]

Murchison returned with the man to his house and saw the three men who had committed rape on the man's wife. The three, officers of the 25th Ohio Regiment, were under the influence of liquor. They had alcohol with them and had given some to Mitchelville men. The officers claimed they had a paper authorizing them to enter the village to recruit colored soldiers, but Murchison gathered five witnesses to the crime.

"We have been trubled very often by these officers & Sailors & I think a stop aught to be Put to it," Murchison wrote Major General J. C. Foster.[16] The reverend said he did not think any of these officers or sailors should have night passes to come over to the Village "for they will not Behave them Selves as men."

Upon reading the letter, the provost marshal thundered, "The rule is for no men to be allowed to visit Mitchelville at night. Why is not this carried out? And who gives passes for this purpose?"

Murchison said that he had several men willing to assist him in keeping order in the village "if you will give me permission."

Murchison became magistrate of the village and the provost marshal general ordered the guard of black soldiers stationed at Mitchelville be directed "to arrest persons" whom Rev. Murchison "may designate for any riotous or disorderly conduct."[17]

Mitchelville, thus, gained a way to protect its residents from unwelcome intrusions.

The Greaves family, including their son Renty, moved into Mitchelville. Blacksmith Caesar Wright moved into the village at some point, as did Adam Jenkins, once enslaved at Fish Haul, Israel Ferguson, Mary Miller, Alfred Smalls, Mingo Brown, two men with the last name of Christopher, among many others.

In addition to having homes of their own, the new freedmen now had choices as to the goods they used. In slavery, they had been forced to rely on their master for what little clothing they had, most of their food and medicine, and such rare luxuries as tobacco. The freedmen now must feed and clothe themselves and buy other necessities from what money they earned.

They had a dazzling array of goods to view, wish for, and buy when they could find the money to pay for them. Store counters, at first on Robber's Row near the post, close to Mitchelville, were piled with ready-made clothing and brightly colored fabric. Sutlers (men who traveled with the army or set up in camps to sell items) also kept on hand everything from pots and pans, coffee boilers, tea kettles, pails, brooms, tubs, wash boards, and rolling pins, to fish nets, cologne, pomade, thread, buttons, thimbles, and even spectacles.

"[T]here is a great demand for plates, knives, forks, tin ware, and better clothing, including even hoop skirts. [Coarse] Negro cloth . . . [is] very generally rejected," an observer noted. "But there is no article of household furniture or wearing apparel, used by persons of moderate means among us, which they will not purchase when they are allowed the opportunity of labor and earning wages."

Even when the contrabands had lived in the barracks and wore tattered clothing, some of them had managed to taste freedom's wares.

A reporter noted that, "All were decently dressed; some of the women indulging in jewelry and hoops that might have excited the admiration of those of pale complexion. The distinguishing feature in their dress was the turban, which is generally worn, and with a good deal of grace, giving to them an oriental and picturesque appearance. These head-dresses are of all colors, from the neutral tint up to the flaming red, and not infrequently combining half a dozen colors in a plaid."[18]

Nordhoff predicted that "the day which sees the introduction . . . of the itinerant Yankee peddler will be an important one. If he is only moderately honest, and quick-witted, he will be a valuable helper in advancing civilization here."[19]

Arm in arm with advancing contrabands, many in the North viewed contrabands' purchasing power as a way to enlarge markets for goods from northern factories.[20]

At least four stores run by northern sutlers, as they were called, later opened in Mitchelville. Two quickly went out of business, apparently for price gouging. An unnamed colored preacher behind Union lines felt compelled, "to preach against the extortions of the sutlers from which his flock had suffered. He announced his text as follows: 'Now de serpent was more sutler than any beast of the field which the Lord hath made.'"[21]

Rampant consumerism never took place though. The freedmen lacked money for that. The only store to last throughout the 1860s was a small one opened in Mitchelville by contraband March Gardner. This store would continue into the 1890s.[22]

As a model for freedom, Mitchelville worked.

Mitchelville would become known as the first self-governing community of former slaves in the country. The village showed that people of African descent could govern themselves. It left a legacy for the future, and perhaps inspired one man living there who would later run for county-wide office.

Chapter Six

FIGHTING FOR THE UNION

SIMON GRANT stood on the riverbank waiting for a boat to transport him on a night expedition to Confederate-held James Island. It was the first week of July 1864.

Grant had been enslaved at Otter Hole Plantation on Hilton Head before the "Big Gun Shoot." He now was Private Grant in Company E of the 21st Regiment of the United States Colored Troops (USCT) Infantry, stationed on Morris Island.[1] From there, the Union was conducting a siege on surrounding Confederate-held islands and the city of Charleston in hopes of eventually capturing Charleston.

A boat filled with soldiers of the 21st Regiment USCT had just departed. Grant watched as the boat, pulled by a tug, cut a path through the evening darkness.

What Grant did not know was that the boat, after disappearing from sight, capsized, tossing colored soldiers into the Stono River. Some clung to the boat in hopes of rescue. Others floundered in the water. Many faced a watery death under a night sky.

Samuel Christopher of Hilton Head was on that boat. He fell overboard but survived.[2]

Christopher's and Grant's paths seldom crossed before the Union invasion, but they knew each other well now. Both served as musicians in same company of the 21st Regiment USCT. Grant was a fifer and Christopher a drummer.

Christopher had just gotten out of the camp hospital on Morris Island, where the 21st Regiment USCT and other regiments were stationed. The bright sun and intense glare from the sand had taken a toll on Christopher as he stood picket. His eyes swelled so badly he could hardly see. He stayed in the hospital for three weeks until his eyes no longer hurt and then returned to duty. Almost immediately Christopher received orders to go on the military expedition to James Island.

"I went over on the next boat," Grant said, "and after we got started, I missed Christopher."

Where was Christopher?

Harriet Tubman, a thin woman who dressed in high-neck blouses and billowing long skirts, once posed for a photograph holding a rifle half her size. She was, hands down, the most famous woman to step foot on Hilton Head during the Civil War. Her fame had spread North and South, though not under her real name.

Her work freeing slaves as the first black conductor on the Underground Railroad was attributed to a mysterious woman said to be "the Moses of her people," while those who knew her simply called her "Moses."

Tubman had arrived in the spring of 1862. She spent some time on Hilton Head, but more time in Beaufort

Harriet Tubman, ca. 1871–1876. Harvey B. Lindsley, Photographer. *Library of Congress*

where she nursed black soldiers in a military hospital established during the war. She tended the soldiers well, often concocting her own medicines from local herbs, and bided her time. She had other work to do.

She obtained authority from Secretary of War Stanton to organize and command a spy ring to infiltrate the rich heart of South Carolina's rice district along the Combahee River. As she gained intelligence, she reported directly to Generals Hunter and Saxton.

The contraband spies she organized blended in easily behind Confederate lines. They memorized river inlets, discovered where underwater torpedoes lay, learned the size and placement of rebel troops, and identified points along the river for slaves to gather to be freed when Tubman felt sure the mission would succeed.

Tubman's espionage led to a raid that had freed close to seven hundred and fifty slaves. The "Combahee River Raid" began on the night of June 2, 1863. Three Union gunboats with a hundred and fifty colored soldiers of the 2nd South Carolina Volunteers aboard slipped away from Beaufort, reached the Saint Helena Sound, entered the mouth of the Combahee, and quietly pushed upstream.[3]

Colonel James Montgomery, commander of the 2nd South Carolina Colored Volunteer Infantry Regiment was officially in charge of the Combahee River Raid, but "Moses" guided the way and the 2nd S.C. Volunteers fulfilled their part. At one point colored soldiers held off rebel sharp-shooters, "keeping up a sharp, effective fire, for half an hour," the *New South* reported.[4]

Union boats anchored offshore at pickup locations, then raised the Union flag and blew their whistles. Slaves poured from fields and cabins down to the river-side to climb into small rowboats that would carry them to the gunboats.

One woman arrived with a pot of smoking rice on her head fresh from the fire, a young one hanging on her neck with one hand and the other grabbing rice to eat out of the pot.

"Sometimes de women would come wid twins hangin' round der necks . . . bags on der shoulders, baskets on der heads, and young ones taggin' along behin', all loaded; pigs squealin', chickens screamin', young ones squallin'," Tubman said.[5]

Men, women, and children crowded into the row boats in fear they would not get to the gunboats anchored offshore to make their escape from slavery. They clung to the sides of the rowboats after the rowboats were full.

Montgomery suggested to Tubman that she lead them in song when a rowboat filled up.[6] Tubman did so. At the end of every verse, black men and women clinging to the rowboats released their grasp and threw up their hands to shout, "Glory!" The rowboat immediately pushed off, rowed the contrabands already on board out to the larger boat, and then returned for more escapees.

By late morning on June 3, Tubman and the Union soldiers, including the men of the 2nd U.S. Volunteers, arrived back in Beaufort. The soldiers burned fields of rice and cotton and set torch to storehouses, plantation buildings, and homes, including those of "Mr.

Middleton," one of the richest and most aristocratic families in the rice country. Outraged Confederates realized they had been outwitted by superb intelligence and "a parcel of Negro wretches calling themselves soldiers, with a few degraded whites."[7]

The mission's main objective was to gather new recruits for the 2nd South Carolina Volunteers. Many of the fresh contrabands enrolled in Beaufort, but Tubman would recall taking one hundred men to Hilton Head to sign up with the army.

Renty Franklin Greaves's enlistment was a far cry from that of the other men. At eighteen years old, he no longer was the child who had fallen into the boiling pot of plantation soup. He was trading and trafficking among the islands, apparently delivering produce and other needed goods. His health had improved somewhat, but he knew he was unfit for military service.

His life changed on June 24, 1863.

Soldiers broke into his house at midnight one night and forced him to go to the base and enlist.

"I was physically disabled when I was compelled to join. I was suffering from a weak back and general disability. I was not stripped and the medical examination was so casual that it was a mere mockery. They measured me and that was all they did except to ask me my age," Greaves said.[8]

He might have been less shocked if he had known

of an article in the *New South*, "The Draft of Camp-Followers." It informed readers that under "General Orders, No. 41, current series" of the Department of the South, lists of draftees were being prepared of men considered to be able-bodied camp followers.

"Gen. Hunter . . . fails to see in the class of unauthorized traders, hucksters, land speculators, bill-discounters, and gamblers who infest the various posts of this Department any just grounds of public or private merit upon which they should be exempted from the burdens of the draft imposed by recent legislation upon all citizens remaining in the Northern States.

"They will be seized when they least expect, and will find themselves suddenly elevated, against their wills, to the dignity of armed soldiers of the Republic," the *New South* heralded.

Greaves wound up in Company D of the 21st Regiment. As a conscript, he was not allowed to enlist as Renty Greaves. He was Private Renty Cruel to the army.

Cruel's company stayed on Hilton Head until January 1864. Company D then went to Jacksonville, Florida. "Then we went to Olustee but were ordered to retreat before we got there," Greaves said. The bodies of black Union soldiers lay strewn on the battleground, some with twigs of the herb Life Everlasting—said to foster long life—tucked into their uniforms. The Union had lost the Battle of Olustee in North Florida. Greaves and others in his company were fortunate that a retreat was called.

His company returned to Jacksonville and stayed there until the early spring of 1864, and then went to Morris Island. Greaves's back and overall health had been further weakened by military duty by that time. The glaring summer sun proved the last straw. "I was sunstruck on Morris Island while I was on picket duty," Greaves said. He was relieved from duty and carried to the post hospital. Six weeks later, on July 22, 1864, "Cruel" received a disability discharge.

It took the army fourteen months to recognize what Greaves knew from the beginning.

An officer noted on the discharge papers that Renty Cruel never had been able to do duty as a soldier, "except a little light fatigue duty, and now is unable to do any duty whatever as a soldier."

While "Cruel" lay hospitalized, the expedition to James Island, in which twenty men in the 21st Regiment drowned in the Stono River, took place.

Morris Island looked like any other long sandbar from the distance, but its location made it a linchpin in the Union campaign against Charleston. In July of 1864 the Union controlled the island. The Confederate army had abandoned the island following long and arduous Union sieges.

The island lay on the main shipping channel to Charleston. Fort Wagner, on the narrow northern end of Morris Island, sat just twenty-six hundred yards from Fort Sumter. The massive fort had been built as part of the defenses of Fort Sumter and the Charleston Harbor. The city of Charleston was so close that anyone with field glasses standing near the fort on a clear day could see men working at the Charleston wharves.

The previous July, the Confederates had held Morris Island. On the eighteenth day of July 1863, the Union waged a bloody battle to capture Fort Wagner. Approximately five hundred members of the all-black 54th Massachusetts died or suffered serious injuries in the failed attempt. Colonel Robert Gould Shaw, the unit's white, twenty-four-year-old commander, had rallied his men by shouting, "Forward, Fifty-Fourth, Forward!" As Shaw mounted a parapet, a bullet struck his heart and he died. His men kept on fighting, even as more died.

The North recognized the valor and sacrifice of the men of the 54th. The fighting spirit and the loss of so many men in the 54th lent support to add more colored troops.

This July, the tents of several Union regiments, plus artillery units and other detachments, lined the beach, with their tent doors facing the sea to catch breezes. With so many troops present the island resembled a small town.

The 21st Regiment USCT sat near the center of the other regiments. The booming sound of shells from Union and Confederate cannons jarred the air. Men ducked as shells flew overhead. The Union battered away at Fort Sumter with little effect.

In addition to holding Morris Island, the Union held Folly Island, a barrier island immediately below Morris, and Coles Island, just inward of Folly. Both lay to the south of Morris Island. The Stono Inlet, fresh from the Atlantic, ran along the lower edge of Folly Island and around Coles. Here, the inlet became the Stono River. It ran a curving course between James Island and Johns Island, both Confederate-held. A battery on James Island lay above the Stono River. The boat that Samuel Christopher boarded was headed to a location near there when it capsized.

As Samuel Christopher was thrown overboard into the Stono River, a gun fell between his legs and mashed his right testicle. He took in saltwater in his stomach and eyes and feared he would drown, but "caught hold of the boat." He managed to hang on and that saved him. Somehow Christopher and other survivors were taken on shore—possibly by men who had been pulling the boat he was on.

"We spent the night on Folly Island," Christopher said. "The next morning I was sent back to camp by the officers of [a] New York . . . regiment who were on Folly Island." Someone, he never knew who, took him to a landing on Morris Island. "I walked from there to camp, only about three miles. When I got to camp I went to the [doctor] of the 3rd Rhode Island Regiment and he gave me some medicine and told me to bathe in cold water."

His testicle remained "swollen and a little painful . . . causing me to walk with a limp for awhile."[9]

The Union army and navy continued to try to take James Island until July 11, when they returned to Morris Island. At least three white soldiers died of heat stroke during the campaign and numerous white troops disappeared, possibly to become prisoners of war. An army officer concluded that the Union lacked enough manpower and boats to capture James Island at this time.

When Simon Grant returned to Morris Island on July 11, he found Christopher in his tent. Christopher had suffered damage that would lead to life-long afflictions, but at this moment he felt simply lucky to be alive.

The army first reported that eighteen men of the 21st Regiment USCT drowned in the Stono River on July 2. A second report upped the number to twenty.[10]

Nine men, either born on Hilton Head or living there, drowned. Of these, eight were privates. Among them was twenty-one-year-old Private Napoleon Harris. His army record stated that he "has received clothing from us amounting to $73.02 since enlistment" and that he owed a sutler the sum of $1.50. The space to be checked to indicate whether or not Harris had received his initial bounty advance was blank.

Sergeant Rueben Pope was the only man of rank among those who drowned.

Pope's wife, Clara, had birthed four children by him, all of whom had died. She was pregnant with another child when her husband drowned. In three months'

Pension record for Samuel Christopher for his service in the Civil War. *Courtesy of the Heritage Library, Hilton Head, SC*

time, Clara would name her newborn son Reuben in honor of his father. The second Reuben would die at age four. Sergeant Pope's line, like that of many men who died during the war, ended then.

A pall hung over the camp of the 21st Regiment USCT.

Esther Hawks, a teacher on Hilton Head and wife of the regimental surgeon, wrote in her diary that the capsizing of the boat was "occasioned by the carelessness of the Capt. of the steamer [or tugboat] who attempted to tow the boat across the river.

"This cast gloom over the regiment, which would not have resulted had they fallen in battle."[11]

Their deaths had been in vain.

The war dragged on.

The steamer *Arago* that brought William Lloyd Garrison and others to Hilton Head Island. *Library of Congress*

Chapter Seven

JUBILEE

UNION SOLDIERS rushed across the Charleston Harbor, each regiment vying to reach the fallen city before other regiments did. The 21st Regiment USCT won the race and entered the city first.

The black soldiers of the 21st marched in as liberators of Charleston's enslaved black population—the largest slave population in South Carolina.[1]

Hilton Head freedmen such as Matt Jones, James Drayton, Polido Fields, Moses Brown, Prince Brown, Samuel Christopher, and father and son Thomas and Renty Miller well remembered their own liberation—the day the Union had seized Hilton Head nearly four years before.

Now, on the afternoon of February 18, 1865, their turn came. The soldiers from Hilton Head and other Sea Islands were the liberators—black liberators liberating other blacks. This was an honor so high that the men of the 21st Regiment USCT could not have dreamed of it in their old lives as slaves.

Joy spread among Charleston's black populace, who for years had endured Union guns raining destruction upon the city. Throughout it all, black citizens of Charleston prayed freedom would arrive.

One elderly black woman had gone to bed the night before fearing that her master would carry her off with him as he fled into the interior. At daybreak, she still feared, but she fretted less as the morning passed. Then, in the afternoon, as if in answer to her prayers, she heard shouts coming from the street and hundreds of voices lifting the cry, "Liberty."

Looking out, she saw a soldier riding a mule, "dashing up Meeting Street at the head of the advancing column, bearing in his hand, as he rode a white flag, upon which was inscribed, in large black letters, LIBERTY." She rushed outside with outstretched arms to hug the soldier. As the soldier, mounted atop the mule, was out of reach, she hugged the mule around the neck, shouting, "Thank God! Thank God!"[2]

The woman's gratitude drew tears to the eyes of bystanders. Nothing could curb the woman's joy, or that of thousands of other black residents whose enslavement ended as the soldiers marched in.

After spreading the joyful news of liberty, the men of the 21st Regiment USCT, along with other black and white troops entering the city, turned to fighting flames leaping from cotton warehouses, buildings, the railroad depot, and bridges. Fleeing Confederates had set the city afire in an effort to slow the Union's entry.[3]

The raging firestorm threatened to destroy all of Charleston. Despite the Union's efforts to quell the flames, four square miles of the city lay burned at the end of the next day.[4]

When the flames died down, the role of the men of the 21st USCT went from that of black liberators and saviors of the city to that of laborers cleaning up debris from the fire and years of Union bombardment. Large parts of Charleston lay nearly demolished by Union shells.[5]

Two moments of shining glory, however, awaited the Hilton Head black soldiers, as well as other men of the 21st Regiment USCT from Georgia, Florida, and other parts of South Carolina.

The first occurred after Union General Ulysses S. Grant ordered all white soldiers in Charleston to leave the city and pursue the fleeing rebels. Grant then instructed General Gillmore to keep the 21st Regiment USCT in Charleston. As a result of Grant's decisions, for nearly a week the 21st controlled Charleston.[6]

Some soldiers in the 21st Regiment USCT had been raised in Charleston. Others had relatives in the city. Many more had ties to the city's entrenched slave past.

Slavery in Charleston had been a way of life since 1670.[7] Over a two-hundred-year period, many of the soldiers' ancestors would have been sold on Charleston's infamous auction block. Fort Moultrie, on nearby Sullivan's Island, was the largest port of entry on the North American continent for the African slave trade. Fresh Africans, offloaded from slave ships, were held at the fort to insure they were free from disease and then taken in chains to Charleston's auction block.

Every man in the 21st Regiment USCT knew Charleston's history. The colored soldiers could not fail to marvel that they, former slaves on the coastal islands—for a brief few days—controlled the city.

Within a week, the Union command placed the 127th New York Volunteers, organized on Staten Island, in charge of the city. A portion of the 21st Regiment USCT then became part of the garrison force. Colored soldiers no longer needed on provost duty were sent outside the city to support white regiments or work on strengthening fortifications and other labor details.[8]

The 127th New York Volunteers had participated in the siege of Charleston and seen service in the Sea Islands but showed racial sympathies akin to those of many whites in Charleston. An observer said that members of the 127th "insulted the colored people" and on occasion, "stoned them, knocked them down, and cut them."[9]

The Union quickly moved to restrict white provost guards to white neighborhoods only, and assigned black provost guards to patrol black neighborhoods. The men of the 21st Regiment USCT then stepped into the role of protectors of the black populace, reducing racial tensions in the city, at least temporarily.[10]

The crowning moment of glory for the men of the 21st Regiment USCT happened a few weeks after their arrival as black liberators. In late March, Charleston's black men and women organized a huge parade to celebrate their emancipation.

In the words of the correspondent for the *New York Daily Tribune*, "It was a procession of colored men, women and children, a celebration of their deliverance from bondage and ostracism; a jubilee of freedom, [and] a hosanna to their deliverers."[11]

First came the marshals on horses "decorated with red, white and blue rosettes," followed by a rousing band, and then the 21st Regiment USCT marched in full form, along with one hundred colored marines. Clergymen carrying their Bibles came next, then a procession of twelve hundred black children of Charleston, many of whom had begun school since the Union had conquered the city. The children sang "John Brown's Body," repeating again and again the refrain, "Glory, Glory, Hallelujah! We go marching on."

The black tradesmen of Charleston came next, with the fishermen bearing banners welcoming General Saxton, the people's favorite in the Union Department of the South. Black carpenters carried their planes; masons, their trowels; teamsters, whips; barbers, shears; blacksmiths, hammers; painters, brushes; wheelwrights, a large wheel; bakers had crackers strung around their necks; and hosemen of ten fire companies bore trumpets.

A hearse followed, bearing signs proclaiming the death of slavery, while fifty women wearing black, in false grief for slavery's death, marched behind with "joyous faces."

Then came Charleston's black societies, bearing banners.[12]

We know no caste or color
Our past the [auction] Block, our future the School
We know no master but ourselves
Our reply to slavery, Colored Volunteers
The Heroes of the War: Grant, Sherman, Sheridan
. . . *The Privates.*

More than fifty-five hundred people, in addition to the soldiers of the 21st, marched in the parade. The procession took one hour and twenty minutes, the *Daily Tribune* reported, and on its return to the citadel square, more than ten thousand people waited to see the marchers and hear General Saxton and the other speakers. The jubilee of freedom ended with one long cheer for President Lincoln.[13]

If Matthew Jones and the other Hilton Head men ever doubted that their black brothers and sisters appreciated their service, they would not after this day. The people took pride in the colored troops, and showed this pride throughout the parade. The triumphal march instilled respect for the colored soldier's role in securing freedom for all enslaved people.

On Hilton Head on April 13, 1865, William Lloyd Garrison, editor of the Boston antislavery newspaper the *Liberator* and the most famous white abolitionist in the North, stood behind the pulpit of the First African Baptist Church in Mitchelville—where General Mitchel once had expressed hope that the day of jubilee would come "to God's ransomed people."

Jubilee had arrived.

With the North winning the war, slavery soon would be abolished in the reunited nation. The spirit of Jubilee—the season of celebration in the Old Testament set aside in honor of the Israelites being set free—rocked the four walls of the First African Baptist.

The people of Mitchelville—"those clean, neatly, handsomely dressed people," as a letter in the *Liberator* had described them[14]—crowded into the densely packed church and "rapturously welcomed" Garrison and other members of his party.[15]

Garrison and other Northern dignitaries, each handpicked by Secretary of War Edwin Stanton, had arrived on the steamer *Arago* out of New York, en route to Charleston. On a stop at Hilton Head, Garrison and those with him wanted to see "the first self-governing settlement of freedmen in the country."

The list of those onboard included such notables as orator Henry Ward Beecher, brother of Harriet Beecher Stowe, author of *Uncle Tom's Cabin*; General Robert Anderson, U.S. commanding officer of Fort Sumter

The steamer *Arago* that brought William Lloyd Garrison and others to Hilton Head Island. *Library of Congress*

when the Confederates captured it in April of 1861; a member of the House of Representatives; U.S. Senator Charles Sumner, of avid antislavery sentiments; a British abolitionist; and Northern editors and reporters.[16]

Standing behind the pulpit, Garrison, a balding, bespectacled man in his fifties, looked out upon the colored congregation of the First African Baptist with amazement. He had fought for emancipation for thirty-five years, been deemed a dangerous radical by many Northerners and an outlaw in the South, been imprisoned, and physically attacked by a lynch mob. Through it all, he never missed getting out an issue of the *Liberator*, the gospel of the antislavery movement.

Now, Garrison was getting to see emancipated people in the flesh, such people as Abraham Murchison, preacher of the First African Baptist Church, as well as a village official, and such Mitchelville residents, perhaps, as Lucinda Greaves, wife of George Greaves and mother of the soldier Renty Greaves. Seeing people he had long fought for filled Garrison with delight.

"But I never expected to look you in the face, never supposed you would hear of anything I might do on your behalf. I knew only one thing . . . that you were a grievously oppressed people; and that on every consideration of justice, humanity, and right you were entitled to immediate and unconditional freedom."[17]

Garrison chose as his text Moses parting the Red Sea for the children of Israel, the very chapter in Exodus that had brought hope for freedom to Sea Island slaves.

William Lloyd Garrison, abolitionist, journalist, and editor of the *Liberator*, ca. 1870. *Library of Congress*

Then Garrison spoke for thirty minutes, informing the congregation of the long history of the antislavery movement in the North that led to Lincoln's Proclamation, "which had answered all their prayers."[18]

Tears flowed and emotions ran high among both visitors and congregants. Island residents sang with fervor old hymns and songs they had sung in bondage. Then they launched into a song fitting to the hearts of all present: "The Day of Jubilo hab' come."

The people of Mitchelville had worked hard, cultivated their crops, strengthened their families, and either worked or fought for the Union. They had succeeded in each charge General Mitchel had laid on them when he told them that "all the people in the Free States are looking at you, and the experiment now being tried in your behalf . . . if you are successful, this plan will go all through the country."

Garrison and his fellow abolitionists left Mitchelville impressed by the "thriftiness and comfort such as is suggested by a quiet New England village."[19] Convinced after his visit to Mitchelville that "the freed slave can govern as well as support himself," Garrison foresaw a bright future for the village residents.

At daybreak the next morning, the *Arago* reached Charleston. Entering the city, Garrison called it "smitten with dust."

News swept Charleston of General Robert E. Lee's surrender at Appomattox, raising excitement to a fever point. The end of the war was at hand.

Laura Towne, founder of the Penn School on Saint Helena, had come for the ceremonies. She first made a pilgrimage to a site that bespoke the cruelties of slav-ery, the workhouse—or "old sugar-house" as it was called—where slaves were sent to be whipped. The whipping room, as Towne noted, had "double walls filled in with sand so that the cries could not be heard in the street."

Towne asked an old colored woman if she was looking at the right building. "Dat's it," the woman said, "but it's all played out now."[20]

The few remaining white citizens in Charleston seemed to Towne "as full of spite as they can be." She heard one woman say, "see those nasty Yankees." A second woman remarked, "I wish I had their winding sheets [burial sheets] to make when the yellow fever comes."[21]

Upon reaching Fort Sumter, Towne saw that the side of the fortress that lay within gunshot of Fort Wagner and other Union forts was "a mass of ruins and big balls."

She judged the ceremonies uninspiring, labeling the oratory of the main speaker, Henry Ward Beecher, "without fire."[22]

But the Stars and Stripes flew again. General Anderson carefully carried the tattered flag that had flown over Fort Sumter at the time of surrender and raised it back atop the fort.

"Then the same old flag went up again . . . amidst the shouts and tears of the audience," Ester Hills Hawks, wife of the surgeon of the 21st Regiment USCT wrote. "It was a scene never to be forgotten!—and we all hope, never to be repeated. The glorious old flag floats once more over the spot where it was for the first time humbled!"[23]

The evening of the ceremony at Fort Sumter — Good Friday, April 14, 1865 — President Lincoln and his wife, Mary Todd Lincoln, sat watching a play at Ford's Theatre when Confederate sympathizer John Wilkes Booth broke into the presidential box and fatally shot the president.

Lincoln died the next morning at twenty-two minutes after seven as a light rain fell on Washington. Bells tolled, announcing his death. On Pennsylvania Avenue in front of the executive mansion, Secretary of the Navy Gideon Welles saw "several hundred colored people, mostly women and children, weeping and wailing their loss."

In Charleston, a freedmen's celebration at Zion Church Saturday morning, the finale to the flag-raising festivities, went on as planned. No one knew that President Lincoln lay silent in death. Days would pass before a steamer carrying the news arrived.

Later, at the Charleston Harbor, as the steamer of Northerners prepared to depart, black abolitionist Major Martin R. Delaney — a former editor of Frederick Douglass's *North Star*, a recruiter for two new regiments of the USCT, the first colored soldier ever to receive a field-grade commission in the Union army, and a man soon to be known on Hilton Head — seized the moment to yell out into the crowd of emancipated blacks: "*Do anything; die first! But don't submit again to them — never again be slaves!*"[24]

When the news of the Great Emancipator's death reached Hilton Head and the other Sea Islands, grief struck the freedmen, along with fear for their futures as well. If Lincoln, the head of the government, was dead, wasn't the government dead too? One freedman spoke for many when he asked, "We going to be slaves again?"[25]

Jubilee — so short — was over.

New battles loomed.

Chapter Eight

A NEW WORLD

WITH THE WAR NOW OVER, Hilton Head's black Union soldiers came back to shape a new way of life on a twelve-mile island bounded by salt-water rivers and the ocean.

James Drayton had blown the bugle in battle on James Island. He was mustered out of the 21st Regiment USCT on April 25, 1866, in Charleston, and returned home to farm with his father, Simon.

Once home, he found his father had exercised one of the most basic rights of freedmen: that of selecting his own last name.

"I don't know how my father got the name of Grant," he later said, "but when I came back from the war I found him with that name, and then I took up the name."[1] Henceforth, except to men who had known him in the army, James Drayton was known to most people on the island as James Drayton Grant.

Within days of his discharge, James Drayton Grant exercised a second right of free men and women: to marry when and whom they pleased. He took his sweetheart as his wife, Mary Ann Mathis. Their first child, a son they named Richard, burst forth squalling into a new world.

The couple's children and grandchildren and future descendants would live "forever free." The Union had won. Forced bondage on Hilton Head had ended. This, the men of Hilton Head had helped to ensure.

William Simmons came home in good shape. He was

just recovering from smallpox when he enlisted. After the army took Charleston, Simmons was assigned to the military hospital there. With his acquired immunity to smallpox, Simmons nursed men stricken with the disease. He also could drop his wartime name, "Ira Sherman."

Other Hilton Head men began their postwar lives bearing wounds or afflicted with lingering ailments incurred in the army.

Aaron Christopher, who had joined the First South Carolina Volunteers on November 1, 1862, before it became the 33rd Regiment, served under Higginson before Higginson was wounded and left the regiment. At the time of enlistment, Christopher listed his occupation as "waiter," which meant that he had been hired to serve a well-to-do soldier. Christopher had a checkered career, including a stint recruiting soldiers, a brief confinement in the provost guard house, and daily duty in a boat.

He received an honorable discharge in January 1866, shortly before his regiment was mustered out, after getting a gunshot wound in his right foot.

Christopher Green came back with his left arm amputated below the elbow. While on guard duty in Beaufort in early April of 1865, a stack of guns fell to the ground. One discharged, sending a ball through his left hand from a distance of six feet. In warm weather, his arm swelled and ached. In cold weather, his arm severely pained him.

The Freedmen's Bureau (officially titled the Bureau of Refugees, Freedmen, and Abandoned Lands), issued a pass to Butler Seabrook in 1866 to return from the military hospital in Charleston to his home on Hilton Head. Seabrook required assistance on the trip as his feet had been amputated. He disappeared then from history.[2]

Some men did not make it through the war.

David Pope of Jenkins Island died of brain fever. Mike Robertson died of pneumonia. Josiah Symons died of inflamed lungs. Sussex Brown died of complications from a varicose vein.

Andrew Baynard, brother of Mary Brown, who lived on one of the Baynard plantations on the Day of the Big Gun Shoot, died of smallpox in the Hilton Head Hospital. A smallpox epidemic had broken out during the war, killing many soldiers. Baynard's body was buried the same day he died to prevent the spread of smallpox.

Baynard's brother-in-law Prince Brown also contracted smallpox on Hilton Head, though he did not die.

Those were in addition to the Hilton Head black Union soldiers who drowned on the Stono River in July 1864 on their way to do battle at James Island. Of the Hilton Head men who drowned, all but one had enlisted in the 21st Regiment on the same day: April 24, 1863.

General Saxton, now head of the Freedmen's Bureau in South Carolina, Georgia, and Florida, raced for time.

Illustration representing the mission of the Freedmen's Bureau, drawn by A. R. Ward in 1868. *Library of Congress*

With Andrew Johnson now president of the United States, Saxton feared his assignment would end too soon. Missionaries in the Port Royal Experiment, as well as abolitionists elsewhere, had thought ahead as to what would happen to the freedmen if the Union won the war. They believed that the freedmen needed to come into freedom with some economic security in order to have a good chance of succeeding.

Saxton's assignment was to resettle and allot acreage of ten to twenty acres to freedmen in the three states that had formed the Department of the South. General William T. (Tecumseh) Sherman had appointed him to this task.

Sherman had just completed the March to the Sea, from Atlanta, Georgia, to Savannah, in December of 1864. Thousands of black refugees had fallen in behind Sherman's troops, to the displeasure of some of Sherman's officers. Many refugees had died along the way and more would as they followed Sherman into Beaufort, Hilton Head, and farther into South Carolina.

Secretary of War Stanton arrived to seek the freedmen's opinion on issues involving their future. A meeting occurred with twenty black leaders and Stanton and Sherman in General Sherman's headquarters on January 12, 1865.[3]

Stanton posed a question to the assembled black ministers, barbers, pilots, sailors, and former overseers of cotton and rice plantations: "Would they prefer living scattered in communities of mixed white and black settlements or in an area totally restricted to Negroes?"

All but one of the assembled black leaders said that they preferred to live by themselves, "for there is a prejudice against us in the South that it will take years to get over."[4]

Out of that meeting grew Sherman's "Special Field Order Number 15," issued in early January 1865. Under the order, the Sea Island region, from "Charleston southward to the Saint Johns River [in Florida], and the coastal lands thirty miles to the interior," were set aside for Negro settlement only.[5] The area covered lands that planters had abandoned during the war. Saxon had helped freedmen buy land and, as time ran out, simply let them stake out land on which they would like to live.

Thousands of freedmen received land, including small lots on Saint Helena and in Beaufort.

Following Lincoln's assassination, President Andrew Johnson repealed Special Field Order Number 15. This led to turmoil that swept the surrounding Sea Islands, except for Hilton Head.

Two thousand people on Edisto assembled in a local church to protest the loss of land they had believed they would permanently own.[6] The news that they would lose their recently gained land preceded the arrival of the head of the Freedmen's Bureau, General O. O. Howard.

Howard told them they must sign labor contracts with their former white owners or be evicted from the land. He urged them not to be bitter and to reconcile with their former masters.

"No, never," shouted the freedmen. "Can't do it. Why, General Howard," an Edisto Island freedman protested, "do you take away our lands?"[7] But the Freedmen's Bureau was powerless now. Neither General Howard nor Saxton could help any longer. President Johnson was focused on reuniting the country as quickly as possible, and did not consider the freedmen of importance.

General Saxon was replaced by General R. K. Scott, who devised a compromise. The white planters would reclaim their former lands, but they could not forcibly remove the freedmen living on the land except for cause. President Johnson let Scott's solution stand.

The Freedmen's Bureau switched from handing out homesteads to supervising labor contracts between the freedmen and the planters—which usually were with their former masters. If the freedmen refused to the terms of the contracts, they could be evicted.

On Hilton Head, freedmen had been spared the bitter upheaval of losing Sherman homesteads.[8] Little, if any, land was distributed. The government planned to keep possession of Hilton Head until certain that the war would not reignite.

Thus, former plantation owners could not return to Hilton Head at this time. In their absence, the crops still grew. Men and women were needed to plant, cultivate, and harvest them.

The Hilton Head plantations once owned by Graham, Steward, and Dr. Pope were marked as property of the Sea Island Cotton Company or, later, the U.S. Cotton Company, on Freedmen's Bureau reports.[9] Hilton Head freedmen who could scrape together money to rent land farmed for themselves. Others worked as wage hands.

At the old "Drayton" Fish Haul plantation, a portion of which Mitchelville occupied, freedmen had farmed the land on a cooperative basis beginning in 1862. They did so under a rental agreement with the U.S. Direct Tax Commission through 1867. The agreement resembled a labor contract, except that the freedmen did not farm under the thumb of a former plantation owner.

Half the rent was due to the Direct Tax Commission-

Tabby fireplace ruin for former dwelling for families enslaved on Fish Haul (Drayton) Plantation on Hilton Head Island.
Photo by Will Warasila

ers in January and the remainder in June. The rental terms allowed the government to take a lien on the crop, specified that no one then living on the property could be forced off, and required that the laborers perform their fair share of the work. The tax commissioners further specified that any government workers living on the land, but not part of the rental agreement, could cultivate up to three acres per hand at a cost of $2 per year.

By February 1867, more freedmen leased acreage on Hilton Head. "The freedmen on all of these [plantations] are engaged in cultivation, having been leased this year to them . . . an acre," Major Martin Delaney, the

Freedmen Bureau's agent on Hilton Head, reported in February of 1867. He noted with pride that the freedmen "are mainly self supporting."

Saxon had handpicked Delaney for the position on Hilton Head, and Delaney endeavored to support the freedmen. But Delaney's optimism over the freedmen's self-sufficiency died when the cold weather of 1867 ruined Hilton Head crops. Hunger set in.

The American Missionary Society purchased hominy and distributed it to teachers to give to the freedmen. A Missionary Society teacher, Eliza Ann Summers, who taught at the old Lawton plantation, divided the two large bags of hominy she received to families in need. Some of the people, she wrote to a sister in the North, "are suffering very much for want of something to eat. Many of them go a day or two with nothing in the world to eat but blackberries. One of my girls has been missing for over a week.

"She had been hoeing all day with her sister in the field, when her sister left her to go home for a short time. When she came back she could find nothing but the hoe her sister had standing in the row where she was at work. She did not mind it for she knew that her sister had had nothing to eat that day, and supposed that she had gone to pick blackberries as usual. But she did not come back and has not been heard of since. . . .

"She probably wandered off . . . in search of food or else she is lying around the field dead some where. I think the latter."[10]

"A fact to which attention is invited," Delaney wrote in his report for March, "that in consequences of the small quantities of land taken by each family, it is very evident, that the people will not be self supporting the current planting year."

To avoid this in times to come, "all working families of four must have ten acres to farm," Delaney said. "It will require from ten to twenty acres to support each family on cotton land."

Land restoration began creeping close to Hilton Head now. The former owner of a plantation on nearby Spring Island regained his former land. Across the Calibogue Sound from Hilton Head, two plantations on Daufuskie Island had been "redeemed" and Daufuskie freedmen worked under labor contracts.[11]

In mid-1867, change hit Hilton Head.

The army began pulling out. With the war nearly two years over, the army had little reason to stay. Many freedmen began leaving too, following the army and jobs, or moving to the mainland.[12] The population was in such a state of flux that Delaney could not get an accurate count of how many people were on each plantation. He estimated a third of the population had picked up stakes and gone.

In July, with the census complete, Delaney reported that seventeen hundred and fifty freedmen remained on the plantations. The largest number recorded at any of the plantations, three hundred and forty-four freedmen, lived on the Seabrook plantation. The former Elliott plantation had two hundred and twenty-four freedmen, the second highest number of freedmen. The smallest number of freedmen on any of the plantations, twenty, farmed one of the Stoney plantations.[13] Fish Haul had a hundred and twenty.

By January 14, 1868, the army, whose 1861 invasion had sent the planters fleeing and contrabands rushing to Hilton Head from Confederate-held areas, had left Hilton Head. Horses no longer whinnied in their stables. Saws no longer screeched. Sergeants no longer bellowed orders. A strange quiet fell over the island. For freedmen, the quiet signaled they were on their own.

A joyful event had occurred in the fall of 1867, one that Hilton Head freedmen could not have foreseen in their youth. They registered to vote.

Lawrence Savannah Barnwell, father of six-year-old Freeman Barnwell, registered. Father and son, George and Renty Greaves, joined those registering. Simon Grant, a free man for just five of his approximately sixty-three years, registered. Caesar Kirk, now Ceasar Jones, also registered.

Polido—"Paul LaDoe," as the army had listed him— a corporal who may have called the morning roster for Company "C" of the 21st Regiment, registered. His brother, Cuffy Fields, registered, too. The two brothers may have thought of their father, Peter, who had been

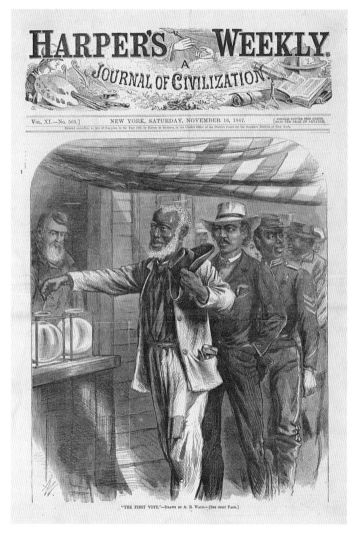

Print of wood engraving depicting African-American men, of various professions, lined up to vote, drawn by Alfred Waud. *Harper's Weekly*, November 16, 1867. *Library of Congress*

born on Hilton Head, and how he would have rejoiced in the day.

Among the many others in line to register were Alfred Mike, Israel Ferguson, Christopher Green, Primus Green, Joseph Riley, William Oriage, and Abraham Jones.[14]

Then, in November, Hilton Head freedmen were able to vote for delegates to the 1868 constitutional convention. When the delegates met they framed a new state constitution that would adopt a congressional requirement that no racial restriction be placed on suffrage.

This same year, James Drayton Grant farmed more than seven acres. He planted three acres of cotton, four acres of corn, and one-fourth acre of rice. His fields produced seventy-five pounds of cotton, thirty-five bushels of corn, and two bushels of rice, enough to feed his family.[15]

Alfred Mike farmed eight and a quarter acres. His two acres of cotton produced one hundred pounds; he yielded sixty bushels of corn on four acres, and ten bushels of rice on half an acre. Poldio Fields netted two hundred pounds of cotton from three acres of cotton he planted. He also grew thirty bushels of corn, two bushels of rice, and one bushel of peas.

The new citizens turned a corner. Starvation had been pushed back.

Bit by bit, parcel by parcel, freedmen scraped and sacrificed to buy a few acres of land whenever they could. A few would manage to buy large land tracts.

After the war, Caesar Jones had happily dropped "Kirk" from his name as that was the surname of his former master. From then on, he was Caesar Jones, as he had always considered himself to be. He settled in an area that became known as Jonesville.

Within his lifetime, Jones would acquire more than one hundred acres of land and his family would eventually acquire more than two hundred and seventy-five acres on the island.

The men and women freed from slavery shaped what came next on Hilton Head for generations to come: tilling the land and harvesting fish and shellfish from the sea; forming close family and community ties; living in small settlements scattered across the island near former plantation sites; observing church laws; and holding to old African customs.

Chapter Nine

REDEMPTION HITS MITCHELVILLE

THE NORTHERN MISSIONARIES and some of generals of the Department of the South never expected Mitchelville to disappear. But somehow the Union army neglected preparations needed to safeguard the freedmen's village.

Seven years after the Civil War ended, former Confederate General Thomas F. Drayton launched a new battle: recovering property he once managed on Hilton Head.

In March of 1873, Drayton wrote two Charleston attorneys seeking help in reclaiming Fish Haul plantation.[1] The land was now eligible for recovery by former owners under a congressional act applying to lands that the federal government still held title to.

"When we get the Right and Title of the U.S., the former general asked, 'Will there not be much trouble in rejecting the [N]egroes who hold titles . . . [through] sales made under Gen. Sherman's Order?'"

Drayton assumed that Sherman's Special Field Order Number 15 had affected Hilton Head in the same manner that it had affected other Sea Islands and coastal lands up to thirty miles inland. This part of Drayton's concern was not relevant. Hilton Head, as the headquarters of the Union Department of the South, was a different case.

But the redemption of Fish Haul to the Drayton family struck at the very symbol of freedom on Hilton Head — Mitchelville. The freedmen's village of Mitchelville sat on the site of an old cotton field at Fish Haul Plantation, and now Drayton wanted the land back.

Mitchelville's glory days ended when the army began pulling out in 1867. Military laborers began leaving the island, following the jobs. Other freedmen moved onto the island's plantations and took wage jobs. Then, the American Missionary Association School closed.

Freedmen continued to walk from miles away or ride in buggies or carts to attend the First African Baptist Church in Mitchelville. Several stores still hawked their wares, and families who lived in the village remained there. The people who continued to live in Mitchelville simply spread out their quarter-acre lots. There was plenty of vacant land.

The army barracks stood empty, and "the people gone then . . . and just broke them down. It was nothing to it. Nobody bother you. They go on through and they do just what they wanted to do and plant what they want to plant," Naomi Frazier remembered her mother saying.[2]

Caesar White, a blacksmith by trade, had lived on Fifth Street for years. Adam Green lived on Fourth Street in a one-story house measuring twenty by eighteen feet. He also had three smaller buildings on his lot and an enclosed orchard containing thirty-five fruit trees—enough to harvest fruit and take it to market.

The village included people with the family names of Smalls, Ferguson, Christopher, Jenkins, Miller, and others. Renty Greaves lived here. March Gardner lived here, as did his son Gabriel, who managed the property for him. A large barn, ninety by thirty feet, an engine

Sign for park marking the original Mitchelville site on Hilton Head Island. *Photo by William Edmunds*

and boiler, and a gin and two mills made March Gardner the most prosperous person in the village.[3]

Drayton faced two major obstacles in his quest: the freedmen and a shortage of money. For the Drayton family to recover the land they had to pay federal taxes and back interest, stemming from the federally imposed last tax of 1861. Drayton lacked the money to pay the federal taxes. As for the question of whether he could force the freedmen off the land, his lawyers may have informed him that federal law would not let him kick them off of Fish Haul after the land was repossessed.

Drayton and a son, William Drayton, decided on an expedient approach: sell some of the land to freedmen living there to raise the tax money they owed. Then the Drayton heirs, as the "rightful" owners, could redeem the land.

Their plan took two years.

The Internal Revenue office in Washington, DC, required the Draytons to resurvey the land as the freedmen who had lived on the plantation before the war remembered the plantation's boundary lines as different from the old land plats Drayton remembered.[4] William Drayton and a surveyor hunted for lines for days, he said, "sometimes up to our waists in water."

The former general and his son learned that even though the army had left Hilton Head, the federal government intended to retain more than eight hundred acres for use as a military reservation in case it was needed in the future. Eighty-four of the acres were on their land.

The Drayton family also learned that the government had sold houses to some people who still lived in Mitchelville and had not finished paying for them. Unless a solution was found, they would need to pay off that debt.

Renty Greaves and two other freedmen put in claims for improvements on the land they occupied in Mitchelville to the local Internal Revenue officer in Beaufort, Silas Wright. William Drayton suspected that Wright, a Negro, had put them up to the claims of improvement, and suggested "greasing" him to secure their path.

The Draytons also hired a "disinterested party" [from the Kirk family] to affix values to the residents' property. They decided to sell on terms of one-third cash down and two equal installments. White's property was valued at $769, Green's at $245, Brown's at $60, Noble's at $200, and Greaves's at $40. The Gardner property was valued higher, at $2,705.

The Internal Revenue officer, Wright, gave the Draytons the go-ahead to sell the property, as those living in Mitchelville were anxious to have the matter resolved. Months later, William Drayton wrote that of the men who bought property from them, only Gabriel Gardner had paid some of the note.

"The [N]egroes are miserably poor," he said, "and had I known as much at first, would never have incurred the expense of cutting up lands."[5]

Finally, in 1975, the heir of Mary B. Pope redeemed Fish Haul and the Pineland tract, including the village of Mitchelville, by paying the back taxes and interest of $407.83.

Mitchelville, the first self-governing town of former slaves in the nation—heralded in the national press as an example to be adopted elsewhere, visited by leading abolitionists at the end of the war, expected to accomplish great deeds—began to fade away.

William Drayton's transactions would create a tangled tale in the far-off future. It seemed that the former general's son earlier had sold the Mitchelville property to March Gardner, before redeeming the property was permitted.

The heirs of March Gardner—the father, and his son Gabriel—would see each other in court approximately forty years later.

Robert Smalls, S.C. M.C., born in
Beaufort, SC, April 1839. *Brady-Handy
Photo Collection, Library of Congress*

Chapter Ten

THE PINNACLE

E LECTION DAY 1876 DAWNED. Excitement, tension, heated tempers, and an attempt by a Democrat to hoodwink freedmen into voting for his party—Hilton Head Island would experience all of that on this day.

Nationally, Republican Rutherford B. Hayes and Democrat Samuel J. Tilden were slugging it out to win the U.S. presidency.

In South Carolina, the stakes also were high. The Democratic Party, composed almost entirely of southern whites, sought to overthrow what they considered "[N]egro rule" created by Reconstruction. They stood poised to be swept into power.

Confederate hero Wade Hampton was running for governor on the Democratic ticket. Northerner Daniel Chamberlain, governor since 1874, was the Republican nominee.

In black-dominated Beaufort County, Republican Robert Smalls, called "the King of Beaufort" and the "Gullah Statesman" by local newspapers, was waging a hard re-election fight for Congress against Democrat George D. Tillman, a former Confederate.

If that was not enough to spark islanders' interest, one of their own—Renty Franklin Greaves—was running on the Republican ticket for a seat on the Beaufort County Commission. He may have been the first Gullah man on Hilton Head Island to run for a political seat on the county level.[1]

Hilton Head had only one voting precinct: Mitchelville. No place could be more fitting, since residents of Mitchelville had learned how to vote in their own civic elections during the Port Royal Experiment, years before the coming of black suffrage in South Carolina.

Fifty-two-year-old W. H. Peeples, who identified himself as "a licensed minister of the Bible," arrived at the schoolhouse in Mitchelville at 4:00 a.m. to set up the polls. Peeples was an election manager for the Republican Party. A second election manager for the Republicans, Gabriel P. Gardner, arrived a little before 6:00 a.m.

The polls opened at precisely 6:00 a.m. Gardner sat by an open window through which the election tickets were to be given to men who did not already have one, and then the men, after marking their tickets, were to pass them back through the window. From there they would be deposited in the ballot box.

The election managers kept the schoolhouse door closed to keep tight control of the ballot box.

Perhaps ten men had voted by the time the main Democratic manager arrived. "Mr. Drayton came and knocked at the door. We opened the door and he came in," Gardner said. "He said he was a little late."

William S. Drayton, a son of former General Thomas Fenwick Drayton, thus entered the room.

After the Drayton family had redeemed much of its land, including Mitchelville, William Drayton had moved into Fish Haul. He had been living there for nearly two years.

Former soldier Simon Grant of Otter Hole, along with Isaac Jenkins and Edward Murray, stood outside the polls distributing "tickets" for the Republican Party—a card listing the slate of Republican candidates for election. This was the straight Republican ticket.

The tickets were both practical and a necessity. Only a small number of freedmen were literate. Having a ticket allowed men to cast their vote for Republican candidates. To vote for the entire Republican slate, a man simply cast the ticket as his ballot.

But that was before John McFall threw a wrench into the election.

Some said McFall voted a little after 7:00. Others said he cast his vote close to 9:00. But everyone knew that McFall, a white Democrat, was here this day of November 7, 1876.

"Captain" McFall, as one freedman called him, looked to be a man of about fifty years or more. He recently had moved to Hilton Head and lived, some said, near Drayton Place (Fish Haul). Few islanders knew much about him. McFall said little about himself. But by the end of this day, many freedmen regarded him a dishonest man.

McFall distributed the Democratic "ticket," a white

card printed with black ink, and also handed out a card labeled "Union Republican." That ticket was white but printed with red ink. It looked exactly like the Republican ticket freedmen were distributing.

A few people took McFall's Republican ticket. Others wondered why McFall was distributing tickets for the Republican Party, as he was not a Republican.

That struck freedman Thomas Bell as suspicious. Bell was in his seventies and known "to be a particular man." As he could not read, he liked bringing someone to the polls with him to make sure he cast his vote right. He did not have anyone with him this time, but his mind was sharp. He felt something was wrong with McFall's tickets.

Bell took his ticket to Gabriel Gardner and asked if this was the right ticket. Gardner looked at it, read the heading, "Union Republic," and said it was. Bell still was not satisfied, so he took the ticket to Renty Greaves, who was at the polls for most of the day.

Greaves read it and quickly saw that the ticket looked right, but all the names on the ticket were Democratic candidates. It listed Samuel Tilden for president at the top of the slate instead of the Republican candidate Rutherford Hayes, and farther down the slate, G. D. Tillman for Congress instead of Robert Smalls. Thomas Bell threw this ticket away and got a proper Republican ticket from Greaves.

That was how "the cat got out the bag," as one person put it. The ticket McFall was handing out was a good imitation of the Republican ticket. It was the same size, bore the Republican label and an eagle, and was printed in red ink.

The fake ticket could fool anyone who was not literate. The only difference Greaves found between the proper Republican ticket and the imitation one was that the paper used for the fake one was "not as stout" as the genuine Republican ticket.

Alfred Noble spoke harshly of the fake tickets, saying they were printed "on weak, sickly-looking paper, like the man that was issuing them."

No one knew how many men McFall might have fooled.

Earlier in the morning, disagreement arose on whether several men were eligible to vote.

A Mr. Pollitzer, a white Democrat and a landowner on Hilton Head, came to the polls to vote. Men standing outside the polls challenged him.

A group of twenty or more men from Spanish Wells stood on the precinct grounds. "I think Campbell was the name of one of them," McFall later recalled. "They were speaking hot words," he said.

Some people thought Pollitzer too young to vote. Others protested that Pollitzer lived in Beaufort and should vote there: "You belong to Beaufort. You belong to Beaufort. You shan't vote here," the men from Spanish Wells chanted.

The men asked Mr. Pollitzer if he was a citizen of Hilton Head. "I heard Mr. Pollitzer say he would vote where he damned pleased," Grant said.

Gardner asked William Drayton to read aloud the law on elections so that the men would know who had a right to vote. Drayton went to the door and read the law.

After Drayton read the election law, Pollitzer was sworn in, voted, and rode off on horseback, angry at having been challenged.

Several sailors arrived at the polls. Some of the men outside the polls said that the sailors should be allowed to vote since their wives lived on the island. Landowner R. C. McIntire opposed this.

One of the sailors, a man called Lightburne, worked for McIntire and was not from Beaufort County. A white Democrat, McIntire owned most of Seabrook Plantation and recently had acquired a sizable part of the Drayton land. He insisted that Lightburne could not vote on Hilton Head. The sailors gave up and left.

Another oddity occurred.

When McFall voted, he scratched off Tillman's name, and yelled to Greaves that he was going "to give you a lift."

"All right," Greaves said, Gabriel Gardner would remember. McFall wrote in Greaves's name for governor and deposited his ballot. McFall probably hoped to gain popularity with the freedmen by his action. If so, it did not help him for long. Thomas Bell had seen to that.

McFall later claimed that some of the freedmen "got

in a muss with Renty Greaves. They found out that he was scratching Robert Smalls's name off the Republican ticket and Greaves had to give up his tickets."

Smalls was a Civil War hero who managed to capture a boat from the Charleston Harbor and deliver it to the Union army on Hilton Head. He was recognized by President Lincoln, and later fought in seventeen battles. Greaves was a political associate of Smalls, who had helped him get on the ballot. It would have been political suicide for Greaves to scratch off Smalls's name.

If such a rumor circulated, McFall was the likely person to start it. He may have given Greaves a "lift" of one vote, but McFall hadn't gotten anything from it.

McFall repositioned himself about halfway between the polls and Gardner's store in Mitchelville and apparently continued to peddle his false Republican ticket. He approached Isaac Jenkins with one of the fake tickets. "He said I needn't mind; it was the right ticket. . . . He knew I wouldn't vote a Democratic ticket."

McFall offered Jenkins a dollar to vote his ticket. Jenkins took McFall's money. When he went to the polls, he discovered the ticket was for the Democrats. He threw it away in disgust and voted a Republican ticket. He did not give McFall his money back.

Frederick Orage also said that McFall offered him a dollar to vote what turned out to be the imitation ticket. Orage took the money and then voted the way he wanted. Both Jenkins and Orage apparently deemed it unnecessary to return money to a trickster.

McFall then got in trouble with some of the women over near Gardner's store. Grant thought McFall might have said something indecent to one of the women. Others thought the row occurred because the women grew angry over McFall's fake tickets. The women could not vote, but the election affected them as well as the men — and the women knew it.

With few (if any) exceptions, Hilton Head freedmen were Republicans. It was the party of Lincoln, the party of the Northern abolitionists, and the party of the teachers and missionaries in the Port Royal Experiment. It also was the party that had brought about the freedmen's right to vote and had put black men in office. Many feared they would be swept back into slavery if the Democrats won.

After Gardner's store, McFall apparently went to Drayton Place. He claimed that Summer Christopher warned him that a procession was coming down the road to get him. According to McFall, Christopher locked him in the lumber house for two hours until all danger had passed.

McFall left the island soon after that and did not return. He later testified in *Tillman v. Smalls*, an inquiry into the congressional election, that the Democratic Party in Beaufort had asked him to hand out the fake ballots.

William Drayton decided to leave Hilton Head altogether. "After having lived nearly two years upon the island in friendly relations with all the colored people and then to be cursed and abused as I was on election day for only carrying out my duties as manager of elections was enough to disgust me," Drayton later said. He moved to Rose Hill on the mainland near Bluffton.

Gardner said he saw no abuse or hostility during the day. If such occurred, he said, he was busy tending to his duties and did not see or hear it. He also denied a charge by McFall that only Republicans were allowed to vote and that any freedmen who wanted to vote for the Democrats was not allowed to.

It was "quiet and orderly all day," said W. H. Peeples. "There was no hindrance; all voted together peacefully," Alfred Noble said. "The boys took it easy and cool," Edward Murray said. Isaac Jones, who had almost fallen for McFall's ticket said, "It was the most peaceable voting I ever saw."

When the votes were counted, the Republicans took Hilton Head by 476 to 12, Gardner later recalled. Only one of McFall's imitation Republican tickets showed up in the Democratic tally. The others were cast by white Democrats and possibly (though unlikely) one or two freedmen.

In their testimony in *Tillman v. Smalls*, Gardner and other freedmen appeared to overplay the calmness of Hilton Head's election. But in some areas of South Carolina, Democrats stuffed the ballot box, and used intimidation, terror, and even bribery to prevent blacks from voting for the Republicans.

One of the worst outrages occurred at Edgefield, in the up-country, where Martin Gary, a former Confederate brigadier general, lived. Gary and his followers donned red shirts and paraded with Wade Hampton during the election. Several groups of Red Shirts invaded Republican meetings in order to intimidate them.

At the Edgefield Courthouse, as soon as the polls opened, Democratic managers seized the ballot box from the portico of the courthouse and put it in an interior room. Armed whites, who had filled the courthouse the night before, remained inside, packed so close that no one could pass without approval. In addition, "several hundred horsemen were crowded around the Court House steps that colored men could not approach the Court House." Two hundred and fifty black men who were qualified to vote did not.

In contrast, Hilton Head's election truly was calm during what became known as the most corrupt election ever in South Carolina.

The U.S. presidential election fell into a tailspin. Tilden won the popular vote and had more electoral votes than Hayes, but twenty electoral votes were in dispute. In three states, both the Republican and Democratic parties reported their candidate had carried the state.

South Carolina was one of the three; the other two were Florida and Louisiana. Months would pass before the nation knew who would be the new president.

Both Hampton and Chamberlain claimed victory. South Carolina would have two self-acclaimed governors until the presidency was resolved.

Robert Smalls held onto his congressional seat, though the Democratic candidate, George D. Tillman, claimed victory. He contested Smalls's win in *Tillman v. Smalls*. Upon winning the battle, Smalls would return to the U.S. House of Representatives. He remained "King of Beaufort."

Of the candidates that the freedmen were most interested in, only Renty Greaves had a clear-cut victory. Greaves won election to the county commission and would soon become its chairman.

He had been enslaved until he was sixteen years old, when he and his family fled to Hilton Head Island. Now, at age thirty-one, Greaves would sit at the helm of the very county in which he once had been the property of another man.

This was the pinnacle, the political high point for freedmen on Hilton Head and throughout Beaufort County. In 1876, freedmen had the right to vote, hold political office, and be treated equally under the law. The long march out of slavery into citizenship had borne fruit. This was a time to celebrate, and a shining moment to hold in their hearts.

Chapter Eleven

RECONSTRUCTION ENDS

RENTY GREAVES SAT HIGH. As one Hilton Head islander put it, he was "a big man." Greaves lived on Hilton Head and traveled to the port city of Beaufort to conduct county business. The Beaufort County Commission had authority over everything from taxes to roads and ferries. As chairman of the commission, everyone in Beaufort County knew Greaves's name. Greaves must have relished this.

Beaufort County was the strongest black Republican center in the state. The black population outnumbered the white population seven to one. That, coupled with the assurance of political equality under Reconstruction's 1868 state constitution, had eased the way for Greaves to win.

The city of Beaufort, once a home of aristocratic white Sea Island plantation owners, bustled with black political activity. Even the mayor, police, and magistrates were black. Black state representatives and other office holders came to and from the state house in Columbia, and Robert Smalls went back and forth to Congress.

Greaves was highly literate, sharp, and ambitious. So it seemed a good bet that Greaves could keep his position on the county commission and lead the county for years to come.

Good bets don't always come true, and in this case, the unexpected would happen.

No. 3331 Record for *Renty Cruel*

Date of Application, Feb 24th 1869
Where born, Bluffton S. C.
Where brought up, Same place
Residence, Hilton Head S. C.
Age, 26. Co 9. 21st.
Complexion, Brown
Occupation, Farming
Works for, Himself.
Wife,
Children,

Father, George Graves
Mother, Lucinda
Brothers,
Sisters, Sylvy Ann Graves
Called Renty Franklin Graves
sometimes. Is separated from
his Wife Sylvy Williams.
Signature, Renty Cruel

Application for bank account in Beaufort, SC, made by Renty Greaves, also known as Renty Cruel, February 17, 1869. Greaves lists his residence as Hilton Head Island. *Records of the Office of the Comptroller of the Currency, RG 101*

At noon on April 10, 1877, federal troops marched out of the state house in Columbia, in cadence to the tolling of the city hall clock.[1]

President Rutherford B. Hayes had been inaugurated in early March, a few days after the presidential election was resolved. After bitter negotiations, the Democrats agreed to accept Hayes, in part because Hayes recognized that the North was tired of Reconstruction and the South's problems. The country also was in a severe economic depression.[2]

The new Republican president backed Hampton's election for governor of South Carolina and pledged to remove federal troops from South Carolina. Hayes favored local control in the South and promised that the federal government would not interfere in the affairs of the South. He thus handed the reins of power to the Democratic Party, allowing Democrats to turn their back on black citizens.

In Columbia, as the twelfth chime of the city hall clock struck, federal soldiers departed the state capital. Reconstruction ended at that minute.[3]

Republican Governor Daniel H. Chamberlain closed his office in the state house, and Wade Hampton soon moved in. During the disputed election, the two governors had not only set up separate offices, but had held separate inaugurals and sent out separate tax bills to state residents.

Chamberlain had abdicated his office of governor on the advice of leading Republicans. In his farewell speech, he addressed black Republicans, telling them that they had been victims of persecution during the 1876 election. "From authentic evidence it is shown that not less than one hundred of your number were murdered because they were faithful to their principles and exercised rights solemnly guaranteed to them by the nation."[4]

He had begun his term as a moderate, determined to end any taint of corruption in his party. He and his aides aired every piece of dirty laundry they found. The tactic backfired. Rather than assuring the public that Chamberlain was eliminating corruption, press reports convinced white Democrats that all Republicans were hopelessly corrupt. The Democrats made hay out of the charges while downplaying corruption within their own party.

Chamberlain left behind a tattered party torn by infighting but wrote a message to William Lloyd Garrison concluding instead that "the undereducated [N]egro was too weak, no matter what his numbers, to cope with the whites."

With Chamberlain and the federal troops gone, and Hampton in office, the Charleston *News and Courier* stated that Republicanism was dead in South Carolina.[5]

Crowds of jubilant whites, and a few blacks, cheered Hampton in Columbia and elsewhere. Most white citizens considered him the "Savior of South Carolina," and felt that they at last had their state back. Hampton repeated a previous promise that he would protect the equal rights of black citizens. He did, however, advise blacks to join the Democratic Party "or perish like the Indians."

Robert Smalls said that Hampton had kept his promises. He referred to the "just and liberal course of the Governor, which has recommended him to the confidence of the people."[6]

In May, the first sign of trouble for the 1878 election popped up. From Edgewood, Martin Gary pronounced "that we regard the issues between the white and colored people of this State, and of the entire south, as an antagonism of race, not a difference of political parties." Gary further said that "white supremacy is essential to our continued existence as a people."[7]

While Gary had been an ally of Hampton's in the 1876 election, Hampton had not been able to control outbreaks of violence committed by the Red Shirts. Determined to see an all-white Democratic government in power, Gary and the Red Shirts would be a key factor in the 1878 election.

In August, Hampton's attorney general James Conner sent a confidential memo to W. D. Simpson, the lieutenant governor, outlining a plan to smear as "corrupt" every man who was a Republican or had ever voted for one. They would get indictments on Chamberlain and other Republican politicians who had moved out of state, but they would not extradite them. Conner reasoned that if the men did not return to South Carolina to refute the charges, they would be guilty in the public mind.

The Hampton administration already had set up a legislative committee to investigate frauds committed by the previous government. The committee was said to be bipartisan, but the Republicans who testified against their former associates were already switching over to Hampton's side. The same men testified time after time.

Hampton's men decided to publish the testimony "in the shape of a Report." "[T]he most captivating parts are historical & would not stand test as legal evidence, but the moral evidence would be crushing," Conner said. "The press would revel in it & we would politically guillotine every man of them."[8]

Among Conner's targets was Robert Smalls, who had won his disputed 1876 election and was running for an additional term in Congress.

In October, Smalls came back from Washington to face trial on charges brought by the Democratic Party that he had taken a $5,000 bribe while chairing the South Carolina printing committee. He was convicted and spent three days in jail before he was released, pending appeal to the state supreme court. Then he returned to Congress. Smalls later would be pardoned, and historians would view the charges against him as not strong and highly political.

Election time arrived again. The Republicans could not find anyone popular enough to beat Hampton in the 1878 election, so they did not run a gubernatorial candidate. Hampton ran unopposed. The governor continued to make campaign stops, hoping, in part, to convert some Republicans.

Hampton rode into Beaufort in late October of 1878. The *Beaufort Tribune*, previously a Republican paper but now aligned with Hampton, reported that, "Large numbers of colored people were kept away through the *machinations* of Smalls and Whipper [another black politician], who industriously circulated the report that there would be a row."

The *Tribune* further reported that, "The effect of the meeting today has been to create a better feeling between the whites and blacks than has existed here since reconstruction."

The following day the *Tribune* ran a longer piece on Hampton's visit including the text of his speech, which included the following: "The Governor produced a huge package of documents containing the evidence in black and white, of the infamy and rascality of every Radical [Republican] leader in Beaufort County who had ever held office in South Carolina. He did not choose, he said, to dwell up this subject at length, because he had never held the rank and file of the party responsible for the misdeeds of the party. If the colored people desired to see for themselves these evidences of crime, he would be happy to show them to them. He could show them that their chosen leader, Smalls, their candidate for Congress from the First District, was nothing more than a common bribe taker, and had, on one occasion, sold his vote as low as $200."

The attorney general's report had come in handy.

Less than two weeks before, Smalls had gone to Gillisonville, a former seat of Beaufort County, for a 10:00 a.m. campaign speech. Union General Ulysses S. Sherman had burned much of the town in 1865, which gave the local populace a right for bitterness. But what occurred this day was due to outsiders. Smalls and about forty followers were at hand the time when the meeting was to begin. He was to speak in front of a storefront. Men and women were arriving to hear Smalls when "eight-hundred red-shirt men, led by former Confederate colonels, generals, and many leading men of the state, came dashing into town, giving the rebel yell," Laura Towne recorded in her diary.[9] They drew up in front of the store and remained there. Every few minutes, a few men would go through the crowd to "lick off the hats" of colored men or slap the faces of colored women.

The colonel leading the charge demanded the right to address Smalls's meeting. Smalls said he was cancelling the meeting. The leader insisted there should be a meeting; Smalls said no. The colonel gave him ten minutes to decide. "Smalls withdrew into the store with his forty men and drew them all up . . . behind the counters. His men had guns. He told them to aim at the door, and stand with a finger on trigger but on no account to shoot unless the red-shirts broke in."[10]

When the ten minutes ended, some of the Red Shirts began trying to break down the door. "They called Smalls and told him they would set fire to the [store] and burn him up in it. They fired repeatedly through the windows and walls. . . . [Smalls] would not come out, and the leaders led off part of the Red Shirts and began to make speeches, leaving the store surrounded, however, for fear Smalls would escape," Towne recorded.

Something remarkable occurred then. Black citizens who had come to hear Smalls ran off and raised the alarm in every direction. "[I]n an incredibly short time the most distant parts of the county heard that their truly beloved leader was trapped in a house surrounded by red-shirts, and that his life was in danger.

"Every colored man and woman seized whatever was at hand—guns, axes, hoes, etc., and ran to the rescue. By six o'clock . . . a thousand negroes were approaching the town" and the Red Shirts decided they would leave. Twenty of their men stayed behind in case Smalls attempted to make it to the train that ran to Beaufort. If so, their instructions were to "attend to him."[11]

Smalls outsmarted them. He waited until darkness fell, managed somehow to get ahead of the train, "jumped on the tender in the dark" and made it back to Beaufort alive. Smalls said that he thought the visit from the Red Shirts was prompted by comments Hampton had made about him.[12]

Renty Franklin Greaves was about to be thrown into jail like a common thief. He had just been arrested on a Saturday night, the one night of the week he could count on being seen by men who were drunk or had stabbed someone at a bar. Here he was, the county commission chair, wondering what was going to happen to him.

The charges against him were trumped up. He knew that. He apparently did not publicly record his emotions and thoughts, though some were predictable based on his history.

First came shock, then anger. Then a twinge of fear crept into his mind.

He remembered the Union soldiers breaking into his bedroom at night and forcing him to enter the army in 1863. He had learned at that moment that he could be overpowered by events and men.

That was more than a decade ago, but Greaves still resented his conscription and the fact that military service had set back his health. He had worked to control his life ever since.

Now "Judge M," as Laura Towne called him in her diary, was his opponent—and a formidable one. The description of Judge M. fit the profile of Judge T. F. Mackey, a native white South Carolinian who lived in Beaufort. He had long been a Republican but had switched his allegiance to Hampton and the Democratic Party.[13]

Even before that, Mackey had acted as if Beaufort County was his own, pledging once, in a political campaign, to virtually run the county single-handed. He also had said that, "Reform on the local level could be achieved by electing one or two large property owners as county commissioners."

For years, even while a Republican, Mackey had been one of the most aggressive reformers in the party, seeking out black officeholders he decided were corrupt.

Mackey now had declared that, as the bridges and ferries on Saint Helena were in bad shape, it was the commission's fault. He ran the charge through a grand jury, and then had all three commissioners jailed at once.

Bail was set for the other two commissioners at $1,000. As Greaves was the chairman, his bail was set at $5,000.[14] The three men found bondsmen.

Mackey then told Greaves that he would have to serve a term in jail unless he resigned as county commission chair in favor of a man that Mackey wanted on the board.[15] The man Mackey desired to put on the commission, Dr. White, was a plantation owner on Saint Helena, a white Democrat, and fit the bill that Mackey once had prescribed of a man of property.

Greaves did not trust Mackey. He did not know how far Mackey might go to get him out of the way. Robert Smalls had almost been killed by Red Shirts.

How long would the judge leave him in jail? What

would happen during that time? No one would rush to rescue him, as Smalls's supporters had. If the Red Shirts broke into the jail, his life would not be worth a plug nickel.

He wanted his freedom.

He resigned and was released.

Greaves returned to Hilton Head and its safety. Black citizens on Hilton Head had lost their key spokesman. The Democrats held the power now.

Laura Towne on Saint Helena wrote of Renty Greaves in her diary:

> Renty Greaves, chairman, and the other county commissioners were all arrested for not keeping the roads and bridges on Saint Helena in order, and were held on $5,000 bond for Renty, and $1,000 for the others, including even the clerk — our school commissioner. Besides this, they arrested them late on Saturday night so that they should have to spend Sunday in jail. But they found bondsmen. Then the Judge bulldozed Renty Greaves — told him he would have a term in jail, but that if he would resign his chairmanship to Dr. White [a man who a large property owner as Mackey had wanted], he should be set at liberty at once, and his bondsmen released. Renty, by virtue of his office, was one of the Board of Jury Commissioners, and the only Republican on it. If he resigned to Dr. White, all would be Democrats and the juries chosen by them. He was scared into doing it, and so we have three Democrats in that office, where the whole county is Republican![16]

Storm damage in nearby Beaufort from the hurricane of 1893. *Library of Congress*

Chapter Twelve

STORM DAYS

THE WOODEN CABINS of Hilton Head Gullah people trembled and quaked as the storm of 1893 descended on the island. The tropical cyclone came on a Sunday night: August 27, 1893. Except for a sudden calm settling over the island turning the air still as death, Gullah people had little way of knowing a huge storm was coming. Even if they had, they had no place to go.

By nightfall, winds up to one hundred and twenty miles battered Hilton Head, bringing with it a huge tidal surge that immersed the island in water. Island creeks swelled. Broad Creek turned into a raging river that nearly cut the island in half.

"The island covered wid water," Laura Mae Campbell remembered her grandmother telling her. "Water come from all sides. All the river' be together."

Gullah men and women fled to tall trees, clinging to them and tying children to large limbs to prevent them from drowning. "They had to git up on the trees behind the water," Miss Laura said.[1]

Even so, the winds uprooted giant oaks and pines at will, or shook and broke tree limbs. Some Gullah parents saw their children disappear into the raging sea.

One two-year-old boy faced the storm alone in a kitchen attached to the house. His parents were at a prayer meeting and the storm had "take' the top of the house off," Joe Walters later said. "Cousin Tim came and pick me up. They thought I would drown."[2] Walters would grow up to be a good fisherman and oysterman.

Others lacked his luck.

"My grandmother lost some chil'ren in that one," Miss Laura said.

She said that after telling how Hilton Head islanders got up into trees. She paused then and said nothing more, except for four words: "That was a *storm*."

When a Gullah person says, "That was a *woman*," or "That was a *man*," the expression referred to an exceptionally strong person, so Laura Campbell's words reflected the strength of the storm that brought such devastation and loss of life.

The storm killed somewhere between a thousand and twenty-five hundred people in the Sea Islands. No official count was undertaken, nor could be. With bodies lying in marshes and graves to be dug, no one had time to take an accurate count.

After the storm, news from Charleston soon reached the outside world. News of devastation in Beaufort followed. Reports from Saint Helena, Edisto, and a few other islands drifted in. No word reached the outside world regarding the fate of Hilton Head for nearly two months.

Clara Barton, now head of the American National Red Cross, had spent nine months as a nurse on Hilton Head during the Civil War. After reading newspaper accounts from New York; Boston; Washington, DC; and London of the storm—all of which painted a scene of total devastation in the Sea Islands—she thought it useless for the Red Cross to attempt a relief effort there.

She knew how flat the islands were and how nothing could stop the sea from sweeping over them. There would be too little to save.

Governor Ben "Pitchfork" Tillman asked Barton to come.

Tillman did not care for Beaufort County, the Republican stronghold in the state. A Democrat and a white supremacist, Tillman believed that black citizens were inferior to whites. At first he harbored doubts that the black populace of the Sea Islands truly needed help, but eventually became convinced that aid was needed. As the state house declined to provide immediate relief, the Red Cross was the only hope.

By the time Barton arrived on the first day of October to set up office in a Beaufort warehouse, refugees from nearby islands had crowded into the town, hoping to get help. Soon after her arrival, four Gullah men respectfully asked to see her. The tallest of the four was the leader.

"Miss Clare," he said, "we knows you doesn't remember us. But we never fo'gits you. We all have somethin' to show you."

He pulled up his shirt sleeve and showed her "an ugly scar above his elbow, reaching to his shoulder."

Storm damage in nearby Beaufort from the hurricane of 1893. *Library of Congress*

"Wagner?" Barton asked.

"You dressed it for me that night, when I crawled down the beach—'cause my leg was broken too. All of us was there, and you took care of us all and you [dressed] our wounds." They had been with Colonel Robert Shaw, in the dreadful slaughter of black soldiers during the attempt by the 54th Massachusetts to capture Confederate-held Fort Wagner on Morris Island. The tall man had reached the outside of the fort when Colonel Shaw was killed while urging his soldiers on.

"One by one [the men] showed their scars—bullet wounds and saber. . . . The memory, dark and sad, stood out before us."[3]

The memories took her back thirty years. She also had been on Morris Island after the Union finally captured it. She remembered freezing rains and the scorching sun and the large number of regiments there, including ones in which Hilton Head's black Union soldiers had served.

The former black Union soldiers said they had talked

Clara Barton, ca. 1890. *Library of Congress*

each district, keep nationwide appeals going for relief donations, oversee a system of food rations for thirty thousand people (a number that grew larger), find a way to get a million boards of lumber so that islanders could rebuild their homes, obtain seeds for the next year's planting, and assure that three hundred miles of ditches were dug on the Sea Islands in order to provide flood drainage. And Gullah people would take pride in their accomplishments.

John MacDonald stayed "lashed to a ship's rigging without food or water . . . hourly expecting death." He was at sea the night of the storm, en route from Boston to Savannah, aboard the steamer, *City of Savannah*. The steamer, caught in the storm's fury, wrecked on a shoal off Fripp Island.

"On the third night, when all hope had died out," the ship sent up its last signal shot, "and in a few moments, another light shot out into the sky about two miles away; our cry for help was answered."[4]

He went on to Savannah, but when he learned of Barton's call for volunteers, he joined up. After having survived the fury of the storm, his sympathies "had been aroused," he said, for others who had been through the storm.

MacDonald, a white Northerner, made his way throughout the islands on a steam launch from the U.S. Navy Yard. He sought the spot where he could be of

of her "a heap of times," but "we never expected to see you again."

She was seventy-one years old and full of energy. After the men left, she went back to organizing the Sea Island Relief.

Under the banner of the Red Cross, Barton would divide the Sea Islands into districts, find volunteers for the most help and found Hilton Head. The island's isolation — like that of Pinckney, Daufuskie, and smaller islands — made Hilton Head the choice for a Red Cross camp.[5]

As MacDonald was a doctor and his wife, Ida B. MacDonald, was a nurse, Hilton Head got a storm-relief team and medical help wrapped into one.

MacDonald went home to home on Hilton Head, talking to families, inspecting whether houses were safe to live in, if there was any sickness, and whether islanders had food to eat. Out of a population estimated at two thousand and fifty people, slightly more than half required assistance.

Many people had been eating salt-ruined corn. "This accounts for much of the stomach trouble I found," he told a *New York World* reporter. He advised islanders "to burn what was rotten, and issued grits to them" to replace the ruined corn.

"With the exception of two wells . . . there is no water on either Hilton Head or Pinckney Island fit to drink, all of it being brackish. . . . [A] majority of the people are suffering from 'storm sickness' (contusions, colds, rheumatism, and the effect of exposure)."

He also wrote in his district field report to Barton that, "Malaria is at its worst form . . . was general amongst the people."[6]

Tents rose on Hilton Head for the first time since the Civil War, providing shelter for islanders whose homes had been lost. MacDonald acquired the tents through Barton's relief effort. Once, contrabands fleeing to Hilton Head to gain freedom had slept in tents before housing became available. Now, it was the turn of people whose homes were destroyed to live in army-issue tents.

The MacDonalds received additional tents to use as hospital rooms and their living quarters. Under Ida's directions, sewing tents were added too. Clothes were in dire need. The storm had whipped clothes off of people's backs, and she found some islanders "practically nude."

After the tents were up, Gullah people jumped to work, "making cupboards, desks, stools, benches, and bedsteads from old packing boxes." Some gathered moss to put on tent floors as a carpet. Then, "the Red Cross flag was unfurled to fly in the breeze over the camp."[7]

Gullah people soon called MacDonald "Mr. Red Cross." He called on the sick or dying at any time in the night, riding up to seven miles on the island in a cart pulled by an ox or a mule.

The Red Cross required that people work in return for food rations and provided lumber and nails, saws, and other tools so that people on Hilton Head could rebuild homes. The entire island pitched in, even people whose homes had not been destroyed.

Flood water still stood on the island, and as long as it did, crops could not grow. The men dug deep, wide drainage ditches.

One man became a local hero. While many boats were damaged or destroyed, Ben Green had a boat that could be rowed.

Friday was the most important day of the week. On Friday, MacDonald went to the distribution point in Beaufort to get food rations for people—a peck of corn and one pound of pork per family—with double rations for the men digging ditches or building houses.

Getting to Beaufort and back without a boat would have been impossible. MacDonald singled out Ben Green for praise in his field report that Green "placed his boat and the services of himself and men at my disposal and, without fee or reward of any kind, for several months, during good and bad weather, brought over the large amount of supplies required for this district."[8]

Upon their return to Hilton Head, "waiting recipients" from several islands handed in their Red Cross relief cards and stood with their bags open to receive their weekly ration of grits and pork. The hungry included healthy and weak, old and young and tottering elders.

Ida MacDonald's sewing circle excited people.[9] She borrowed a sewing machine from a woman on the island, pored through clothes in the relief warehouse in Beaufort, and took barrels of clothing back to the island. The garments usually needed buttons, patches, or even total re-makes before they could be handed out. Many Gullah women devoted a full week to working in the sewing tent.

The sewing circle repaired more than three thousand clothing items. Each item was given to someone on Hilton Head or on Pinckney, Daufuskie, or nearby smaller islands.

John MacDonald took down the Red Cross flag on May 20, 1894. The couple's work was finished. They stayed on awhile, watching new crops flourishing in the soil and getting to see "people again prosperous and happy."

James Drayton Grant already had turned to the future. His first wife, Mary Ann, no longer lived. He and Emma Chisholm exchanged wedding vows at the First African Baptist Church on September 20, 1893—less than a month after the storm. The former solider and his bride marched forward.

Those men who had been Union soldiers resumed their meetings of the Grand Army of the Republic (GAR) in the Grand Army Hall on Hilton Head. Before the storm came, they had printed their own letterhead for the GAR post on the island. In May 1893, that letterhead listed officers of the Abraham Lincoln Post 12, Hilton Head Island. By 1905, the post would have thirty-two members and would meet on the second and fourth Saturdays of every month.[10]

Storm clouds gathered again. This time they were political and were aimed at black disenfranchisement. Everyone, white and black, sensed this. The dark clouds had been building for years.

In July 1895, Governor Benjamin "Pitchfork" Tillman convened a constitutional convention with the intent to finish stripping away the voting rights of South Carolina blacks.

Strict voting restrictions already had stripped many black people of the vote. Under an 1882 "eight box law," for instance, a voter must place separate ballots in boxes for eight classes of national, state, and local offices. If a voter couldn't read the label on the boxes, registration officials helped him — if they thought he voted "right." If not, they let him cast his ballot in the wrong box. The vote then was tossed out as not valid.

When Tillman's constitutional convention opened, only six black delegates had been elected to participate. Five of the six (Robert Smalls was one of the five) came from Beaufort County. The other black delegate was from Georgetown. The six black men were the only Republicans at the convention.[11]

The day after Robert Smalls protested a bill designed to strip all voting rights from black people in South Carolina, or as Smalls said, "two-thirds of the qualified voters of the State," a white convention delegate burst forth, saying, "We don't propose to have any fair elections. We will get left at that every time. . . .

"I tell you, gentlemen, if we have fair elections in Berkley we can't carry that. . . . The black man is learning to read faster than the white man. And if he comes up and can read, you have to let him vote. We are per-fectly disgusted with hearing so much about fair elections. . . . [M]ake it fair and you'll see what'll happen."[12]

Smalls's protest did no good.

To disenfranchise blacks, Tillman sought a way that would not violate the U.S. Constitution. He turned to Mississippi's example, borrowing planks from there. The harshest was a literary qualification. In order to vote, a man had to show he could read and write any section of the U.S. Constitution. This blocked the state's many illiterate or near-illiterate blacks from the polls.

The law would have two exceptions. If a man owned $300 in taxable property and could show the registrar that he had paid his yearly land tax, he could vote. The second exception required a man to understand anything in the U.S. Constitution read to him [by a white registrar].

Also, the poll tax would have to be paid six months in advance of the November elections. Crops were still in the ground in spring. Few black farmers — or white farmers of small farms, for that matter — had enough cash to pay the tax six months before voting.[13]

"We took the government away," Tillman later bragged. "We stuffed the ballot boxes. We shot them. We are not ashamed of it."[14]

Disenfranchisement went into effect on January 1, 1896.

Dr. Wilder holding a rattlesnake, Hilton Head, SC, 1904. *American Museum of Natural History, Library: Julian Dimock Collection*

Chapter Thirteen

AN OUTGOING TIDE

ISENFRANCHISEMENT TOOK a steep toll with political gatekeepers making sure few black men voted. In October 1903, Neil Christensen, Jr., editor of the *Beaufort Gazette*, wrote that majority-black Beaufort County had 3,434 literate Negro males and only 927 white male voters, but that "registration officials do not allow registered Negro voters to outnumber the whites."[1]

Church bells pealed that same month for Renty Franklin Greaves.

"R. F. Greaves, age about 66, an esteemed colored citizen, died on Wednesday morning," the *Beaufort Gazette* reported on Thursday, October 29, 1903. "He had been in poor health for several years."

Ill health had grayed his hair and damaged his body.

Yet the term "an esteemed colored citizen" showed genuine respect for Greaves in the first decade after disenfranchisement.

Renty Franklin Greaves had ridden the incoming tide of freedom, reaching Hilton Head two days after the Union invaded. He grabbed at previously unheard-of possibilities for a people who had been born in slavery, including that of a school teacher and an assistant lighthouse keeper.

He rose, at the tide's crest, to chair the county commission of Beaufort County. He won electoral office again in 1888 as the coroner for Beaufort County. He later became a shopkeeper and a pension attorney.

He also saw full equality for black people washing away with the outgoing tide.

Through his accomplishments, Greaves stood as a symbol of what might have been if disenfranchisement had not come to pass. No other Gullah person on Hilton Head had been elected to public office on the county level as Greaves had, not once but twice. No one else on Hilton Head would, for more decades than the islanders could foresee.

Beaufort County would remain a power base, to a lesser degree. A few local officials would continue to be elected, but even Smalls, who had served additional terms in Congress following his loss in 1878, could never be elected again. He would, however, gain a federal patronage post as the U.S. Customs Collector in Beaufort, serving from 1889 to 1911.

The gate to elected position had been locked. The chance to sit in electoral office, and represent and lead Gullah men, women, and children was gone. The roar of the outgoing tide silenced the islanders' political voice.

Greaves had led an up and down life. The year before he died, he met one last time with a pension examiner conducting a periodic review of his pension claim.[2]

"I am a recognized attorney before the Interior Department and am actually engaged in the prosecution of pension claims," Greaves told the examiner who wrote down his words.

"I was born on the Linden plantation near Bluffton, SC. My owner was Nathaniel P. Crowell. My father was George Greaves. My mother was Lucinda Greaves. They both belonged to my owner . . . [who] is dead."

He then made an extraordinary remark.

"He [Crowell] had two sons, Beech and Savage, but they are living up north somewhere. The last time I heard from Beech he was living on Staten Island."

That hint of a cordial correspondence with the son of his former owner raised questions as to Greaves's childhood on the Crowell plantation.

Had he and Beech been friends when they were young? A small number of slaveholders permitted their sons and daughters to befriend a young enslaved person. As soon as a white child reached maturity, however, parents ended the friendship in order to enforce the master-slave relationship.

If Renty and Beach had been friendly, did the friendship occur because Greaves, frail after he fell into a pot of boiling soup, had been allowed to spend time with his master's son?

Was Greaves the rare enslaved man who learned how to read and write on the plantation? Or did he learn at a freedmen's school on Hilton Head? He spent less than two years on the island before he was conscripted into the army. Was that enough time for him to acquire penmanship more legible and more elegant than any other freedman on the island, including W. D. Brown, the postmaster, or the pension examiner who recorded his words?

He never said.

Following his funeral at the First African Baptist Church of Beaufort, where Greaves had been a deacon, his body was laid to rest in the Beaufort National Cemetery, where he lay alongside comrades who had fought in the Civil War.[3]

Renty Greaves had not lived on Hilton Head for years. His two sons, Joseph and Franklin, and his first wife, Sylvia, were dead. He and his second wife, Elizabeth, had no children.[4] Greaves might have faded from Hilton Head history except for one fact: he had fathered a son on Hilton Head Island, outside of marriage.

Benjamin W. White, Sr., had been born to Hannah White in 1881.[5] Hannah had worked and raised Benjamin until she fell seriously ill. Realizing death was close, she sent for her closest relatives, Peter and Clara Chisolm, and made the couple promise to raise her son. They did as Hannah White asked. Benjamin grew up in the Chisolm household on Cherry Hill Plantation.

White, now twenty-two, owned ten acres of land on the island's former Grasslawn Plantation. He had set out to succeed, and on Hilton Head, this meant farming.[6]

White would become the biggest and most successful farmer on the island, and his grandchildren—the great-grandchildren of Renty Greaves—would surpass even Greaves's dreams of educational achievement.

Caesar Jones died two months after Greaves. Jones had remained on Hilton Head ever since the Civil War.

Jones did not know his exact age, but likely he was about seventy-nine at the time. Toward the end of his life, he had poor eyesight, rheumatoid arthritis, and heart disease, yet remained a giant of a man. He measured nearly six feet tall.

He left a widow, Lavinia; five grown children by Mariah, his long-deceased first wife; grandchildren; and a step-brother, Thomas Young. The flourishing community of Jonesville bore his name.

He had done well. The county tax records listed Caesar Jones's property that year as consisting of a hundred and eight acres of land, four buildings valued at $375, and personal property valued at $250.[7]

"I paid $15 for my father's coffin," his son, William Jones, said, and rather than placing the customary wooden marker on a grave, "we children paid $18 for a headstone and fence around his grave."[8]

Both Greaves and Jones had been pivotal figures after the Union invaded. Their deaths foreshadowed the time when all the island's black Civil War soldiers would pass on, but this was not that time.

Former soldiers—such as Renty Miller, Joseph Riley, Edward Lawyer, Simon Grant, James Drayton Grant, and Matt Jones, and their wives, children, and relatives—still populated the island.

If anything, disenfranchisement forced Gullah people to turn inward, to strengthen family and community bonds, and rely on their praise houses, churches, societies, clubs, and folk beliefs. Adversity made them hold onto their African customs.

A bateau carrying black men in dark suits and hats and black women in their Sunday best rowed out to a steamship bound for Beaufort. A man with a mule plowed a field for spring planting. A woman sowed watermelon seeds. A fisherman looked toward shore from the bow of his sailboat.

In those images and others a young white Northerner captured Gullah life on Hilton Head shortly after disenfranchisement. "Camera-man," as his father called him, had come to Hilton Head. From April 6 through April 10 of 1904, Julian Dimock turned his lens on people living on Hilton Head. Dimock, a New York resident, had become the landowner on the island as a result of his father financially aiding an old friend.[9]

Anthony Dimock had been a leading Wall Street financier. When a trusted friend on Hilton Head opened a deposit account with his Wall Street firm and soon thereafter issued an overdraft, Anthony Dimock guaranteed the overdraft without hesitation. The friend's debts mounted. Dimock kept signing for them. By the time he took notice, he had jeopardized his own financial security.

His friend had been a principal in the Sea Island Cotton Company, which later merged into the U.S. Cotton Company. Land holdings of the company turned out to be the only security Dimock could get for the debts he had guaranteed. The company bankrupted in 1896.

While he did not say so, his friend was Dr. Francis E. Wilder, one of the principals in the cotton company. A well-known figure on the island, Wilder had arrived in the spring of 1864 from Syracuse, New York. The *Palmetto Post* immediately hailed the twenty-seven-year-old man as "a gentlemen well known for his wealth, intelligence, and enterprise," as Wilder (and his investors) had just purchased Leamington Plantation "for a larger sum" that had yet to been paid for any "confiscated estate" in the Department of the South.

Two women from Massachusetts already lived in the residence at Leamington, teaching thirty adults and children to spell and read, "a good work which [Wilder] so warmly approved that he invited the good ladies" to continue living there. With the assistance of a farmer who came with Wilder, and twenty-four islander residents, Wilder began seeding a hundred acres of cotton. He also acquired, on behalf of the Sea Island Cotton Company, Gardner's, Muddy Creek, and Otter Hole.

The first year's cotton crop earned a 25 percent profit, in part because of well-heeled Northern investors. The price for cotton then began a downward slide from a dollar a pound to four cents a pound by 1890.

The cotton company, by one name or the other, had lasted thirty-six years, enough time for more than one generation of Gullah people to work those fields. During this time, Wilder engaged himself in island life.

He had been elected to serve as a delegate to the critical 1868 constitution convention, and, as he lived on Hilton Head, Gullah people likely voted for him. He also served as a county commissioner at one point, and school commissioner at another. As a doctor, he often treated Gullah men and women on Hilton Head, and had attended Sylvia Greaves in her last illness. He lived at Otter Hole and would live out his life there.

When U.S. Cotton bankrupted, 1,200 acres of company land at Gardner and 700 acres at Muddy Creek were recorded as sold to Anthony Dimock's son, Julian.[10] Within a year Julian Dimock sold twenty acres of land at Gardner's to Namon Singleton and twenty acres at Muddy Creek to Stephen Hamilton.[11]

Anthony Dimock had left Wall Street and become a well-known travel and adventure writer. Later, he would note of this stage of his life, "We were interested in the dependent peoples and we visited, studied, and pictured them," from the Native Americans to Ellis Island immigrants to "the descendants of the victims of the last slave trade shipment to the Sea Islands of South Carolina."

Julian Dimock's photographs, however, did not show a dependent people on Hilton Head. His camera showed people working for themselves, making do on little money, and leading full lives.

In one image, women work in the fields, sewing watermelon seeds, a big cash crop on Hilton Head. In an-other, several young women, dressed in their Sunday best, lean against a buggy in conversation. A young girl stands in front of them, leaning forward, as if to gain a word or two in their conversation.[12]

A boy wearing a moth-eaten sweater, suspenders, and rolled-up pants, one hand tucked in his pant's pocket, the other holding a farm implement, beamed a cocky smile. As a gaggle of less adventurous boys watched from the side, the youth assumed a confident stance with no hint of servility to the white photographer.

John Ford wore a patched wool jacket and a dark cap as he gazed unflinchingly into the camera. His bushy gray beard testified to his advancing years, but he appeared strong, a man who could do it all—fish, farm, and swap tales with the men.

A slight furrow crinkled the brow of an attractive woman, perhaps a teacher, as she posed while looking into the sun. Bands of handmade lace adorned the bodice and sleeves of her striped, high-neck cotton blouse.

A woman sat on the stoop while two others stood in the doorway of an aging one-room cabin with ragged shingles and a crumbling brick and mortar chimney. A row of sun-bleached shells lined the path to the door, a testament, perhaps, of an urge to beautify her home.

In a second field, a woman strode to a newer house with painted shutters and tight shingles on a high-pitched roof. A grape harbor in her yard awaited summer fruit.

"Camera-man" also photographed one of the few

Planting watermelons, Hilton Head, 1904. *American Museum of Natural History, Library: Julian Dimock Collection*

Young women with horse and wagon, boy looks on, Hilton Head, SC, 1904. *American Museum of Natural History, Library: Julian Dimock Collection*

Dr. Wilder holding a rattlesnake, Hilton Head, SC, 1904. *American Museum of Natural History, Library: Julian Dimock Collection*

white men on the island: Dr. Wilder. Julian's camera showed Wilder, a short, bespectacled man in his late sixties wearing a dark suit and a Panama hat with a black band. In one photo, he held a live rattlesnake at arm's length. In a second photo, Wilder was looking down at the rattlesnake while he extracted its fangs.

❖ ❖ ❖

Matt Jones stood on his land on the former Stoney plantation, the plantation where he and his family once had been enslaved. He wore a broad-brimmed felt hat with the insignia of the Grand Army of the Republic and the regimentals he would wear in the Decoration Day parade of veterans in Beaufort at the end of May.

Matt Jones in his regimental uniform, Hilton Head, SC, April 6, 1904. *American Museum of Natural History, Library: Julian Dimock Collection*

A longtime officer in the GAR post on Hilton Head, Matt Jones held an officer's saber in his left hand. A medal pinned to the chest of his uniform bore a delegate badge proclaiming "Abraham Lincoln, Post No.12, Hilton Head, S.C."

He had dressed with care for this chance to show the outside world the pride he and his former comrades took in their service in the U.S. Colored Troops. The outgoing tide may have washed away much of their gains as citizens, but freedom on the island, and the ability to work for their own gain, remained a precious thing.

Booker T. Washington, ca. 1895.
Library of Congress

Chapter Fourteen

BOOKER T. WASHINGTON COMES TO HILTON HEAD

TWO YEARS AFTER a photograph was taken showing Matt Jones, outfitted in regimentals for his pride in the black Union soldiers who helped secure freedom, famed black educator Booker T. Washington and steamship magnate William P. Clyde launched a project to uplift Hilton Head's black farmers.

Clyde agreed to set aside one thousand acres of land on Hilton Head to start an agricultural colony based on Washington's beliefs of how to advance the race. People could buy a farm of up to thirty acres, paid for at low interest over seven to ten years. No more than thirty farmers perhaps could buy land under the plan, but with family members added in, between one and two hundred people stood to benefit. And Clyde pledged to set aside more land if the colony worked.

It was a generous offer, and Clyde could afford it. He now owned nine thousand acres on Hilton Head.

From Tuskegee, Alabama, where Washington presided over the Tuskegee Institute, the industrial school he had founded, he and his colleagues honed the details that Clyde and his son, William P. Clyde, Jr., signed off on.

Each farm was to sell for about $520. The price included a frame house with a wood-shingled roof and two or more rooms (depending on the size of the family), an outhouse, and a decent well. The children of the colony would attend their own school. Clyde would pay to build the schoolhouse and provide the salaries of teachers, each of whom would be a graduate of Tuskegee or Hampton Institute.

On paper the plan sounded great, as it increased opportunities for people to acquire land, live in new, improved houses, and gain a better education for their children. But it is doubtful that anyone fully gauged whether Hilton Head citizens, who valued their independence, cared to live, work, and buy a farm in a colony run by outsiders.

The colony sprang to life without Washington, his partner in the project, W. T. B. Williams of Hampton Institute, or Clyde attempting to build trust with the people. They ignored or did not know the Gullah expression *com ya can't tell bin ya how to do*—"come here" cannot tell "been here" how to do.

In the aftermath of disenfranchisement Washington had observed, "Every day convinces me that the salvation of the [N]egro in this country will be in his cultivation of habits of thrift, economy, honesty, the acquiring of education, Christian character, property, and industrial skill."[1]

The teaching of practical skills and the molding of good behavior became the guiding principles behind Tuskegee, other industrial schools modeled after it, and outreach projects Tuskegee undertook.

In line with those principles, Washington envisioned the Hilton Head colony as "an ideal settlement" illustrating "what Tuskegee graduates can teach the people to accomplish."[2]

Besides introducing modern agricultural techniques, the men and women sent by Washington were to serve as models of the cleanliness and neatness, and other examples of good character, upon which he insisted.

Tuskegee had experimented with three agricultural colonies in Alabama with less than outstanding results. That the new colony was larger than the other colonies and located on an isolated island in the Atlantic Ocean, farther away from Tuskegee than previous efforts, did not dampen Washington's enthusiasm.

Clyde had made a small donation to Tuskegee in 1904.[3] Now, at age sixty-five, he stood ready to "give back" to the island he used as his personal retreat and hunting preserve by putting a portion of his land in Washington's hands, along with his trust.

Like other wealthy Northerners who supported Washington's projects, Clyde respected Washington as an example of what the Negro race could achieve. The prospect of Negroes holding powerful positions was not altogether new to him. He had corresponded briefly in

1890 with Frederick Douglass, the well-known black abolitionist. At the time Clyde contacted him, Douglass served as U.S. minister to Haiti, appointed by President Benjamin Harrison.

Clyde sought Douglass's support to open steamship service from New York to Haiti in order to expand his company's business. But his letter also noted, "I am sincerely glad that you see evidences of present prosperity and future promise in the condition of these people, who have suffered so grievously both while bound and free for more than [a] century past."[4]

His words showed concern for those who had endured slavery and its aftermath, and whenever he came down from New York to stay at Honey Horn, his home on Hilton Head, he saw people working hard to eke out a living. He knew they needed a hand.

To people on the island, however, Clyde was the wealthy man who owned more land than anyone else. Within a year's time, he and his son would begin placing restrictions on deeds of land they sold to Gullah people to forever reserve exclusive hunting rights for themselves and their heirs.[5]

The new restriction would allow the Clydes to prosecute anyone hunting game animals or birds on Clyde's land without Clyde or his property manger's permission. It allowed the Clydes and their guests to enter the premises of the new landowners to hunt whenever they choose.

Although not specified in the deeds, Clyde would let black people raise crops on his land. Even so, it residents were disrespected when a group of white hunters rode up to shoot game in someone's front yard.

Clyde also had sat for his photograph with fifty or so black men and women who labored for him at Honey Horn. Seated in the center of the first row, surrounded by his hunting guides, field hands, cooks, maids, and laundresses, the silver-haired Northerner looked as paternal as any plantation master of old. This was the man people knew.

Georgianna Barnwell, the daughter of a Civil War veteran, John Miller, would remember "Purry," as she called him, for the rest of her days. She was about twenty-five in 1906 when Washington sent Stephen Gordon Powell, a recent Tuskegee graduate with only a few years of farming experience under his belt, to set up the colony at Seabrook.

His marching orders were to grow Sea Island cotton, which Washington knew once had brought wealth to the island. Washington hoped that reviving the fabled, long-stapled cotton would make the colony prosperous.

Powell visited Georgianna Barnwell's mother, Katie Miller, and bought his rice from her. "We were just like that [close]," Barnwell said. In addition, Josephine

William T. Clyde, surrounded by black men and women who worked for him at Honey Horn. *Courtesy of Hack Family, Coastal Discovery Library*

Clayton, a white woman Washington sent to teach in the school at Seabrook, boarded with Barnwell's mother.[6]

The new school struck Georgianna Barnwell, known to islanders as "Miss Mimi," as so advanced that she considered it a college. "Booker T. Washington build a college, build a college for the colored," she would remember seventy years later at age ninety-three.

The new school had two rooms, compared to the one-room schoolhouses on the island, and it offered more grades than the other schools did. After disenfranchisement, the state of South Carolina put less money into colored education than it did into education for white students. At the turn of the century, Hilton Head schools provided three to four years of education. If the

Georgianna Barnwell. *Collection of Thomas C. Barnwell, Jr.*

new school allowed students to get as much as a sixth-grade education, it would have seemed like a college to many black people.

Squire Pope, where Miss Mimi lived, did not have a school at the time. Under customs in the black community, if a community did not have a school, children walked to the nearest community that did. Pope sat near Seabrook.

Some parents in Squire Pope and other nearby communities wanted to send their children to Seabrook so they could get a better education. Tommy Wright had to intervene first.

A light-skinned black man, Wright worked for Clyde. While Clyde had white property managers at Honey Horn, Wright was his black overseer. People knew Wright as a wood rider. He would ride through Clyde's land, find trees that had fallen or needed to be chopped down, and let people know where they could come to get wood. People relied on wood to cook their food and heat their houses, so Wright provided a service.[7]

Wright lived across the road from Powell at Seabrook on land Clyde had sold to him. He served as Clyde's point man for the uplift settlement and he objected to the school excluding children from Squire Pope.

"Tommy didn't like it. . . . He say you must give the people here some of the school." So a new arrangement began. In exchange for attending the school, the bigger students, the ones Miss Mimi called "young lad-like," worked in the colony's fields.

In Alabama, Washington grew impatient for results.

"I am very anxious that the industrial, moral and religious conditions of the people be improved as fast as possible," he instructed J. R. E. Lee, the head of Tuskegee's academic department in the spring of 1908, before sending him to the island to advise Powell for a few days.

"For example," Washington continued, "I want them to begin the whitewashing of their houses and fences, planting better crops and making better farms. They are a very primitive, backwards people and cannot take on new ideas very fast."[8]

He had adopted the idea that Gullah people were "primitive," just as some of Port Royal missionaries had thought.

Hilton Head blacks held to their African ways because they had served them well over the generations. They needed to see good reason to change before considering new ways. Otherwise, their attitude was, "What you in such an all-fire hurry for to change me?"

Lee wrote Washington that Powell was setting a good example in farming methods. Some men who used hoes to cultivate their fields wanted to try plows after watching Powell.[9] Lee was mistaken, however, if he believed no one on the island used plows. Whoever owned a work animal or could borrow one did so. One of Julian Dimock's photographs taken four years earlier showed a black man plowing his field with a mule.

Lee also recommended adding a two-room school, five or six miles away, to expand industrial education. The school at Seabrook had proved popular. Islanders knew the advantage of education.

Washington stepped foot on the island for the first time in early June 1908. He came on the first Sunday following Decoration Day, with its annual veterans' parade in Beaufort in which people marched.[10]

He was the spokesman of the people, a celebrity who had dined at the White House with the president, a man who had written a best-selling autobiography, *Up from Slavery*, that convinced Andrew Carnegie and J. P. Morgan and other captains of industry to underwrite his uplift projects.

People on Hilton Head were eager to see the great man in person.

When Washington got off the boat, Georgianna Barnwell was waiting at Honey Horn. She had raised the turkey Washington was to eat. Powell bought it from her, and Miss Josephine and another teacher cooked it.

Tommy Wright drove Washington around the island in a horse and buggy,[11] and Washington spoke to people at the First African Baptist church. At lunchtime, he and several men who came with him to the island had lunch with Mrs. W. D. Brown, the wife of the white landowner and storekeeper.

"He didn't eat the lunch what Miss Josephine fixed for him," Miss Mimi said. "He eat lunch to Mrs. Brown. Then he tell them [Powell and the teachers] to let the boys have [the] lunch what they had for him. That was

Sollie [Solomon] Campbell, Reggie Park and some more of them. They eat the lunch."

Washington would write Clyde that the white people were enthusiastic and wanted the colony to succeed as much as the blacks, and that the land was more fertile than he had expected. Then he turned to his assessment of the islanders. "We shall have to, in my opinion, greatly interject a little new blood into the island. The people are about as run down as the animals," he said, "but there is a foundation for good work here."[12]

He did not wait for Clyde's approval. He acted while he was at Honey Horn.

"He said he want all the people what he bring there, must come there," Miss Mimi said. She was there, listening.

"I ain't going," one of the men said. "Well, I ain't."

Arguing with Washington did not get him anywhere.

"They all stand up in a row and Mr. Booker T. Washington look at them and talk to them . . . and talk to them. He been up on the porch [at Honey Horn] and they been on the ground."

Washington was to spend the night in Clyde's home at Honey Horn, the last antebellum plantation house left on the island. The maids had made up the bed for Washington in a special room. Washington, however, did not spend the night. He left the island by boat before the day ended.

The maids were disappointed, but Washington at least had tried out the bed. His imprint was on it. They appreciated this. The great man had lain on the bed they had made up for him.[13]

Washington sent money for lime for black people to whitewash their houses. Powell had whitewashed the houses in the colony, and Washington wanted other black people to whitewash their homes, too.

"And all the house, he said he wanted every house whitewash. He said if it's holey [has holes in it], let it be clean. That was his word. That was his word. And he was deep brown skin—he wasn't a white man," Miss Mimi said.

Georgianna Barnwell's family owned twenty-five acres of cleared land and ten acres of wooded land. Her husband, Jerry, was the son of Savannah Barnwell, who rowed his family to freedom after the Union invaded. Jerry's older brother had been the infant his parents named Freeman even before Lincoln signed the emancipation proclamation. She was not used to being told what to do.

A breach grew between black people and the colony on Hilton Head.

Washington decided to inject more new blood.

He ran an article in the *Tuskegee Student* in 1910

informing Tuskegee graduates of an opportunity "to either buy or rent land and settle down as successful farmers on Hilton Head." He wanted a "first class" Tuskegee colony on the island.[14]

His first injection had resulted in some black men on Hilton Head being replaced by Tuskegee men. The colony was becoming less focused on black people on Hilton Head and less centered around land ownership. Tenants were now welcome.

The breach widened at the end of 1910 when the cotton raised by one of the men in the colony matured late. The farmer, a man by the name of Stanfield, had been among the men Miss Mimi remembered as accompanying Washington on his trip to the island.

None of the residents would help Stanfield pick his cotton, nor could Stanfield persuade them to hold off on releasing their horses, cows, and hogs to forage. The first of December had come, the time when, by tradition, islanders released their animals to forage each winter. The residents released their stock. The hogs ate Stanfield's cotton.[15]

Washington and Clyde had hoped that the colony, once the cotton thrived, would also grow winter crops for Eastern markets, but foraging animals killed the prospect of growing winter crops. From the residents' viewpoint, though, they had to let their animals forage during the lean months. Otherwise, their stock starved.

Washington sought funding for the uplift project for 1911. Clyde responded that the colony had one year to

begin resolving its problems. Otherwise, he might end his support.[16]

The tensions between the residents and the colony worsened.

Blacks were used to rowing their own crops to market, where they sold the fruits of their own labor. Powell was keeping all the cotton in the barn, apparently to sell after the final harvest at a better price. In the meantime, however, this created a financial hardship for many farmers in the colony.

"And you hear say," Miss Mimi said, "they most starve to death. If the children didn't have a boat and catch fish and sell them, they would have starved because that [the cotton] was their living."

"Tommy Wright told Purry share the bread," Miss Mimi remembered. "Don't let some get all the bread and some don't get none."

Powell did not listen to Wright.

"People got disgusted with the Seabrook Center," Miss Mimi said. "They used to have to steal the cotton and bring [it] to Ben Jones's shop and sell it.

"They would pick so much, they would put it yonder [in the barn], and in the night they go and get a wagon, pulling it and pulling it [by hand], going to Ben to sell the cotton. That was the only way 'cause Purry wouldn't want to give them nothing."

Powell blew the whistle.

He wrote Washington that the colonists were stealing the cotton. "It seems impossible to get in a full set of

tenants who will not fall into the hands of the islanders," he said.

"I have found that even the people who are suppose[d]
to administer the law have received cotton which was
thrown over in their yard by night. That is the system of
delivering it. Just throw it over in the yards and whoever
calls for pay[ment] for the right number of sacks will get
the money."[17]

The breach between Powell and the colony and rest of
the island had grown too wide to bridge. People began
to be suspicious that the colony was a trick to get them
back into slavery.

If disenfranchisement had occurred, why couldn't
the clock be turned back further to slavery? They didn't
want to get sold down that river again.

Clyde and his son ceased paying the teachers' salaries
and other costs of the colony at the end of 1912. The
colony shut down, and the school ended, by April 1913.[18]
Washington told Clyde's son he thought they had done
the best they could under the circumstances.[19] But what
began with hope had ended in failure.

"It just become a mix-up," Miss Mimi said.

Washington never knew Hilton Head's black people's
point of view.

He did not see that the very quality he sought to ig-
nite in black rural southerners lay behind Gullah stub-
bornness: self-reliance. The Port Royal Experiment had

Thomas Robinson, PhD. *Courtesy of Thomas C. Barnwell, Jr.*

helped forge islanders' self-reliance, and the war had
strengthened their steel. Even life during slavery had
not altogether stripped away their independence, in part
because the plantation owners had been absent most of
the time.

In most of the rural South, black farmers now worked
the soil as sharecroppers on a white man's land, often

leading lives of bondage almost as severe as if they still were enslaved. Washington sought opportunities for blacks to buy land, believing that as they cultivated their land, they would catch the spirit of freedom and stand on their own two feet.

A sizable number of Gullah people on Hilton Head owned land. Those who did not either rented land or worked as wage laborers for other farmers. They did not farm for shares and did not want to. To islanders, this was a matter of pride.

The odds of the colony at Seabrook succeeding had been slim from the start. Washington wanted to see the people advance to the next level, but he used a one-size-fits-all approach that lacked sufficient flexibility to adapt to local situations. Even though Hilton Head blacks wanted and needed an economic boost, they were determined to control their own lives.

Powell and the other men and women who had come to Hilton Head to join the colony left the island and scattered.

Tommy Wright, who had sat on the hot seat, answering to Clyde, the colony, and the islanders, wound up being called by some islanders "Uncle Tommy," a pointed reference to the main character in Harriet Beecher Stowe's *Uncle Tom's Cabin.*

But several students who graduated from the school at Seabrook picked up an appetite for education. Thomas H. Robinson graduated from the school and went on to the Penn Normal and Industrial School on Saint Helena Island and then to Hampton Institute, a college the American Missionary Association founded after the Civil War in 1868 in Hampton, Virginia, to provide education to freedmen. He would become the first black person from Hilton Head to earn a PhD.[20]

Had the focus been strictly on education rather than growing cotton, black people likely would have gained more. It was sad, as the Clyde and Washington plan would be the last uplift attempt on Hilton Head.

Chapter Fifteen

THE 1920S DIDN'T ROAR

THE TWENTIES DIDN'T ROAR on Hilton Head. Post–World War I euphoria, speakeasies with flowing liquor, and flappers dancing the Charleston had not reached the island. There was plenty of moonshine on the island, though, and people kept busy.

Blow after blow hit Hilton Head in the 1920s: the boll weevil, a lawsuit over who owned the land in the former freedmen's village of Mitchelville, and the murder of a white storeowner.

A monumental change was also underway. Only a few black Union soldiers still lived, and they would die in this decade.

By 1921, the boll weevil reached Hilton Head and started eating up the cotton. Over a period of years, the voracious insect had marched from Mexico, crossed the Rio Grande, and invaded cotton fields in the South. The small, grayish, long-snouted beetle wounded cotton buds and laid their eggs in the buds. By the time the cotton bolls ripened, boll weevils sat on top of the squares chomping up the cotton.

The boll weevils were another peg in the coffin of King Cotton, though a cotton company from Savannah, spurred by the World War I demand for cotton, managed to continue growing cotton for a while. After that only Gullah people would persist in growing cotton. A number of blacks would continue to plant cotton, as a cash crop, for decades to come.

The Mitchelville lawsuit was like a Gordian knot. The two branches of a feuding family could not untangle the knot. Church elders lacked authority to settle a legal dispute. For many years, it also appeared that a Beaufort County court would fail to untangle the knot.

Both the heirs of March Gardner and the heirs of Gabriel Gardner testified before the clerk of Beaufort County Court of Common Pleas in 1911 as part of the lawsuit.[1] Ten years would pass before the lawsuit's resolution in 1921.

Even in majority-black Beaufort County, a lawsuit involving Gullah people arguing over ownership of a sizable amount of land had to be unusual. The land in question had been the village of Mitchelville, a model of freedom.

Much testimony relied on forty-five-year-old memories of a land sale to March Gardner and whether March's son Gabriel later had been sold the same land. The shadow of William Drayton loomed in the background, at the root of the dispute. But as he was not a party to the lawsuit, he remained simply a figure from the past. When plaintiffs mentioned Drayton's name, the opposing attorney cried, "Objection."

The offending statement then was stricken from the record.

The meat of the testimony went like this: March Gardner arrived on Hilton Head with a bag of money

African Americans working in a cotton field, ca. 1920. *Library of Congress*

from the up-country in about 1863. After working as a carpenter during the war, he built and opened a store on Mitchelville Road. He also had a gin and a grist mill, which made him the most prosperous man in the village. When Drayton, son of former General Drayton, offered to sell Mitchelville to March Gardner, Gardner saw an opportunity.

Joseph Riley, a former soldier; John Nesbitt, a preacher who lived at Mitchelville; and Clara Wigfall went to the place where Gardner kept his money safe. Riley counted out the money. Clara Wigfall saw her father hand over the money to William Drayton. "[March] took his money and bought Mitchelville," Thomas Wigfall, Clara's husband, said.

Clara Wigfall remembered the date as being either 1865 or 1866.

Both dates were odd. The war had ended in April 1865. Most Hilton Head soldiers came home in 1866. Hilton Head blacks knew of the chaos on other Sea Islands, as pre-war land owners reclaimed their former lands. But land on Hilton Head was not open yet for redemption.

At best, William Dayton erred in believing that Fish Haul could be reclaimed anytime soon. The federal government had not made land on Hilton Head open to redemption at that time.

Drayton did not give March Gardner a deed and was not able to. March trusted the word of a Drayton and did not grasp the importance of deeds. He thought his son, Gabriel, who was literate, could write a deed for him. That, of course, was impossible.

March Gardner believed he owned Mitchelville, however, and took possession of the village. He rented lots to some islanders and sold lots to others. Linda Perry, another of March's four daughters, said that March told his daughters that would be passed down in the family. She said her father said, "the land was for us all."

Hannah Williams, whose husband, Joe, ran a boat for Gabriel Gardner, believed that Gabriel bought Mitchelville from William Drayton. That would have been during the Draytons' efforts to redeem their land, or slightly afterwards. Hannah Williams remembered her husband taking Gabriel and Drayton to Beaufort to deposit the money to pay Drayton so that Gabriel could purchase Mitchelville.

A fair number of people still lived at Mitchelville at that time. Two family names particularly stood out. One was Pinckney. Charles Pinckney was the father of Dr. E. M. Pinckney, who often gave medical examinations to former soldiers as part of the process for seeking a federal pension for Union soldiers. The other was Wiley. Robert Wiley was either the father of or a relative of Cyrus Wiley. Cyrus Wiley had graduated from Georgia Industrial School in Savannah by now, and soon would go on to greater heights.

March died in 1889, according to Clara Wigfall, and Gabriel Gardner took over the possession of the village. Gabriel continued to retain someone in the village to collect rents from people who lived there, and the money to pay villagers' land taxes. Adam Jenkins did that at one time. Thomas Wigfall later took on the job. He continued after Gabriel died, which according to Clara Wigfall was in 1893—the year of the big storm. Gabriel's wife, Susan B. Gardner, continued to run the store, and Thomas Wigfall collected the rents and the money to pay the villagers' taxes.

In 1910, everything came to a head. Susan Gardner died. James Heyward, the husband of Susan's daughter, Sarah Heyward, took over possession of Mitchelville. Heyward kicked Thomas Wigfall—"a man of good repute," Dr. Wilder testified—off the job. Heyward had decided that he and his family owned Mitchelville.

He also declared that Clara Wigfall and her sisters and grandchildren did not own Mitchelville, but instead lived on the old Fish Haul tract. Heyward may have believed that as Gabriel had built a large house on "Pope land" after March Gardner died. The Wigfalls had lived in Mitchelville for more than forty years, though. Heyward was younger and had less knowledge of Mitchelville's history.

Everything came to an impasse. Thomas Wigfall said that James Heyward pushed many Mitchelville villagers off the land. Heyward would later respond that a probate judge had told him to. At this point, Clara Wigfall and other plaintiffs filed suit.

The court apparently believed that Mitchelville had been sold to both March and Gabriel Gardner, but it was still impossible to untangle, as disagreements extended to which parcel of land was Mitchelville and which was the Fish Haul tract.

A special master had the land surveyed, with the costs to be paid by both the plaintiffs and defendants. He then divided the land into parcels, allotting Clara Wigfall, for one, thirty acres in the original village of Mitchelville, and allotting land in the Fish Haul tract to the Heyward heirs—a solution to which all agreed.

His action was similar to how Alexander the Great dealt with the original Gordian knot. After several tries to untangle the famous knot, the famous conqueror pulled out his sword and sliced through it.

Mitchelville would never be a working village again, but its legacy as most likely the first freedmen's village in the nation would remain.

W. D. Brown, a well-regarded figure on Hilton Head, had come to the island soon after the Civil War and had stayed. A Northerner, he was among the small handful of white families on the island. He had acquired a great deal of land through the government tax sales, and he sold some land to Gullah people.

He owned the largest store on the island and his wife, Lulie, served as postmaster, beginning in 1907. They raised two daughters on the island. Booker T. Washington, on his one visit to Hilton Head, chose to have lunch with the Browns rather than with the teachers at the new school William P. Clyde had financed as part of Washington's plan for an uplift colony. Georgianna Barnwell always stayed a little miffed that her turkey was not served at the lunch that the teachers had planned for Washington. Other than that, she liked Brown. Most people did.

He was important to the island's black former soldiers in their pursuit of receiving a federal pension for a war injury; an application for status as an invalid, which also entitled them to a pension; or an old-age or widow's pension.

Brown served as a witness to former soldiers' written testimonies that were to be mailed to one of the large pension firms in Washington, DC. For a minimal fee, regulated by the government, the pension attorney then would put a soldier's paperwork in proper form and submit it to the U.S. Pension Bureau.

Other times, Brown served as a notary public, writing down the words of men seeking pension aid. At times, he testified on behalf of a pensioner before a special examiner who would recommend whether the pensioner merited receiving an increase in his pension.

He was more than a cog in a wheel. On the fourth day of every third month, a pensioner appeared before Brown to sign his name to his quarterly pension voucher.

The government sent the vouchers to Brown.

Each man who appeared before him had to present his pension certificate in order to receive his voucher, which would be exchanged for cash. Brown conducted a short ceremony required to receive his voucher. The pensioner tipped a pen to his certificate, swore that he was the soldier whose name was on the voucher, and saluted the flag of the United States of America. Everything had to be done just so. Brown made sure of it.

That came to an end on July 3, 1923. It was a Saturday evening, a holiday weekend on the mainland, but Hilton Head was quiet. Both Brown and his wife were asleep when two Negro men broke into the store, took the money in the till, killed the Browns, and set the store on fire. The blaze burned so bright that people in Beaufort could see the fire.

Black people on the island, alarmed by the murder of the Browns, searched for the two strangers. They knew the terrain well, but the two men — both strangers to Hilton Head — had escaped in a small wooden boat that they managed to steal.

Ben White had been the last person to pass the store that evening. Some said that he stayed low for a few days afterwards. With a prominent wife and husband killed, events could have gotten out of hand if white citizens on the mainland turned vigilantes and came to Hilton Head looking for Negro criminals.

The two outsiders later would be caught off-island and executed. But the death of Willie Brown and his wife remained a loss to black people and shifted the pattern of life.

Joints wear out, limbs stiffen, eyes dim, hearts deteriorate, and minds wander. The last of Hilton Head's Civil War soldiers ailed in ways reflecting those and other injuries.

Their ailments came, in part, from the hard, physical work of farming and old age. Yet their war-time experiences often had compounded their aliments in ways that the federal pension bureau sometimes recognized, and sometimes did not.

Federal pensions had existed before the Civil War, but the federal government initiated a new statute in 1862, specifically for Union veterans of the Civil War. Confederate veterans had their own pension system.

The 1862 statute had strict rules. It aided only Union

soldiers whose disability was "incurred as a direct consequence" of their military duty or developed after combat "from causes which can be directly traced to injuries received or diseases contracted while in military service." Pensions allotted to veterans depended upon a veteran's military rank and his disability.

The Grand Army of the Republic successfully lobbied Congress to drop the requirement that veterans could receive a pension only if their injuries were a direct consequence of their military duty or if their diseases were contracted in military service.

The new 1890 stature was simple in comparison. It allowed any veteran who had served honorably to qualify for a pension "if at some time he became disabled for manual labor." He did not have to prove that his condition related to his military service.

But therein was the rub. Most former black soldiers on Hilton Head continued to try to prove that their injury resulted from military duty, and most of the special examiners sent out by the Bureau of Pensions kept stating that a former soldier had not proved that his injury resulted from military duty. It followed the old biblical saying that "many are called but few are chosen." It usually took several tries to get a pension, or, later on, an increase in the pension size.

The fiftieth anniversary of the Union's capture of Hilton Head had occurred on November 7, 1911. So it was not surprising that only two of Hilton Head's former soldiers remained alive during the twenties.

Many of the former soldiers had enrolled in the army at age eighteen. Others, including Caesar Jones, who died in 1903, had been forty years old at the time they enlisted.

Just as the soldiers had answered the daily roll call during the Civil War, they had, as the old spirituals decreed, answered the roll call in the sky. When they had enrolled in the USCT, often two or three men enlisted at the same time. For this roll call, they went one by one.

Many were men, or their widows, who had lived on plantations on the day of the big gun shoot. Prince Brown was among them. He had lived on one of the Baynard plantations on the day of the big gun shoot. Through the U.S. tax sales of 1876, he achieved the dream of every freedman — acquiring land of his own. He lived on his land in the Marshland/Chaplin area for twenty-two years. In 1893, when Hilton Head's GAR post had its own letterhead, Brown was listed as quartermaster.

As old age hit, Brown testified before a pension bureau special examiner that he suffered "from weakness in my back and pain around my waist which came from the smallpox [that he had during the war]. . . . I am now almost helpless and I am not able to do but very little manual labor." He died at age eighty-seven.

Mary Barnard, wife of Prince, died in 1913. Earlier, her house had blown down in a storm, and her land was deemed practically worthless. She had no way of contacting her son, Jacob Brown, for help. He was "somewhere in Texas teaching school," she testified before a special examiner.

Martha Fields, who along with her husband, Polido, had watched over their seven children on the day of the big gun shoot, died in 1907. She outlived her husband Polido by fifteen years and all but two of her children had died. She did raise a grandson, Frederick Oriage, who produced a long line of islanders with his last name.

Both Polido and Martha lived out their lives on Cotton Hope plantation, which soon became Squire Pope. They were thought to have lived in the same house that they were in during slavery.

Polido died on September 22 of the "year of the big shake"—the 1886 massive earthquake that destroyed much of Charleston and caused aftershocks for weeks.

It seemed as if everyone on Hilton Head came forth to sign either an affidavit or to testify before a special examiner to prove Martha's identity.

As Polido (or Poledo) had not been seriously injured in the war, he had not filed for a pension and the army could not find Polido's name on its record. Some records turned up a "Pauldo." Other records found a "Paul LaDoe." He had been known by both names on some records, but Martha Fields had never heard either of those names. She knew that her husband was a corporal in Company G of the U.S. Colored Troops, and would see the stripes on his uniform whenever he could come home.

Martha eventually got an $8 monthly pension. With it, she bought the land she and Polido had lived on. The affidavits, testimony, and comments of the special examiner would stack two inches high before she got her pension.

Simon Grant, who had been the first person to notice that Samuel Christopher was missing when he reached James Island and could not find Christopher (whose boat had wrecked), died in 1905 of pains in his heart. He and his wife, Maria Bryant, had lived at Otter Hole on the day of the big gun shoot.

Joseph Riley, who counted out the money so that March Gardner could buy Mitchelville, did not live long enough to see the outcome of the court case. He had been friends with Simon Grant and Maria Bryant, long before the day of the big gun shoot.

And there were more.

Riley's wife, Emma, spent eight years trying to get a widow's pension. The last special examiner Emma went before said that the "Claimant is very lame and infirm and lives alone in a little cabin in a lonely spot." He recommended that she receive a pension. After eight years of trying, Emma Riley would receive a pension in 1922. The pension came late in her life. She died two years later, in 1924.

Matt Jones in his regimental uniform, Hilton Head, SC, April 6, 1904. *American Museum of Natural History, Library: Julian Dimock Collection*

Chapter Sixteen

THE LAST BLACK UNION SOLDIERS

MATTHEW JONES, often called Matt or Mack, had stood on his own land when "Cameraman," Julian Dimmock, photographed him in 1904. That was a bright point in his life. He wore a broad-brimmed felt hat with the insignia of the GAR, as well as a ribbon on his chest proclaiming "Abraham Lincoln, Post No.12, Hilton Head, S.C."

Anyone seeing his photograph at that time could find it hard to believe that Jones was in his late fifties. And ten years earlier, in 1894, Jones's appearance was one of several barriers to his gaining a pension increase.

Jones held a $6-a-month pension in 1894 for rheumatism and other ailments that he believed stemmed from his military service. He hoped to get a bigger pension. Jones received a doctor's examination, ordered by the Bureau of Pensions, to verify the extent of his disabilities. Then the Bureau sent a special examiner to Hilton Head to recommend whether Jones deserved an increase.

The special examiner, J. G. Gibbs, Jr., arrived in 1894.

People on Hilton Head had long known Jones was not a well man. Millie White, who had raised him on the Stoney Plantation, had always said that he went into the service healthy "and broke himself down in the war." She now was deceased, but her sister-in-law, Amelia

Amelia White Cemetery, with graves dating back to the 1800s. *Photo by Will Warasila*

White, who had also helped raise Jones, testified that Jones complained of pains in his shoulder and back from the time he got back.[1]

York Williams, a near neighbor, recalled that in the last nine or ten years Jones was laid up sometimes for several weeks at a time with pains in the back, side, and

head: "I know that he has not been a man I would care to hire and pay a full day's pay to for a day's work."

Jones stated that he was a farmer and about forty-nine years old, though army records put him at fifty. As with many former soldiers who never had a record of their birth, he had difficulty knowing his age.

"I enlisted in August 1864 and was mustered out in April 1866, and there was no doubt I was a healthy young man at enlistment," Jones said. "I was given a musket at once and did my duty right along up to Dec. 1865. The USCT 21st regiment was then stationed at Morris Island, and there was no other regiment there, and the enemy was all around us.

"We had severe picket duty to perform, and during that month I was on picket duty for ten nights running and it was very cold . . . and there was little protection. I was exhausted, and the captain increased the guard to four men to the post.

"That night I was relieved about 10 o'clock and went with my oil cloth into a shell hole and went to sleep. Before morning I woke up soaking wet and nearly frozen. I got up, and it appeared as if my whole left side was paralyzed. I went along for a day or two and had chills and fever, and the doctor, a colored man, gave me something to keep the chill off. That was in December 1865.

"I did my duty right along and the regiment was sent [back] to Hilton Head. While there, I took sick again from that same cold. . . . The doctor excused me from duty, but [I] was not put in any hospital. After I got some better I was given light duty as watchman at Fort Howell on Hilton head. I watched there a month or two and got better but still had that rheumatism in my left arm. The regiment was sent back to Morris Island where we were mustered out in April [1866].

"I got the frostbite of right big toe also on Morris

Depiction of black Union soldier at site of Fort Howell, by artist Mary Ann Browning Ford. *Photo by Will Warasila*

Island during the winter of 1864. Yes, sir, it was the same winter I enlisted. I was frostbitten on the beach while doing guard duty. That toe has been stiff ever since. . . . No, sir, I was never in any hospital.

"My rheumatism was bad at discharge, and it has gotten worse ever since. The toe only gives me trouble from the stiffness. . . . I have a swimming in the head, which gives me trouble and keeps me with a constant headache and thumping.

"I have a wife and seven head of children, and if it was not for my wife and large children there would be suffering in my family. I cannot work in the hot sun and can do nothing in cloudy and rainy weather."[2]

Moses Brown, a Hilton Head farmer and disabled soldier with a $12 pension, backed up Jones's testimony.[3] Brown served in Company H at the same time Jones had.

"The first that I remember of any sickness Jones had in the service was in the winter of 1865 on Morris Island. I had been made corporal and had charge of a squad of men on post. The regiment was divided at that time, and it threw double duty on the men who were on Morris Island.

"We had a hard time all around at that time, and I remember one severely cold night. I had relieved Jones from duty on post, and he retired to a shell hole to get some rest. A shell hole was a hole made into our sand breast works by a shell from the enemy's fort. I knew Jones had gone into the hole, and when I went to call him to go [back] on guard, it had rained in the meantime, and he was soaked.

"I woke him up and told him he would take his death of cold. He got up chilled . . . and in a week or ten days he complained of a hacking cough and went to the doctor. I know the doctor exempted Jones from duty several times. I never knew him to go to the hospital but know he was on the sick list. I don't know where that cough settled, but since the service I have heard Jones complain of a ringing in the head [and misery]. I never have lived near to him or worked with him but have seen him off and on at church."

Upon question, Brown added, "I had forgot about the rheumatism. I live within six or seven miles of Jones. I am no relation and have no interest. The above is correctly set down to the best of my belief."

Thomas Young, who had lived within sight of Jones ever since the war, also recalled the night Jones took ill. Young said that a rain came up that night, and Jones got soaked in the shell hole and "he commenced having chills and fever and cold that seemed then to settle in his left side and back. . . . These pains in back and side went along with him while he remained in the service."

"After service I knew Jones here on Hilton Head, and he had that same back and side complaint. . . . We belong to the same church, and if I don't see him at church on Sunday he is sick. He is . . . an afflicted man and has been for years."[4]

Aesop Singleton, called Dick Perry in the army, who now lived on Saint Helena Island, also remembered that night of severe weather. He said that Jones always complained of pains in his left shoulder after that night in the shell hole.

Each man recalled the incident with varying details. Jones's night in the shell hole had occurred twenty-nine years before.

Gibbs did not believe them.

"Claimant is a young looking very black man with a large family. He walks with a limp and may have at times some rheumatism.

"In my opinion, the 'shell hole' cause of rheumatism advanced by Claimant and Comrades Perry, Brown and Young cannot be relied on. The former has talked over the matter with claimant, as also the two latter, who have resided near claimant since discharge and as a matter of course were prepared for the coming of the Special Examiner. I believe that very few of this class of colored claims are meritorious.

"A portion of this testimony was taken in the wilds of Hilton Head and Saint Helena Islands, and I was often unable to secure attesting witnesses.

"I recommend the rejection of the claim under the general law for the reason that the disabilities were not of service origin."[5]

Jones lacked military hospital and doctor records to present as proof. Under the 1890 pension act, though, he did not have to prove that his ailments stemmed from his service. And unknown to Jones, the physician's affidavit that the pension bureau required "stated that Jones had chronic rheumatism afflicting shoulders, hips, and left leg, and failure of eyesight and an affliction of the heart."

By 1905 he managed to get his pension raised to $8 a month. Two months after Jones was photographed in 1904, Jones's wife Tena Middleton Jones died. A few years later he married Flora Williams. His health remained bad, and in 1914, under a new 1912 "old age" pension act, he received a pension of $16.50. Matthew Jones died in his early seventies on December 22, 1917.

Flora Jones applied for a widow's pension. She first had to prove that she was the wife of Matthew Jones.[6]

R. D. Jones, from the Jonesville community, filled out a 1918 affidavit stating that as treasurer of the Young Star of Bethlehem Society he had charge of the society's books and records. The records stated that Matthew Jones's first wife, Tena Jones, died June 14, 1904.

Flora Jones received a pension in 1919 (back dated to 1918) of $25. For the rest of her life, she kept hold of as much of Matthew Jones's land in Stoney as she could.

When James Drayton returned from the army and changed his last name to Grant, as his father had, he had no idea how tricky it would be to make his new name stick. The question of whether he was "Drayton" or "Grant" followed him to his grave—and beyond.

The army knew him as Drayton and some people called him Drayton because he had grown up at "Drayton Plantation" (Fish Haul). He decided to state his name as James Grant and insert the letter "D" for Drayton as his middle initial.

For some reason, possibly because a special examiner did not understand his Gullah speech, his name on pension records became James "B." Grant. James Grant accepted it and went on. Even then, some continued to call him James Drayton.

Over time, he and his wife, Mary Ann (Mathis), had eleven children. Several died young. One daughter, Caroline, would marry Ceasar Johnson, known on Hilton Head for his basket-making skills. A second daughter, Violet, would marry islander Jacob Green. A third daughter, Henrietta (Martin), would live in Brooklyn, New York, in the 1920s.

Mary Ann was visiting a daughter in Savannah when she took ill and died in February 1889. She was buried on Hilton Head without a headstone, as money was scarce. One islander later testified about Mary Ann's death before a special examiner, "I know for a fact that she died because I was present at her funeral and I saw her laid a corpse."

Grant later married nineteen-year-old Emma Chisholm of Hilton Head. This was her first—and only—marriage. Grant was forty-seven and was feeling his age, but he and Emma would have nine children. Midwife Nancy Christopher, whom Grant had known ever since she was a child, delivered two of their children. She also recorded their births in a bible.

Grant had a pension for rheumatism in his left side and heart disease, and in 1896 a special examiner asked him whether those ailments still troubled him. He replied that sometimes he had pains from the rheumatism and if he did "any swift work, his heart jumped." He eventually received $14.50 per month under the 1912 "old age" act.[7]

The pension bureau seemed to forget him after that. Grant should have been receiving automatic increases in his pension at this point, but he heard nothing from the bureau, and his condition had worsened.

He wrote the pension bureau a desperate appeal on November 15, 1917. The letter, in his handwriting, asked the pension commissioner to look up his pension record and reminded him that he had served in Company G, USCT, for eighteen months. Then Grant, who had lapsed into calling himself James Drayton, added the following:

Have pity on me for God Sake. I have writen [sic] to the commissioner and he told me he would give me . . . [his] Best and not yet any answer. Please sir to help me By give me the increase. I so much in need. Please, my health is So Bad. All of the old veterans have received increases and all the old widows getting increases and I have not received any increase since May 1912. Believe my name must Be over look.

Sir, for God Sake, I am a Poor old veteran and yours Respectfully, James Drayton

I am only getting $14.50.[8]

Grant was buried on October 25, 1922, at age seventy-eight. The cause of death was listed as "pains in the head."

Emma Grant applied for a widow's pension in November of the same year. She was farming at the time. She testified before a special examiner in January 1924 that she no longer had her marriage certificate and the minister who married them had died.

"I had a certificate of my marriage, but I gave it to W. D. Brown . . . who was supposed to have sent it into the Pension Bureau. If you say the paper is not there it must have got burnt up in his house when he was killed and his house set on fire . . . last July.

"I suppose my correct name is 'Grant,' but in case my pension is allowed I want my name to appear in the certificate as 'Emma Drayton,'" she stated. She preferred that name in part because he had enlisted with it.

"Renty Miller is the only Civil War soldier now living in this part of the country. He served with Dray-ton, and he can testify that the soldier of record was my husband.

"I don't know of any other old-timer who was acquainted with the soldier in earlier days, the most of the people of the island have known him [Renty Miller] all their life."

Emma Grant got her name changed to Drayton on pension papers before she died of paralysis in 1927. Rebecca Drayton, who had been at the bedside of Samuel Christopher when he died, was born to Emma and James. Julia Grant, named after a sister of James, was another.

Renty Miller may well have been the best known of Hilton Head's soldiers, not for valor in wartime, but for the care he took of his comrades after the war ended.

Former soldiers always wanted him to testify in their pension cases, hoping that Miller's testimony would help them receive a pension increase. He was forthright and told the truth as he saw it, which made his testimony valuable. Special examiners who listened to testimony of soldiers and witnesses day in and day out considered him credible.

That did not necessarily assure Miller of getting an increase, however. Special examiners were as tough on him as everyone else.

When Miller got back from the war, he complained of

severe pain in his left knee, according to Moses Polite. While on Morris Island, Miller had been detailed to pile up some old lumber. While engaged in piling the lumber, "the lot that had been piled toppled over on top of him, and an old rusty spike penetrated his left knee."

Matthew Jones was present and remembered that the spike broke off in Miller's knee, about an inch below the knee cap. James Drayton was working alongside Miller when the lumber tumbled and remembered that Miller was under treatment by the regimental doctor (Dr. Hawks) for over two months.

After that, Miller began to develop rheumatism. He managed to get a pension of $8 in 1892 for injury of the left knee and rheumatism but could not get a pension increase for many years. His neighbor, Thomas Frazier, who plowed Miller's field, said in 1897 that Miller could not perform more than one-third of the manual labor he previously could. A panel of doctors examined him that year and confirmed Miller's injuries.

Miller was about fifty-five in 1901. His hair had turned gray, and his pension still was $8. He sought a pension increase due to trouble with his left knee and loss of sight. A special examiner asked questions that had been covered many times.

Q. What disabilities are you pensioned for?
A. For rheumatism and injury to my left knee.
Q. What is the trouble with your left knee?
A. It was hurt on Morris Island while piling lumber, and a spike in the timber stuck in my knee.
Q. Does it trouble you?
A. Whenever there is a change in the weather I can hardly walk with it.[9]

The pension bureau decided that a small increase was warranted but then denied the increase, writing that there was no medical proof that Miller's disability happened in the army.

Two years later a surgeon's certificate added a new ailment to Miller's list. He was beginning to develop senile debility.

The year 1907 arrived. The pension bureau asked Miller for a record of his birth to determine whether Miller was sixty-two, and based on his age was eligible for an increase. Miller sent a notarized affidavit that he was born on or about February 1, 1848, but was "unable to furnish record evidence . . . for the reason that no such records are in existence." His affidavit also stated that he "gained a knowledge of his age from his uncle, who was overseer for the man he was working for, after his discharge from the Service of the U.S."[10]

Further, his uncle had since died, along with that part of the family. His statement about his uncle was not clear: Could he have been an overseer for one of the cotton companies during the war? That information was lost to history, though of little interest to the pension bureau.

Finally, under the old age act of 1912, Renty Miller received a pension of $14.50 a month.[11] His pension automatically increased each year for the rest of his life.

Prior to receiving his pension increase, Miller scraped to find ways to bring in a little money. Farming was hard for him because his rheumatism had spread down his entire left side.

He had a small store at Point Comfort, the former plantation where his father, Thomas Miller, had lived before freedom. He also worked with pensioners. That helped them and also him.

He did some business with S. I. Wright, his pension attorney in Washington, DC. As Miller did his own writing, he could act as a sub-agent for Wright, doing pensioners' writing for them on affidavits and other items. Miller sometimes got $5 for doing their writing for them. When Wright received an affidavit Miller prepared, he might change some writing to be more lawyer-like, and then forward it to the pension office.

Miller had about twelve pensions he regularly worked with. The pension bureau would send out quarterly vouchers rather than cash, which could easily be lost, and Brown would execute Miller's vouchers on the fourth of each quarter for twenty-five cents. The vouchers required the signature of an official witness, and Miller could assume that role, as could W. D. Brown. Miller would "sign and swear to them, first showing my certificate."

By 1912, Miller had become the post commander of the GAR Abraham Lincoln Brigade on Hilton Head. Everyone on the island knew him. He continued his work with former soldiers until W. D. Brown died in 1923 and the store was gone. In 1924, he was said to turn eighty. Then his health grew worse.

His wife, Roseanne (Mills) Miller, whom he had married when he first got out of the army, may not have been alive now. His children, now adults, had moved out on their own. No one later would remember exactly what happened or why. A nephew, Abraham B. Miller, who he and Roseanne had helped raised, knew he was ill. He came to the island and took Miller back to Savannah with him. Miller lingered on there for a while and then went into a Savannah hospital.

He died in October of 1926.

Abraham, a preacher in Savannah, made sure that Miller's body was brought back to the island for burial. Renty, his father Thomas, and his grandfather Renty, then represented at least three generations buried on the island.

Abraham Miller had put himself in charge of Renty's affairs. The Red Cross in Savannah had helped to pay for Renty's hospital stay and wrote the pension bureau about this. The undertaker who had brought Renty's body back from Savannah charged a large amount. The pension bureau paid about $60 in such cases, to at least temporarily reimburse a family who could not afford burial expenses.

Abraham made a list of property that could be sold

to reimburse the pension bureau. Renty's property, as stated on the list Abraham prepared, consisted of two horses, valued at $20 each. It was a sad ending for a man who spent much time trying to help others. He had always had more respect than money though.

Miller, said to be the last of the black Union soldiers on Hilton Head, was definitely respected.

Then they were gone, the soldiers who lived in amazing times: the Union invasion, their time in the war, freedom at last, Reconstruction, and finding their own way. The soldiers left adult children and grandchildren closing in on adulthood. Those who came behind them would stand on the shoulders of the black Union soldiers, just as they had on those of their African ancestors. And a new age began.

In 1926 Cyrus Wiley had been president of Georgia Industrial for five years. Under his administration, girls were admitted as boarders to the school, and other worthwhile changes occurred. It now was his last year at Georgia Industrial. He soon moved to Atlanta, where he died at the age of thirty. But Wiley had won a place in the history of early black educators.

Charlie Simmons, this same year, got the first boat on Hilton Head with a motor. Others would follow him, and motorized boats would ease islanders' trips to Savannah and other places to sell produce. Meanwhile, the Hudsons and the Toomers ran oyster factories in the 1920s. Men and women both turned to oystering for winter income. And unknown to them, the Great Depression would soon sweep down over the nation.

Chapter Seventeen

SHADOWS UNDER THE TREES

WHEN THE SCORCHING summer heat hit, men and women took breaks under big live oak trees with large branches and long tendrils of gray Spanish moss. The air felt a little less steamy there, especially if a slight breeze came up.

"Let's go in the shade" someone would say when the heat rose and they were ready to knock off from their morning work in the fields. In the shade, people would sit on old chairs or stools and mend cast nets or do other work.

To break the monotony one of the men might say, "You know why the cat doesn't wash his face until after breakfast?" "No," the others exclaimed, and the story began:

The mouse and the cat were out there looking for breakfast. The mouse went first. He saw a barrel and he climb' up, just looking to see what kind of breakfast he could get. The barrel was half full of water, and the mouse slipped and fell in and couldn't get out. He was splashing around trying to get out.

The cat came along, heard a noise and looked in the barrel, and saw the brown mouse. "How did you get in there?" the cat asked.

"Oh I was looking for breakfast and fell in and now I can't get out," the mouse said. "But if you take me out I'll let you eat me."

Sun shining through Spanish
moss on Hilton Head Island.
Photo by Will Warasila

The cat took him out and got ready to eat the mouse.

"Wait," the mouse said. "My hair will choke you to death if you eat me like this. Let me dry and you can singe it off and eat me. Why don't you go wash your face while I dry?"

The cat laid him on a board to dry and went to wash his face, and the mouse took off quick as a flash. And that's why the cat never washes his face before breakfast.[1]

No matter how many times that story got told, everyone laughed. A story was never told the same way twice. The storyteller put a new twist on it every time and kept the story fresh.

The cat and the mouse was a trickster tale in which a smaller animal uses its wits to out-smart a bigger one. Africans had brought the memories of trickster tales with them and substituted different animals for ones in their new environment.

Shadows crept between the tree limbs as dusk—fus' dark—settled in, and talk could turn to the past. Some spoke about "rebel time" or "rebel time people," which to Hilton Head blacks meant the entire Civil War period, rather than just the period of secession.[2]

Elders told stories from their parents' times, their grandparents' time, or farther back. They were memory keepers, passing down knowledge suitable for children's ears.

As the sky darkened, sometimes a particularly wise man or woman might stare deep into the shadows, studying them almost as if it were possible to see all the way back to Africa. Their roots to Africa ran deeper than the roots of any ancient tree they sat under. Traces of Africa spilled from their tongues as they spoke.

Lorenzo Dow Turner stared into the shadows, too. He did so throughout the Sea Islands of South Carolina and Georgia.

Turner, a college professor who graduated from Howard University and then earned a master's degree from Harvard and a doctorate degree from the University of Chicago, was the first scholar ever to take Gullah links to Africa seriously. That he was black, friendly, and respectful of Gullah people made them open up to him more than they ever had to anyone else.

Turner's deep interest in Gullah language came about by happenstance. While waiting to join the Fisk faculty in Nashville, Tennessee, in 1929, he took a summer teaching job at South Carolina State College in Orangeburg, the state's public college for blacks. At South Carolina, Turner, fluent in several languages, heard two students speaking in a dialect he barely understood.

When they told him that they were from Johns Island, South Carolina, Turner asked if he could visit them and their families.

On Johns Island he heard something—what seemed to him a rapid African rhythm to their speech—that excited him. He also found that people there used basket names: naming practices based on a baby's appearance, order of place in the family, or any of a variety of other traditions. The names often were African, and sometimes were known only to members of the family. People outside the family sometimes knew only a child's public name, usually a "proper" English name.[3]

As a result of his experience on Johns Island, Turner became determined to investigate links between Gullah speech and West African languages. He would spend years interviewing Sea Islanders, followed by study at the Department of African Languages at the University of London, where he learned West African languages. This helped him determine that words he had found in the Sea Islands had definitely come from West Africa.

Later, Turner would seek out African "informants" to verify whether some African-sounding words, whose origins he had not yet identified, could have been used as personal names, or expressions, in African speech.

He had embarked on a massive task at a time when most scholars totally dismissed the possibility that few, if any, traces of African languages could be found in Gullah speech. Some believed that the harshness of slavery had erased all of their African past and left them as "a vacant slate." One bluntly said the Gullahs had contributed only one word to the English language: *buckra*, the word for a white man, usually one who held power or was unpleasant.

Most believed Gullah speech was derived from peasant English. Some called it "baby talk" taught to Africans by plantation owners. Others labeled Gullah speech "debased English."

South Carolinian Ambrose E. Gonzales, while intrigued with Gullah speech, rendered a harsh depiction, saying "slovenly and careless of speech, these Gullah seized as they could an enriched peasant English used by early settlers and by the white servants of the wealthier colonists."[4] He believed, however, that Gullah people did use "certain expressive African words."

Gonzales, born in 1857, four years before the Civil War began, grew up on Edisto Island and had ties to Hilton Head. His mother, Harriott Elliott Gonzales, was a daughter of William Elliott, owner of Myrtle Bank Plantation up to the day the Union captured Hilton Head.

Gonzales's great-grandfather was the William Elliott who raised the first successful crop of Sea Island cotton, setting off the rush by other coastal planters to raise the lucrative crop and causing a new wave of importation of enslaved Africans to raise and harvest the exceptionally fine long-fiber cotton.

Gonzales considered himself to be a Gullah expert, as he had grown up playing with Gullah youths and surrounded by Gullah "family retainers." He found it curious that so few true African words had been passed down, since Africans had been illegally imported as late as 1858. His family's servants had mentioned knowing Africans who used African words, but they never told him any.

Wanting to record the oddities of the dialect, Gonzales compiled a glossary of seventeen hundred words as used by Gullah speakers.[5] He had some Gullah pronunciations right, such as "swimp," for shrimp, but Turner would find most of his interpretations to be incorrect.

Gonzales, for instance, listed the English phrase "done for fat," and said that Gullah people used it to mean that a person is very fat, and therefore his life would be short—he was done for.

Turner wrote that if Gonzales had had "sufficient training in phonetics to reproduce accurately what he supposed was the English phrase, done for," and had then used a dictionary of Vai—a language spoken in Liberia and Sierra Leone—"he would have discovered that the Vai word for fat is 'dafa, literally 'mouth full.'"

"When the Gullah speaker says 'dafa fat,' he is merely adding the English equivalent of 'dafa' to make sure the word is understood," Turner said. He was astounded that previous scholars had not bothered to study West African languages before making their pronouncements. West Africa had been the largest source of enslaved people imported to the Sea Islands.

Turner began interviewing Gullah people in 1931. Over time, he spent a total of nine months or more in the Sea Islands of South Carolina and in the Georgia Sea Islands, where the islanders are usually called Geechee. In all, he interviewed people in twelve coastal communities.

He told everyone he interviewed that he wanted to hear about their lives rather than saying he was interested in their speech. He felt that would make Gullah islanders less self-conscious, as they knew that most outsiders thought they "talked funny."

The more Turner heard words spill from Gullah mouths and listened to the islanders' beat, tone, and how words were pronounced, the more Turner thought their speech reflected connections to an African past. He learned all he could about their lives, present and past, including slavery and freedom, and their culture. On the Georgia coast he watched islanders doing traditional ring shouts used in praise-house meetings.

Turner did not hear many African words when he first started interviewing. Only after he came to know people well did he gain their trust. He had to break through an entrenched barrier: wariness of outsiders.

A tall, brown-skinned man with wire-rim glasses, Turner often was photographed wearing a suit. But summertime in the Sea Islands, with temperatures of ninety degrees and above, high humidity, swarms of mosquitoes, and hard, pounding rain demanded simpler clothing. Besides, Turner lugged a thirty-pound wire recorder with him.

Sometime around August 1933 Turner interviewed three Hilton Head Gullah islanders: Ruben Chisolm, Dave "Rufus" Singleton, and Lewis Wright.[6]

Ruben Chisolm had never seen a recording machine before and now he was speaking into one that used a fragile, steel magnetized wire the size of a strand of hair.

Actually, Chisolm was talking to the brown-skinned man who was running the recorder, an energetic man of thirty-nine years, who got him talking, listened closely to him, and asked questions.

Chisolm, a fisherman, liked to be in a creek somewhere, not inside. He always wore bib overalls, like a lot of men on Hilton Head did. Some even wore starched and ironed overalls to church. In the winter, Chisolm wore a long denim jumper over his overalls that went below his hips, where it squared off. It gave him a more polished look.

Chisolm was a bit nervous, frequently saying "uh" after a sentence or two, so this likely was their first meeting.[7]

After Turner completed each wire recording, he usually stayed up late at night marking words to show tone, pronunciation, cadence, and Gullah grammar. He used the linguistic style recommended by the International Phonetic Association of the U.S. and Canada with a few alterations to accommodate Gullah speech.

Farmin' and fishin' is my occupation, in, uh, Bluffton, Beaufort, and Savannah. When you get to Bloody Point [Daufuskie Island], there's a different tide.

The tides are goin' out when you get to Bloody Point. Sometime when you get there, well, accordin' to what kind of wind you have, you have the tide with us.

And, uh, bring your produce to Savannah and decide you couldn't get no price on it, according to the difficult time now [the Depression], and take what you could get for it. . . .

The island of Hilton Head, they had us working on the road over there, and uh, was no price for that, fifty cents a day was all you could get, fifty cents a day. I make eight days on the road. And I never see a penny yet. When I went to draw my money, there was no money.

And it turns out something's going on; you get something [script, used as cash in some stores during the Depression] you glad you spent it where you don't want to spend it at.

Will it get you more satisfaction out of work from Savannah, but 'cording to how I consider it, when you spend at the store, everything you get to the store they sell kinda high. [Sentence paraphrased.]

Later on, I haul oyster to the factory on Hilton Head. You couldn't demand no price for that. You carry oyster there and couldn't get a good price. But they give you what they please, you gotta take that.

We was poor salary we was making at this time according to the difficult time. I was very glad for a little instruction to see if [Roosevelt] couldn't make the time a little better than it is with us.

I'm a man with a wife and, uh, six, nine head of children: six head of boys and three head of girls.

But I haven't got any job, you know exactly how it is to live to provide bread for those children, yes.

[*Question by Turner*]

In the sailboat sometime i' blowing a real storm. And sometime you figure you lose your life. But then you have to make money, be glad for contribute; tryin' times, but the Lord provided it, make it safe sometimes how I'm gonna get near port about two miles before I go to anchor in about three, four hours.

So I lay dead [a sailing term] until the storm over sometimes. Sometime I haven't got any wind at all, just gotta row it. Sometime the storm comin' and tear the sail off the boat, drive it over.

Time good; time to make honest bread.[8]

Before Turner and Chisolm finished talking, Chisolm also told stories of Brer Rabbit and Brer Wolf.

Among the contributions of Rufus Singleton and Lewis Wright, the two sang a lively spiritual, "Tell Me What More Can Jesus Do."

Turner later would say that Hilton Head was one of the South Carolina islands with the most distinctive examples of the Gullah dialect. He also found that people who lived on islands that did not have a bridge to a mainland had kept more African language traits in their speech.

Turner finished interviewing the three Hilton Head men. Chisolm went back to the creek to fish. He had, as he said, a wife and nine children, all of whom needed to eat.

Turner opened a treasure chest. He would discover more West African influences on Gullah speech than he had dreamed. He made a list of approximately three thousand six hundred personal names used by Sea Islanders, that had come from West African languages, as well as other words and terms used in conversation.[9]

Among the many were: *kuta* for tortoise, *hu'hu'* for owl, *bidi* for a small chicken, and *pojo* for a heron (later called poor Joe in English). *'Nanse* (*a'nanse*), a spider, figured in many Gullah tales.

Gambo was okra, and later became known as gumbo, and there was *yam* (yambi) for sweet potato, *bene* for benne (sesame), and *pinda* for peanut, although other names existed for the peanut depending on which West African language was used.

Juk meant a disorderly house, a word that transferred over to "juke joint." Several words referred to

Close-up view of tabby, a building material composed of shells. *Photo by Will Warasila*

black magic, including *hudu*, which meant "to cause bad luck," and *fufudas*, a fine dust used with the intention of bewitching or causing harm to someone.

Tabi was a house made of cement and oyster shells, in which pieces of brick were frequently mixed. On Sea Island plantations, this word became "tabby."

Bento was a wooden box in which a dead person is buried. *Ban!* meant "It is done! It is finished! The end!"

Turner also recorded some stories told by Gullah people on Edisto and other South Carolina islands, including their memories of the Charleston earthquake and the devastating 1893 storm.

Turner, however, missed hearing stories on Hilton Head that he might have recorded if he had had more time. Such stories included the selling of enslaved people on Hilton Head and the beginning of freedom on Hilton Head in 1861, on the day the Union captured the island:

> "You see that shanty tabby over there?" Naomi Frazier asked. "She [her grandmother] . . . said that was the [banju] selling table. They would put you up on the banju table and you were bid and you were sold. . . . My grandmother's oldest sister was sold to Alabama. Some men came down from Alabama and bought her. . . . They [the people] all cried but that did not make no difference."[10]

> Well, all I know is, in slavery time, what Mosiah [master] used to do. Put you cross a ban and lick you during those times."— *Thomas Holmes*[11]

Mrs. Frazier also recalled a story told by her grandmother, who lived near Talbot (also called Talbird) Cemetery, a Gullah cemetery located on the banks of Skull Creek marsh, in keeping with the Gullah belief

Talbird Cemetery, on Skull Creek. The cemetery, damaged in 2016 by Hurricane Matthew, remains an active site for burial of Hilton Head's Gullah citizens.
Photo by Will Warasila

that the souls of those buried near water would be able to travel back to Africa in peace.

Her grandmother said "when peace declared that day [the day the Union captured the island] she was in back of the cemetery, but it wasn't no graveyard then. But they used to walk down . . . in a drain there and catch crabs. And they were catching crabs. . . . And they heard all that shooting and hooraying and going on." You could hear all the bomb' shooting . . . that was the beginning of the Freedom.[12]

Talbird Cemetery, on Skull Creek. On the day the Union took Hilton Head Island, the siege could be heard from this spot, which is now adjacent to development in Hilton Head Plantation. *Photo by Will Warasila*

"That must be the war when they freed the slaves," Isabel Brown, born 1894, recalled:

> That's the war. That's a long time ago. My mother was just three weeks old when the gunmen [Union gunboat] take them from Saint Simon' Island and bring them here on Hilton Head. Hilton Head was the first place free during the slavery time. And then the mainland people . . . come down here . . . because this was the first place that was free.[13]

Turner's book, *Africanisms in the Gullah Dialect*, would not be published until 1949, by which time Ruben Chisolm was no longer alive. Some of the personal names Turner found were disputed, but he laid the foundation for the field of Gullah studies. Overall, his work was well received, though decades would pass before his book came to the attention of Gullah people. When it did, Gullah speakers would find a new sense of pride in their culture.

If all the personal names that came from West African languages and all the other words Turner found in Gullah speech were inscribed on slabs of stone and stacked pyramid-style, they would form a sizable monument. The monument would bear testimony to the resilience of the men, women, and children who endured the brutal voyage across the water, began anew on Hilton Head and other Sea Islands, and held onto vital pieces of their African past.

Original landing point for Captain
Charlie "Sims" Simmons's
ferry, now dedicated to him.
Photo by Will Warasila

Chapter Eighteen

OLD MAN DEPRESSION

DAILY LIFE CONTINUED as usual on Hilton Head, filled with little events and big ones. A few girls played in the surf and slid down the dunes at "the Folley" in the Chaplin area, fronting the Atlantic Ocean.

Charlie Simmons's boat plied the waters between Hilton Head and Savannah three days a week. He took islanders to Savannah to sell their crops, and he brought back groceries islanders had ordered.

Meanwhile, the Great Depression rendered havoc throughout the United States. Old Man Depression hit everyone, big or small.[1] On Hilton Head, people grew their own crops, so they usually had food to eat, and they could get fish from the creek. This made them bet-ter off than many people in the nation. But they still needed money to buy supplies, ranging from oil lamp fuel to rice, and to pay their property taxes.

Women, in addition to working in the fields and over-seeing all the house chores, continued making quilts to keep their families warm. They used every scrap they had of cotton or other fabrics, often cut from clothes too worn to patch, and made rugs out of burlap (croker) sacks, dying strips of the sacks and working with the col-ors. Nothing got wasted. Thrift ruled more than ever.

With work scarce on the island, one youth, fourteen-year-old Charles "Fuskie" Simmons, a nephew of is-land entrepreneur Charlie Simmons, went from street to street in Tybee Island, selling vegetables. He got the nickname "Fuskie" by traditional naming practices—a place name, in this case.

Since he had gone to school on neighboring Daufuskie Island, he became known as Fuskie. The name stuck. If someone mentioned Fuskie, everyone knew who was meant.

Fuskie went by boat to Savannah, where he got work from a man who bought vegetables at the Savannah market. He took Fuskie to Tybee Island, a small island about eighteen miles away, and dropped him off. Simmons walked the streets selling watermelon, corn, okra, butter beans—whatever people wanted, usually for a nickel or a dime. People were happy to get good produce, delivered straight to their doors. And vegetable men often hawked their wares in a raised voice and an entertaining style.

I's got okra, tomata an' sweet pubtatuh!
Soo-oup! Carrot! Carrot! Carrot!
Fresh Cabbage! Veg-e-tubble!
Veg-e-tubble man![2]

Fuskie Simmons earned three dollars a week, a good amount for a teenager in the early 1930s. Then, when his work finished, he would return to Savannah and catch a boat back to Hilton Head.[3]

Arthur Orage of the Squire Pope Community and Ben Miller, Jr., of Jonesville, along with other islanders, joined the Civilian Conservation Corps (CCC). Started by President Franklin D. Roosevelt, the CCC became the most popular program of the New Deal. Early on, the men who joined had to be at least eighteen years of age.

The program provided manual labor jobs for young men in order to relieve families who had difficulty finding jobs. The men who participated got food, clothing, shelter in a tent or a barracks, and a small sum of money. Under CCC rules, most of the money had to go back to their families in order to help them. The work the men in the CCC did, including cutting trails in forested areas and state and national parks, boosted public appreciation of the United States' natural beauty.

Orage—whose father was Paul Orage but was called Pauldo—was a descendent of the black Union soldier Polido Fields. "I was seventeen years old but I tell my momma to put my age up to eighteen so I could go to the CC Camp."[4]

He got $30 a month for working for the CC Camp. "And that's all you would get. Thirty dollars a month, fifteen come home to momma . . . I get seven and put eight aside for when I come home." When he went home with $300, "boy, you rich," Orage said.

The Depression caused William ("Jesse") Holmes to drop out of school after the second grade. He had been promoted to the third grade but did not go. "I had to stop because my mother wasn't making nothing. . . . I had to do something because the depression been on."

Holmes did a bit of everything. He got sixty cents

a day, three dollars a week, working on the Beaufort County roads for a while; he patched wagon spokes so islanders' wagons could keep rolling, and he made new handles for hammers. And, like a lot of people on the island, he started oystering—going out on the water in a homemade boat, picking oysters from the oyster banks, loading them up in his boat, and taking them back to the oyster factory.

The ownership of thousands of acres of Hilton Head had changed hands in 1931.

Roy Rainey—a Northern industrialist who had acquired the holdings of William P. Clyde on Hilton Head, plus additional land—had used Honey Horn for hunting and entertaining guests for perhaps twenty years.

The year before W. D. Brown's death, Rainey bought four hundred and fifty acres of Brown's land at Possum Point. Rainey also bought most of Cherry Hill from Brown's heirs, and some land in Stoney.

Rainey bought big and small parcels. When Eugenia Heyward, the granddaughter of Gabriel and Susan Gardner, could not afford to pay her land taxes at Fish Haul, Rainey bought her land for a small sum.

But Rainey, a free-spending New Yorker, who loved hunting, gambling, and entertaining friends in a lavish style at Honey Horn, lost his money in the 1929 Wall Street market crash.

He sold his estate on the Long Island shore in 1930 to an exclusive Long Island club.[5] He was also forced to sell Honey Horn and his other holdings on Hilton Head.

Thorne and Loomis, as the new owners were called, were partners in one of the most successful New York investment firms. They also were brothers-in-law.

Unlike most investors, Landon K. Thorne and Alfred Loomis had realized that stocks had become dangerously over-inflated. By the time the stock market crashed in October 1929, the two men had converted all of their investments into cash. After the market bottomed out, they bought more stocks cheaply and added millions to their robust wealth.

Thorne had been born in Connecticut but had ancestors who had owned plantations in the South Carolina Sea Islands. The two men previously had bought land on Hilton Head: eight hundred and fifty acres on Coggins Point, including the former Confederate fort, Fort Walker. The federal government had declared the land a military reservation in 1874 and held onto it for fifty-three years before deciding to sell Coggins Point in 1927.

The news of Rainey's fall caught Thorne's attention. He suggested to Loomis that they buy Rainey's holdings on Hilton Head and make the island into a hunting and fishing resort for family and friends. Loomis liked the idea.[6]

While Thorne was a financial whiz, Loomis was

devoted to science. He had already begun bankrolling the work of a few well-known scientists, and as a result, at least one magazine had labeled him "the Scientist of Wall Street." Loomis disliked the limelight. He could use a get-away.

Buying out Rainey was easy. Thorne and Loomis paid cash.

The two men would continue living in New York and spend time on Hilton Head as they could.

Loomis soon entrusted Thorne to handle the two men's investment firm. He then "retired," at age forty-five to focus totally on scientific research. He lived in Tuxedo Park, an elite community outside of the city of New York, whose residents included J. P. Morgan and one of the Astors. He also had bought a separate mansion in Tuxedo Park and transformed it into the "Loomis Laboratory," a fully equipped private research laboratory.

The mansion provided space for scientists to work and live there full-time. Loomis brought in more scientists to speed up the rate of inventions, and to develop inventions of his own. Albert Einstein, along with other famous scientists, gathered there periodically and named the stone mansion "a palace of science."

Radar detection systems used to detect low-flying airplanes grew out of the pioneering research projects of Loomis's scientists. (The U.S. further developed it and used the technology to good effect in World War II.)

On their early visits to the island, Thorne and Loomis began repairing and enlarging the old Honey Horn house. Since both men loved yachting, they also had a new yacht built and brought it to the island. On Hilton Head, Loomis and his sons played on the beach, having found the island the right place to relax.

Those were the two men behind the label "Thorne and Loomis." Their goal was to buy more property on Hilton Head and have their own private island.

The old Myrtle Bank plantation, often called "Elliott," became one of their first land acquisitions after their arrival on Hilton Head. Some land on Elliott had been sold to Gullah islanders long ago. Two unmarried daughters of the Elliott family held the rest.

The sisters willed Myrtle Bank to the heirs of a third sister, Harriott. She had died of a tropical illness in Cuba after moving there with her husband, a former Cuban-patriot, General Ambrosio Jose Gonzales.

The Gonzales heirs sold Myrtle Bank to Thorne and Loomis in 1934. Ambrose Gonzales, the writer who relished the speech of Gullah people but derided what he called their "clumsy tongues," would have been one of the heirs had he not died a few years before.

Thorne and Loomis also made it a practice to buy land from Gullah islanders, including land sold at tax sales. Their first year on the island, they bought several parcels of land in Fish Haul.

Honey Horn required a sizable staff, especially when Thorne and Loomis were on the island. Guests were fed and entertained—sometimes on short notice—and the house and grounds needed constant attention; the horses and dogs needed training and care, stables had to be kept clean, and hunting guns kept oiled and ready. Gullah islanders held those jobs.

Georgianna Barnwell, who had helped at Honey Horn as far back as Booker T. Washington's visit to Hilton Head in 1908, continued to work in the laundry. "Old man Dempsey Frazier" took care of the milk cows. Chamberlin Robinson—whose son Thomas had attended the Booker T. Washington school and was on a path leading to a PhD—took care of the horses and a large vegetable garden. Another Gullah islander raised the chickens. Joe Cohen was a professional hunting-dog trainer.

James (Jim) Cohen also took care of the horses while the men shot the birds. John Miller took the men out on horseback, to where they could shoot quail. Other islanders held jobs there, too.

Ben Jones and Josephine Jones were head cooks, along with Annie Driessen, and others. They prepared succulent meals, using fresh duck, quail, and other game birds, seafood fresh from the water, and seasonal produce and fruit, all from the island.

A visitor described the elaborate dinners this way: "The big kitchen at Honey Horn sent out a tempting fragrance of roast turkey and venison, of duck with orange sauce made from bittersweet island oranges, Carolina shrimp pie, oyster stewed with crisp bacon and onions and served with fluffy rice. There were crunchy benne seed candy in the crystal dish, or perhaps of pecan pralines, with the nuts fresh and crisp from island trees."

At the end of the evening, the two men brought out what Thorne called "sippin' whiskey," the alcohol brewed by Gullah people, which was quite strong.[7]

Gullah Islanders worked at Honey Horn over several decades. Undated photo. *Courtesy of the Coastal Discovery Museum*

Young boys with dogs in front of Honey Horn house. Undated Photo. *Courtesy of the Coastal Discovery Museum*

ful on Honey Horn's hunting preserve, let it be known he would pay a penny for each rat islanders caught and brought to him—*dead* rats, that is.

A penny motivated people during the Depression, and lots of rats lived on the island. So people started bringing in sacks full of dead rats to the gamekeeper. The gamekeeper's staff counted the rats and paid whoever brought them in.

The rats got pretty much wiped out, but a few people didn't want to give up getting those pennies. Some of the younger guys began cheating. They rowed boats all the way to Daufuskie to catch rats and brought sacks of rats back to get paid.

The man found out they were going to Daufuskie and stopped that project.[8]

If that sounds like another kind of trickster tale—where a Gullah man or woman slipped one over on the white man in power—it definitely had the makings. Years later, a few islanders remembered the story with amusement.

Oystering had become the biggest business on Hilton Head. For Gullah people, it provided a seasonal job, after the spring and summer crops were in. Come late fall and winter, Gullah men became the oyster pickers, and Gullah women usually shucked the oysters.

Oysters had always been a part of Low Country life, as far back as the Native Americans who had lived on

As Thorne and Loomis came and went at will, they probably never heard of one of the few hitches that occurred at Honey Horn during the Depression.

The gamekeeper had to keep the hunting fields and nearby wooded areas stocked with game, but there was a sudden onslaught of rats.

The rats had to be caught because they were eating the quail eggs, and quail was a favorite game bird for the hunters who came to Honey Horn. So the gamekeeper, whose job it was to make sure game was plenti-

Hilton Head and other coastal lands. They ate oysters and used the oyster shells in building large mounds known as shell rings.

When the planters arrived on Hilton Head, they also ate oysters and then used the oyster shells, (mixed with other shells, sand, and lime) to make tabby, the building material frequently used for everything from houses for enslaved people to foundations for some of the planters' island homes.

The sweet morsels, nestled in gray, razor-sharp shells, also were a welcome food source for Gullah people. Oysters with grits or rice and a little gravy made a much-favored Gullah meal.

The Hudsons and the Toomers, white families long a part of island life, ran oyster factories on Hilton Head. A third oyster company, L. G. Maggioni & Company, had been started by an Italian immigrant in Florida and had expanded along the Atlantic coast.

Based in Georgia, Maggioni had become well-established throughout South Carolina. The Jenkins Island's oyster factory that employed many Gullah islanders was controlled by Maggioni & Company on nearby Lady's Island. The Jenkins Island factory had a large raw shucking operation. (There was also a steam oyster plant on Jenkins Island.)

The oyster factory of Ben Hudson, Sr., was in Squire Pope, in a location known as Bull Point. He also had a smaller oyster factory at Gardners.

S. V. Toomer had a steam-shucking operation in

Restored structure made of tabby, now known as the Barnwell Tabby (after Thomas C. Barnwell, Jr., who owns and has restored it). This structure, thought to have been used for domestic purposes, stands on the land that was formerly the Cotton Hope Plantation. *Photo by Will Warasila*

Stoney and later started a raw oyster business on Jarvis Creek.

There were a few independent operators too, but the Hudsons, Toomers, and Maggioni employed the most Gullah people.

Women from Baygall, on the north end of the island, walked to Jenkins Island, above Stoney, early in the morning to shuck oysters, then walked home late in the day, and packed a lunch for the next day. A few walked from the south end, miles away.

"I work in them factories and shuck oysters," said Regina Bennett. "I walk all the way from Braddock's Point.

We left home around six in the morning and walked all the way from there and go from them factories and shuck oysters the whole day until about seven o'clock."

Most oyster houses had concrete floors with high tables, long enough to accommodate perhaps fifteen women on each side. The women stood on wooden benches, twelve to eighteen inches high, so they were not on the floor. The edge of the table was about hip-high when they stood on the benches. The empty shells were thrown down a hole in the table at each worker's position.

Men called shell rollers would bring in wheelbarrows full of oysters and dump them beside the shuckers. The women picked up an oyster, banged its mouth against a metal post, and popped an oyster open with a knife. The meat went into steel pails, and the oyster shell roller would come in with an empty wheelbarrow, shovel them up, and take them out.

Then the shell roller would bring each woman another wheelbarrow filled with oysters. The clang of the oyster shell hitting the metal post and the shell rollers coming and going went on all day.

William Holmes, Sr., born in 1915, was one of the few men who shucked oysters. There was no food at home one day, and he told his brother he'd let him finish school and he would go and shuck oysters.

"It was in the twenties when I started. I went to the oyster factory on Jenkins Island. Say, I can learn to shuck. I had to shuck 'em . . . you see."

The pay was better for shucking raw oysters, as they took more work than shucking oysters that had been steamed.

Holmes said he made ten cents for every gallon of steamed oyster meat he shucked "and if I shucked four cans, that's forty cents" a day.

Thomas Holmes, born the same year, said that if he harvested oysters for steaming, he got six cents a bushel. The woman who shucked the bushel of steamed oysters would get ten cents for opening them.

But for raw oysters, he said, it was fifty-fifty. "If the oyster is two dollars a gallon, the woman would get one dollar and the man get one dollar."

Many men rowed out to the oyster banks in their homemade boats to gather oysters at low tide and bring them back to the oyster factory.

Maggioni had a permanent fleet of large sailboats, as well as a huge canning operation at Lady's Island. Men stayed out on the water in the sailboats up to a week at a time gathering oysters. Sometimes a string of small boats was connected to a sailboat. Hundreds of gallons of oysters were gathered. Steamed and canned oysters often were shipped throughout the country.

The work was hard, and the water could be treacherous if a storm came up. But the money helped islanders get through.

Workers often received small round coins, instead of cash, which they used to buy items at stores run by the oyster factory owners; this was a common currency practice during the Depression.

"Was I happy in those days?

"Well, I had to be happy," Thomas Holmes said, "cause I couldn't do no better. That's right."

He was working for the oyster dollars.

It was never all work and no fun. Church groups picnicked on the beach at times. There were jokes and laughter. They held community baseball games at Squire Pope and at Jonesville for several years.

They sang at church and in the praise houses and were uplifted. The Mothers' Union held a special "All White Day" once a year, on which the members dressed all in white from their hats down to their shoes, read inspirational poems out loud, sang hymns, lauded the young girls who one day would join the club, and ate every morsel of the potato salad, fried chicken, and a table loaded with desserts.

The Boys of Pleasure had their own building and held dances there. The Farmers Club held parties, too, as did the Brownville Social Club.

They had holidays to celebrate, each marked in its own way. On the Fourth of July, the men on Hilton Head rode their horses to fields throughout the island, inspecting the crops to see whether the fall harvest would be good. Every holiday was celebrated on the island, except for one: Decoration Day, and it came around like clockwork.

Isabel Brown, born in 1884, always remembered going to Decoration Day as a young girl. She lived at Braddock's Point on the south end of Hilton Head in a two-room house built by her great-grandfather. Only a handful of families lived on the southern tip of the island.

Brown liked watching the sun and the stars and the water at Braddock's Point. "You could see when the water was rolling, and you could see when it looked like a looking glass. It seemed like you could walk on it."

Braddock's Point was home but going to Beaufort for Decoration Day in the 1890s made for an exciting change. "You know those days little children don't go everywhere," Brown said. But her parents took her to Decoration Day.[9]

The commander of the Grand Army of the Republic, in 1868, proclaimed May 30 as Decoration Day, a day to honor deceased Union and Confederate soldiers of the Civil War. He advised grieving family members of the late soldiers to commemorate the day by "strewing with flowers or otherwise decorating soldiers' graves."

White southerners usually attended a separate holiday to honor their war dead, but majority-black Beaufort differed somewhat. Some descendants of white Northern Unionists, who remained in Beaufort after the Civil War, participated in Decoration Day initially.

Decoration Day was an important black holiday, especially for Gullah people on the Sea Islands, as so many black men served as Union Soldiers under the Department of the South on Hilton Head. (The Grand

Army renamed the holiday Memorial Day in 1882, but most Gullah people still called it "Decoration Day.") It was the only public recognition given to the contributions of the black Union soldiers.

"We used to go from here on sail boat," Brown said. By the time she was twelve years old, she recalled, a special steamer began going from Savannah to Beaufort to pick up passengers going to Decoration Day. "You could catch it down Spanish Wells landing. But most of the time you would go in the sail boats."

Her family had to get from the south end of Hilton Head to the Port Royal Sound, enter the sound, reach the Beaufort River, and follow the river ten miles inland to the city of Beaufort. The journey took time, wind, and the knowhow to sail a boat through large waters and tidal channels.

"You would leave here on the twenty-ninth [of May], and you would have to leave that night to be there by morning [on May 30]," Brown said. The Beaufort National Cemetery had been established in 1863, as one of six national cemeteries to honor the Union dead.[10] Deceased soldiers from Hilton Head and other islands in the Port Royal Sound, Charleston, Savannah, and East Florida were among the first men re-interned in the national cemetery. Almost every family on Hilton Head was related to soldiers buried there.

When the young Isabel Brown, under the wings of her parents, reached the Beaufort National Cemetery and stared through the main gates of the cemetery, as most people did, she saw a towering twenty-foot-tall granite obelisk. The obelisk, erected in 1870 by a woman renowned for caring for ill soldiers in Beaufort's military hospitals, was dedicated to "the Defenders of American Liberty Against the Great Rebellion."

Inside the gates, burial sections were arranged in the shape of a half-wheel with roads forming spokes from the "hub" at the cemetery entrance. Erect white grave markers lined the roads, almost as if the soldiers still stood at attention. On Decoration Day, however, the deceased soldiers were the ones saluted for their deeds.

A large parade kicked off the May 30 events, often led by the famous black Allen Brass Band of Beaufort, one of the high-stepping, often-uniformed military-style brass bands that paraded streets in Northern cities, Southern cities such as Charleston, and rural communities around the turn of the century.

They earned the name "jump-up" bands for the stirring effects on parade watchers. The Allen Brass Band was so well-regarded that the *Indianapolis Freeman*, a nationally distributed black newspaper, noted in December of 1890 that "Allen's Brass Band of Beaufort, S.C. has just returned from filling an engagement at Augusta."

In 1897, the year Brown turned thirteen years old, ten to twelve thousand black people thronged the streets of Beaufort on Decoration Day. Beaufort's two colored militia companies turned out, along with colored military companies from Columbia and Augusta, Georgia.

Steamboats, packed with riders from Charleston and Savannah, as well as from Hilton Head and other islands, delivered passengers to Beaufort. Others from South Carolina towns, including Greenville—more than two hundred miles away—arrived on special excursion trains.

Vendors set up tables on the streets with all kinds of food for sale, including pork, fowl, fish, and "pink, blue and vari-colored tartaric acid iced lemonade . . . at three glasses for a nickel."

A huge parade, including bands, military units, Grand Army members, other veterans, relatives, and the Women's Relief Corps proceeded to the cemetery for the speechmaking and "the planting of small United States flags and flowers on the graves." Some strewed flowers in the river.[11]

Decades had come and gone since Isabel Brown had been a young girl. She had reached her fifties in the 1930s. But Hilton Head islanders still grew excited when Decoration Day rolled around. The American Legion now sponsored "Memorial Day," but it remained "Decoration Day" to Gullah people.

"Are you going to the twenty-ninth?" men and women asked each other, weeks ahead of time. Those who were going still left on the twenty-ninth of May in order to reach Beaufort in time for the festivities. Everyone rode the steamer now, the *Cleveland*—also called the *Clivedon*. But on Hilton Head the ceremonies started two full days before May 29.

(*Top*) The steamer Clivedon at the Hilton Head dock. *Courtesy of the Coastal Discovery Museum*

(*Bottom*) Loading the Clivedon. *Courtesy of the Coastal Discovery Museum*

Preparations began a few weeks before. Gullah people gathered blackberries from the fields, crabs from the rivers, and other seasonal food, took them to Savannah by boat, and sold their wares. They used the money to buy shoes, pants, or dresses so that children and adults could dress up for a pre–Decoration Day event—a special treat for everyone on Hilton Head.

Hilton Head's own homegrown band marched from the Brownsville Club to the Central Oak Grove Baptist Church on May 27. Even people unable to go to Beaufort could celebrate on May 27 and, later, at parties on the island on the day of the Beaufort celebration.

And for those going to Beaufort, the music of the homegrown band—many of whom were members of the Brownsville Social Club—heightened islanders' excitement.

The Brownsville Club Band had begun in the 1920s, formed by Gullah men in the Marshland/Chaplin area. Among its members were Abe Johnson on the trumpet; John Patterson, drum; Rubin Green, "bass horn" (tuba); Sam Christopher, little drum; Jake Riley, "the slide" (trombone); and Raymond Perry, French horn.

The band played at picnics as well as at parties where people would dance to both waltzes and lively tunes. But the pre-Beaufort celebration was the best-attended event.

The men in the marching band did not wear fancy uniforms. They did not bother with any uniforms at all. They had something better. Family names that went way back on Hilton Head. And they played a rousing rendition of "Tiger Rag."

Catch that tiger!
Catch that tiger!

Hilton Head's Gullah people had one foot in the past, one in the present, and played a jazz tune as they marched forward.

Chapter Nineteen

THROUGH THE EYES OF A CHILD

THERE WERE ALMOST fifty marsh tackies in the Spanish Wells community. Emory Campbell, born in 1941, knew the names of all of them. Anna Belle, Susie, Iris, Lucky, Peanut, Sworee, Maggie, Paul, Alice, Hannah, and Trolley were among them.

The small, wiry marsh tackies were believed to be descended in part from Arabian horses left on Hilton Head Island by Spanish explorers in the 1500s. Spanish ships sailing from Florida to Virginia stopped at a bluff overlooking Calibogue Sound to fill their ship casks with sweet water from wells they dug, and it is thought that some of their horses got left there. The area where the Spanish got their water became known as Spanish Wells, and while every Gullah community on the island used marsh tackies, people in Spanish Wells had particular reason to take pride in them.

Herds of marsh tackies had once run wild on the white sand beaches of Hilton Head Island, but that was long ago. Every family had a marsh tacky, including Emory's, and many families had two or more. No one owned a mule. Mules were larger and sturdier and could work harder, but they cost more. Buying a mule was like buying a Cadillac. It was beyond islanders' means. They stuck with marsh tackies.

Gullah speakers are thought to have originated the term *marsh tacky*. On other sea islands in Georgia and South Carolina where small horses roamed beaches and marshes, islanders also called them "tackies." The term appears to be a part of Gullah African heritage—a West African word, "taki," refers to a horse.

A marsh tacky helped your family in almost every aspect of life, from birth to death and in between. A man might mount his marsh tacky in the middle of the night to get the midwife when his wife was ready to give birth. When someone in the family died, the marsh tacky would pull the wagon that took the deceased to the burial ground.

If a serious emergency came up in your community, someone would jump on a marsh tacky and ride through the community like Paul Revere on his steed, delivering the message house to house. Come Sunday mornings, hitched to a wagon or carriage, your marsh tacky carried the family to church.

It was a real privilege for a young boy or girl to ride a marsh tacky to school or two miles away to the post office. "You can walk," a parent said, and usually young boys and girls walked everywhere. Come courting time, a young man who got to ride a marsh tacky to see the girl he was interested in made a good impression.

But you always had to be careful not to use your marsh tacky for unnecessary tasks, and you never ran him on a hot day. You usually saved your marsh tacky for work that helped ensure your family's survival.

Each spring and fall, whoever in the family could plow the straightest line would hitch the marsh tacky

to a plow, mount the horse, and cut long rows in the field. The extended Campbell family, young and old, shared the work and their ancestral land. The crops they planted fed them throughout the year. They had plenty of sweet potatoes (a favorite treat), field peas or red peas, corn, sugar cane, squash, butter beans, bush beans, okra, watermelon, and more.

When a son (or sometimes a daughter) got old enough to hitch the marsh tacky to a cart, he would ride the tacky out to the forest to gather wood to cook dinner in the wood stove, to keep the family warm on cold nights, and to heat water for bathing and washing clothes in a big iron pot.

So a marsh tacky was a true beast of burden, but more than that. A marsh tacky was pretty much a member of the family.

The first marsh tacky Emory Campbell knew as a child was Sworee, a tacky passed down to his father, Reginald Campbell, by Emory's paternal grandfather Solomon. But Sworee was up in age and slowing down. Reginald started looking around for a marsh tacky of his own. He came home with a spirited young stallion with a good-looking brown coat and a white streak on his face. The Campbell men named him Trolley. Like all young horses, Trolley, who stood about five feet tall, needed to be broken before anyone could safely ride him.

You could hire someone to break a horse for you, but Reginald picked Emory's brother George and a first cousin, Clarence, to do the job. "Breaking" a marsh tacky was essential if your horse wasn't going to wreck your wagon or plow or hurt you.

George and Clarence harnessed Trolley to a tree and made him pull weights and objects around (called a trace chains-singletree unit) to teach him to use the right muscles to pull a plow or a wagon without wrecking it. After a while, Trolley got the hang of it, and he could be ridden without bucking.

Trolley was temperamental. He showed his displeasure by pawing Emory's brother, Herb, in the face, leaving an angry lump on his forehead. And during his long years of service to the Campbell family, Trolley occasionally would try to bite family members. Somewhere inside him, Trolley had an independent streak as pronounced as the white streak running down his face. But he became domesticated. A few marsh tackies never did; they just lived off the land.

Emory's love of marsh tackies continued for decades. He knew every marsh tacky that regularly passed his home by the sound of its gallop. Peanut, a small marsh tacky, had a real short trot. Paul, a large marsh tacky, had a big, heavy gallop. The gallops and whinnies of marsh tackies were part of island life.

"You knew every sound on the island. You knew the sound of the few cars that there were on the island. You knew the birds. You knew where they were when they were singing. You knew the sound of the cowbell, calling you to school or to evening meetings in the praise house. When you heard a loud horn blow, the men would say,

'That's the *Bessie M. Lewis*.' The *Bessie M. Lewis*, the last steamboat to stop at Hilton Head, anchored off of Spanish Wells. People wanting to board the steamboat would row their bateaux out to the steamboat."

These sounds filled everyday life. To families in Spanish Wells, the sounds said, "This is home."

Ancient moss-draped oak trees, tall pines, palmettos, cedars, and other trees lined the dirt roads and cart and wagon trails, some of which dated back to slavery time. In the Spanish Wells community, vines twined around trees, and wild flowers, from Cherokee roses to yellow jessamine in the spring, bloomed. Large forests held deer, rabbits, wild turkey, and other game. Cleared fields dotted the land, farmed by several generations of the same family who lived close to each other in kinship groups. They lived cheek by jowl, as the saying goes, treading worn footpaths to each other's doors.

The traditional Gullah communities on Hilton Head had much in common. Each community differed a little, just as the pre–Civil War plantation communities had, depending in part on when Africans had arrived and meshed their languages and traditions.

Likewise, each Gullah community had members with the skills and knowhow to make the community thrive: farmers, fishermen, carpenters, boat builders, net makers, and, often, owners of small stores; women, who carried the main responsibility for raising children,

Ruins of a neighborhood store that was owned by Gullah native Herbert Chaplin. *Photo by Will Warasila*

making quilts, and putting up food for the winter; and praise-house leaders and teachers. A few communities also had a blacksmith and midwives. Everyone had value. Together, they formed a community and helped each other out.

The communities included Stoney, the first community visitors entered from the Buckingham Landing on the mainland; Jonesville; Spanish Wells; Gardner; Marshland; Chaplin; Grassland (aslo known as Grasslawn/Big Hill); Cherry Hill/Mitchelville; Baygall; and Squire Pope. Squire Pope likely was the largest community in terms of land and the number of people living there.

In addition to the Campbell family, there were other family names among Spanish Wells landowners:

Painting of Charlie Wiggins's roadside market in the Stoney Community on Hilton Head Island, by Walter Greer, Hilton Head artist. *Courtesy of the Coastal Discovery Museum*

Chisolm, Frazier, Graham, Anderson, Albright, Cohen, Holmes, Williams, Jenkins, Young, Washington, Bryant, Johnson, Smith, Mitchell, Brown, Chaplin, Hamilton, and Simmons.

The Spanish Wells community lay on the grounds of the old Spanish Wells Plantation, said to predate 1792. The six-hundred-acre plantation had stretched from Broad Creek to Calibogue Sound on the western shore of the island. Cotton flourished here before the Civil War, as it did on other Hilton Head plantations worked by enslaved men and women.

The Baynard family, owners of Spanish Wells and Braddock's Point, reclaimed the two plantations in 1875 after Congress passed the federal Redemption Act.

Later, in 1893, a court ordered Spanish Wells and Braddock's Point to be sold to satisfy the claims of additional heirs to share in the estate.

William P. Clyde bought both plantations the following year. He would sell land in Spanish Wells to at least three men whose descendants would continue to live in Spanish Wells: Stephen Hamilton, Paul Brown, and Minus Graham.[1]

The community of Spanish Wells probably was well-established by then, since many Gullah people stayed on their old plantations after the war. Walla Campbell, the first of the Campbell line on Hilton Head, may have been among these. Walla is said to have arrived on Hilton Head from Edisto Island around 1820.[2]

Whether Walla Campbell lived at Spanish Wells before the war, he lived out his life there afterward. Walla, a name other enslaved men in the Beaufort District also bore, may well have been African.[3] Walla's family later called him Wallace. Wallace was the great-great-grandfather of Emory Campbell.

Wallace's son Phillip was a child at the time the Union captured Hilton Head. Growing up in freedom gave him the leeway to speak his mind and to be a full person. Phillip would have been a tall teenager (as all the Campbell men were) at the time of the heated election of 1876. He may have been the Campbell man from Spanish Wells that John McFall (the white man who handed out fake ballots designed to trick Gullah island-ers into voting for the Democrats) accused of "speaking hot words" about a Beaufort man that Campbell felt was not entitled to vote on Hilton Head.

Phillip knew that the key to independence lay in owning land. When a chance came his way to buy land, he grabbed it.

The opportunity came about through a string of events. The pre-war owner of Possum Point Plantation on Hilton Head never stepped forward to redeem his land. As a result, the U.S. tax commissioners put the plantation up for sale in an 1876 tax auction.

W. D. Brown, the late white store owner, had picked up the one-thousand-acre plantation for $150 in a federal tax auction. The former plantation included three hundred and twenty-three cleared acres and heavily wooded land.

Brown decided to sell five hundred and forty-two acres of Possum Point in 1893. Four Gullah islanders bought the land. Each paid a slightly different amount, depending on the total acres of land he acquired. Phillip Campbell bought one hundred and fifty acres for $100. Brown made a hefty profit, and Phillip Campbell got a well-situated tract of land that began at the public road on the island (running from the north to the south end) and ended at Broad Creek, the huge tidal creek that flowed off of Calibogue Sound.

William P. Clyde bought Phillip's share of Possum Point in the early 1900s for a hunting preserve, but Phillip apparently lived there until 1916. Selling his land at Possum Point allowed Phillip to continue being an aggressive land buyer. He and Benjamin White, Sr., would ride out on early mornings to look at land they were interested in. Phillip came to own large parcels of land in Spanish Wells.

People called him "Friend," in part because, while he kept some land, he also sold some to Gullah families, several of whom still were living in Spanish Wells.

Phillip may have been proud of his land purchases, but he also was proud of his son Solomon. Solomon graduated from South Carolina State College in Orangeburg, founded in 1896 as the state college for colored persons. A tall, lean man whose looks probably came from his grandfather Wallace, Solomon became a legendary teacher on Hilton Head in the post-Reconstruction era. Likewise, Julia Aiken Campbell of Saint Helena Island, the wife of Solomon, was known as a great teacher. She had graduated from Barber-Scotia College in North Carolina, founded after the Civil War for the daughters of former slaves.

Gullah people still spoke of Solomon with great respect, and Phillip held great importance for the Campbell family. Phillip had bought and passed down the land on which the extended Campbell family lived. Emory and his brothers and sisters marked the fifth generation of the Campbell family on Hilton Head, and the fourth generation to live on the land Phillip had purchased.

Passing land down within the family was a long-held practice on Hilton Head. Gullah families lived on "heirs'" land that their forbearers had worked for, bought, and passed down to their descendants. Whether the descendants stayed on the island or moved away, they knew there was a place called home if they wanted to return.

In Emory's family, his father, Reginald, and Reginald's siblings jointly shared about fifty acres of heirs' land. Solomon died before Emory was born, but Emory's paternal grandmother, Julia Campbell, lived close by on land initially purchased by Philip Campbell. Emory's maternal grandparents, Rosa Chisholm Williams and Perry Williams, who made nets, lived on their own five-acre parcel. Other relatives lived nearby.

The Campbell children grew up surrounded by parents, siblings, grandparents, aunts and uncles, and a line of cousins stretching from first to second, third, fourth, fifth, and beyond. They farmed the land cooperatively under the leadership of Reginald, the oldest of Solomon's sons. Altogether, they farmed about forty acres of ancestral land.[4]

As with the Campbell family, numerous men and women who worked hard and managed to buy land after freedom were considered heroes. Families remembered who bequeathed the land that sheltered them. Land was the basis of everything—your home, your food to eat, your ability to be as independent as possible, and your opportunity to live on an island where Gullah islanders formed the majority and Jim Crow slights seldom touched them.

The roll call of such heroes included Martha Fields, who used the widow's pension she received to buy land on Cotton Hope Plantation (later known as Squire Pope). Martha, Polido, and their children had lived in bondage at Cotton Hope. Her heirs held twenty acres of land in the late 1940s.

Nancy Christopher, who as a child had been enslaved at Fish Haul, became a midwife and delivered babies all over the island. She passed down twenty acres to her heirs. Matthew Jones, enslaved at Stoney (Fairfield Plantation), bought land where he had lived. His heirs owned twenty-five acres.

Likewise, the heirs of the soldier Mingo Green owned twenty acres, heirs of Backus Ferguson owned forty acres, and heirs of Diana Singleton owned one hundred and three acres. Edward Lawyer, who arrived on Hilton Head during the war, left twenty-three acres to his heirs. The heirs of Christena Murray held more than one hundred acres. The heirs of Clara Wigfall, in the old area known as Mitchelville, had twenty-eight acres. Among many others, Caesar Jones, founder of Jonesville, handed down land, as did his sons and daughters. His two daughters Katie and Ammie had been aboard the boat with Caesar and his wife, Mariah, when they fled to Hilton Head after Emancipation. Katie and Ammie had married two Miller brothers,

John and Gilbert. Katie and the Miller brothers were no longer living, but Katie had bequeathed thirty acres to her descendants. Her sister Ammie still lived. Now in her late eighties, she owned eight acres.

Reginald and his brother, Solomon, built the house in which the family of Reginald and Sarah Campbell lived. A wooden frame house set on wooden blocks, it had five rooms at the outset: a kitchen, a dining room, a living room that nobody used unless company came, and two bedrooms. It was a one-board-thick house with gypsum board on the bedrooms' walls to cut down on drafts.

People of status on the island, including Solomon and Julia, usually had a chimney and a hearth. The house Emory grew up in did not. Either the chimney was too hard to build or cost too much.

Reginald added a third bedroom, a lean-to with a single-pitch roof attached to the side of the house. As often is the case, the lean-to leaked during heavy rains. His father plugged the leak with pine tar each time. The tar held for a while, and then the leak came back and the rain dripped in again.

They needed that lean-to. The family kept growing. Sarah Campbell birthed thirteen children—nine boys and four girls—of whom the last child, a girl, unfortunately died within months. With twelve children, Reginald piled as many of his sons as he could in the lean-to and dubbed it "the bull pen."

One of Emory's sisters went to live with their maternal grandparents. "I want to stay with Mama Needie," which is what they called Rosa Williams, she said. "You want to stay? Okay," Rosa Williams said. Two of Emory's brothers eventually went to live there, too.

Reginald was working on the dredge in Savannah, helping the U.S. Corps of Engineers build the Savannah Port, and Sarah Campbell had her hands full. So Sarah's mother helped raise the children. Under the Gullah way of life, families pitched in to raise children, and they shared children with relatives and friends who did not have children.

"We were always around our grandparents. We worked with them, and we went to the river with them—they were always around. We would run errands for them, and we spent the night with them sometimes. We were one family," Emory Campbell recalled.

But Emory, the sixth child in the family, did not volunteer to live with his grandparents or anybody else. He decided to stay right where he was.

"Every time I saw a certain truck drive up to the house, I ran and hid under the house. I wanted to stay with my parents." The truck belonged to Emory's aunt and uncle who had no children and wanted to adopt him. They also were Emory's godparents. "I knew that if I were willing, my mother would let me go."

"I was four years old, and I was terrified. I ran for my life."

The couple finally found a hand baby—a baby so young you held it in your arms—to raise, and that ended that. Emory did not leave his mother.

You lived by the rhythm of the tide, and you ate by the rhythm of the tide. The men in Emory's family would fish, but so would Rosa Williams. Rosa was a tall, strong woman who spoke traditional Gullah and loved her Gullah life. She bragged of her third-grade education, which was the standard on Hilton Head when she went to school. Her husband Perry Williams could read and write.

On summer days Rosa Williams loved to take her grandchildren fishing. "You got up as early as four a.m., depending on the tides, and sometimes earlier than that." Rosa was the captain. Emory, still a young boy, was the bailer.

The sky was dark when they reached the landing on Broad Creek, pushed the bateau into the water, and entered the tidal creek. From his seat in the middle of the boat, Emory watched the sky gradually lighten to dark gray, then to a lighter gray. The first birds chirped next, and it was "jus fo dayclean," as Rosa Williams said, using the old expression that the Africans had brought to Hilton Head and most islanders still used. Just before dayclean.

The sun began to rise, bringing rosy streaks that filled a child with wonder. The sky grew blue then, and

Emory Campbell's paternal grandparents, Perry and Rosa Williams. Picture taken on the veranda of their home in the Spanish Wells neighborhood, Hilton Head Island in the 1960s. Perry was a WWI veteran, retired U.S. Corps of Engineers dredge hand, and fish net knitter; Rosa was an expert fisher and homemaker. *Collection of Emory S. Campbell*

an hour or so later the sun glinted down on the water, turning ripples golden.

"It was beautiful," Emory would remember, a pure beauty that would stay with him for life.

Some of the Campbell men built their own bateaux. They put sails on some for sailing to Savannah to sell crops and seafood and used the ones without sails for fishing. Perry Williams hand-knitted cast nets, too, a skill in high demand in the community.

Each spring, he repaired any leaks he found in the bateau Rosa used, though a few leaks always remained. He added some cypress siding he bought in Savannah to make the bateau more rot resistant. Cypress swells tight after a good soaking, which keeps water from coming in, but if Rosa Williams had not used the boat for a while, water seeped in fast. But most of the water that came into the boat did so when she stood in the boat to cast her net. Water splashed among the bait or fish as she pulled up her net. Emory had his hands full bailing water.

They worked the tide in Broad Creek until the water started coming in from Calibogue Sound. They rowed back and ended their fishing trip.

By getting up early, Rosa Williams could work the tide all week on summer days. She did not do much fishing in the winter. The community fish man took over then, coming to your door with fish on a palmetto frond, strung through the gills. He might bring all mullet, a mix of mullet and spots, or sometimes trout.

"After an early morning tide, you had fish for breakfast. If you had an afternoon tide you had fish for dinner." They ate fried and stewed fish. Leftover fried fish might be refried in the morning. Stewed fish came with onions, pepper, and flour, browned and smothered.

"If you have gumbo over rice on Sunday, you could have gumbo over grits on Monday morning as a leftover. We always thought that was a poor man's food," Emory later would remember.

The Campbell kitchen had a metal-top table, a wood stove, a big dipper hanging on the wall, and a bucket to hold water from the hand pump outside. Pots hung on the wall around the stove. A wood box held the wood that fed the stove. A little pantry in the corner of the kitchen held grits and rice and spice, including the hot pepper they grew. Not everybody liked hot pepper, but Reginald did. "After we had taken up our food, he'd add

hot pepper to his, particularly when we had fresh fish or stewed mullet."

They had plenty of sweet potatoes, greens, and cornbread. On Sundays, their table included turnip greens, collards, or cabbage, or greens mixed with cabbage. Summertime brought green butterbeans and okra fresh from the fields. Winter brought dishes of field peas or red peas with rice. They always had "sumptin" to eat.

With no electricity or refrigeration on the island, Sarah Campbell found ways to put up food for her family. "She would fry shrimp, seal them in a jar, and we'd have them later. They were delicious," Emory said. She also preserved peaches, pears, figs, and watermelon rinds. "Peel that thing, cut the rind up into pieces, and that could make a good dessert in the winter."

Reginald was still working the dredge on the Savannah River, moving pipes that pumped sand from the river bottom, thus deepening the channel for ships and helping the U.S. Corps of Engineers build the Savannah Port. Many Hilton Head islanders worked in Savannah at one time or another in their lives. More jobs were available there.

Several men from Spanish Wells, including John Young, Perry Williams, and John Holmes, Jr., worked on the dredge. Men from other communities did, too.

Reginald would be out on a boat working on the coldest day of the year, trying to put pipes in the right place so they could vacuum up debris from the river bottom.

He wore hip boats to keep his feet and legs dry, and the boots came close to killing him one day when he fell overboard into the freezing river.

"The men on the boat thought he was a goner. They thought those heavy boots would drag him under, but either he got lucky or they may have helped hold him up," Emory recalled. His crewmates managed to pull him out. Sometime after that, Reginald Campbell moved back to Hilton Head permanently.

By the time Emory reached third grade at the Spanish Wells combination praise house and elementary school, Reginald was the teacher. Reginald had attended Hampton Normal and Industrial in Virginia (later to become Hampton University). He had more education than most people on the island, was a notary public, and was a deacon at First African Baptist, so he was a natural choice for the job. For Emory, this meant that his father would be his teacher for grades three through five.

Mornings for Emory—and all Gullah children on the island—started with greeting everyone they saw. "Good morning, Bubba," he said to his father. "Good morning, sista [sister]," he said to his mother. Respect mattered. Manners mattered. Children learned this young.

He made sure he said good morning to everyone he saw as he walked to school. "Some of the people deliberately made it hard to get their attention. There was a man out working in the field in the morning, and I would have to interrupt him. I'd say, 'Good morning!'

again, louder and louder until he stopped working and looked up to acknowledge me."

An older woman whose home he passed every day was half deaf. Emory went closer and closer to her house yelling, "Good morning." He often had to say "Good morning" three times to get her attention. Usually, she would be going to his mother's house later that day, and if Emory had not succeeded in getting her attention, she would tell Sarah Campbell, "That Emory went right through my yard and didn't say good morning."

"Sometimes they knew you were speaking to them but wanted you to really show respect. It was like a test to see if you were respectful."

The Spanish Wells praise house was a simple one-room frame structure built by men in the community. It did not matter whether you were Baptist or Methodist, the praise house was for everyone, and it bonded the community together. Then, at 9:00 a.m. on weekdays, the praise house turned into a school house for children in the community.

His uncle Saul had built heavy, long tables that seated ten to twelve students and equally heavy benches with backs for the students. He was a perfectionist, having studied carpentry at Voorhees, a black industrial school that followed the model of Tuskegee Institute at the time he attended. He built tables for every grade. Then he painted a wall black, and that served as a chalkboard. Students used a damp rag to clean it.

As was the practice in most one-room school houses, the teacher would teach four or five classes at the same time. The teacher might be giving a lesson to the young children while older students might read an assignment the teacher had given them or do an arithmetic exercise.

Discipline was strict. Only the class getting a lesson from the teacher could speak. No one else could. Students caught talking might have to stand in the corner with one foot up for thirty minutes. Other times, the teacher might decide to switch a student's hand. Corporal punishment was common and acceptable.

The students gathered switches from the forest and took them back to the school. The teacher always had a jar of switches at hand. Some were cut from tall blueberry bushes. "They made a nice slender but sturdy switch," Emory recalled. "Sometimes the heat from the stove in the schoolhouse hardened the switches, and they could be hurtful. There were certain people that you knew would get a switching, but most students didn't get many. We had to behave."

Reginald was good at teaching the three Rs: reading, writing, and arithmetic. Emory learned quickly. He would have, anyway, but he could not shame his father.

Something puzzled Emory, though. Why did they have those *Dick and Jane* primers? The kids pictured in them were always white. He lived on an island with about eleven hundred people. Everyone on the island was black, except for five or six white families, and he did not know any of them. He thought whites must be a minority.

At school in the second or third grade, he argued about it with his first cousin Solomon, Jr., whom he affectionately called Junior. Junior insisted that white people were in the majority. "Naw," Emory scoffed. He couldn't believe it, but his cousin kept insisting it was true. Emory would have to be older before he learned this for himself.

The morning sun came into the Campbell's front bedroom, at the northeast corner of the house. The kitchen got some morning sun, too, although everyone rose before the sun. On winter mornings, Emory or one of his brothers or sisters would go out to the corn house and get some corn to spill for the chickens. Then one of the kids would go in the chicken house, check the chickens, and prepare them for laying, if any were about to. You could tell by feeling their hind end for eggs. They left those about to lay eggs in the chicken house and let the other chickens out to range.

With turkeys, you had to dog that turkey—watch that turkey to see where it went and where it was going to lay its eggs. You would go out every day in the field until the turkeys hatched their eggs, gather them, and take them back to the coop. You also would chop up certain plants to go into their feed to help prevent disease. With your cattle, you let them range during the winter. When spring came, you corralled the cows with ropes and moved them around to fresh ground so they could graze.

The chores didn't stop there. Someone in the family had to take out the slop jars each morning. Come washing day, you had to pump the water from the outside pump and get a fire going under the big iron pot to get that washing done.

After school you had more tasks. Emory's time came for grooming and feeding Trolley and taking him out to the forest for gathering wood and then chopping it to fit the wood stove. The Campbells divided up the labor, depending on who was good at what, which was fortunate for Emory. He didn't like planting and working in the field. There was too much sun and hard work, so he learned how to do other things.

"I built things. Chicken coops and outhouses and whatever was needed, and I learned to cook." He learned how to cook rice early. He'd wash that rice and scrub it between his fingers to get rid of husks or other debris. He'd put the rice and water in the pot and measure it by putting his finger into the water to make sure the water did not go beyond the first joint of his index finger.

That way the rice "would not jump the fence," his mother said, meaning the rice would not be soggy.

When the rice boiled, he would let the heat subside on the wood stove and then moved the rice to a cooler part of the stove. Your rice had to be perfect. They ate rice with every meal, as Gullah people always had.

After dinner the children did their studies. They could not get away with saying they did not have any. Sarah Campbell knew better. The Campbell house was a popular place. The Campbell children, along with friends who came over, studied around a kerosene lamp with a shade. They had two or three lamps in their home. The lampshades got sooty, and you had to shine them every few days.

Some people had a lamp in every room, including Julia Campbell, whose house also had a chimney. Reginald and Sarah's family moved lamps around when they needed light in another room. "You'd say, 'I got to use that lamp awhile,' and then you'd bring it back," Emory Campbell said. "People were careful with the lamps, kids too."

Two houses on the island burned down, but the fire always came from the fireplace chimney—never from the lamps. Solomon and Julia's house once caught fire. People came running from everywhere in the community. They formed a bucket brigade and saved the house. But from then on, Reginald and Sarah may have thought that the lack of a chimney was not so bad after all.

Chapter Twenty

CIVIL RIGHTS AND LAND

WORLD WAR II had come and gone, but the memories remained.

The Coast Guard had monitored the eastern Atlantic shore along Hilton Head for a while during the war. U.S. Marines had set up base on Hilton Head, putting in new gun emplacements near the Leamington lighthouse to help protect the Atlantic shore. Black residents called the base Camp Dilling; officially, it was Camp McDougal.

The dirt road that ran from Lemington northward was paved for the marines. Jeeps filled with marines drove to "Downtown Stoney," the business center of Hilton Head. The noise and the white men in uniforms always frightened Emory's oldest sister. Whenever she heard the marines coming, she hid somewhere in the house.[1]

Living on an isolated island, no one could overlook the presence of the marines. They never forgot that a war was going on overseas.

A number of Hilton Head Gullah men joined a massive work force on the Savannah ship docks, building a total of eighty-eight Liberty ships for the war effort.[2] The U.S. Army drafted other islanders.

Elijah Jones, Jr., whose father Elijah (Massey) Jones had been in World War I, did not wait for a draft notice. At seventeen, Jones volunteered for the navy, as did his brother Joseph Jones. Eugene Wiley; Abraham Lawyer; Jacob Driessen; Thomas Barnwell, Sr.; James Lee Frazier, Jr.; and Clarence Ford, Sr., as well as others, also joined the navy.[3]

When Jones joined the navy in 1943, he encountered discrimination. "People treat[ed] colored people like, oh my Jesus; although you in the service . . . they was mean to us," Jones recalled. One obstacle Jones faced was that he "wanted to work on the deck of a ship. But see, at that time they only wanted colored men as cooks and stewards."[4]

By the time the navy began to let black men work on the deck, Jones was married to his wife, Viola Holmes Jones of Hilton Head, and wanted stability. He decided to stick with cooking and make the best of it.

Most of the men from Hilton Head Island came through the war alive. Jones's cousin, James Lee Frazier, Jr., was aboard a ship during intense bombing. "He came home clean, but his ship got bombed. They had a rough time saving the ship," Jones said. Viola Holmes Jones would remember that "several men came back to the island shell shocked, and they never were able to function again."

Jones, however, spent twenty years on active duty with the navy, followed by ten years as a reservist. "I was an all-around man; I bake, butcher, and cook. See that was my job all my life, and I take pride in that. I knew cooking outside and inside."[5]

But the war left a bitter aftertaste in the mouths of many black veterans who came home to find that the freedom they fought for overseas did not exist for them in the U.S. Jim Crow segregation legally ruled the workplace, public life, and education, and, especially in the South, still denied black men of their right to vote.

The unequal treatment of black soldiers returning home from war pushed the issue of inequality to the forefront of the nation's conscience.

Locally, the Hilton Head branch of the National Association for the Advancement of Colored People (NAACP) organized in the early 1940s. Luke Graham of Spanish Wells served as president, and others such as Arthur Brown and Reverend William Ford played instrumental roles.[6]

The local branch sought quality education for black children under the "separate but equal" law. The Graham family, and other leaders on the island, understood the need for improved education on Hilton Head. Graham had seen his son, a respected minister in Miami, benefit from educational opportunities available off the island. Luke and Florence Graham owned the land on which the Spanish Wells combination praise house/school house sat.[7]

Meanwhile, voting rights litigation topped the national NAACP's agenda. Of the many barriers designed to prevent Negroes from voting—poll taxes, literacy tests, arbitrary requirements set by local registrars, and racially discriminatory Democratic primary elections in the South—the NAACP labeled the southern Democratic primary election system "the most effective and the most widely used tactic to disenfranchise blacks."[8]

The NAACP determined to overthrow the southern Democratic primary election system and to start by filing suit against the Texas all-white Democratic primary.

Black citizens were restricted from voting or running for office in southern Democratic primaries. Only white citizens were allowed. As a result, some called the southern Democratic primaries the "white primary."

The South had a one-party system—and it ruled with a tight fist. By barring blacks from participating in Democratic primary elections, the South prevented blacks from gaining electoral power.

The Republican Party in the South had never recovered from Reconstruction and ceased holding state primaries for federal and state offices in the early 1920s.[9] Majority-black Beaufort County and a few other places in South Carolina continued to have Republican voters. But the South's Republicans were too weak to field more than a few candidates in the general election after disenfranchisement.

South Carolina's white primary had begun the year after Governor Ben Tillman ushered in disenfranchisement.[10] After that state legislators and governors, and U.S. representatives and senators in the South, were white Democrats.

White candidates vied against each other in heated races in the Democratic primary election. The winners knew they would face little opposition in the general election. They were as good as elected.

Blacks able to pay a poll tax and pass the literacy test could vote in the general election held in November, as federal laws regulated that election. But black voters had little impact in most cases. Their numbers were small. Only three thousand blacks were registered to vote in South Carolina in 1940.

On Hilton Head, blacks who had a general election certificate (sometimes referred to as a federal election certificate), valued and held onto it. Emory Campbell watched his father starting off to go vote one time, and then coming back to get his federal election certificate. That piece of paper showed he was eligible to vote in the general election. The ability to do so was precious, even if he was shut out of the Democratic primary.

He and other Hilton Head black residents who stood in line with their election certificates in hand provided visible proof that blacks wanted their voices heard. They wanted a say in who made the laws under which they lived. They wanted to regain the fruits of emancipation for themselves and their children.

South Carolina blacks, including some in Beaufort County, engaged in fundraising for NAACP litigation against the Democratic primary system. Some members of the Hilton Head Island branch of the NAACP likely contributed. Black South Carolinians knew that if the Texas Democratic primary fell, the South Carolina all-white primary could fall too.

The suit against the Texas primary wound its way through the judicial system and landed in the U.S. Supreme Court. The time for oral arguments came.

Thurgood Marshall, the grandson of a slave, stood before the Supreme Court justices, arguing against the Texas Democratic Party's all-white primary. The ruling in the landmark case *Smith v. Allwright* could open all southern Democratic primaries to black voters before the 1940s ended. But before that could happen, the NAACP needed to convince the justices of the merits of its case, and then set foot on a path that wound back to South Carolina and ended in Beaufort County.

The case centered on Lonnie Smith, a black dentist in Houston who tried to vote in the 1940 Texas Democratic primary but was prohibited from doing so on the basis of his race.

Marshall, a young attorney in charge of legal cases for the NAACP, had argued Smith's case before the Supreme Court in 1943. It was now 1944, and attorneys on both sides had been called back to answer further questions, as the case lay in uncertain territory. Did federal jurisdiction and federal laws extend to primary elections? The issue had been debated in previous cases.

Marshall and other NAACP attorneys argued that the Texas Democratic primary barred black citizens from voting in what amounted to the real election in Texas, thereby preventing blacks from having a voice in electing their representatives in government and allowing whites to structurally dominate the politics of the state.[11]

At the heart of the case lay one question: Does the Texas Democratic Party's racial-exclusive policy violate the Fourteenth and Fifteenth Amendments of the U.S. Constitution? Both amendments had been passed during Reconstruction to protect the rights of freedmen as full citizens. The Fifteenth Amendment specifically affirms that "the right of citizens of the United States to vote shall not be denied or abridged by the United States or any State on account of race, color, or previous condition of servitude."[12]

On the Texas side, Allwright's attorneys argued that the Texas Democratic Party was a private organization. Therefore, they argued, the Democratic Party could set its own rules of membership and deny Smith the right to participate in the party's primary election without violating the Fourteenth and Fifteenth Amendments.

The Court found on April 3, 1944, that Smith had been denied his right to vote and ruled the Texas primary unconstitutional.

The Court reasoned that the Democratic Party's primary elections are operated in association with state government machinery set up to choose state and federal officials. Thus, the Fourteenth and Fifteenth Amendments to the U.S. Constitution could be used to protect Smith's right to vote in the primary election.

The Court also stated in *Smith v. Allwright*: "The United States is a constitutional democracy. Its organic law grants to all citizens a right to participate in the choice of elected officials without restriction by any State because of race.

"This grant to the people of the opportunity for choice is not to be nullified by a State through casting its electoral process in a form which permits a private organization to practice racial discrimination in the election. Constitutional rights would be of little value if they could be thus indirectly denied."[13]

Marshall called the ruling "so clear" and "free of ambiguity" that the right of blacks to participate in primary elections was established "once and for all." As the ruling was directed solely at Texas, however, the NAACP would have to file suit against additional southern states to force compliance.

Shock waves hit southern Democrats when news of the ruling broke. Just nine years prior, the Court had ruled the racially discriminatory Texas Democratic Party's primary constitutional.

In South Carolina, Governor Olin D. Johnston said, "History has taught us that we must keep our white Democratic primaries pure and unadulterated so that we might protect the welfare and homes of all the people of our State."

The governor called for an "extraordinary" session of the state General Assembly to convene on April 14, 1944, "for the purpose of safeguarding our elections" and "the repealing of all laws on the [State's] statute books pertaining to Democratic Primary elections."[14]

"After these statutes are repealed, in my opinion," Johnston said, "we will have done everything within our power . . . insofar as legislation is concerned."

The General Assembly struck down approximately a hundred and fifty laws tying the State of South Carolina to the state Democratic Party and its primary.[15] Johnston and the General Assembly hoped to transform the South Carolina Democratic Party into a private organization whose primaries would remain white.

"White supremacy will be maintained in our primaries," Johnston said. "Let the chips fall where they may!"[16]

The 1944 Democratic Party, now organized as a "private organization," held true to its course. The Democratic primary remained all white.

Two years later in South Carolina, the Negro Citizens Committee decided to try to open the Democratic primary to blacks. The committee organized teams of potential black voters in Columbia to try to vote in the Democratic primary. George Elmore, manager of a five and-ten-cent store, cab driver, and NAACP member, agreed to attempt to vote in the primary of August 13, 1946.[17] The ballot included candidates for the

U.S. House of Representatives and various state offices. When Elmore and others got to the polls to vote, Richland County Democratic officials turned them away because they were not white Democrats.

Elmore became the plaintiff in a class-action case to test whether it was legal for election officials to refuse to let qualified black electorates vote in the Democratic primary. Filed by Harold R. Boulware, legal counsel for the South Carolina NAACP, *Elmore v. Rice* landed in the Federal District Court for the Eastern District of South Carolina before a white federal judge, J. Waties Waring, who recognized that South Carolina's primary election defied the Supreme Court ruling in *Smith v. Allwright*. Boulware, Marshall, and another NAACP attorney argued the case before Waring in July 1947.

Democratic officials argued that a private club has a right to choose its membership. Waring's ruling stated that while private organizations have that right, "private clubs and business organizations do not . . . elect a President of the United States, and the Senators and members of the House of Representatives."

"It is time for South Carolina to rejoin the Union," Waring wrote.[18]

The Democratic Party appealed the *Elmore* ruling and lost, and the U.S. Supreme Court declined to review the case.

Waring's pro-integration stance in *Elmore* angered whites who felt he should be on their side. A member of the elite white aristocracy, Waring's roots in Charleston went back to the 1600s. Colleagues, friends, and some family members ostracized him. At this point, he felt the need for armed guards at his house.

Elmore bore the brunt of acrimony. Crosses burned on George Elmore's lawn. He lost his house after a bank called in his loan. White vendors no longer would stock the shelves of his store, completing his financial ruin.

The South Carolina Democratic Party devised new rules to evade the *Elmore* ruling. Delegates to the spring 1948 Democratic convention set up two standards of voting—one for whites and one for blacks. The delegates limited membership in the Democratic Party to white Democrats. "Qualified Negro electorates" would not be members of the state Democratic Party. They could, however, vote if they presented their general election certificates and took a loyalty oath to the Democratic Party.

The oath required both black and white voters to swear that "I believe in and will support the social and educational separation of races. I further solemnly swear that I believe in the principles of States' Rights." The purpose, Judge Waring later ruled, was "to require an oath supporting segregation . . . and [overrule] discrimination, according to race."

Some blacks in Beaufort County managed to enroll on the enrollment books, but their names later were stricken. Black citizens were told they were "not accepted as enrolled members of the Democratic Party," but could vote in the primary if they produced general election certificates (which required paying a poll tax and owning a certain amount of property), and took the loyalty oath.[19]

David Brown stepped forward. Brown, a black resident of Beaufort County for more than fifty years, had paid his poll tax and was a legally qualified elector under the Constitution and the laws of the United States.[20]

Brown became the plaintiff in *Brown v. Baskin*, a class-action suit questioning the legality of Negroes not being able to enroll as members of the South Carolina Democratic Party. Thurgood Marshall argued the case before Judge Waring.

Upset with the South Carolina Democratic Party's continuing efforts to maintain the white primary, Waring issued a temporary injunction requiring the state Democratic Party to open its membership rolls and freely allow all citizens the right to participate in the August primary "without discrimination of race, color or creed."

"South Carolina Negroes voted freely last week . . . in the Democratic primary; by evening of election day nearly 35,000 had cast their ballots," *Time* magazine reported.[21]

It was the largest number of Negro voters since Reconstruction. The South Carolina white primary be-

came the last of the South's white primaries to fold. With its disappearance, the white primaries ended. This was the beginning of reclaiming the right to vote. Negroes as a total group no longer would face voting discrimination.

It was, however, still far from perfect. The pressure on individual Negroes in South Carolina and elsewhere would increase. Black citizens remained subject to literacy requirements, poll taxes, and arbitrary requirements set by local registrars. That would not begin to change for almost twenty years, until the Civil Rights Act of 1964 and the Voting Rights Law of 1965. But for the moment, the horizon had lifted a bit.

The fall of 1949 arrived, and with it the time for Gullah people to pay their Beaufort County taxes for the year. In communities such as Squire Pope, where pecan trees had been planted for this purpose, heads of families assembled children and grandchildren to gather pecans. They filled burlap bags with one hundred pounds of pecans, closed them up, marked the owners' initials on each bag, and sold them in the Savannah market. The money helped families pay their taxes, and the children who picked pecans learned the importance of paying taxes.

The value of land varied on Hilton Head, depending on its quality, use, and location. In the community of Spanish Wells, for instance, Emory's family and close relatives shared ten acres of land taxed at $60. Solomon's house was taxed at $100, so the land plus the house put the real estate taxes at $160.

Beaufort County taxed personal property too, which included almost anything that could help a family earn a living: horses (marsh tackies) were taxed at $10 up to $20, or $25 for an exceptionally fine one, cattle were taxed at $10 each, hogs at $5 each, and dogs—as they could be used for hunting wild game—at $3 each. Carriages, carts, drays, wagons, trucks, and automobiles also were taxed, along with farm implements, machinery, mills, or gins.

The heirs of Solomon Campbell had a marsh tacky taxed at $25—an amount slightly exceeding the tax for four acres of land. The Campbell heirs lacked elaborate farm machinery, a car, or truck, but owned two cows, hogs, and a cart (or wagon). This put their combined real estate and personal property taxes at a total of $292. (The tax bill was equivalent to $2,859 in 2013.)[22]

Reginald Campbell's five-acre parcel of the family land was taxed at $40, and his total tax bill was $144. (The tax bill was equivalent to $1,414 in 2013.) Perry Williams, Emory's maternal grandfather, also owned five acres of land taxed at $40 and a home taxed at $30 for a total tax bill of $288. (This was equivalent to $2,865 in 2013.)

Charlie Simmons, the largest Gullah entrepreneur on the island, easily owned the most land of anyone in the Spanish Wells community. He owned seventy-four

Charlie Simmons, Sr., known as "Mr. Transportation," ca. 1990, in the sanctuary of First African Baptist Church on Hilton Head Island. *From the Collection of Ayoka A. Campbell*

acres altogether. A good deal of his land lay outside of Spanish Wells, in his boat landing along Broad Creek, and a lot in Stoney for his variety store. He owned two trucks and a car, three buildings, and boats, including the *Alligator*. His tax bill totaled $5,472, more than any other Gullah taxpayer on Hilton Head. (Simmons's tax bill was equivalent to $53,686 in 2013 dollars.)

The only white man on the island whose county taxes exceeded those of Simmons was S. V. Toomer. His 1949 county tax bill, including a general store he owned, was $7,344. (The amount was equivalent to $71,883 in 2013.)

Among other Gullah entrepreneurs, Arthur Frazier of Jonesville, also a store owner, had the second highest tax bill among Gullah islanders, $2,736. Ben White, Sr., who had fifty-three acres of land and three buildings, paid $2,412.27.[23] Henry Driessen owned a small store that sold gas and basic items such as rice, grits, and flour, a produce stand, and thirty acres in the Chaplin community. His taxes were $1,512. (His grandson, also named Henry Driessen, worked on his grandfather's farm in the 1930s and 1940s, and later would go on to the Penn school, followed by college. He would become prominent on Hilton Head in his own right. The younger Driessen inherited and expanded the business his grandfather started. He also became the first black councilman in 1983 when Hilton Head residents voted to make Hilton Head Island a town.) William Aiken, who gathered and mixed herbs to concoct remedies for islanders' ills, owned nine acres of land, and had a home taxed at $150 and a total property tax of $1,153.

Abraham Grant of the Chaplin Community had a tax bill of $108; his grandson, born in 1937 and named after him, would join the next generation of entrepreneurs and become a successful business owner.

Everyone paid county taxes. Almost all Gullah families owned some land on Hilton Head. In the rare instance when a family did not own land, the family still paid taxes on farm animals, farm equipment, and other items. Whatever the amount of the tax bill, families worked hard to pay it.

Gullah families owned approximately thirty-two hundred acres of land on Hilton Head Island in 1949.[24]

Thanksgiving came and went. Christmas was almost upon them. Families who had raised turkeys for sale at the Savannah market hoped they would make good money when they made the boat trip there—enough to buy a few presents for the children and put a jingle in the adults' pockets.

Men started hunting for game for the Christmas table. Children went into the woods to gather sprigs of yaupon, a small-leafed native holly with red berries their mothers used to decorate mantles. Laura Campbell, an aunt of Emory's, went to people she worked for in Savannah and got magazines from them. Then she pasted Christmas scenes on her walls, making her "whole house pretty."

Women began gathering the ingredients for their tastiest dish or dessert for Christmas Day, when everyone in the community visited house to house to eat, talk, and have fun. When the day came, anyone who went to enough houses and visited got their choice of pies, cakes, chicken, raccoon, deer, possum, pork, gravy, corn bread, fried cracklings, and, for adults, home-made moonshine.

Many women and men, including members of such clubs as the Boys of Pleasure and the Mothers' Union, went around in separate groups, singing spiritual and secular songs, and feasting at each stop. People kept visiting for days until they had been to every home in the community. Sometimes that took a full week.

Watch Night came next, the old praise-house ceremony that ushered in the New Year. Gullah people crowded into small praise houses to sing hymns and spirituals, tell of the blessings they had received this year, and wish each other well in the coming year. A "watchman" stood outside each praise house. From time to time, the praise-house leader called out to the watchman to ask how much time remained before the new year came in. The watchman yelled out the remaining time in count-down fashion: fifteen minutes, ten minutes, five minutes, one minute.

As the watchman announced the arrival of a brand-new year, joyful shouts broke out accompanied by the clapping of hands and the sound of feet stomping on a wooden floor. Celebratory shouts carried throughout Gullah communities from the small praise houses set under the blanket of night and a starry sky.

People, some carrying oil lanterns, then walked home to eat their hoppin' John: field peas and rice cooked with salt pork or ham hocks. You had to eat hoppin' John on New Year's to make sure you had good luck in the coming year.

Nationally, broadcast from New York, Guy Lombardo sang a clever new song with lyrics crafted to remind everyone that the years speed by quickly, so "Enjoy yourself, enjoy yourself, it's later than you think."

Watch Night occupied Gullah people's attention, not the radio. Yet the new song carried a message worth heeding, even on Hilton Head. With the year 1950 now ushered in, time was running out for Gullah families on Hilton Head. It was far later than they knew.

That is how Gullah people on Hilton Head had lived as far back as memory went on a boot-shaped island on the edge of the Atlantic Ocean.

Chapter Twenty-One

THE TIMBERMEN COME

THE *ALLIGATOR*, owned by Charles Simmons, Sr., one of the island's Gullah businessmen, cut across the water bound for Hilton Head Island, a timber scout from Georgia aboard the dark gray boat.[1] The 1950s were roaring in toward Hilton Head like a tidal wave cresting in the Atlantic, threatening to sweep over the island.

In the waning days of 1949, Thorne and Loomis, the largest landowners on Hilton Head, had issued a thunderclap announcement. They would sell eight thousand acres of their land on the south end of the island. In Hinesville, Georgia, a small town forty miles southwest of Savannah, Fred C. Hack heard the news on December 20, 1949, and rushed to the island.

On Hilton Head, Hack saw huge forests with first-growth trees dating back to plantation days and before—trees that had sprung up in deserted cotton fields after the Civil War and Northern-owned cotton efforts ended and trees that had grown in the former small plots of Gullah islanders who had since moved to the north end of the island. The amazing stands of trees filled Hack's thoughts on his way back to Georgia, but Hilton Head's twelve-mile pristine white beach running along the Atlantic Ocean dazzled him even more.

Before going to Hilton Head, Hack had told Joseph B. Fraser, Sr., of the Hinesville Lumber Company that he planned to check out the timbering potential on Hilton Head. Now he sought Fraser's help in buying the

Present-day site on Broad Creek of the landing for Charlie Simmons's boat that transported people and goods to and from the mainland. *Photo by Will Warasila*

Thorne and Loomis land. Fraser and C. C. Stebbins, Hack's father-in-law, accompanied Hack on a return visit to the island. The quality of the timber and the island's natural beauty amazed Fraser. They signed an option on the spot for the eight thousand acres at an average of $60 per acre.[2]

By the end of December, they had lined up additional investors, including Olin T. McIntosh, and formed the all-white Hilton Head Company to harvest timber. The sale would not close until March 1950, but the deal was solid. The new company now owned the southern end of the island.

Thorne and Loomis had been land owners on Hilton Head since 1931. Like William Clyde and prior big land owners on the island, they lived in the North and had come and gone as they wished, mainly for the hunting seasons or to celebrate holidays. They had a yacht, a ground generator, and a caretaker who tended the woods and fields to ensure good hunting for themselves and their guests. They spent their free time on Hilton Head but still were absentee owners.

Black people had little reason to believe the timbermen's arrival signaled the beginning of irreversible change for Hilton Head and for themselves. They hoped jobs would come but were suspicious of outsiders.

The Hilton Head Company set up three sawmills on the island, two on the south end and one on Broad Creek, in the area called Shelter Cove.

The screech of the saw at a lumber mill on Broad Creek filled the air. The screech began at eight in the morning and lasted to four or five in the afternoon. Emory Campbell could hear the screech from his home, clearer than people in Spanish Wells used to hear the bell of the last steamship, the *Bessie M. Lewis*. The steamship no longer came. Its era had passed.

Tall pines crashed in the forests as men operating nearly two-foot-long gasoline chainsaws cut the trees close to the ground. Felled trees were hauled to the lumber mill and put on a long belt powered by diesel engines.

The saw's loud screech began. "It hit a high note as the saw bit into the wood," Emory Campbell said, "then lowered as the saw went through the length of the wood. They'd put the wood on the belt again to run the length at another spot, and that high note — you'd hear it again. Day in and day out."

Campbell, then nine years old, could imitate the screech of the saw from the high note to the low one. The screech was the sound of 1950.

Lumber crews from Fraser's sawmill came for the timbering, and many Gullah people worked in timbering, too. The timbering paid good cash. Charles "Fuskie" Simmons, a nephew of Charlie Simmons, became something of a right-hand man for Hack.[3] Some islanders found ways to earn money besides working at the mills. Campbell's grandmother, Rosa Williams, for one, earned money housing people from Daufuskie who came over to work at the mill. They would stay all week, then row their bateau home for the weekend.

Charlie Simmons bought a forty-ton barge. He kept the *Alligator*, continued his transportation services for islanders, and hauled saws and sawmill parts and huge amounts of gasoline for the sawmill operation.[4]

By this time Simmons kept a truck at Buckingham Landing and one on Jenkins Island. He crossed the water to Buckingham Landing by boat, used his truck to get to Savannah and other places he needed to go, returned to Jenkins Island, unloaded the supplies he had picked up into the truck he kept there, and then drove to his landing on Broad Creek for the final stop. His son, Charles Simmons, Jr., later joined him. They provided transportation for Hack, and later for Charles Fraser, for almost ten years.[5]

"People were happy to make some cash," Campbell said. "They thought of the screech from the mill as the sound of money, the sound of change. Some folks kinda welcomed that industrious sound."

"Look at Hilton Head," they said. "We're moving."

The 1950 timber harvesting was the first time in history that Hilton Head trees were marketed. Gullah islanders had only cut trees to build their small houses and homemade boats. In six months' time, the timber company cut enough trees to make a profit. Millions of board feet were shipped off-island from Broad Creek.[6]

Some large pines were shipped whole—presumably the most valuable ones—and were likely dressed another way.[7] Thomas Barnwell, Jr., a teenager at the time, remembered how the trees had looked huge when he was a child. "They stood way up. They were beautiful."

Gullah people never knew where the lumber went or how it was used.

A second land sale occurred in May of 1951. This time, Thorne and Loomis sold their holdings on the north end of the island. The purchase included Honey Horn, the former estate of Thorne and Loomis. Hack,

McIntosh, and Stebbins formed a new company, Honey Horn Plantation, for the sale. Fraser had a smaller share in the new company than in the first.

The timbermen now owned two-thirds of the island—more than thirty square miles.

Fred Hack and his family had moved into a vacant house at Honey Horn. Hack ran the day-to-day business of the Hilton Head Company, as well as Honey Horn, in Fraser's absence.

One Sunday, Mr. Hack, as everyone called him out of politeness, respect, and his status as a major white landowner on the island, attended a Gullah church service. He likely went to First African Baptist, the oldest and most popular church on the island. But there were four Baptist churches and an African Methodist Episcopal (AME) church on Hilton Head, and the churches rotated holding the Sunday service.

Whichever church he went to, Hack had a large audience of men in their Sunday best and women in their Sunday dresses and favorite hats.

"He showed up because he wanted to develop a real relationship with the people," Campbell said. But as Hack knelt down to pray, he pulled out his prayer book to read.

A stir occurred among some of the older islanders, with Campbell's deeply religious grandmother among them. Rosa Williams was taken aback to see their visitor relying on words in a book to pray.

Gullah people prayed spontaneously. People clapped their hands, stomped their feet, and called out as the spirit moved them. "That's God talking to you . . . you listen to God," Campbell recalls his grandmother saying. "God gives you the words. If you're a strong Christian, the words come to you; why you having to read?"

Watching Mr. Hack read from a piece of paper meant to Campbell's grandmother that "Mr. Hack wasn't a strong Christian."

"She came back suspicious of that man."

Hack, a quiet though friendly man, had grown up in a small southern town. He knew the importance of Sunday church service. But his background in white churches failed to prepare him for Gullah spirituality.

Small signs of a cultural divide continued.

Orion Hack, the younger brother of Fred Hack, got a flat tire while driving on the island. Benjamin White, Sr., and one of his sons happened along and changed the tire for him. Orion Hack offered to pay them.

"Don't you ever do that again," White flared. "We don't do that here. We help one another here."[8]

White was instructing a new resident on island rules. But something else hung in the air. Gullah islanders had no intention of being subservient. Accepting money for fixing a tire implied otherwise. The Hacks and other newcomers had entered a world foreign to them, a

Barge with poles—part of project to bring electricity to Hilton Head. *Courtesy of Palmetto Electric Cooperative*

black world populated by independent Gullah men and women.

Lights began shining through the windows of Gullah homes in late 1951. Electricity reached Hilton Head Island.

Electricity had been a dream for years, but stringing power lines on an island as remote and sparsely populated as Hilton Head had seemed impossible. Extending electricity to Hilton Head would be a money-losing operation for a large utility company. But a small electric membership cooperative, Palmetto Electric Cooperative, took on the job.

Black and white residents worked together to bring electricity to the island. Thomas Barnwell, Jr., remembered his father and other Gullah people traveling to the Jasper County office of Palmetto Electric Cooperative in Ridgeland to meet with the director to try to bring electricity to Hilton Head.

Palmetto Electric had been organized by rural residents and farmers in 1940 and soon brought electricity to nearby Hampton and Jasper counties.

"Every Gullah native who got electricity traveled to Ridgeland at least once and some went more than that," Barnwell said. Going to Ridgeland, the county seat of Jasper County, took money and commitment. "Gullah islanders had to hire a boat to get to Buckingham Landing on the mainland, then hire a truck to take them to Ridgeland, about thirty miles away. They went on that voyage to express their desire to have electricity on Hilton Head Island, pay their membership fee, and to give permission to Palmetto Electric to run power lines across their land."

Almost everyone on the island applied, black and white. The board of directors of Palmetto Electric formally accepted Hilton Head Island applicants as members of the electric cooperative in a meeting on September 26, 1951. Of the eighty-one applicants to the cooperative, at least four-fifths were Gullah islanders whose family names had been known on Hilton Head for generations.

Families like the Edward and Rosalie Barnwell family (ca. 1950) took the opportunity to apply for electricity. *Courtesy of Nell Barnwell Hay*

Among the Gullah names were Chisholm, Holmes, Bryan, Rivers, Barnwell, Jones, Johnson, Frazier, Murray, Robinson, Ford, Cohen, Campbell, Patterson, Samson, Green, Singleton, Grant, Kellerson, Driessen, Bligen, Wright, Brown, Owens, Drayton, and Williams. Four

Gullah churches—Queen's Chapel, Mount Cavalry Baptist, Church of Christ, and First African Baptist— joined. The White & Patterson Hall (a funeral home) also joined.

The long-time white families on the island, the Toomers and the Hudsons, as well as Maggioni & Company, became members, along with W. L. "Bill" Robinson of the Hilton Head Agricultural Society, a white hunting club that had been on the south end of the island (near Leamington) since 1917. Fred C. Hack and Charles Fraser, son of General Fraser, became members, too, as did the Hilton Head Company and Honey Horn Plantation.

"The majority of the people were rural Hilton Head Gullah farmers [the focus of Palmetto Electric], so their applications helped bring electricity to the island," Barnwell said.

Gullah residents began getting electricity within a few months. People started slow and added more outlets as they could. Many families got one cord hanging from the ceiling and a naked light bulb. The Barnwell family had two sockets and light bulbs, one in the living room and one in the dining room, to supplement their oil lanterns and fireplace flames.

Night-time farm tasks grew easier, children bent over their lessons had more light to see, and with the wonders of electricity, the night's deep darkness began to fade.

Gullah people worked for this change and welcomed it. Electric lights fulfilled the magic catchword of the 1950s—"Progress." To some it was the most exciting thing that had ever happened on the island. Gullah children and grandchildren could say with pride, "My family helped bring electricity to Hilton Head." A biracial effort had made obtaining electricity possible, and that was a source of pride to Gullah people.

Things were looking up at the end of 1951.

Timber cutting ended on the north end in 1952. Timbering on the south end stopped, but would resume later, to a lesser degree. Gullah islanders had not thought too much about what the timbermen would do with the land after they finished timbering.

Each major new landowner who came to Hilton Head had ended up wanting more land and eventually turned his eyes toward property owned by Gullah families. Blacks saw no signs of that this time. They did not know that Hack and his partners had decided to develop the island as a seaside resort.

Middle-income and affluent white families throughout the South had fallen in love with beaches in the 1950s. The partners knew that Hilton Head's beaches would prove too attractive to resist.[9]

At first, life went on as usual for Gullah people. Families kept plowing with marsh tackies. One farmer now had a strong mule. Ben White, who had owned a tractor for years, grew tons of watermelons and other crops for the Savannah market. Charles Simmons continued to make trips to Savannah aboard his boat, the *Alligator*, carrying crops to market and bringing back provisions for everyone who needed them.

A North Carolinian arrived with plans to grow tomatoes on a large scale. Yellow blossoms sprouted in huge tomato fields on land leased from Honey Horn and from Seabrook and Talbird. The timbering had left the last two almost clear-cut. But with the timbering over, the tomato fields employed a lot of people for a short time. Deacon William "Jesse" Holmes, who early in life worked in the CCC camps, and his wife, Laura Holmes, joined those who worked in the tomato fields.

The Holmeses started early in the morning, around seven or seven-thirty, got off for lunch, then went back till five or five-thirty. "You'd set out the tomato vines and then go back to hoe them. Then when they get ready, you went to picking." They filled half-bushel basket after basket with tomatoes.[10]

After the tomatoes were picked, the North Carolina man trucked them off. Agricultural crops had dominated Hilton Head since the late 1700s. No one realized that tomatoes would be the last big agricultural crop on the island.

Emory Campbell and other youths his age entered Robinson Junior High, a fairly new school on the island. The school had taken over responsibility for the sixth grade from the Gullah community schools.[11]

The new junior high ran through the eighth grade, providing Gullah children two more years of education. Then students could attend public high school in Bluffton, though they had to cross the water to get there.

As most Gullah families could not afford to send their sons and daughters to the Penn School or Mather School, the public high school in Bluffton instilled hope that more children could get a high school diploma.

Located in the middle of Gullah communities and not far from the First African Baptist Church, the junior high school was named for Bill Robinson, who owned a house on Hilton Head and provided substantial funding toward the cost of the school.

The school had three teachers. Each teacher had a separate classroom, along with a small side porch. For the first time, all grades were not crowded into one room. The gray-painted school had a nice architectural style, and a post to hitch marsh tackies, but it lacked indoor plumbing. A parade of students continued to go to and from the outhouses, as they had in the community schools.

Local teachers Ruth Jones, Rosalie Barnwell, and Diogenese Singleton taught at the school, along with a few teachers from off-island. Miss Jones was one of the first women on the island to earn a college degree in education.[12] Early in her life, she had been a student

Robinson Middle School. *Courtesy of the Coastal Discovery Museum, Ed Wiggins*

Ruth Jones. *Collection of Thomas C. Barnwell, Jr.*

at the Seabrook School that Booker T. Washington and William Clyde had established in the early 1900s.

An attractive woman, Miss Jones wore her hair back in a bun most of the time. She had milk white teeth, a dark brown complexion, and, to her students, always seemed to be made up.

After growing up on Hilton Head, she had lived in New York and changed her speech. She did not speak Gullah. "She spoke very crisp. She was quite a teacher," Campbell would recall, "and gosh, what a talker. She seemed so worldly. She taught English well, and she taught social studies."

Miss Jones had a large roll-down map of the world. She would unroll the map, point to Hilton Head, and then point to Africa. Her students had never seen such a map or known where Africa was. Sometimes she walked down the classroom aisles and said to a student, "You look like you could have come from Ethiopia," and then told the next student where his family may have come from.

She also helped spearhead the annual Emancipation Day on January 1. People in the Sea Islands had celebrated Lincoln's Proclamation of Emancipation every year since 1863, and still did.

"She instilled pride in us. Whenever we talked about black history, black heroes, and emancipation and slavery, there was always a sense of accomplishment," Campbell said.

Miss Jones was a stickler, though, when it came to grammar. She had her students diagramming sentences and learning how to use subjects and verbs. "She was very tough . . . we had to put Gullah on the back seat. If she heard someone say, 'He dah bother me, Miss Jones,' meaning he is bothering me, or 'turn round, stop look at me,' she would ask, 'Now how do you say that?'"

The students listened. Whether they wanted to or not, many knew they had to learn "proper" English. Even in the 1940s, some students knew that they would need to go off the island to find work and be able to send money back to their families, and then, if they could, return home someday. The money helped Gullah families have enough to live on. Getting rid of some of their Gullah speech would allow them to hold better jobs off-island.

The boys and girls were young, though. At recess time, when they rushed out to the playground, they would sneak in some Gullah.

About this same time, Tom Barnwell was in Orangeburg at Claflin College, a historically black college founded in 1869 and affiliated with the United Methodist Church. His teachers found "something a little different" in the way he talked and worked with him to change his Gullah.

The few new white residents on Hilton Head would look at each other and say, "The people talk funny." The language Gullah people had spoken since their forced arrival on Hilton Head would begin to fade away.

Jake and Eliza Brown, who opened the first juke joint on the island. *Courtesy of the Coastal Discovery Museum*

Time moved faster and faster. The slow island days of the past disappeared. Juke joints set the tempo. Back when the marines had been stationed on the south end of the island, Jacob "Jake" Brown and his wife, Eliza, had opened the first juke joint on the island. It served

Buckingham landing, the *Pocahontas* ferry, 1953. *SCDOT Archives*

Buckingham landing, the *Pocahontas* ferry, 1953. *SCDOT Archives*

good Gullah cooking and had a fancy jukebox with colored lights. The marines had flocked to the juke to listen and dance to music from a genuine jukebox. Put a nickel in the slot and music, music, music poured out.

Most Gullah communities had juke joints now; they were simple buildings, sometimes set under sprawling oak trees, usually just a few yards away from the owner's home, and popular with adults and teenagers alike. A juke could be so small that only one couple could dance at a time, or have space for many couples trying out new 1950s dances.

Juke, an African-derived word, means *disorderly*, as Turner had learned. Hilton Head patrons usually were more fun-loving than disorderly, but some teenagers

began to skip evening prayers at the praise house to go to the jukes. This was a major departure from traditional Gullah life.

A small state-run ferry began running between the mainland and Hilton Head in 1953. Olin McIntosh built twenty beach cottages at Folly Field Beach. The cottages sold, and the ferry could not handle enough passengers in the weekend stampede to get back to the mainland.

Gullah families owned between one and a half and two miles of beachfront in the Chaplin area. Folly Field had long been a favorite for islanders. Gullah families often went there for picnics at least once a year, as did big gatherings of church groups.

Other than those gatherings, Gullah people used

the beaches for fishing. People in Chaplin traditionally caught fish from the beach, including huge drums, twenty to thirty pounds or more.

After the ferry started, the Bradley, Ferguson, and Singleton families opened their beach property for recreation. Black families from Savannah, who had little or no access to beaches under segregation, frequented the Chaplin beaches. Singleton Beach had a pavilion and a coin-operated juke box, which attracted both islanders and visitors from Easter to Labor Day.

The Gullah community schools closed in 1954, replaced by a consolidated elementary school for all black children on the island. The new school was all brick with central heat and shining tile floors. It held about two hundred children, grades one through six, and had a cafeteria and an auditorium. It was a huge change from the five one-room schools with outhouses and wood stoves.[13] Arthur "Sonny" Brown, a Gullah man, helped make it possible by selling some of his land at a price the school board could afford.

When the Beaufort County area superintendent of schools came to Hilton Head to tell blacks they would be getting a new school, Ben White respectfully told him that he did not believe it.[14] White had reason to say so, given the county's history of paltry funding for Gullah schools on Hilton Head. That he was wrong was a rarity due to outside events.

Determined to head off school desegregation, South Carolina Governor James F. Byrnes had convinced the General Assembly to levy a 3 percent sales tax to fund an "Education Revolution." Millions of dollars were poured into an effort to make black schools equal to white ones. Byrnes wanted to show that "separate but equal" schools could work.[15]

Byrnes also knew that the NAACP Legal Defense Fund had brought suit against a South Carolina school board in the U.S. District Court in Charleston the previous year.

Parents in Summerton, South Carolina, had asked the school board to provide school buses for black students, as they did for whites. Some black students walked up to eight miles to get to school. The school board ignored the request. Parents then complained of inadequate school buildings.

By the time the suit was filed in 1950, it had blown into a full attack on school segregation, based on the equal protection clause in the Fourteenth Amendment. The NAACP lost the case but appealed to the U.S. Supreme Court. The South Carolina case would become one of five suits rolled into *Brown v. Board of Education*.

Black residents were proud of the new school, even though they knew it was an effort to stave off integration. In addition to being a fine facility, the school attracted talented teachers and a new principal, Isaac Wilborn, a black educator originally from Elloree, South Carolina.[16]

In the five years since the timbermen had come,

Bridge construction, 1956. *SCDOT Archives*

ger would need to row their bateaux to the mainland nor pay a small amount to ride in a Gullah-owned motorboat or on the state-run ferry. Most people thought of the bridge as an improvement, so the bridge by itself did not cause a ruckus. Everything came to a head when Gullah people learned of developers' plans to zone the island.

one change after another had occurred. A much bigger change was on the way. A bridge connecting Hilton Head to the mainland was under construction.

Everyone could see the pilings for the bridge going up in March 1955. Black workmen in denim jeans, heavy shirts, and work boots worked on the bridge day after day.[17] The developers had found private financing for the bridge and contracted with the State Department of Transportation to supervise the work.

When the bridge was finished, Gullah people no lon-

Completed Old Hilton Head Bridge, officially named the James F. Byrnes Bridge. *From the collection of Vernie Singleton*

Chapter Twenty-Two

THE BRIDGE ARRIVES

A RUMOR SPREAD of some Gullah people setting fires on the north end of the island, on land owned by the Honey Horn Plantation. Tom Barnwell was in college at the time but heard the rumor on a visit home. Emory Campbell was still on the island but did not hear the rumor.

No one was ever caught. But whether or not the rumor was true, Gullah people's tempers boiled over in early 1955.[1]

State legislator J. Wilton Graves had sponsored a bill in the General Assembly to reshape land use on the island. Gullah people believed that the bill would force people who lived along the road in Stoney off their land.

Graves was no stranger. He first came to Hilton Head in 1950, an ambitious young white man seeking a seat as a Beaufort County state representative. Since Gullah people now could vote in the Democratic primary, he sought their vote.

The state capitol did not have any elected black officials. Black candidates could not get enough votes in the Democratic primary to be elected. But the votes of black voters could influence which white candidates won.

Graves had promised he would be a good state representative. Gullah islanders who were registered to vote gave him their votes. Graves also promised the timbermen-turned-developers that he would support their development efforts. He won the election, returned to Hilton Head, and opened the island's first real estate office.

When the bridge was completed Stoney would be the first community that people would see as they drove onto the island. "Downtown Stoney" was the pride and joy of Gullah people. Charlie Simmons brought the mail from Savannah to the post office, where it was handed out three times a week, and Gullah people rode their marsh tackies into Stoney to get their mail. The new elementary school increased the number of people coming and going to Stoney. Kinley's, a combination neighborhood store and juke joint, kept people coming weekdays and weekends.

Businesses lined the blacktop road the marines, with the help of some black men in the community, had built during World War II. A barber shop cut hair, roadside stands sold home-grown produce and other items, and the small wooden houses of Gullah people dotted the roadside.

The bridge would allow well-heeled people to drive to the island, but a developer still had to entice people to buy beach houses or land. Outsiders saw the small houses as shacks and eyesores. In the view of Gullah people, the new zoning would give developers a way to get rid of the small houses and make the entrance to the island more acceptable to the public.

The land meant something different to the people who lived on the island. They'd whitewashed their houses while they'd plowed their beans. To them their house was not a shack. It was home.

Graves's bill would create the "Hilton Head District," including Hilton Head Island, Jenkins Island, and Hog Island, between Skull Creek and Jenkins Island. A three-member planning commission, approved by the governor, would govern the district.

One provision dictated that no buildings or structures could be built within one hundred feet on each side of the center of existing (or future) state highways or other major thoroughfares on Hilton Head, Pinckney, and Jenkins Islands.

"Existing structures" within the buffer zone could not be enlarged by more than 20 percent, nor rebuilt if the cost was more than 100 percent of the assessed value of the building at the time of the passage of the act.

The planning commission for the island had the power of eminent domain to remove or purchase buildings in the buffer zone. The use of any structure erected, altered, or maintained in violation of the act would be a misdemeanor, punished by not more than one thousand dollars or by imprisonment for not more than six months. The bill also included an appeal process.

As the commissioners and their employees would have salaries and expenses, sufficient millage would be levied, "upon all taxable property in the Hilton Head District" and collected by the treasurer of Beaufort County.

No one had discussed the proposed bill with Gullah

residents, who would not have agreed with the provisions, or in many cases, been able to pay the new tax. They had been ignored and completely discounted on the island where their ancestors had lived for up to two centuries.[2]

The bill had been introduced in the state house on January 11, the first day of the 1955 session. On February 19, the governor signed it into law. It went into effect on that date, before Gullah people had even heard of it.

Graves got a telephone call from someone on the island telling him he needed to get back to Hilton Head and talk to black residents of the island.[3] Whoever called convinced him. He arrived for a meeting with islanders in early spring while the General Assembly was still in session. They met in the new consolidated elementary school.

Fourteen-year-old Emory Campbell attended the meeting with his brother Herb and his father Reginald. "It seemed like everybody on the island who was old enough to be there was there, it seemed like a huge number of people," Campbell said. The auditorium held two hundred people. It was packed.

The ever-present American flag with its stars and stripes stood on the auditorium's wooden stage, flanked by the state flag, with its crescent moon and palmetto tree on a blue background. The wooden stage rose an impressive three feet above the seating for the audience.

Graves, Hack, and at least one other man, sat on the stage in brown folding chairs, which were considered an improvement over the wooden benches in the old community schools. The men on the stage were white. The audience mainly was black.

Graves, a man with a receding hairline and eyeglasses, rose to speak—and listen—to islanders. He stood behind a podium. Campbell would not remember what either Graves or Hack said. He was more impressed with listening to four members of the audience.[4]

Benjamin White, Sr., who always spoke loudly and eloquently, could be outspoken if he saw the need. "He saw the need this time." He spoke against the plan "with his mouth wide open," Campbell said.

James "Son" Frazier, a short man with a way with metaphors, who lived down the way from the Campbells, was there. He had been in the army in World War II and said he would fight again.

"Mr. Toomer was there. He definitely was with us." S. V. Toomer, Jr., a longtime white islander, lived in Stoney, and was concerned about his neighborhood and his oyster business. Gullah men went out to get the oysters in their own boats, and Toomer bought oysters from them. "He needed them, and they needed him. It was a mutual need."

Charlie Simmons, whom Graves had asked to vote for him in 1950, said, "Mr. Graves, you told us you were gonna do right. This isn't right."

"Graves's face blanched. He could count the voters in the auditorium," Campbell said. "He was between a rock and a hard place, and he was about to lose his constituency. He had black voters and three white men with money. Not enough white people had moved to the island yet to re-elect him."

The entire county was majority black. Bluffton was 60 to 70 percent black. Some Gullah islanders rowed their boats through the waterways to Bluffton and sold their oysters to an oyster factory Graves's brother owned. Others shucked oysters on Bluffton. Word of Hilton Head Gullah islanders' discontent would spread throughout Graves's district.

Graves had heard enough. He went back to Columbia and got the law establishing the Hilton Head District repealed. The governor signed his name to repeal the act on April 22, 1955.[5]

It was a red, white, and blue moment: a rare moment of democracy in the segregated South. Had it been a decade later, with the civil rights movement in full swing, had news cameras been whirling, audiences would have seen black citizens politely, but firmly, presenting their grievances, and their legislator returning to the state capitol to change the law. As it was, no record or minutes were kept.

"We knew the civil rights movement was coming. We were living our rights," Campbell said. The Supreme Court had ruled against school segregation in *Brown v. Board of Education*. In December, Rosa Parks would refuse a Montgomery bus driver's order to give up her seat in the colored section of a public bus to a white passenger. Her arrest for civil disobedience would trigger the Montgomery Bus Boycott.

Gullah people went home euphoric over their victory.[6]

Their voting power would lessen as more newcomers moved to Hilton Head. But they were safe for now.

The big day arrived—May 19, 1956. The bridge connecting Hilton Head to the mainland would be dedicated at a noon ceremony.

The crossing consisted of a causeway and two sets of bridges: a low bridge over Mackay Creek and a drawbridge over Skull Creek.

Officially, the crossing was the "James F. Byrnes Crossing" in tribute to the former governor. Most people simply referred to the crossing as "the bridge."

A brief morning ceremony took place first at Buckingham Landing on a small piece of land near the new causeway. Governor Byrnes watched the unveiling of a roadside plaque honoring him, as a photographer snapped pictures. The plaque, set in a vertical stone slab, bore an engraved portrait of Byrnes, his name, and his biographical details.[7]

Byrnes wore what appeared to be a white linen suit, popular among white southern politicians. He held a hat in his hand, with the crown turned toward him. His wife, Maude, held a huge bouquet of flowers with stems that ran down her waist.[8] They then were rushed

Bridge construction, James F. Byrnes Crossing, 1956.
SCDOT Archives

across the bridge to Hilton Head, with enough time only for Byrnes to shed his white suit for more comfortable clothing.

Lieutenant Governor Ernest (Fritz) Hollings read aloud a list of Byrnes's many accomplishments. A native South Carolinian, Byrnes had served in the U.S. House of Representatives from 1911 to 1925, the U.S. Senate from 1931 to 1941, the U.S. Supreme Court from 1941–1942, and then headed the Office of War Mobilization. He had so much influence with President Roosevelt

that some dubbed him the "assistant president." After Roosevelt died, Byrnes became secretary of state under President Truman from 1945 to 1947. *Time* magazine had named him the man of the year in 1946.[9]

Byrnes had left much unfinished. After *Brown v. Board of Education*, he had stopped pouring money into black education. His efforts, and all state efforts, switched to maintaining school segregation as long as possible.

He stepped into the waiting car and was whisked to Hilton Head, across the bridge that bore his name.[10]

Everyone had been invited to the main ceremony, Gullah people included. Hundreds of cars sat on the grounds of Honey Horn Plantation. A thousand people crowded onto the grounds for this day. More white people were gathered on Hilton Head than at any time since the Civil War.

South Carolina elected officials arrived in full force, with their numbers including Hollings, who would become the next South Carolina governor; Mendel Rivers, longtime member of the U.S. House of Representatives; and Strom Thurmond, who eight years earlier had lost his run for president on the States' Rights Democratic (Dixiecrat) Party ticket and was again a U.S. senator. The presidents of the University of South Carolina and Clemson University, both all-white institutions, also attended. Wilton Graves was present as a member of the Beaufort County delegation and the island's new toll-bridge authority.[11]

The political big guns came out of respect for Byrnes, hailed as "Mr. South Carolina," but May 19 also was Armed Forces Day. The developers got full cooperation by tying the bridge opening to a patriotic day.

A parade of military units representing the army, the air force, the Parris Island marine depot, the Citadel, and Clemson University kicked off the ceremony. "As the troops passed in review with massed colors flying," the *Charleston Evening Post* reported, "a silvery Navy blimp floated overhead and soon made way for a fly-over by a roaring jet aircraft."

Gullah teenagers, including Emory Campbell, watched the bands and the roaring jet with excitement, but did not pay much attention to dignitaries' speeches. Speeches could not compete with marching bands.

The president of the University of South Carolina, Donald S. Russell, praised Byrnes for championing the principles of states' rights, and mentioned Byrnes's desire to see the power of the Supreme Court curbed.

Russell did not appear to find it odd to praise states' rights, a term frequently used to defend segregation, while on a majority-black island.

The next day's newspapers would err in their reporting about Gullah people.

The *News and Courier* would write, "Most of the 1,000-odd inhabitants are Negro farmers, the majority of whom own small acreages . . . and after the [Civil] war a large part of the land was given to the Negro in-habitants by the federal government." The *Evening Post* report would vary only slightly, saying that "much of the plantation land was divided among the former Negro slaves by the federal government."[12]

The federal government had never "given" or "divided" a large part of Hilton Head's land into small plots for formerly enslaved men and women. The federal government had held onto much of the island for many years after the war.

Few outsiders knew how Gullah families had scraped and pinched to buy and hold onto land for close to a century. Few outsiders knew anything of the numerous accomplishments made by Gullah men and women of Hilton Head. Most knew almost nothing about the Gullah history of Hilton Head.

But the *Evening Post* was correct in one observation. The new crossing would make Hilton Head Island's "twenty miles of wide beaches easily accessible for the first time." Hilton Head's isolation ended this day. Gullah people did not know it yet.

Some Gullah people were happy to see the bridge come, and some were not. Arthur Frazier, store owner and entrepreneur, said in a booming voice, "Let the people come." His father, Daniel "Lemon" Frazier, didn't want to see the bridge come to the island. He said people were going to get their property for little or nothing. Ben

Completed Old Hilton Head Bridge, officially named the James F. Byrnes Bridge. *From the collection of Vernie Singleton*

White, who did not live to see the bridge come, had long predicted that someday every square inch of Hilton Head would be valuable. He would be proven right.

Most islanders saw the bridge with optimistic eyes. They saw convenience and the freedom to leave and come back to the island as they pleased. Emory Camp-bell and other students soon would cross the bridge to attend the Michael C. Riley public high school in Bluff-ton. For one woman, the bridge made the difference be-tween life and death.

Mary Lawyer Green, in childbirth with her first child and attended by a midwife, underwent serious compli-

View of current bridge
from mainland to Hilton
Head from Skull Creek.
Photo by Will Warasila

cations, passed out, and opened her eyes in a Savannah infirmary. Thomas Barnwell, Sr., took her across the bridge and on to Savannah in his green truck, the "Carry All." Her doctor said that if she had gotten there thirty minutes later, she probably would have died. She fared well, and her son would grow up to be a corporal in the U.S. Army.[13]

Almost two hundred thousand people paid the $2.50 toll to cross the bridge the first year. When the summer of 1956 ended, the developers had sold three hundred homes to visitors.[14] More than one beach house sprang up the next year.

Tolls were cut in half in mid-1957. Up to fifteen thousand visitors came on peak summer days, a huge increase over the resident population, which had numbered slightly more than one thousand before the bridge. Tolls ended in December of 1959. People moved freely across the bridge. The real development began then.

PART II. GULLAH CULTURE AND COLLECTED MEMORIES

Row boats in Skull Creek. *Photo by Will Warasila*

(*Overleaf*) William Kellerson with marsh tacky horse plowing his field along U.S. Highway 278, the main road traversing through the Chaplin community on Hilton Head Island. In the background is the first store owned and operated by Abraham Grant, Kellerson's nephew and father of author Carolyn Grant. *Collection of Abraham Grant and Charliemae Grant*

GULLAH CULTURE

I was nearly a half-century old when I realized that the culture in which I was born, Gullah, contains uniquely rich folklore and a fascinating distinguished idiom.— *Emory S. Campbell (born 1941, Spanish Wells Community)*

Gullah culture combines folk beliefs, spiritual beliefs, music, crafts, foodways, and language traits into a distinctive way of life stamped with West African influences. This culture was introduced by West and Central Africans brought to the United States of America along the coasts of North Carolina, South Carolina, Georgia, and northern Florida during more than two centuries of the African slave trade. African descendants continued to practice their beliefs in their new homeland, kept as many traditions alive as possible, adapted them to their new environment, and shaped them into an enduring culture.

The more isolated the island, the more traditions held. Hilton Head Island (between Savannah, Georgia, and Charleston, South Carolina) long remained one of most isolated of the sea islands.

The Gullah way of life thrived until a bridge from the mainland to Hilton Head opened the way for massive development in 1956. But aspects of the Gullah culture still exist.

GULLAH LANGUAGE

The word *Gullah* often is used interchangeably to describe both the people and the way they speak.

"Enty?"

Enty in Gullah means "Is it not so?"

Add the word *oona*, which means *you*, and a Gullah person might say, "Oona gwine chu'ch enty?" The English equivalent is "You are going to church, aren't you?"

It once was commonplace for a visitor to Hilton Head to hear the word *oona* used in a greeting. "We glad fa see oona," means "We [are] glad to see you."

Gullah speech lay at the heart of Hilton Head's African-influenced culture before the island's isolation

Trees and Spanish moss on Hilton Head Island. *Photo by Will Warasila*

During the Civil War, northerners who arrived on Hilton Head and other sea islands had trouble understanding the newly freed men, women, and children, also referred to as "contrabands." Likewise, the contrabands had trouble understanding the speech of northerners.

Even famed Underground Railroad conductor Harriet Tubman had difficulty talking with Gullah people at first. Tubman spent time on Hilton Head and in Beaufort while serving as a scout for the Union. Her dialect carried the accent of the Eastern Shore of Maryland where she grew up as a slave. "Dey laughed when dey heard me talk, an' I could not understand dem, no how," Tubman said.[1]

Missionary Elizabeth Botume said her head "grew dizzy with the speech."

A teacher working on sentence structure with Gullah students during the Civil War instructed his students to look out the window. He then asked, "What color is the sky?"

He expected his students to answer him in a complete sentence. But no one spoke. Finally, one student said "white" then "red."

A former house slave walked by the window, looked in at the baffled teacher and the baffled students, and asked what the problem was.

The teacher explained, and the man grinned and asked a student, "Tom, how sky *stan'*?"

"Blue," Tom shouted.[2]

The phrasing was peculiar English to the teacher, but

ended. Gullah people spoke to each other in Gullah, shared their joys and grief in Gullah, and dreamed in Gullah. Gullah speech bound them together as a people. But the way Gullah people spoke mystified outsiders for well over a hundred years.

the students understood it at once. To a Gullah speaker, the word "stand" referred to "the state or condition of a person, place, or thing." So the former house slave's question made perfect sense to the students.

The sentence, "Tom, how sky *stan'*?" also lacked a verb, which did not faze the students. Gullah people grew up speaking short, rapid phrases rather than straight-out, full sentences. They appreciated "efficient English."

The roots of Gullah speech go back to the African slave trade. When the British dominated the slave trade in the 1700s, they needed to communicate with African traders. Because of their need, an English-based creole sprung up along the West African coast. The creole blended elements of English and African languages.

English words formed the base of the creole, but African languages changed the pronunciation of most of the English words and "influenced the grammar and sentence structure, and provided a sizable minority of the vocabulary."[3] The Gullah pronunciation of shrimp as "swimp" shows how African languages changed the pronunciation of English words.

The new hybrid language successfully allowed British and African traders to conduct business with each other. Soon, some African people adopted it as a "common tongue" to communicate with other African ethnic groups.[4]

Whether any enslaved Africans who arrived on Hilton Head were familiar with this common tongue is unknown. It is certain, however, that enslaved Africans had to surmount huge language barriers.

Speech traits varied on each sea island and even on different plantations on the same island, depending in large degree on how many speakers of the same African language group were represented on a particular island or plantation and when they arrived.

Imagine being offloaded from a slave vessel after weeks or months at sea, sold on the auction block, and brought to Hilton Head. A "fresh" African saw dark-skinned people who looked as if they were pure-blood African, but he or she might not understand what they were saying. If that were the case, the fresh African had to quickly learn the local speech in order to get along with others and to become a member of the plantation community.

At least twenty-seven African languages were blended into Gullah as it developed on the sea islands. Among others were the Wolof, Malinke, Mandinka, Bambara, Fula, Mende, Vai, Twi, Fante, Ewe, Yoruba, Bini, Hausa, and Kongo languages.[5]

The creole resembled an African language, yet it differed from any single language found in Africa. Gullah eventually became a language of its own.

Outsiders often labeled Gullah or "Geechee" as everything from "bad English" to "broken English," "peasant English," or "corrupt English." Even outsiders who considered Gullah picturesque often failed to understand what they were hearing. Many were convinced that the harshness of slavery had destroyed all memories of an African past.

Then Lorenzo Dow Turner came to the sea islands. Turner was the first African-American researcher to study the sea islands. The child of an enslaved mother and a freeborn father, he was born in North Carolina. He and several other members of his family moved to Maryland while he was still young. Turner eventually earned a master's degree from Howard University and a PhD from Roosevelt University in Illinois.

Turner remembered the South and the realities of segregation and was able to relate to members of the Gullah community more than most white researchers had been. This proved an advantage, as Gullah men and women opened up to him more than they had to former researchers. He interviewed Gullah people for several years, spending a total of fourteen months in the sea islands of South Carolina and Georgia.

In the summer of 1933, he interviewed three Hilton Head residents who spoke to him about hard times during the Great Depression. The more Turner met the people, the more he realized that their speech differed from anything he had heard before, something that could only be explained by African roots. He then set out to study African languages and make connections.

Some of the words that Turner identified were private "basket names," the names Gullah people for generations had given their children after they were born. These names often were not revealed outside the family and had been largely unheard by white researchers. Turner linked about three thousand personal names and words to West African languages.

Turner's 1949 book, *Africanisms in the Gullah Dialect*, stirred controversy, but also eventually made Turner known as the "Father of Gullah Studies." As the result of his work and subsequent research by other researchers, the Gullah Geechee language became recognized as the only "distinct African-American creole in the United States."[6] The recognition increased the Gullah marvel that their African ancestors had managed to pass down language traits that have persisted for more than two hundred years.

FOLK STORIES

Gullah people were prolific storytellers. It was almost as if you could shake a person and the stories would come tumbling out—if the setting was right and the storyteller was among Gullah people.

Folklorist Elsie Clews Parsons found that out when she came to Hilton Head Island in 1919 to compile tales told in the sea islands. She stayed in the Marshland community, in the home of Gullah residents James and Pinky Murray, to whom she in part dedicated the book she wrote. Murray, about thirty-five years of age, was a farmer and a former boatman.

"James Murray, in whose cabin I had been enjoying a very good and fruitful time, told me that, had I staid on in the house of the white-man where I first suggested storytelling, he would not have told me no tales," not "fo' no money, not fo' a week. . . . We don' boder wid dem, and dey don' bother wid us. We wouldn't tell riddle befo' dem, not even if we was a servan' in deir house."

However, with guides like the Murrays and Miss Justin Brown of Spanish Wells, then about sixty-five years old, Parsons managed to gather tales. Those she got ranged from animal stories to tall tales and a few tales Murray said were only fitting for men to hear. The following tale from James Murray fits into the category of a tall tale.

Once I was goin' in de woods, an' I had a muskit-gun. An' I look down de riber, an' I see a duck. I look up on de hill, an' I se a rabbit. I look down in de woods, an' I see a drove of wil' turkey. Now, I study how I was goin' to get all dese t'ings, an' I didn't have but one gun. So den I say, "Well, I take my chances, I shoot down de riber at de duck." De shot kill de duck. Ramrod come back up an' kill de wil' turkey. De hammer jump off de gun an' kill de rabbit. I t'ought to myself dat was well done.[7]

The first Africans brought animal stories to Hilton Head, and the stories told on the island evolved from there. Many were "trickster" stories in which the mischievous Bro' Rabbit easily outwitted Bro' Bear, Bro' Fox, and other animals.

Bro' Rabbit, small as he was, used his wiles to outwit larger animals having more brawn. That was a message for adults as well as for children. Similar stories developed about slaves outwitting their masters.

In those stories, the masters had the power, and enslaved persons were the ones who thought on their feet to outwit their masters and gain a little something for themselves. That "little something" might be a rare piece of meat in their diet or getting out of a whipping. Whatever stories were told, the enslaved person usually came out on top.

No two storytellers told the same story alike. Each one delighted in adding twists and changes to an old tale, putting a personal stamp on it, and delighting listeners with the storyteller's ingenuity. Pitch, tone, faster pace, slower pace, and emphasis on certain words combined to keep people laughing. Hilton Head storytellers were performers, and storytelling was both an art form and an oral tradition.

The stories were for amusement, but they also helped islanders endure hard times.

Mama was really my first storyteller 'cause she told me stories, stories I remember up until today. I mean exactly how she told 'em. A lot of times it wasn't a sitting, it was just like a teachin', you know, but you hear and you store it.—*Louise Cohen (born 1943, Squire Pope Community)*

The following tales are from Hilton Head Gullah native and storyteller Louise Cohen:

Hilton Head Island native Louise Miller Cohen, Gullah storyteller and founder of the Gullah Museum of Hilton Head Island. *Photo from Gullah Museum of Hilton Head Island website*

The Crane and the Eel

[Mama] say, "Well Louise, you know the crane got straightgut?" It probably got one intestine, right? There was the one crane in the pond and the one eel. The crane would eat the eel and the eel would suck right on out the rear end and the crane would eat the eel and the eel would slip right on out the rear end. And the crane keep right on eating the eel, the eel kept on sliding out, and the crane look around and say, "God, plenty eel in this pond today."

Cow Guts Creek

Massah come looking for this man, this slave, one day. He asked his little boy, "Johnny, where is your pa?" So Johnny said, "Pa gon' for throw the cow guts in the creek, suh." Ma heard him, said, "Johnny, turn 'round, turn 'round." That mean turn the story around. So then when he ask again, "Boy, I said where is your pa," Johnny said, "Oh, Pa gon' to Cow Guts Creek, suh."

Many Americans are just now coming to appreciate that the animal tales Gullah people tell have deep African roots. In 1880, when Joel Chandler Harris's, *Uncle Remus, His Songs and His Sayings* was published, Harris, a white journalist, wanted to preserve the stories he had heard in the 1840s from two elderly black men on a cotton plantation. A myth took hold, however, that Harris had created the tales himself. This made Gullah people even more wary of sharing their stories with outsiders.

FOLK BELIEFS

Many elements of the Gullah belief system likely came from Africa or were adapted from African beliefs. Some related to Gullah spirituality. Others were based on observations of natural occurrences, such as those relating to the moon and the tides.

Signs and sayings provided guidance for a people who lived close to the land. People lived by them. They helped people make it through tough times and good ones. And if you were a youngster, you didn't ask "why" questions about a belief. You did as told. These were beliefs that everybody followed.

Before the bridge to the mainland was built, many signs were handed down on Hilton Head Island. Among these were:

- Most children are born when the tide is high or flooding.
- If born when the moonshining [the moon is full], it will take a while for a child to open up its eyes. [The light from the moon prevents the child from doing so.]
- Dream of fish, somebody in the family is pregnant.
- If you plant off the sign, all you get is vine. [This refers to the stage of the moon.]
- Crab on high tide are not as fat. They're just floating along the water. Crab on low tide in spring have more meat on them, are fatter.
- Rooster crow in the middle of the day, a stranger coming.
- Rooster come right to the door, somebody strange is coming and bad news gonna follow. [Then someone will say, "Oh, yeah, that rooster sure came with bad news. I knew that was gonna happen!"]

- If a woodpecker starts tapping on a tin roof, it's a sign somebody's gonna die. [Someone will say, "get that broom and knock that woodpecker away from here."]
- A certain way a dog would howl [a slow, mournful howl] if death coming. ["Stop that dog from howling out there," people would say.]
- A certain way a dog would get down and crawl meant that one would be measuring the grave.
- Airplane sounds a certain way when death's coming.
- If a black cat runs in front of you [signifying bad luck], turn around and go back unless it's running from right to left.
- If you stumble on your left foot, that's bad luck. Right foot, that's okay, but if you stumble on the left foot, turn around on the right foot around that stump you stumbled on.
- Point your finger at the graveyard and it will rot off unless you put it in water or in the ground.
- First day of the New Year—first thing in the morning, if a man who is not in the family crosses the doorstep and comes into the house and says good morning and walks out, then you will have good luck for the year.
- Pass baby over the grave [so the baby won't be bothered by the spirit of the dead].
- Don't sweep the dirt outside after dark. It's bad luck.

- Dream about water means rain.
- Dream about snakes, you have something to fight, some kind of temptation.
- Dream about a single snake, you have an enemy.
- Dream of a funeral, sign of a wedding. Dream of a wedding, sign of a funeral. [Some dreams meant the reverse of what the person dreamed about.]
- Dream that somebody is dead, they will live a long time. See anybody very sick and dream he is better, he is dead. Dream he is dead, he will be better.
- Dream of a man dying, it's a woman; dream of a woman dying, it's a man.
- Dream of family gathering interpreted as a funeral for someone in your family.

SPIRITS, HAGS, AND "ROOT"

Gullah people were fervent Christians and the church was the most important institution on the island. But they did not totally turn their backs on African spirituality. They believed that the two could exist together and blended both into their belief systems.

Examples of African-based beliefs were spirits (also sometimes called ghosts), hags, and "root." Early on, most people believed in these, although well-educated persons might put aside such beliefs.

Gullah people believed that the spirits of the dead could travel. They could visit you, provide you guidance, indulge in mischief, or, if restless or angry, trouble or haunt you. And sometimes, spirits just wanted to be noticed.

The people used to say when wind [was] spinning that was [the] old people' spirit come 'round. That's the way they figured it. "Oh, that's somebody coming now, see that wind blowin'. All the sand kickin' out. They just want let you know they in the yard." That's way they put it.—*Laura Mae Campbell (born 1918, Braddock's Point Community)*

In her mid-eighties, Laura Mae Campbell still recalled a woman named Georgie who saw ghosts.

Ooooh, Georgie could see the ghosts. You know when they used to have dances and thing[s] in the hall . . . Georgie and Richard, my uncle, use to come from Braddock's Point. And Richard would ride the horse, and Georgie would walk. And in the night, when the hall closes and [it was] time to go back home, it was dark.

Uncle Richard and my father and the horse [were] ahead of us. Now we can't see them, and they can't see us, but they know we behind.

Georgie tell me hold her han[d]. "You hold me, Laura, hold me." And I'm holdin' her. Then Georgie tell me the next day—Georgie say, "You know one thing? Ghosts walk with us all the way." I say, "What?!"

"Yes, the ghosts walk; somebody walkin' alongside. . . . That the old people guidin' us because it were dark. Mae, the road be full of ghosts, and they walk with us all the way until we get in our island gate."

Yeah, I know all about those things. I know about all the ol' people; I know about them. I came up with 'em.—*Laura Mae Campbell*

A hag was an old woman, sometimes the eldest community member. She could leave her body, enter your home through any small opening, jump on your back while you were sleeping and ride you, and you couldn't breathe. The next morning you'd wake up tired. A hag could come back night after night and even try to smother you. Some people believed you could trap a hag in a jar if you tricked her in and closed the lid. Older people in Hilton Head believed in hags; the younger ones loved hearing tales about hags. It was great entertainment to them.

I had an old cousin, old Betty, down in Savannah. She look almost like a man. She couldn't see. She was blind and she was a big lady too, no small lady. And myself and Stella, and Mary, we spend the night [there with an aunt and uncle].

"Oh my gosh. I know she gonna ride us tonight," we said. "You see that woman? She gonna ride us tonight!" And we go to bed, and you know she did ride one of us! She ride one.

We say, "I tell ya so. That ol' lady was gonna ride us." Lord, we had fun with that. . . . Did we believe? We had to believe it. Older people believe, so we believe it too.—*Laura Mae Campbell*

Gullah people on Hilton Head were great herbalists. They arrived from Africa knowing how to use herbs to heal illness. They made herbal remedies from plants and roots that grew on the island, much as their ancestors had in Africa.

The word *root* covered the use of roots and herbs in healing *and* in witchcraft, another practice that came from Africa. But when people spoke about "root" they usually were talking about witchcraft. Just as Africans had identified poisonous herbs in their homelands, some Gullah people knew the dangerous ones too. Thus, the idea that someone could do you harm held some truth to it. It was part of the Gullah belief system. Many people respected and feared "root workers" or "root doctors." A particular root doctor's potions might not be dangerous, but when people believed in them, root held power over them. A root doctor could mix up a potion that someone would buy to "fix" you (put a spell on you)—by slipping it into your food, for instance, or burying it in your yard.

Then if you went to a root doctor, he or she could sell you something to lift that spell off you and give you something to protect yourself from evil.

Many Gullah people believed in root well into the 1940s and 1950s, though some people stayed away from it and did not believe. As time went on more people began to scoff at root.

We hear about it, but we haven't had it happen.
—*Julia Grant Bryant (born 1915, lived in Squire Pope Community)*

I heard of some people do it [root]. Can't call [speak] the people' [names] . . . Some of 'em already done gone. Some people just believe in that. I know a lady right there not too far from me. They believe it. . . . And some might be true.—*Laura Mae Campbell*

[My maternal grandfather] . . . believed that a witchcraft worker inflicted the epilepsy that he infrequently suffered.—*Emory S. Campbell*

COMMUNITIES

Everybody knew everybody. It's a disgrace you pass somebody and didn't say "Hi" and didn't say "Good morning." You in a heap of trouble.—*Charlie Simmons, Jr. (born 1928, Spanish Wells Community)*

The freedmen's village of Mitchelville—the first village for freed slaves—had been a huge success in the 1860s, celebrated by northern newspapers, missionaries, Union army officers, and Gullah people. Built on an empty cotton field on Fish Haul plantation, it had become a model for freedom: Mitchelville proved that

Gullah people could conduct their own lives and live and work independently.

No one expected Mitchelville to disappear, but it almost did. Many of the people who lived in Mitchelville had been contrabands who had fled to Hilton Head in search of freedom. People born on Hilton Head made up a smaller proportion of Mitchelville residents.

After the Union left Hilton Head, many who had lived in the village and worked for the Union left in search of jobs elsewhere. The village dwindled, although some people always remained.

Other freedmen fanned out across the island. There was plenty of room for them, as the plantation owners were gone. Some freedmen moved onto plantations where northern cotton companies needed workers. Still others who had grown up on the island before the Civil War returned to their home plantations. And some Gullah families never left the plantation that was "home" to them.

As hard as it might be for outsiders to fathom, Gullah people felt a sense of community on the plantations where they grew up. They knew each other, had stood by each other during the war, and felt attached to the land where their families lived and their ancestors were buried. Leadership already existed in these communities. Each community had respected elders and praise-house deacons. In addition, Hilton Head's black Union soldiers returned from the Civil War with military experience that equipped them to be leaders.

Gullah people apparently did not see the need to change the names of some of the plantations they lived on. It did not, for instance, appear to matter to Matthew Jones—a former house servant of the Stoney family—that the area where he bought land was still called Stoney. Everyone who had grown up on the island knew the plantation as Stoney (or possibly Fairfield, another name for it). The name Stoney was by now traditional, and Gullah people held onto tradition.

Cotton Hope Plantation, owned by Squire Pope, the largest landowner on Hilton Head before the Civil War, got a minor tweaking of its name. Islanders began to refer to the plantation as Squire Pope instead of Cotton Hope.

Plantations had been owned by one landowner and then another for more than a century, and the land had been bought, sold, and inherited by a small, elite group of planters. The Stoneys, for instance, had once owned Otter Hole and sold it to the Stuarts (also spelled *Stewart*). William Seabrook had assembled the Seabrook plantation by buying tracts of land from other planters, including the Talbirds, or Talbots, as they were often called. Gullah people used the name "Talbot" to describe an area near Skull Creek where they maintained a burial site.

So the land had a layer-cake history. If Gullah people had decided to change the names of all of the plantations, choosing names would have required a good deal of thinking. Overall, it likely was easier to stay with the names they knew, get on with life, and then let some name changes come about gradually.

Only one community introduced an altogether new name—that of Jonesville. Caesar Kirk Jones and his sons acquired more than one hundred acres of land in an area near a small stream called Jarvis Creek. The area did not have a pre-set identification, so it was called Jonesville after the Joneses. It was the only community on the island originally settled and owned by Gullah people.

Meanwhile in the late 1920s and 1930s, several small communities disappeared after northern land barons bought the land. A number of people moved from Braddock's Point and the former Lawton plantation on the south end of the island to the north end of the island, where churches and other institutions were established.

Those who lived at Joe Pope/Leamington, bordered by the Atlantic Ocean and Broad Creek, also moved to the north end of the island. Among those was the family of a Gullah man who had served as lighthouse keeper.

Pre–Civil War plantations such as Possum Point and Point Comfort also fell off the list of places where Gullah people lived. Wealthy northerners bought the land from the families of former white planters and from Gullah people. A northern landowner—William P. Clyde—began to assemble a private retreat with hunting grounds on Hilton Head. Some former Gullah landowners in those areas moved to Spanish Wells or Jonesville.

As each change occurred, more Gullah people congregated on the northern end of Hilton Head. This became the area where Gullah communities dug in deep. Gullah communities have since remained on the north end of the island.

In the days of slavery, each plantation had been a village of its own. Enslaved people likely saw similarities between this and African village life. After freedom came, freedmen realized that each community needed to be a complete working unit. Every skill necessary for the community to exist had to be present among community members. That, plus the necessity to get along with each other, resolve disputes, and help each other in times of need, became bedrock principles for community life.

In addition, in each community Gullah people managed to buy a considerable number of acres, from twenty-five to fifty or sixty. The families that were able to purchase a significant amount of land clustered together, farming the land together and living in neighboring houses. Most communities also had access to waterways.

The communities that remained include Stoney, Jonesville, Spanish Wells, Gardner, Marshland, Chaplin, Grassland/Big Hill, Cherry Hill/Mitchelville, Baygall (which included the smaller settlements of Drayton and Fish Haul), and Squire Pope, which included Gumtree and Wild Horse. Each community was known for its distinct strengths and characteristics.

STONEY

Civil War veteran Matthew Jones was among the first black landowners in Stoney. By the 1900s, Stoney was filled with industrious people and entrepreneurs, making it the island's most vibrant business district. Some called it "downtown Hilton Head."

Between the 1900s and 1950s, several confectionaries and other businesses emerged. The island's first consolidated public school serving all black children and other businesses were established in Stoney. There were many black store owners, including Peter Drayton, Florence Robinson, Alex Patterson, Jr., and Arthur Frazier.

The most popular store was owned by Charles (Charlie) Simmons, Sr., and was considered so grand when it opened in the 1940s that local people nicknamed it after a well-known store chain in Savannah. It became the island's "Big Star."

"Big Star sold blue jeans, wood-burning stoves, and other items unavailable elsewhere on the island," his son, Charles Simmons, Jr., recalled. It was also the place to go for lantern oil, rice, turpentine, socks, and sundries for people living in the surrounding communities.

When the U.S. Postal Service decided to offer direct mail service to Hilton Head, a post office was located along the main thoroughfare of Stoney. People walked or rode horses for miles to pick up mail.

The midwife Adrianna Ford also lived in Stoney.

SQUIRE POPE

Neighboring Squire Pope, possibly the largest community in both population and area, was segmented into small areas. Gumtree, which later became known as Gumtree Road, took its name from a large gum tree that stood on one end of the road.

Squire Pope was known as a community of fishermen, boat operators, farmers, net makers, and others whose occupations stemmed from the proximity of the area to Skull Creek, the body of water that hugs the land near Talbird Cemetery (also known as Talbot Cemetery). Bountiful catches of fish, shrimp, and oyster came from Skull Creek. An oyster factor in the community, owned by a member of the Hudson family, a white family that had long lived on the island, provided jobs for many community members. Squire Pope also had a grits and corn mill, social clubs, a praise house, a church, burial societies, and several stores owned by William "Boney" Brown and Samuel Bryan.

Mount Calvary Missionary Baptist Church, founded in 1914, remains a defining institution in the community.

While many communities had a one-room school, Squire Pope had a two-room school with two teachers.

One community member, Georgianna Miller Barnwell of Squire Pope, lived to be 107 years old. Her memories of the area are described in chapter 14.

JONESVILLE

After being settled by the Jones family, Jonesville was a prime example of a kinship community, with related families living up and down the riverside, including uncles, aunts, first cousins, and others.

The people were willing to work to start and sustain businesses. Among shop owners was James "Son" Frazier, a blacksmith. In his blacksmith shop next to his home, he made anchors for boats and wagon wheels. The latter were essential items since horse-drawn wagons were the main mode of land transportation for Gullah people through the mid-1950s. He also made and repaired horse plows used by island families.

In addition to farms, stores, a sugar cane mill, and a Farmers Club Burial Society, Jonesville had many enterprises run by entrepreneurs like Daniel Frazier. Frazier was best known as a carpenter with a distinctive style. The roofs on the homes he built, for instance, were pitched higher than other homes on the island, and he added porches to homes, which for most families was a luxury. Other entrepreneurs included store owners Fred Owens and Naomi Frazier, who was known widely for her colorful floral arrangements. As people in Jonesville had often been able to acquire good land early on, many were considered prosperous. Even though there was a sense of equality among community residents, people in need often went to Jonesville for help.

The former community store owned by Fred Owens, near the Jonesville community. *Collection of Carolyn Grant*

SPANISH WELLS

The community of Spanish Wells has extensive access to waterways as the land laps along Broad Creek, Old House Creek, and Jarvis Creek. In the same vicinity were other smaller communities that blacks claimed as home—Muddy Creek, Broad Creek, and Nazarene (originally called Nazarith). The Spanish Wells named derived in the 1500s when Spanish explorers traveled along the local waterways. Spanish Wells was a stopping point for Spanish ships that came up from Florida. The ship crews dug fresh water wells along Broad Creek, thus the name Spanish Wells.

Gullah people in Spanish Wells became known for their maritime activities, including fishing, crabbing, and oyster harvesting. Among prominent people in the Spanish Wells area was Charles Simmons, Sr., who operated a number of boats over the decades that helped islanders travel back and forth to Savannah and transport their produce as well. Simmons was a pillar in the community and in the island overall and for many years also operated the island's main variety store from Spanish Wells. The Campbell family was another prominent family, with family members serving as teachers and church leaders.

School was held at a society hall on present-day Oakview Road, and following a fire at the society hall, it was moved to a praise house on Spanish Wells Road. Although Spanish Wells had a praise house, residents went to church with other congregations on the island.

GARDNER

Gardner Plantation was a large plantation bordering Broad Creek. The federal government sold land here to the Sea Island Cotton Company, thus making it ineligible for redemption by its pre–Civil War owners. The Sea Island Cotton Company in turn sold out to the United States Cotton Company. Both companies were owned by northerners and provided employment for Gullah men and women. When the two cotton companies bankrupted in 1896, the land fell to another northerner, who sold acreage to some Gullah people, and the bulk of the land eventually ended up going to another northern landowner.

Gullah resident March Gardner also had land in this area, as well as land in Mitchelville.

One Gardner family — the Aikens — can trace its history to "Jessie Goodwine Aiken, one of the slaves sold to cotton farmers along the South Carolina coast. . . . Jessie, his wife, Jennie, and their baby daughter, Katie, ran away from Pinckney Island and came to Hilton Head by boat. They settled in an area then known as Brownsville and raised five children: Katie, Martha, William, Peter, and Janie."[8] Later, a descendent of the Aiken Family, William "Brankey" Aiken became widely known for his expertise in using plants and herbs for medicine. Many residents sought his cures for their illnesses.

MARSHLAND

A large amount of land in the Marshland/Chaplin area was sold in an 1876 federal government tax sale to the following Gullah men: Adam Green, Edward Murray, Phoenix Robinson, Chance Ford, Moses Brown, and Prince Brown. This was the largest known sale of land through a federal government tax sale to Gullah people on Hilton Head.

Over the decades, many residents of Marshland made significant contributions to education and the economy. Among them were Alex Patterson, who operated a community store; John Patterson, who later provided transportation to and from Savannah, Georgia; and John's wife, Lucinda Frazier Patterson, a strong teacher who required her students to study hard. Christopher Green, Sr., Walter Green, and Mingo Green were sailboat builders. The Green family, considered among the top boat builders on the island, sold their boats to other people on the island. Their skills were extremely important to Gullah people, as their livelihoods depended upon the creeks, rivers, and oceans surrounding Hilton Head. Mingo Green and another Gullah man, George Murray, used their sailboats to transport loads of island-grown watermelon to markets in Savannah.

CHAPLIN

Among the Gullah families that settled in Chaplin after freedom were the Grants, the Burkes, the Singletons, the Christophers, and the Driessens. Chaplin, straddled between Broad Creek on one side and the Atlantic Ocean on its eastern side, was a four-hundred-acre plantation owned before the Civil War by one of two Chaplin brothers. (History does not record which.)

Gullah families that lived in Chaplin were very skilled at farming and netting large fish from the beach. Fishnet makers and basket makers lived here too. Farmers like James Grant and Solomon Grant eventually set up roadside stands and, along with their wives and children, sold homegrown vegetables, fruits, quilts, and other items.

William Kellerson with marsh tacky horse plowing his field along U.S. Highway 278, the main road traversing through the Chaplin community on Hilton Head Island. In the background is the first store owned and operated by Abraham Grant, Kellerson's nephew and father of author Carolyn Grant. *Collection of Abraham Grant and Charliemae Grant*

People frequently stopped by for freshly picked peas, beans, corn, tomatoes, plums, figs, and more. The scenic beaches at Chaplin provided picnic spots for Gullah people from many neighborhoods.

The community was home to several community stories owned by Henry Driessen, Sr., and Abraham Grant, who was too young to get a business license. His aunt, Beaulah Grant Kellerson, got the license for him. In later years, other businesses that catered to beach crowds sprung up. Popular spots included Singleton's Beach (also referred to as Collier Beach), Burke's Hideaway, and Bradley Beach.

Gertrude and Solomon Grant's produce stand. *Collection of Carolyn Grant*

GRASSLAND/BIG HILL

I always thought of Grassland as the farm and watermelon area. While growing up, you could always get good watermelon from Ben White, who lived and farmed in that community, and his son Johnny.
— *Emory S. Campbell*

Conrad Wiley, William "Kit" Ferguson, Benjamin White, Sr., and his son, Johnny, were large landowners there. They were considered some of the most successful farmers on Hilton Head in the late 1800s and early 1900s.

Ben White, Sr., continued to play a major role on Hilton Head into the early 1950s. Johnny White, his oldest son, became the first black person appointed from Hilton Head to serve a full term on the Southern Beaufort County Board of Education.

Under the leadership of Ben White, Sr., the White family continuously pushed for greater educational opportunities for Gullah people. Of the seventeen children Ben White, Sr., had by three wives, all but two earned college degrees.

While farming his own land, he also rented plots from others so that he could increase his farm yield. He produced a wide variety of crops such as watermelon, sweet potatoes, sugar cane, okra, peas, high and low bush beans, squash, cucumbers, and cantaloupes.

White sold most of his crops off-island. He shipped a lot of produce to Savannah through a ferry operated by Charlie Simmons, Sr., who made his living through boat operations. During the summer, White would charter many of the sailboats available on the island to take his produce to the Savannah Market, where many other farmers sold produce as well. The sailboat owners would be guaranteed to have at least two to three weeks of work from White alone.

White fine-tuned his farming work so that he could stay in Savannah to manage the sale of his produce. His farm crew would consistently send him more produce as it was picked.

White also was the first black man on the island to

Beachfront in the Chaplin community in 2019. *Photo by Will Warasila*

buy a brand-new Ford tractor. The tractor represented the result of years of steady labor. It also represented the shift in time from the horse-and-plow days to the industrialist era of the early 1900s, when machinery began to take the place of manual skills. In addition to using it on his own land, he would cultivate land for anyone on the island, marking off the number of acres he had cut. White's family named a road off Union Cemetery Road in Grassland—Ben White Drive—in his honor.

Conrad Wiley was another community advocate for education. A skilled and successful farmer and a deacon at Saint James Baptist Church, Wiley would give powerful talks to the church congregation to motivate members to send their children to school so they could get as much education as offered.

William "Kit" Ferguson, a large landowner in Grassland, joined the U.S. Army during World War I. Ferguson was known throughout the island for his oratory skills. He was diplomatic and extremely articulate. When others were afraid to speak up, Ferguson was not shy about giving his opinion or leading discussions on issues such as whether to extend the number of months for children to attend school or the responsibilities of parents to haul wood to the community schools to keep the children warm.

One distinct area of Grassland was known as "Sylby Tub"—a Gullah derivative of Sylvia's Tub. The area was marked by a small bridge that became known as Sylby Tub Bridge after a woman named Sylvia who lived near the bridge.

> She washed her clothes on one side [of the bridge] and rinsed them on the other side. When my mother and sisters would go out early in the morning to the field, Sylvia would be down there washing her clothes. And in the evenings, when they would be coming out of the fields, Sylvia would be taking her clothes off of the muckle [myrtle] bush on the side the ditch.— *Thomas C. Barnwell, Jr. (born 1935, Squire Pope Community)*

(*Left*) Benjamin White, Sr. He and his son, Johnny White, owned large parcels of land on Hilton Head and were considered to be among the most successful farmers on the island. *Photo Courtesy of Dr. David White*

(*Right*) Johnny White. *Collection of Maggie White Bruen, artist unknown*

MITCHELVILLE/CHERRY HILL

Long before other communities became permanent homes for blacks on Hilton Head Island, Mitchelville held the distinction of being the island's first township for Gullah families, as described in chapter 5. Churches, schools, stores, and other institutions arose from this experiment, and Gullah people ultimately gained opportunities to buy land in Mitchelville.

Cherry Hill School in 2019. *Photo by Will Warasila*

Cherry Hill was an outgrowth of Mitchelville. The most vivid landmark of Cherry Hill is the Cherry Hill School, a one-room schoolhouse patterned after the Rosenwald Schools that became common in rural communities in the South in the early 1900s.

BAYGALL/DRAYTON/FISH HAUL

The residents of Baygall were drum fisherman and big-game fisherman. The people of these communities displayed a unique cultural linkage to Africa—their speech, their patterns of fishing, their sea-faring way of life. They had a sense of closeness to Africa, and their communities were somewhat isolated from the other communities. The residents seemed isolated because the areas in which they lived were heavily wooded, and the access roads were almost nonexistent.

Fish Haul (also called Fish Hall and Drayton Plantation) had working rice and cotton plantations. After

Reconstruction, it was often referred to as Baygall. And there in Baygall was where Gullah residents Herbert Chaplin established a community store where residents bought an assortment of goods.

This community also stood out because of the number of religious institutions that existed along the nearby roadway. The most prominent was First African Baptist (FAB) Church, also frequently referred to as Cross Roads Church. Originally located in Mitchelville, the church moved to property on this stretch of road, which had yet to be named. The road, at that time, intersected with what was later named Matthews Drive, thereby giving the section its name—Cross Roads.

Other churches along the roadway included Queen Chapel African Methodist Episcopal Church, founded by missionaries in 1865, and Saint James Baptist Church, founded in 1883.

Just beyond FAB Church was Robinson Junior High School, which, in the late 1940s and early 1950s, provided instruction for children in the sixth, seventh, and eighth grades. The school was named for William Robinson, a white man from Gastonia, North Carolina, who often retreated to the island. He gave a large sum of money to build the school.

People in Gullah communities, for the most part, looked out for one another and shared a rich way of life. To them, life was good.

They was just happy people. They had things convenient for themselves. They were happy about it because they know that was their living, so they just live with it. I never was lonely a day. It was always be somebody coming down to see us. They really had everything organized for themselves. They didn't have too much education at that time but they was happy. No, nothing sad.—*Naomi Frazier (born 1905, Jonesville Community)*

Them people never fight and carry on and all kind of things like that. . . . They didn't fight and cut one another and do all kind of dirt and kill up one another like people is doing now.—*Nancy Ferguson (born 1901, Big Hill)*

At that time, to me, it was better than it is now. Because at that time, the people did not rush like they do now. The neighbors would come around when you were sick. They always had time for you. These days people wait until they do everything home before they go to you. But they didn't do that time. They leave everything and go to you to try to do what they can to help.—*Emma Graham (born 1907, Jonesville Community)*

My mother and Miss Helen used to get along when we were coming up. When one was sick, everything goes on. They had a way when we were, like if my mother would go to Savannah grocery shopping

this Saturday, half of what she gets goes to Miss Helen. Miss Helen do the same thing when she go to Savannah. If you go over to Miss Helen and do something, Miss Helen is going to whip you and when you get back home your mother is going to whip you. But nowadays if you spank these people' kids, now they are ready to take you to jail.
—*Elnora Aiken (born 1947, Marshland Community)*

If you were sick or something happened to you, the community would come together, and someone would always be there at that house. I don't care whether they working or what. I can remember that. They would always be there to help that person washing, cooking, whatever. Helping the children [or] whatever needed to be done.—*Mary Lawyer Green (born 1938, Squire Pope Community)*

If people had a problem they would get together and compromise. Most times they would handle it right just like that in the church. They never used to have problems over land and like that. Everybody had their own place, their own homes. I don't remember them ever having that kind of stuff. Not in my time. If they can't, they would go to the judge.

At that time, everybody seemed . . . the same. They never put on like people do now because they have a little. 'Cause they knew in those times that we bring nothing into the world and we carry nothing. They live that way. They don't live now

thinking they going to carry things. I know a couple of years ago, a man was talking to me about this lady that was well off, well to do. And had a lot of family, and none didn't do nothing for that poor woman and she was sick a long time. And after she died, and after the funeral, one of them wanted to know what did she left. So the undertaker said that he didn't see her carry nothing.—*Emma Graham*

FAMILIES AND DAILY LIFE

The people got it good now. 'Cause when we go to lay down [to sleep] we could see the stars out. [At my] mama's house [in Braddock's Point on the south end of Hilton Head]. . . [she would] look up through the loft and . . . see all the stars on the outside and all the water. . . . I don't want to see that now. Oh Lord have mercy.—*Regina Bennett (born 1902, Braddock's Point)*

When freedom came and Gullah people no longer worried about whether their children would be taken from them and sold to another plantation owner, a burden was lifted. There was an explosion of marriages on Hilton Head Island at First African Baptist Church, the only Gullah church on the island at that time.

Couples who had gotten married in the praise house or had jumped the broom got married again in the church, and soldiers returning from the war hugged their sweethearts and went to see the minister. Copies of marriage certificates on the island go back to 1866 or before.

When freedom came, newly married Gullah couples could now stay together "till death do we part." They could eat meals together, build their own houses, and devote more attention to their children.

Enslaved people on Hilton Head had valued family members before freedom. But after freedom, as families got stronger and stronger, family life was taken more seriously. Everyone in the family had their own roles and chores to do. There was little time to be idle.

But before you had a family, you had to have two people courting, and courting was done with the permission of the girl's father. After courting a sufficient time, sometimes six months to a year, the father or both parents would grant permission for the couple to get married.

I believe somebody musta tell 'im, somebody from over [in Spanish Wells] and. . . [he] row to find [me] over here [at Braddock's Point].

I see him comin', and he used to wear a white cap. When I see that cap comin', I run. I don' wanna see him a'tall. Oh then after a time you get used to it, you know.

You had to ask [if you can keep company]. [My daddy] ask, "Who you come to see?" because he got to know who you come to see. You come and sit down like some other chil'en do now? No, you couldn't do that. Couldn't come in and jus' sit down. No sir. You got to tell who you come ta see. Very strict.— *Laura Mae Campbell*

MARRIAGE CEREMONY

After freedom, marriages took place at the church. Friends remembered small things like hitching the horse to the cart for the newly wedded couple to leave the church. Sometimes a party was held back at the parents' home. Later, some couples married at home. One couple, Naomi and Dempsey Frazier, got married at the lighthouse in Palmetto Dunes (now Leamington), where her father was a lighthouse keeper.

By the 1930s, a couple had to get a license issued by the local magistrate, J. B. Hudson. The license had to be recorded in the Beaufort County Courthouse.

Family members made the wedding dresses and clothes. Lemonade, cake, fried chicken and fish, venison, raccoon, potato salad, red rice, and okra were all part of the wedding feast. A chicken or cow was considered a good wedding gift.

The new husband and wife would usually build their own house on land available from either the bride's side of the family or the groom's.

HOUSES

After freedom, most Gullah families lived in simple wooden houses. At first, many houses were even smaller than the cabins they had lived in during slavery. Gradually, the houses got a little bigger, with a living room, a room for the parents, one for the children, and a kitchen.

Most of Gullah peoples' daily activities took place in the yard around their house—from working in a field full of crops that they relied on for food, to washing clothes, sitting under a tree shelling beans, working on a cast net, telling stories, and even sometimes cooking outside. Plus, a family might have a chicken coop and a stable for horses. A few fortunate people had a smoke house to smoke meat. And there usually was a corn house in every neighborhood. An outhouse sat about seventy-five feet away from the family's home.

The yard took on more importance than the size of the house as long as the family could bed everyone down for the night. Wooden-shingled roofs were common on the island at first, giving way to tin roofs when tin became available. Sometimes the tin was salvaged off of old buildings.

Homes sat off the ground, from eighteen inches to two feet, allowing air to circulate, and providing some safety in floods or storms. Carpenters went into the forest to identify trees that could withstand hewing. Later the trees were cut and sawed and used as sills under the houses.

Newspapers and magazines were sometimes glued on the inside walls to cover the cracks and to keep air from flowing in. There might be a sofa (or "settee") in the living room for sitting, and a chifforobe that could be used as a china cabinet or a closet.

The house was built as a straight structure—one room after another in a line. As more children came along, additional bedrooms would be added on to the side of the house, making the house L-shaped. Most homes also had either a front or back porch. The windows would be covered with glass or wooden shutters.

Water was pumped from a hand pump for dish washing, cooking, drinking water, clothes washing, and taking heated baths with a number-two washtub.

Everything was kept simple. The fireplace or chimney usually stood in the center of the house so that two rooms could be heated. Firewood was plentiful in the forested areas and was cut and used in the fireplaces and cooking stoves. The iron wood-burning stoves had four removable eyes on top with an oven for baking. Some had a storage area on top, which served as the bread oven. The stoves were bought in Savannah and shipped by boat to Hilton Head.

Some people also had a trash-burner, which would heat a room quickly and often lasted no more than a season. Other families had a long iron stove that had a removable top lip so wood could be loaded from the top or the front of the stove.

At nighttime people used heated bricks in their beds if the weather was cold. Their mattress might be made of corn chips, cotton, a combination of the two, or corn chips, corn shuck, and cotton. Sometimes parents sprayed the bed with kerosene to keep bedbugs from biting.

HOUSEHOLD CHORES

In the Gullah way of life, every member of the family had chores to do in order for the family to survive and flourish.

The husband was responsible for gathering food, providing money and support for the family, providing shelter, stacking the stove with wood to start the fire in the morning (if not done by the child), heating gallons of water on the stove top, handling outdoor activities such as going into the field with the horse or mule to work the crops, harvesting the crops, repairing fences, doing other household repairs, and going to his normal day-to-day job or employment.

The wife was just as busy. She had breakfast on the table at five or six a.m., lunch at noon, and supper at dinnertime. She had housekeeping chores, cloth-making and sewing, teaching the children to cook on the wood-stove, healing wounds, nurturing the garden, and, if employed, going to her normal day-to-day job.

Children learned respect for their parents and elders in the community and had plenty of chores. Among these were cutting wood and pumping water; cleaning the yard; feeding the chickens, roosters, and turkeys; "dogging" the turkey   watching to see where the tur-

Thomas S. Barnwell, Sr., milking a cow. *Collection of Thomas C. Barnwell, Jr.*

key laid its eggs; staking out the horses; helping out in the fields and at harvest time; and pulling out weeds in the field, including indigo, which was referred to as "poly-po-john."

Other chores included milking the cows and bringing them in at night, emptying the ashes from the wood-stove, and cleaning glass shades on the lanterns used to light the house at night. Boys did many of these, but girls pitched in also, especially with household chores, such as churning the butter and learning to cook. The child's day usually began by 5:00 or 5:30 a.m.

By age five, a child would be expected to help care for younger siblings, too. And in the fall of the year, children picked up pecans that were then sold in Savannah to help the family pay its property tax.

Yet there was also time for sitting around the fire listening to stories about Bro' Rabbit and other folk tales, hearing about your connections to other relatives and ancestors, and waiting for that sweet potato in the fire to be a tasty snack.

Well, mostly the oldest one [her brother] and my father was fishin', plantin' for the lot. My mother didn't do no work; she just take care of chil'en and carried the farm on. And then we older one, we keep the house and help wid the chil'ren.

 Mind the chil'en and keep the house clean and cook. You had to wash in the washing tub wid the washboard. Keep dem chil'en clean. And cook three meals, breakfast, dinner, and supper. We had the fireplace, [the] wood stove. Cook dem big ol' roll bread, flour bread with no grease. Put the flour in the big iron frying pan, put the top on 'um, mix that flour, put 'um in that pan, turn 'em over, then pull out. . . . You got your bread.— *Laura Mae Campbell*

They hook the rug, make them out of croakers bag. Burlap. Cut it up and braid it and make, I remember they dye them, the colors were nice. And they would weave baskets. I believe the Grants have some of them.— *Naomi Frazier*

One of the things my mother teach was how to embroider. Everything you see around here would have a doily on it and it would have some kind of

Naomi Frazier, a Hilton Head native, owned a floral arrangement business. *Photo Courtesy of Patricia Thomas*

embroidery on it. She took a piece of cloth from the rice sack or grist sack or whatever it was and made it the size she wanted it. One rice sack would be long enough to make two doilies. She could cut that straight in half and she seam it up with her machine. Then she take this paper that has the design and press it on the cloth. That's how you stitch, that's how you do your doily. Now crocheting, I learned the crochet from my sister when I was in New York.

We made grass dolls. I could go pull that grass [now] and wash the roots of it and do it like I used to do. You make it as long as you want it and then you cut it all off. I would take a little piece of cloth that my mother was using and made a dress for it.—*Ruth E. Germany (born 1933, Squire Pope Community)*

I used to make dress on the side, dress for my children, little shirts for my boys. I would cut the pants out. I don't know how we does cut them but they was pants, they got them on. I make shirts, some kind of flannel, white flannel, cotton inside and outside plain. I get the material to Savannah and sometimes Beaufort.

We called them the rich ones, the ones could get things. We poor ones, you might have certain dresses. You would have one church dress and one dress to go wear to school. Wash them out that evening, stockings too. You come from school and hang it up. And we always had a chimney or a stove. You know a two-pot stove and you hang the stocking up in the night and let them dry by morning. Then you put them stockings back on.—*Nancy Ferguson*

When I was a little girl, they weren't particular about what they were wearing. What they were particular on is be' clean. They been wearing those long dress, but they used to wear long dress and wear bustles to make them have a big hip. They would call that pad. Some of the women go now, you can see everything. And that is true.
—*Emma Graham*

I guess I was about twelve or thirteen, maybe even before, I would have to wash my clothes. I was never responsible for washing all the bedclothes or washing my mother's or my father's clothes. I would pump my water and use the washboard with Octagon soap.

My mother had the big iron tub with the fire under it that you boil. She had a washtub that she would wash the clothes in with the washboard. You let it boil some in there. You have a stick that you take the clothes out of that boiling water. Nobody ever used that stick for anything else because it's a clean stick and you want your clothes to be clean. When you take the clothes from the boiling water, you put them in a tub with clear water and you rinse them least twice.

You put a little bit of whitening in the water and then you wring it out and hang it on the line and let it dry. And you did the same process with your darker clothes 'cause you did them separately. You cook Argo starch and use it on the collar and the cuffs and down the front of shirts.

It take all day, you couldn't rush it. And then you need to iron. We used two or three flat-face irons.

You put the iron on the stove or, if it's a nice hot day in the summertime, you put it outside. You let the iron get hot and you have to test the clothes first or you may end up burning something.

My mother believed in the cleanliness. She always kept a very nice, a very clean house. We didn't have cobwebs, you had to sweep the house daily. That was what you do. Saturday was cleaning day. We cleaned everything, my room, the living room, the dining room. I had to wash windows and do the front porch. There was no such thing as a mop. You scrubbed the floor with a scrub brush and you dried it with a piece of rag, an old rag from somebody's shirt or flannel pajamas or a piece of a towel.

My mother believed that you needed to take that rake and rake the yard, that there couldn't be a nail or a broken glass or anything in that yard area from the back to the front where we walked barefooted. My brothers would be responsible for that. I didn't have a lot to do with the yard except I love to plant flowers in the front. . . .

I know in the corn house there was rats but we also had cats. We had a piece cut out down on the bottom of the backdoor so the cats could go in and out of the house. The cats was there, not the rats. —*Ruth E. Germany*

We swept the yard and underneath the house and everything else until everything was clean. Yes.

Because most houses then were sitting up. You never find houses on the ground then. Most of 'em were sitting up on blocks or something. I remember that was our duty, rake under the house, swept the yard. And I know you could go under there and sit, do whatever you wanted to. If you were small like two years old or whatever, you could walk under it.

You see the green grass that was dried and piled together? You sweep with that. Then you had to rake. Every Saturday you have to rake the yard. . . . Everything was cleaned that day, the floor, you would use polish and lime or something and scrub the floor. Get on our knees and scrub the floor. It used to be so clean, until you could eat off those. I remember that.

No work was done on Sunday. Everything got to be done on Saturday. You couldn't even cook on Sunday.—*Mary Lawyer Green*

Food on the table was sustenance and a reward for all the hard work that went into growing your crops, harvesting them, grinding your grits, pumping your well water, and on and on. Then people could eat good and relish the food on their dinner table.

Cow give the milk. You save the milk, and let it stay and try to get the cream on 'um. You skim it. The next mornin', you get the cream wid your butter and put it in the cup, then skim the cream off, put some milk in there, and put 'um in a jar, and shake 'um. "Butter, butter. Come, butter. Come, come, come." Then you get de butter, put it in de butter dish, you had butter.

[You sing] a little song. Come, butter, come. Come, butter, come. You shake it up in the cup. In a jar, yeah . . . solid butter, just like the one you buy. And you put it in the dish.—*Laura Mae Campbell*

Oh yeah, we didn't had no grits mill. We had them big stone with the hole in the middle. Yeah, they broke the corn and shell 'em, and then the two people, or one people according to how heavy the stone is, they take a stick and put it in the middle and just bring it round and round and round and round.

They grind the corn, get the grits out it, and then they sift 'em. The wind blow it and put a sheet or something down and hold it up and that hawks will go off the grits. And then we get corn meal from the grits.

We had sugar cane mills, oh yeah. You cut the cane and you take the leaf off 'em and you grind it with your hand. It was two stones, and it had a handle. And you just grind it and get the water out of 'em, and then you have the big iron pot to boil it in. —*Albertha Ruby Jones (born 1918, Pinckney Island)*

You shell until your hand sore from shelling that corn. So we gone and get a pestle and a barrel and we put that corn in that barrel, and you take the ax and you beat that corn off that cob until you have four or five or six bushels. You put it in a sack and you go across the river where the mill been, some way on the other side, and you carry the corn in there and you get it grind. The husk go to itself, the grits go to itself, and the corn meal go to itself. You cook the husk for the hog.—*Nancy Ferguson*

Her parents had a cow, they had horse, they had chicken, they had hog.

They raise cane and would ground them up and make syrup. Hard work. Sometimes you might catch a rabbit or possum, you singe the possum and gut 'em, clean 'em. And the rabbit; you skin the rabbit. Then you carry 'em over there [to Savannah to sell]. The chicken and turkey, you take them over there live. And they do what they wanna do. Theys take 'em, and they pay you for 'em. —*Minnie Holmes (birth year unknown, Braddock's Point)*

Yeah, I used to jar a lot of things. I jar plenty okra. I see my parents jar, and I learn from them. A lot of people blanch that okra, but I don't do it. Just stuff that jar and put 'em in and boil and cook in that jar. Don't screw the jar tight when it be hot. And that okra be good.—*Corrine Lawyer Brown (born 1923, Squire Pope Community)*

My mother jarred very heavily. She never jarred them all mixed together. She would do the early June peas, and then we would get to the okras and tomatoes, white potatoes, greens, lima beans, string beans. Yeah and when you went to the fruit, she would do peaches, pears, figs.

We didn't have a lot of pear trees here on the island, so she would buy a bushel of pears from Savannah when the summer comes on. We had peach trees in the yard but some years some of them would end up having worms in 'em so it would be too many to try to cut around. Now figs, we had a fig tree so we would have figs jarred.
—*Ruth E. Germany*

They would kill hogs and that was the time they would smoke it. That was the bacon from their labor. My old daddy and brothers had labored.
—*Emma Graham*

We planted sugarcane in the spring and then you harvest it in, around October, November. We used to grow a lot of cane and sell it to the market. Then we used to make syrup. Jesus almighty, what a chore.

We had a mill about fifteen inches high, ten or twelve inches in diameter . . . with a horse pulling this thing around. You feed the cane in through the neck, squeeze the juice out of it. We was driving this thing all day for about a week, and as you grind it, you pour it into this pot as big as this table, about forty-eight inches around, maybe two feet deep. You had a wood fire under it. We had no electricity, there's no gas, nothing. Everything was wood back in those days.

We boiled all the water out of it and leave the syrup at the end. . . .

We had barrels of syrup, fifty-five-gallon barrels. The syrup was basically for farm consumption, and [my father] gave a lot of it away to people that he knew.—*Charlie White (born 1929, Grassland Community)*

The well was good water. Running water. A running spring. It was like ice water. Now, right now, I even can't drink the water. I put it in the refrigerator and let it get cold, but if you go to that pump and pump your own water you enjoy it much better. We use to go and get that water. It would rain that water off, and the cool water would come up.
—*Laura Mae Walters Holmes (born 1919, Squire Pope Community)*

You used to could find blackberry, huckleberry, blueberry, figs, plums, nice big plums.—*Ben Miller (born 1925, Jonesville Community)*

We ate fish, crabs, oysters, clam, all of that.
—*Nancy Ferguson*

We'd cook every day. Every morning most times. When you come home from school usually there was something here. My mother made biscuits so there was usually some food. There was always peanut butter and if there wasn't, we used to make a sandwich with the fruits. If we didn't have anything else, we put some sugar on the bread and then put a little water on and make a sandwich. Or you could make cucumber sandwich, or you'd take the saltshaker and you go out in the field and you get a cucumber and you shake and you eat. Or you take a tomato and do the same.— *Ruth E. Germany*

We had three meals a day, and then on the side at night if we get hungry, they would fix us. My daddy would get up at five o'clock every morning and then he would get his crackers and coffee and then he goes to work. He never worked, never in his life work for nobody. He did his own work.

If the children want cocoa, we would get cocoa. And we would get hominy grits, sometimes fried fish, breakfast bacon.

We had dinner in the middle of the day, but when all the children come in from work, Papa and the children worked together, then my sister already done have dinner ready, table set and then all would get to the table. My daddy had a table that was a long table. And he sit at the head of the table, and he got to grace the table. You cannot eat, and you better wash your hand, and you can't start eating until Papa sit at the head of the table.

Didn't have the flapjacks until dinner time. They would have all the flapjacks made in this pot. My aunt used to make it with the fire underneath the pot. They used to fix that in the day. They would put it in a big frying pan, and they would fry up about twenty because it was a lot of children. And they would put it up on top [of the stove].
— *Emma Graham*

People had orange tree, tangerine tree, pecan tree, and all kind of tree. They made marmalade out of the sour oranges. I was thirteen or fourteen years old, but I can remember those times, good old corn bread, that ham hocks and butter beans, get the rice and that bake sweet potato.— *Ben White, Jr.*

You could get a bunch of greens or something for ten cents, and you could get a half of pound of lard for a nickel. And you get a pound of meat for a nickel, two quart of grits for a dime, and a quart of rice for a dime. You could get two quart of grits for a dime and a pound of fresh meat or something or another — you pay a dime for them. Sometimes you pay fifteen cents.— *Albertha Ruby Jones*

We didn't buy no snacks those days. On the weekend they would buy you a box of what that, ZuZus, ginger snaps. You ate solid food. Solid food don't hurt you because you burn it, you work it off. During that time, you work. They had to feed you because nobody can do nothin' on a hungry stomach. You got to feed that soul.—*Henry Ford (born 1937, Squire Pope Community)*

HEALTH REMEDIES

Gullah people on Hilton Head had to be resourceful. For the most part, they relied on themselves and each other for their health care before the bridge came. Except for notable exceptions, there were no doctors on the island throughout most of Gullah history.

During the Civil War, Union doctors tended ill black Union soldiers. Even then, a few soldiers listed as absent from duty on the army roster were found ill and being cared for by their families on Hilton Head. The crowded military hospital sometimes was less appealing than close attention received from family members in a nonfatal illness.

As described in chapter 13, in the late 1800s through the early 1900s, a white doctor by the name of Dr. Frances E. Wilder—remembered as "Dr. Wiley" by islanders—lived at Otter Hole and treated a number of Gullah residents.

Dr. E. M. Pinckney, who was black, often conducted physical examinations of black Civil War veterans for their applications for a Civil War pension from the U.S. Department of War. These examinations helped former black Union soldiers gain a federal pension, keep

it, and make their case for an increase in the amount they received.

The black soldiers who had stepped forward to help reunite the nation inevitably aged. Whether from a war-time disability or age, or a combination of the two, their need for assistance grew. In 1898, for instance, Dr. Pinckney stated in a physician's affidavit that, in his opinion, the former soldier Edward Lawyer was three-fourths disabled for manual work. A few years later, Dr. Pinckney found that Lawyer's condition had worsened. The affidavits from Pinckney and other doctors were critical. Without a pension, an aged veteran was penniless and unable to provide for his family.

For the most part, however, the only way to see a doctor was to travel by boat to Bluffton, Beaufort, or Savannah.

Isabel Brown remembered seeing a white doctor in Bluffton by the last name of Mellichamp who sometimes had treated islanders during slavery. Plantation owners on occasion called in doctors to attend to ill slaves. This particular doctor treated enslaved people on some plantations when white planters called him in.

The first doctor I had was Dr. Mellichamp but that was in Bluffton. . . . You would have to go from here to Bluffton. He didn't write no prescription, he would give you the medicine in his office. That was the first doctor I went to and he was a good doctor. . . . That was the same doctor my mother used to go to. They [in slavery] didn't have no different doctor. He was white.— *Isabel Brown*

Traveling across the water to see a doctor was rare, however. Early on, there was insufficient time in an emergency situation. In addition, few people could pay cash to see a doctor. When a life-threatening illness struck, mutual aid societies on the island assisted families of the ill. Emory S. Campbell remembers his grandmother walking miles to sit overnight to give care to an ill person.

Families kept several common products in the house to cure illnesses. These included Epsom salt, used for soaking hands or feet in a basin (small tub) to cure swellings, and castor oil or syrup of black draught, taken once a year to cure roundworms.

For many health problems, Gullah people relied primarily on herbal remedies. Enslaved Africans arriving on Hilton Head knew how to use herbs to heal illness. A few plants that grew in West Africa also grew on Hilton Head. The fruit of the fig tree, for instance, was used in Africa as a dressing for skin lesions. Figs were also used as an herbal remedy on Hilton Head. Newly arrived Africans searched for plants and roots that looked similar to those they already knew and could be used in herbal remedies.

Much of their knowledge they learned by trial and error, and some from Native American lore. An example is the blackberry plant. Native Americans used it to treat diarrhea, as did the Gullah on Hilton Head. In addition, enslaved people and white Europeans passed some knowledge of herbs and roots back and forth.

So, as in other aspects of Gullah culture, the people blended information from many sources to form their own distinctive use of herbal remedies.

Gathering, drying, and concocting herbal remedies was a necessary part of life. Hilton Head was isolated, and Gullah people rarely saw a doctor. They had to rely on their neighbors to treat illnesses and ailments that resulted from accidents.

During the Civil War, famed Underground Railroad conductor Harriet Tubman, who reached Hilton Head in 1862, used local plants to prepare remedies to treat ill Union soldiers. She was well known for curing dysentery and told her biographer that she once was called away from Hilton Head to go to Fernandina, where she said the men "were dying like sheep" from dysentery. Tubman made a medicine from roots that "grew near the waters which gave the disease."

Generations of men and women gathered healthy herbs and roots on Hilton Head until the bridge came. In the twentieth century, one Hilton Head father and son, James and William Aiken, were especially noted for their mastery of the medicinal power of herbs. William "Brankey" Aiken, born in 1894, was known as "the medicine man" to Gullah people. His knowledge of plants and roots came from older people on the island, as well as from a Savannah herbalist. He knew which roots and herbs to combine to make a remedy, boiled his potions, bottled them, and sold his homemade remedies.

We used to get all the bush medicine out the wood. For cough, garlic and syrup . . . my mother and others would boil it together, [until] it thick. And they give you by the spoonful to carry [away] your cough. Use mullein for swellin', moss for high blood. [Spanish moss was worn in a shoe to lower blood pressure—some believed that an ingredient in the moss travels through the bloodstream.]

Put that old [fever] bush all the way around their stomach, and when that old bush dry up, the fever gone. You hardly can find them now. They have big wide leaves.

You got pain in the side or anything, they cut the pine tree. The parents do that. And then . . . the sap come out. And they take it and roll it as pills, and they give you that for pain.

They got a bush here they give you . . . boil that bush and give [it to] you to chuck your stomach up.

That's what we used to do.
— *Laura Mae Campbell*

Our people had the knowledge of herbs, some right in your back door, some across the fields, some in the woods. We knew what to get for whatever the ailment. They worked. We used this stuff up until the bridge came.

I think everybody reared on Hilton Head had knowledge of these plants, but we had Mr. Aiken—"Brankie" Aiken—William Aiken, the medicine man. He used the gift that he had. He had the knowledge of the medicine, he actually made medicine. Whatever the ailment was he know the herbs to go to address the ailment. So if there was a problem, they talkin' about oh, "Well, I'm gon' get some Brankey medicine, gon' really clean me out good." They say if you can't have no chilluns, get some Brankey medicine. So I think if there was someone that was barren and wanted children, all they had to do is tell him, he know the herb.

I specifically remember his father that we called Cousin James Aiken. When I was little and my throat would hurt, Mama would look down there and say, oh your palette is down, whatever that meant. Cousin James Aiken would run this spoon handle down your palette. He would have some salt and pepper on the end of it. For some reason it work. Someone ahead of him had knowledge of all the plants and stuff that they used for medicine and that person probably studied it. And it was something that was passed on.— *Louise Cohen*

The common (nonscientific) names of some medicinal herbs used on Hilton Head Island, as remembered by Louise Cohen (all quotes in this list are from her):

- **Cow Cabbage:** Used for earache. Looks like cabbage, growing flat on the ground and spreading open. Eaten by cows. Produces a stalk before it dies. So thorny you need to wear gloves to pick a leaf.
- **Life Everlasting**: Sometimes called "life for lasting." Used for colds and coughs. Mint candy was sometimes taken afterwards because of bitter taste. The plant is easily identified in the field: silvery white leaves and white blossoms in the fall. The root was boiled to make tea and sometimes combined with lemon and honey. It still grows along roads and in ditches on Hilton Head.
- **Shoemaker Root:** Sumac. Used for colds. Has clusters of deep burgundy berries. Tangy taste, often used to make sun tea. The root was combined with pine needles and holly for colds.
- **Itchy Berry:** Used for watercourse trouble, probably prostrate trouble.
- **Pine Tree:** Used to treat backache. A slice was cut deep into the tree, a process known as "boxing the tree." The sap was collected with a spoon, rolled in flour, and made into pills that were called "pine gum pills." [This is another version of the remedy Miss Campbell's parents used.]

- **Blackberries Root:** The root was cleaned, steeped, and used to treat diarrhea in children.
- **Catnip:** Given to babies, probably for colic. Minty smell; planted around the house.
- **Mullen:** Used for swelling. Wide leaves, bushy, similar to cabbage but without the head.
- **Fever Bush:** About three feet tall with long, wide leaves. The leaves were tied on a person's head with a cloth to pull fever from the body.
- **Okra Blossom:** The blossom from an okra plant was used to bring boils to a head. Also used "to draw the poison out" from an infection. When wrapped with a penny and the skin from a piece of pork, it also was used to treat an infection when someone stepped on a nail. "It would be pulling, drawing, and as it draw, it would hurt . . . it be doin' so hard . . . it would feel like it actually got a heartbeat to it, and it be like beating."
- **Fig Leaf:** Used to treat ringworm. "Mama and those used to say, 'Go get piece that fig leaf from off that tree,'" and they would put the milk of the fig on the ringworm.
- **Horse Nettle:** A sticky green plant with a little white blossom—if you brushed up against it, it would cause intense itching. [This plant was said by some to be an aphrodisiac.]

RELIGION

First African Baptist was a long ways, and people had to walk. My father had a buggy with an umbrella in the middle, and we had back and front seats, and that is how we went to church. We used to have good times in those days, very good times. I wish many times I could call them days back.
— *Emma Graham*

Africans arrived on Hilton Head with differing belief systems. As with other elements of Gullah culture, a common system of beliefs evolved over time.

The early Africans likely held secret "bush arbor" meetings in wilderness areas sacred to them. They may also have had secret rites such as naming ceremonies when a child was born. Similar ceremonies were performed in African villages.

Missionaries and plantation masters introduced Christianity to enslaved Africans. Africans and their descendants eventually adopted Christianity but infused their faith with strong African influences brought with them to this country.

Methodist missionary Thomas D. Turpin arrived on Hilton Head to provide religious instruction to enslaved people in 1833. The planter William E. Baynard welcomed Turpin and wanted him to return the following year.

William "Squire" Pope, Sr., the largest plantation owner on the island, was not impressed with Turpin's efforts. "If I am not deceived," Pope wrote Baynard, "one or two of [the slaves] will long remember [Turpin] with gratitude . . . but am inclined to think he has not met with decided success . . . he has had to encounter some difficulty, discouragements and prejudices [against Methodists] he has not been able to fully overcome."

Pope withheld his consent for Turpin to return to Hilton Head. He added that there were better "means and opportunities" of religious instruction now that there were "two churches [on Hilton Head] in which there is service at least twice a month." These were plantation churches for white families.

Pope was Baptist, as were many Hilton Head planters, and this may have had an impact on his decision not to allow the Methodist missionary to return. Both Baptists and Methodists wanted enslaved people converted to their denomination.

Planters saw Christianity as essential to plantation discipline and management. The official opinion of South Carolina Baptists was that "slavery was clearly established in the Holy Scriptures by both precept and example."

For the slaves Christianity had drawbacks. It emphasized "obedience to slave masters, punishment for wrong-doing on earth, and inequality between master and slave."

Enslaved people seized onto the story of Moses leading the children of Israel into freedom and other Bible stories that provided comfort and inspiration. They took hold of biblical teachings that they could accept and spread the belief that one day freedom would arrive. They had the perfect mechanism for transmitting their teachings—the praise house, where enslaved people gathered to hold their prayer services.

Planters permitted enslaved people to meet in small praise or "prayer" houses in the belief that this provided a positive influence in the plantation community.

Two small wooden praise houses were built on Hilton Head before 1861: one at Cherry Hill and another at Chaplin. In addition, the cabins of respected elders often served as praise houses, as northern missionaries on Hilton Head discovered during the Civil War. Praise-house meetings offered opportunities to transcend the harsh realities of slave life through the preaching of praise-house leaders, fervent singing of spirituals, and ring shouts in which participants moved in a circle, sang, clapped with an African beat, and shouted their joy in the Lord.

The praise house bonded the plantation community together and developed leaders. The praise house was the first institution for Gullah people.

DEVELOPMENT OF GULLAH CHURCHES

The First African Baptist Church began during the Civil War and was the first black church on Hilton Head Island. Reverend Abraham Murchison, an escaped slave preacher from Savannah, was installed as pastor on August 17, 1862. The church had about one

Historic First African Missionary Baptist Church, 2019. *Photo by Will Warasila*

hundred and twenty members when it was organized, seventy of whom were already Christians, according to the *New South*, a weekly newspaper on Hilton Head that flourished on the Union base.

The church had been authorized by General David Hunter who respected Murchison and suggested and recognized that Hilton Head contrabands needed a formal house of worship. By the time the church was constructed, Hunter was on leave from the Department of the South and his replacement, General Ormsby M. Mitchel, enthusiastically addressed congregants at the formal dedication of the church on October 16, 1862.

First African Baptist (FAB) Church became the first

building in what would become the village of Mitchel-ville. But while two different generals in the Department of the South were briefly involved in the establishment of First African Baptist, the church was for Gullah people and run by Gullah people. This was a departure from the past experience of enslaved people on Hilton Head and other places.

In Savannah, for instance, the former home of Murchison, a First African Baptist Church existed before the Civil War. It had a black congregation and a black minister but was under white supervision. On Hilton Head Island, the apparent independence of the First African Baptist Church represented another taste of freedom. It was one of the many experiments undertaken by the Department of the South, which the *New South*, a newspaper published on Hilton Head, labeled the "Department of Experiments."

First African Baptist would become known as the mother of black churches. Many Hilton Head families found a spiritual start at this church. Some then branched out to form churches closer to their homes or within the communities in which they lived.

Among the churches whose roots started from the First African Baptist Church are Goodwill Baptist Church, which only existed a short period of time; Central Oak Grove Baptist Church; Saint James Baptist Church; Mount Calvary Missionary Baptist Church; and the New Church of Christ on Hilton Head. Church records also reveal that the First Zion Baptist Church

in Bluffton emerged from the First African Baptist congregation.

The roots of a second denomination on Hilton Head, the African Methodist Episcopal (AME) Church, go back to 1865. This church, Queen Chapel AME, is the oldest AME church in South Carolina.

According to church history, several AME ministers arrived on Hilton Head that year in the area called Cherry Hill. As they waited for a storm to pass over, "they decided to have services with prayer and singing under a large oak tree. This was to be an historic event because it was where African Methodism began in the state of South Carolina. A few years later Queen AME Church was built."

W. D. Brown, a northern storeowner on Hilton Head, sold the property for Queen Chapel to the church founders in 1886. The church building was finished on September 11, 1892. Services were held in it before completion. The church sanctuary was rebuilt in 1954. After the bridge, in 2002, the church congregation constructed a more modern sanctuary.

Among the Baptist churches that sprang from the First African Baptist, Saint James Baptist Church was organized in August 1866. Like First African Baptist, this church also began within the Mitchelville community.

Reverend A. C. Abes served as the first pastor of the church. He was succeeded by a Reverend Williams. Little is known about these two pastors, although a

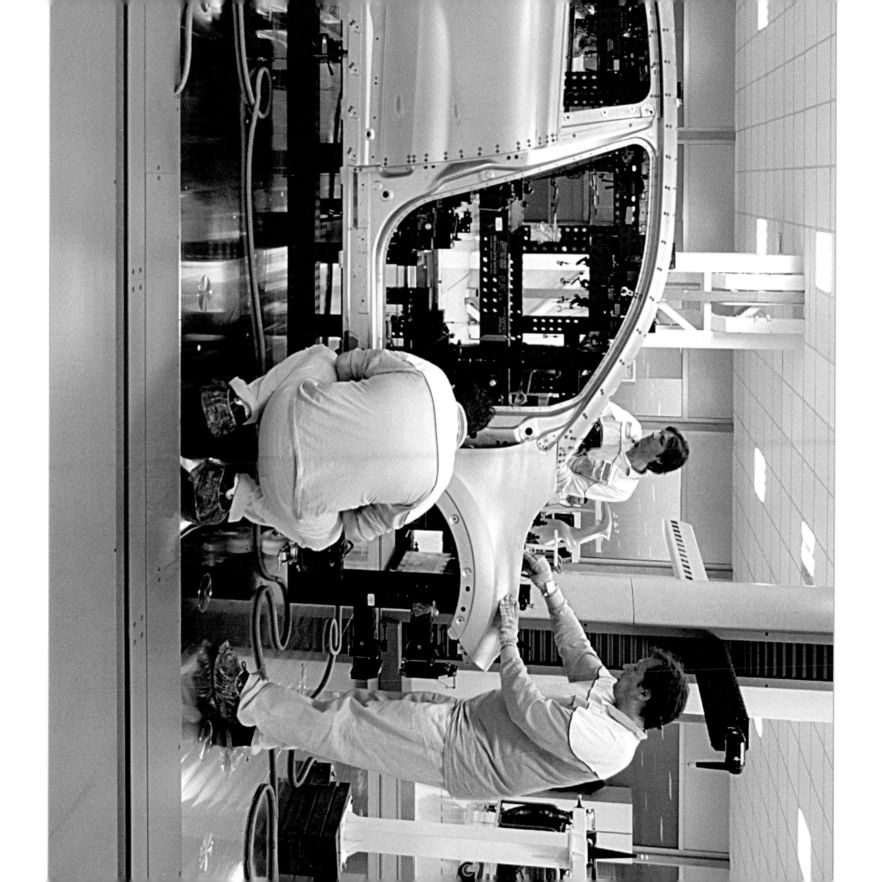

194 ALTHOUGH THE 500 X WAS CLEARLY LARGER, ITS SOFT LINES WERE SIMILAR TO THOSE OF THE 2007 MODEL OF THE 500. THE FIRST SERIES WAS AVAILABLE IN 2-WHEEL AND 4-WHEEL DRIVE.

194-195 MEASURING THE ELEMENTS OF THE ALMOST-FINISHED CHASSIS OF THE 500 X, IN A FACTORY PROTOTYPING CENTER. THE X WAS PRODUCED IN MELFI (PZ).

196-197 THE 500 X MIRROR HAD AN INFOTAINMENT SYSTEM THAT COULD DUPLICATE THE SCREEN AND FUNCTIONS OF THE DRIVER'S SMARTPHONE. IT WAS AVAILABLE IN SPECIAL COLORS, INCLUDING MATTE JEANS BLUE.

Like Mirror versions of other 500s, the X Mirror was designed for an audience of young, tech-savvy drivers. The name "Mirror" referred to the ability of the UConnectTM infotainment system, for Apple iOS and Android, to "reflect" the information on the driver's smartphone and manage apps, music, and information on a 7" screen. The 500 X S-Design presented at the Bologna Motor Show was a descendant of the Cross Look. It was painted matte Alpine green with Myron accents and was available with two- or four-wheel drive.

THE RENEWED OFF-ROAD: THE 500 X II SERIES (SINCE 2018)

In 2018, the 500 off-road underwent a slight restyling, with LED position lights on all three versions: the Urban, which got new bumpers; the Cross and the 4x2 City Cross, with skid plates added to the bumpers; and the 4x4 Sport, which would go out of production at the end of 2019. The taillight units were also modified to incorporate an insert that matched the body color, like the ones on the second series of the 500. Important updates were made to the safety equipment: traffic sign recognition, lane assist, intelligent speed assist, city brake control, adaptive headlights, and blind spot detection. Engine choices included the new Firefly aluminum gasoline engines with variable valve lift and timing and particle filter: a 120 HP three-cylinder 1,000 cc and a 150 HP four-cylinder 1,300 cc. The diesel engines, with a urea Selective Catalytic Reduction (SCR) system, were the 95 HP Multijet II 1,300 cc; the 120 HP 1,600 cc; and the 150 HP 2,000 cc, only for the 4x4. In the fall of 2019, production exceeded the 500,000th mark. The 2020 model, the first that was not available with four-wheel drive, was proposed in two Urban Look versions, the Urban and the Lounge; three Cross versions, the Cross, the City Cross, and the Business Cross, destined for car fleets; while the Sport was offered in just one version. Four engines powered all the versions: the Firefly gasoline engines were a 120 HP three-cylinder 1,300 cc and a 151 HP four-cylinder 1,300 cc, while the two diesel engines were Multijet IIs, a 95 HP 1,300 cc and a 120 HP 1,600 cc. The biggest of both types were available with automatic transmission.

Like the 500 L S-Design, the bold-looking S-Design derived from the Cross. Painted matte Alpine green, it had under-bumper guards. The Cross Mirror was matte blue jeans blue with full LED lights and the smartphone Mirror function. The 500 X was also part of the family that commemorated the 120th anniversary of Fiat. It was presented at the Geneva Motor Show in 2019. It was the first time that the 500 X was presented in a two-tone version, the same Tuxedo livery that had been seen on the 500, 500 C, and 500 L but with the option of replacing the white with metallic grey. It was also equipped with Mopar Connect. The engines available in the 120th anniversary edition were the 120 HP Firefly 1,000 cc turbo and the 110 HP E-torq 1,600 cc, and the 95 HP Multijet II 1,300 cc and the 120 HP 1,600 cc diesel.

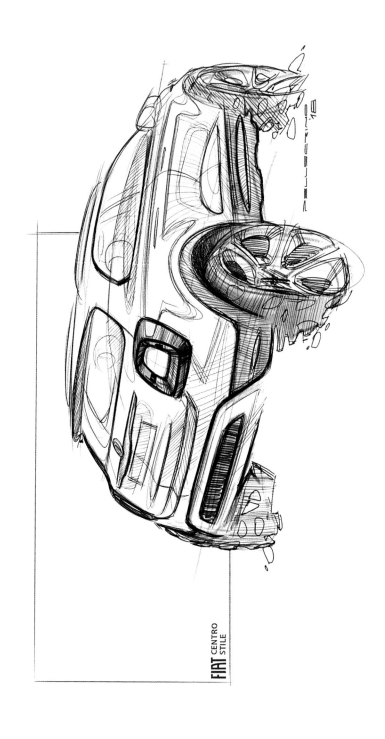

FIAT CENTRO STILE

Present-day St. James
Baptist Church. *Photo
by Will Warasila*

minister whose name had a similar spelling to "A. C. Abes" was mentioned by former black Union soldiers and their widows in pension applications and could be the same man.

In 1942, the church sanctuary caught fire, and the fire destroyed all the church records. It was a difficult time to rebuild, as many of the men had been called to military service in World War II. Building materials also were hard to obtain because of military need. Nonetheless, members preserved and rebuilt the sanctuary the following year. After the bridge, in 1972, members built a new sanctuary. Church members paid off the mortgage

(Left) Present-day Central Oak Grove Baptist Church. *Photo by Will Warasila*

(Right) Present-day Mount Calvary Missionary Baptist Church. *Photo by Will Warasila*

in 1980. Fire again damaged the church a year later. Repairs were made, and the church continued. The church also restored the former one-room Cherry Hill School, located across from the current church building. The former school is still used as an educational building for the church.

Central Oak Grove Baptist Church organized in 1887. Gullah resident Frank Murray donated land in 1886 for the church. Initially members began worshipping at the Saint James Baptist Church. However, many of the members of Central Oak Grove Baptist lived on the south end of the island near Braddock's Point. They therefore wanted a church that was closer to where they lived. The church was built near the Old Baynard Tomb Ruins at the present-day intersection of Matthews Drive and Highway 278.

In the early 1950s, fire destroyed the church. It

was rebuilt on Matthews Drive, across from Broad Creek.

Mount Calvary Baptist Church was founded on March 14, 1914. Charity sisters within the congregation selected the grounds for the church building, located on Squire Pope Road. The church started as a praise house and was then transformed into a wooden, two-story church.

In 1940 a major hurricane destroyed the church. Money was scarce in the 1940s, but the congregation pulled together and rebuilt the church.

The Church of Christ, established in 1938 by Bishop Steven and Sister Dianah Frazier of Savannah, was the last of the island's Gullah churches to be organized. Services first were held at the Charity Hall on Spanish Wells Road, but the 1940 hurricane that destroyed the Mount Calvary Baptist Church building also destroyed

Charity Hall. George Frazier, a resident of the community who operated a store in the community, allowed members to use his store for worship until they could construct a building. Between 1940 and 1941, members built their first church building. Benjamin Jones, a deacon at the church, and his young son David, supplied the first load of building materials for the church. As they were bringing the supplies from the mainland to Hilton Head, their bateau (a small flat-bottom boat built by Gullah men for fishing and other purposes) capsized, and the Joneses had to be rescued. The materials later were recovered by the shore near Spanish Wells. The present-day Church of Christ is on Spanish Wells Road.

CHURCH CONSTRUCTION

Native craftsmen from Hilton Head built the Gullah churches on the island. Between 1930 and 1950, Samuel Holmes, a native carpenter on nearby Daufuskie Island also helped build some of the churches.

All of the Baptist churches originally had balconies, but several of these churches were destroyed by fire or storm. Newer churches were built without balconies. Balconies were common in plantation-style churches, likely built by enslaved Africans. This perhaps influenced the style of early Gullah churches. Lumber to build the churches came from pine trees on the island. Finished framing materials were brought from Savannah by sailboat in the 1920s. Tongue-and-groove was used for flooring and walls inside the churches.

CHURCH SERVICES

The churches were a major part of Gullah families' spiritual, cultural, and social lives. But for a considerable time, churches were unable to regularly conduct services each Sunday. Ministers usually came from off-island, and often one minister served as the pastor of several congregations. In addition, no one church on Hilton Head was able to afford a full-time minister.

In the early 1900s, a rotational system developed whereby each church held service on a particular Sunday of the month and hosted members of other congregations. Services on first Sundays were held at Saint James Baptist; second Sundays alternated between Mount Calvary Baptist and Central Oak Baptist; services on third Sundays were at First African Baptist; fourth Sunday services were held at Queen Chapel AME; services on fifth Sundays were rotated. In addition, the Church of Christ held services on second and fourth Sundays. Some choir members and ushers would participate in services at more than one church.

The church sexton was responsible for ringing the bell to indicate the start of church services. Services typically started at 10:00 a.m. or 11:00 a.m. After worshippers gathered, a church "sister," "brother," or "deacon" began devotional services with singing and testimony.

Two deacons stood at the front of the church to officially start the devotional service. One would be responsible for lining the hymn, which was referred to as long meter or short meter. He would ask for "some sister or brother with suitable voice to sing as I line." The other deacon would lead the prayer, which could range from mellow to fiery, depending on the person praying. Then the congregation would break into song. Following that, the choir and musicians, often called choristers, would stroll in from the church foyer to the choir seating, which was generally behind the pulpit area.

The worship service would then proceed with scripture readings, prayer, announcements, collection of a "missionary offering" and a general offering, preaching, a call for people who wanted to accept Christ or join the church, acceptance (the right hand of fellowship), serving the Lord's Supper, and dismissal. Church services could last from two to three hours.

Before 1954, two sermons would be preached in the course of a day. After the morning service, worshippers would take a recess. Families would bring food to eat after the first service, and some churches had a kitchen. In some cases, people would eat outside or in the rear of the church and socialize until the afternoon service began. Church was a long affair. After the bridge was built, only one service was held.

SPECIAL PROGRAMS

Churches would have special services during the year: fall and spring revivals and Women's Day and Men's Day. Island clubs also would host special services. These clubs included the Mothers' Union, the Boys of Plea-sure, the Lilies of the Valley, the Workers of Charity, the Farmers Club, and others.

Some clubs ceased to exist in the 1950s, and the remaining ones were gone in the 1960s. However, in contemporary times, churches hold annual revivals. The revivals are week-long services held at night. During the revivals, churches conduct services at each other's churches. In addition, Hilton Head's Gullah churches hold large celebrations at Easter and Christmas.

CONTINUATION OF PRAISE HOUSES

Praise houses continued to thrive after the development of churches on Hilton Head. Communities developed their own praise house, built by the men of the community and tied to one of the main churches. Through meetings on Sunday, Tuesday, and Thursday evenings, the praise houses bonded communities together and built a sense of belonging.

In addition to providing a local place of worship, the praise house "always stressed neighborly love at every praise-house meeting. That's why they had the handshake at the end of every service," Emory S. Campbell recalls.

The leaders were looked up to. Many went on to become church deacons. A critical role of the praise house was that of providing religious training to the young people of the community. They prepared youths to be admitted into the fold through the process of seeking.

The praise houses continued to be simple one-room,

wooden buildings, less elaborate than the church buildings. They could seat up to fifty persons. Benches lined the praise houses and buildings, and there was a wood heater in the middle of the room to keep people warm during the cold winter months. Praise-house leaders, mostly men, led services and were responsible for the upkeep of the praise house. They usually were identified by their locations instead of by specific names.

Services, commonly called prayer meetings, were similar to church services with prayer, songs, shouting, and personal testimony from members. Members read Bible verses and lined a hymn. Meetings were "spirit-filled" with people singing, shouting acclamations to the Lord, clapping, and testifying.

Praise houses were located in the Stoney, Squire Pope, Spanish Wells, and Chaplin communities. In the Marshland and Gardner communities, people would walk to the Grand Army Hall, which was used as a praise house.

My family, the older ones in slavery times, were Catholic and Baptist. My great-grandfather was the Catholic, my great-grandmother was the Baptist. The old master, they called him that, he was the thing, and you had to know that. When the master would sell you over, like to Squire Pope, you had to be what religion they was over there.

In my mother time, she walked from Braddock's Point to Mitchelville to church. It wasn't but one

church, and they tell me now that church foundation is to the low-water mark and might be sailing now. That was the First AB. We call it the crossroad church.—*Isabel Brown*

I was a little girl, and I know when Mount Calvary come in. All those people had belong to First AB and when my uncle died, some of the family wanted the funeral to be preached. And Papa was the only brother left after his olderest brother died, my uncle. Papa and them didn't want to go through all of that again. That is how come the church split and that how come it was Mount Calvary happen. —*Emma Graham*

The people at Mount Calvary were originally from First African Baptist Church, "Crossroads Church." They only had one church on Hilton Head and different preachers, everybody wanted to be big shots so then they fall out. They couldn't get along. So that's how come they move and build their own church.

They want me to be deacon, but I say no, no. I was sitting in church one night, they had to grab my father and hold him down. And another man called "Bubba Son," they had to hold him down in church.—*Elijah Jones, Jr. (born 1925, Squire Pope)*

I joined the Methodist church. But they [other people] get out and talk so much about the church then until they got more Baptist churches on the island when it ain't ought to been but one or two. The Methodist stay like it been. Stay like it is right now. One Methodist church. One Methodist church like here now.—*Nancy Ferguson*

My membership was FAB. I went to all the churches on Hilton Head. Back then you go to all the churches. The first Sunday was at Saint James, second Sunday was Mount Calvary, third Sunday was FAB, fourth Sunday was Queen Chapel. If it was Sunday, I went to every church.

I know Mr. James Grant style of prayin'. I remember the songs he sing. I know Mr. Jones, we call him Fruit, David Jones and those daddy, I know his style. I remember Dave White and them daddy, Mr. Ben White. That was the only man that I saw walk and pray with his eyes wide open.
— *Louise Cohen*

Both of us [Laura Holmes and William Holmes] went to Mount Calvary. I asked Armon Frazier to remodel the church with a pew. He was a carpenter, and he build that church. That church had a upstairs. A lot of times I go in and sit there and join in with 'em until I get the anointing.

The pastor preach in the morning, and we used to have Sunday school in the afternoon. On Communion Sunday we had a hour, and like that, you go back in to communion. Stay right to the church.—*William Holmes, Sr. (born 1915, Squire Pope Community)*

They have sermons two times a day, one in the morning, one in the evening. The prayer meetings be on Tuesday night and Friday night and church on Sunday.—*Albertha Ruby Jones*

The first preacher we had when I went came from Charleston. Minister Duncan was the minister when I join in 1932. He came once a month, ride to Buckingham and come cross on the ferryboat. He would come on Saturday and stay with Steven Bryan. He [Bryan] was chairman of the church.—*William Holmes, Sr.*

The minister didn't live on the island at that time. All had to travel back and forth.

As time rolled on, Reverend Jones lived here. But the preachers had to come and go.
— *Emma Graham*

I don't want to say how much training most of them have. They did the best they can with what they had. They had a calling. Maybe they didn't have all the learning and stuff that they should have had but I think if you want to compare times, I think that some were better prepared then than some are now.

They were ahead . . . they were up hill, looked up to 'cause they were deacons.—*Caesar Wright (born 1935, Squire Pope Community)*

At the church the people did some real good singing, now. They did not have any pianos and organs,
but they did a lot of vocal singing. And Sunday
evening when they meet together to the other home
[the praise house] and start to singing vocal note,
you could hear some singing. Old man Abraham
Mitchell, Johnny Grant, and Mingo Green, they
were masters of notes.

They could start you to singing, and they go
outside, and as soon as you would go too high or too
low, they would know who did it. They were professional. Sometimes people would come here and
have music for the young children. I know when my
children were growing up, they didn't have no place
to go, and they would have people come over and
show music pictures with them.

—*Naomi Frazier*

SEEKING

Methodist missionaries introduced the term "seeking"—
or "seekin'," as Gullah people say it—into the sea islands. Gullah people adopted the term but went about
seekin', making spiritual journeys, in ways that likely
included African memories.

One Methodist missionary, irritated at his lack of
control over how enslaved people on the plantations
went about seeking, complained that when youths began
to pray, they selected a spiritual guide by means of a vi-
sion and that the guide often was female. Whether the
guide was a man or a woman, the youths put themselves
under their guides' instruction. The guide also interpreted a youth's dreams—or travels—and decided
when the youth was ready to join the church. The missionary concluded that there was, "in a word, no . . .
element of Christian experience involved in the whole
affair." The entire practice was governed by the praise
house.

Similar, though more elaborate, rites have been found
by scholars among such ethnic groups as the Mende,
Temne, and Gola of Western Africa along the Windward
Coast. Through secret societies, the Poro for boys and
the Sande for girls, youths retreated into the bush into a
"lonely spiritual journey or travel . . . with instructions
not to be afraid." The girls "wore a white head tie, called
'the white thing.'"[9] Both boys and girls reported their
visions or travels to an altar father or mother who interpreted them. In one ethnic group, the Mano, before a
youth had gone into the bush and been initiated, he or
she was called a shadow. In other words, the youth was
"not really a member of the village."

On Hilton Head Island, seeking was a major turning
point in the lives of the youth well into the 1940s and
early 1950s. Youths who were not members of the praise
house were required to sit on the back bench, and they
could not lead shouts or fully participate in other praise-
house functions.

Parents often scolded children that it was time
for them to go seeking in the wilderness. This ritual

occurred when a boy or girl was on the brink of adulthood, often at about twelve years of age. To not join the church was unheard of.

The successful seeker was accepted into the praise house as well as into one of Hilton Head's African-American churches after they were established. Initiation into Gullah religious life also marked the person a full member of the community.

When you was ready to seek, then they would identify you from the other children in the community by putting a string around your head. There were nine knots in the string, and they were suppose' to help you remember your dreams.

You had to go on your own. You know when to go 'cause your parents pretty much guide you. And durin' that time you don't kill the mosquitoes even if the mosquitoes bite you, you don't kill 'em. You just brush 'em off.—*Louise Cohen*

You couldn't be around your other siblings. You have to go outside in the woods somewhere. It was like a quiet place you had to be. You couldn't be around nobody at that particular time. And at night, you couldn't actually be around anybody.
—*Mary Lawyer Green*

You had to sit on a back seat [of the praise house], you couldn't go up to the front if you didn't belong to the church. Then . . . you see some of your friends going up, and then they get up there . . . well that really get on your nerves. . . . So after Clarence [his brother] done get through, when Grandma got to me and say, "Clarence done get through, you got to . . ." so I figger I can get through. So I say, "Well, I think I go right now." I go when it's time to pray, ask the Lord forgive me for my sins.

And after the second night, I found my teacher . . . the Lord did show me a deacon, and it was her granddaddy [Benjie Walters]. Her granddaddy said, "I know you were coming."—*William Holmes, Sr.*

When you were seeking, you had to remember your dream. Then you had to find your teacher. You tell your mom who you dream about, you call that person's name. She a lot of times know you coming, and she would be your teacher.
—*Mary Lawyer Green*

Then when I find my teachin' [spiritual] mother, I had to go all the way to Point Comfort [from Braddock's Point], ride horseback in the mornin'. Five o'clock, I got to be at the spiritual mother. Tell the dream. If I dream something, I jus' dream and go tell her. You see a white horse or somethin' like that, and you dress in white or something like dat, and you tell dem. . . . Then they carry you to conference committee.—*Laura Mae Campbell*

Nora Aiken—she was my spiritual mother. You go there every morning and tell her your dream. They try to discourage you. Say you ain't prayin', to try from your heart.—*Richard Oriage (born 1927, Gardner Community)*

I join the church when I was twelve years old. . . . You have to be there every day, the evening, twelve o'clock at night, five in the mornin', you got to be out der by yourself. I prayed [at] a willow bush until it come day. You had go to kneel down der, and da mosquito, the rat runnin', you got to stay der. Papa say, "You prayin'. You have to stay der. Can't be afraid o' nothin'."—*Laura Mae Campbell*

My sister and those, they started praying, seeking. I went out there and tried to seek because I figure I'm not gonna let my twin sister outdo me. I was sitting out there under a tree at the edge of the bushes. And I was sitting there, just leaning down, and here come a black snake. I run back home so fast, and I was finished. There was no more. They were saying that I wasn't really ready. I did mine the year after.—*Mary Lawyer Green*

Your prayin' ground, the place you went to pray, mighta been your back yard, mighta been a field close to you. For me it was palmetto bushes, and I think Mama had a turkey that nest around there. I mostly went in the morning, the dawn of day, and in late evening.—*Louise Cohen*

Oh, I seek a long time. I seek must be a whole *month*. Aunt Phyllis Ferguson [a church elder from Spanish Wells] came over to Braddock's Point where we [me and a cousin] were on Sunday. I'll never forget that. She say, "You all still prayin'? You all are playin'."

Oh boy, we go and pray then sure 'nough. We go an' pray. We ain't doin' much eatin'. Probably didn't have no time for eatin' then. We pray all day along. Oh we pray. . . . We get through in a little time then because she mean business. We might been *two* months.—*Laura Mae Campbell*

I ask the Lord forgive me for my sins, and I repent of my sins. Before he forgive me for my sins, he [his spiritual advisor] say, "You got to face your wrongs." So I faced 'em. Coming up, I didn't know no better than to kill every green frog I see in our backyard. I spent a heap a time killing them frogs.

But when I go into prayer and I told my dreams, every one of them frog show up on me just as big as that . . . they looked in my face. He say, "Uh-huh, you see you kill them frogs? You had no right killing frogs." After I faced those frogs, I went back on my knees, and I went to pray.—*William Holmes, Sr.*

You go to pray first dark at night and pray until you just feel like it's time to come in. I think it was a lot of being led by the spirit. The Lord would give you dreams. These dreams would tell you who is your spiritual mother and she might have had some kinda dream that you was comin'. I dreamed there was a airplane that land right on my prayin' ground, and this man that came out, that stepped out, he was a olive complexion and dressed—he was draped in a long white robe—and he actually spoke to me. He told me somethin' about my dad. But . . . I didn't ever see him again. That was just one of the dreams, not the one that got me through.—*Louise Cohen*

When you have the [right] dream, they knew, your spiritual mother know. On the island, we didn't have a lot of cars, but I dreamed I had a dime, and it fell down in the car door. I was trying to get it out, and some kinda way, I got it out. And that morning she told me I had found the Lord.
—*Mary Lawyer Green*

I would tell my spiritual mother my dream until she think that I have went through the process which might be findin' something, findin' diamonds or a gift, maybe beautiful white pillowcases. Mine was brushin' off all these things like ants and stuff crawlin' on me but brushin' 'em all off until I was free. They say I was brushin' off my sins.—*Louise Cohen*

When your spiritual mother think that you're ready, then she gon' call in some other people. She ain't gon' just go by herself to determine whether you had gone through the process or not, she gon' call in some other people, the deacons from the church, and then you gon' tell those dreams to them as well. After that, if you pass, you ready for baptism.
—*Louise Cohen*

And those old people were somethin' else. You better not bring nobody else dream. . . . They send you right straight on the way back. No, no. That person yonder dreamed [that], but [you] ain't dreamed dat. You couldn't fool those old people. No two ought to dream the same dream. . . . Those deacons send you back.—*Laura Mae Campbell*

BAPTISM

Baptism traditionally was marked by immersion in water to cleanse one of his or her sins. Charity sisters at the churches made white baptismal gowns as part of the preparation for those who would be baptized. Candidates for baptism wrapped their heads with a small white covering and wore their white baptismal gowns. Baptisms took place in creeks near the churches and usually occurred at low tide. Some locations for baptism included Old House Creek, Skull Creek, Bull Point, Port Royal Sound, and Broad Creek.

After donning the baptismal attire, a pilgrimage of church members, the ministers, and baptismal candidates walked from the church to the creek singing spir-

A group of young baptismal candidates from Mt. Calvary Missionary Baptist Church prepare to be baptized in Skull Creek, October 1994. *Collection of Carolyn Grant*

ituals along the way. A common spiritual sung while baptism candidates were escorted to the river bank was "Take Me to the Water." The second verse ended with the words "None but the righteous shall be baptized."

Accompanied by the minister and a church deacon, the candidate walked into the water until he or she was waist-deep. After reciting scriptures, the minister and the deacon lay the candidate back into the water and lifted him or her up. In the Methodist faith, baptism was conducted with the minister sprinkling water upon the head of the candidate.

After baptism, the new church member would be given "the right hand of fellowship" at the following Sunday church service. During this service, the new member would select or be assigned a deacon to be his or her leader within the church. The new member could also decide what he or she wanted to do within the church, such as becoming an usher, singing in the choir, or serving on a church committee.

We had a lotta people. Thirty-seven head o' chil'ren prayed that year.—*Laura Mae Campbell*

Baptism depends on who was baptizin'. If it's time for baptism, and FAB have some candidates, they call us, and Mount Calvary is baptizing, then these children would go there, and that preacher would baptize them all. I know we went behind Aunt Sadie and them house that day, and you could walk down in that creek. We sang "Take Me to the Water."

When you walk down in the water, there be the pastor and his help, and most times you walk out there to them, and one would be in the front, one in the back, and then you kinda fold your arms, and they go through their whatever they say: "I baptize you in the name of the Father, Son, and the Holy Ghost." Then they would put a towel over your face and dip you down in the water and bring you back up. You would have your baptism gown on, it was white and handmade or machine-made. It would be tied so the girls wouldn't be exposed. They tied your head too. Then they take you down in the water.

Sonya Grant, the niece of author Carolyn Grant, baptized in Skull Creek, October 1994. *Collection of Carolyn Grant*

When you got out of that water, you went back to conference. Conference was you tellin' your dreams and stuff to people there which would be the deacons. They be singin' and stuff like that. After conference, there was time to shop for the clothes and get your hair done.—*Louise Cohen*

Baptism was a Saturday thing and next day is church. They call that big church, I think because you mostly did that in the summertime after school was out. Then that was the time when everybody prayed and join the church. If your church wasn't gonna be held that Sunday, you go through what-

ever church was bein' held, and they did a transfer thing. When it was your church's time, you received the right hand of fellowship.

The right hand of fellowship is after the pastor have said they welcome you in the church, the deacons and the deaconess all come and shake your hand, giving you the right hand of fellowship. They want to know what area in the church you want to work in. You might want to be a choir, or you might want to work on the usher board. If you want to be in the choir then the president of the choir will come, shake your hand, and welcome you in the choir.—*Louise Cohen*

The first thing they . . . put me [on a] committee. . . . And the leader of the church say, I want you to go praise lead prayer meeting tonight right down the street. [He] said God need me to the meeting. *And I shout right through that roof.* . . . I been in church every since then and is there now.
— *William Holmes, Sr.*

You had a sense of somebody when you finish. Man, that was good for you. Then you were able to go into the church and praise him and pray. That was a big thing.— *Richard Oriage*

DEATH AND DYING

After the Union captured Hilton Head, Harriet Tubman attended the midnight funeral of a contraband named David. Night had been the only time slaves had to bury their dead, and the tradition was still followed.

Tubman described a torch-lit ceremony in which the corpse lay on the ground, mourners sat around the corpse, and the preacher stood over the deceased.

"The old Negro preacher began by giving out a hymn, which was sung by all." Then he started his sermon by "pointing to the dead man who lay in a rude box."

"*Shum?* Ded-a-de-dah!! *Shum, David?* Ded-a-dedah! Now I want you all to *flec'* for a moment. Who ob all dis congregation is gwine next to lie deda-de-dah? You can't go nowheres, my frien's and bredren, but Deff' fin' you. You can't dig no hole so deep an' bury yourself dar, but God A'mighty's farseein' eye fine you, an' Deff'll come arter you. You can't go into that big fort [pointing to Hilton Head] an' shut yourself up dar, dat fort dat Sesh Buckner [Secessionist "Buckra," or white man] said de debil couldn't take, but Deff'll fin' you dar. All your frien's may forget you, but Deff'll nebber forget you. Now my bredren, prepare to lie ded-a-de-dah!'

The congregation then "went round in a sort of solemn dance called the 'spiritual shuffle' [a ring dance], shaking hands with each other, and calling each other by name as they sang":

My sis'r Mary's boun' to go
My sis'r Nanny's boun' to go
My brudder Tony's boun' to go
My brudder July's boun' to go

When they came to Harriet (an outsider), they sang:

"Eberybody's boun' to go!"[10]

The body was put in a government wagon, "and by the light of the pine torches, the strange, dark procession moved along, singing a . . . funeral hymn, till they reached the place of burial."

Funerals were an important part of slave life. They reunited a slave with the ancestors.

As in other areas of Gullah culture, rituals surrounding death and dying fused African and Christian beliefs. A central difference, though, was that Christianity emphasized the body and the soul. Africans, however, believed in the body, the soul, *and* the spirit—and brought that belief to Hilton Head and other sea islands.

The body was buried, and the soul went to God. But the spirit remained on earth, usually close to the burial site though it could travel. It "was conscious of all earthly events and had the power to exercise influence over the destiny of the living." Good spirits "appeared only in dreams, giving messages and warnings to the living." Bad spirits "could haunt the living."

Families and community members provided care for the dying so that the slave could die in peace. On some plantations, the whole community became involved in the death rituals. "We got tuh help him cross de ribber," plantation members would say.

When death occurred, a dying person's last wishes were carefully followed out. Then the family gave the deceased as good a funeral as it could to honor the family member and to avoid angering the dead person's spirit.

After freedom came, family, friends, and community members continued to care for the ill and dying. With the passing of time, new ways to assist islanders developed.

When Caesar Jones, founder of the Jonesville community, died in 1903, he left his second wife, Lavinia Jones, a widow. She died the following year. William Jones, a son of Caesar, took charge of his stepmother's burial. "[I] paid fifteen dollars for a coffin, but the society of which she was a member paid me ten dollars back."

Mutual aid and burial societies were part of Hilton Head life. Members paid a small amount regularly to a society, often no more than a dime but a dime was hard to come by at the turn of the century.

In exchange, the society would help care for ill members and provide a financial benefit that helped provide a decent burial. Workers of Charity, Rose of Sharon, Lily of the Valley, and the Sisters (and Brothers) of Charity were among a number of societies.

The Mothers' Union became the largest women's organization on Hilton Head. The club assisted women club members who were ill. They also handled family chores such as washing clothes, tending the field, and platting the hair of any young girls in the family. They continued caring for the family until the time of sickness passed.

Among the various societies for men, the Brownsville Society had as a major purpose the assisting of families when illness occurred. The club was composed of men from Chaplin, Marshland, Grassland, Big Hill, Cherry Hill, Baygall, and Spanish Wells.

Most families in those areas did farming. If, for instance, a family's horse died during the farming season,

Original bell from the First African Baptist Church, which sits in front of the current church building. *Photo by Will Warasila*

remains of a person from the home to the church and then from the church to the graveyard.

The club was made up of men mainly from the north end of the island, but included members from other areas. The Farmers Club had its own building, the Farmers Hall, located in the Jonesville community.

For generations, many people rowed wooden bateaux from other islands or from Buckingham, near Bluffton on the mainland. If family members came by bateau, and the weather was bad or the funeral was held late in the day, they had to spend the night on Hilton Head. The Farmers Club made the arrangements for people to stay overnight and return to Buckingham the following day.

It was important to Gullah families to have a loved one's body properly prepared for burial. Various societies would also assist families with that task.

We hear that church bell ringing at night, you know somebody dead. Yeah, this man is dead. You hear them horse foot. Somebody come and tell you somebody died.—*William Holmes, Sr.*

society members would voluntarily come and take care of the fields.

The Farmers Club dated back to the 1880s or earlier and was best known for assuming responsibility of burying the dead. A primary purpose was to help the family obtain a casket. The club also transported the

Friends and all would come in and do it. Some of them old deacons . . . like if they belongs to the church some of them old deacons would kinda be in charge and see that they get washed and things. Her daddy, God bless the dead, he catch me one day and I had to wash one.—*William Holmes, Sr.*

We had a big old brass tub, and you put water in it, and . . . you wash the body and then take the turpentine . . . I don't know what they did with the turpentine 'cause I ain't never did it, but there's a ointment. And then they dress 'em. One time it got too hot then I get a tub of ice and put under the bed holding 'em 'til what time is the burial. So if the family is off-island sometime they try to keep 'em, and if they can't keep 'em they go on and bury 'em as far as I know.— *Laura Mae Walters Holmes*

That's how my granddaddy was buried. I remember that. Take a white sheet, wind it all around the body, put it in the coffin. Had a cotton towel wind 'round his head. I think they put turpentine in that cotton.— *William Holmes, Sr.*

Wakes were held in the family's home or in the church the evening before burial. Festive memories of the deceased were told, and popular Gullah food was served. Another type of wake existed called a "still wake." This wake was held in the praise house. Family, friends, and community members would sit in silence with the deceased throughout the night.

Burial was often within a day or two after someone died. Bodies were taken to the graveyard by a wagon pulled by a horse.

Burial was held at the graveside with family members and friends attending. The burial usually was a simple one. Last remarks spoken over the grave were performed by local ministers. During the days of slavery, most Africans and their descendants were buried on plantations where they had labored, and this tradition continued. Often the cemeteries were near water, in keeping with the Gullah belief that the souls of those buried near water would be able to travel back to Africa.

Mama had three children just a year apart. And all of us, we three, was small little children when my brother died, and I remember good when Papa and them make the box and they make the mattress and they lined it and made the pillow and everything and they painted it. It looked good. Didn't have no hearses, they put it in the wagon. They had the funeral outside in the yard.

Mother used to take everything so hard, and when she cried, I cried. And I asked her where are they going with my brother. Mama said he is going away, but he is coming back. And I look everyday, I ain't see no brother come back. And she still cry. Walking and walking all over the yard and crying to herself, and then I would cry. So, I quit asking her that 'cause brother didn't come back. And every time I would ask her about it she would cry more.— *Emma Graham*

It was traditional for Gullah people to pass the youngest child across the grave. In early times, the baby of a deceased mother was passed back and forth over the grave. It was believed that otherwise, "Dead moder will

Braddock Point Cemetery in Sea Pines is surrounded by a golf course and condominiums. *Photo by Will Warasila*

hant de baby and worry him in his sleep." A similar custom dated back to the Bakongo, a Bantu-speaking people of Africa.

When my grandmother died, the younger one, they pass it over the grave. You got any loved one died, you pass.— *Laura Mae Campbell (Campbell passed her son, Carl, over the grave of a loved one.)*

A special plate or picture or piece of crockery or porcelain that belonged to the deceased, or a last item the deceased had used often was placed on the gravesite.

Even medicine the deceased had used at the time of death might be placed on the grave. Sometimes water or a dish of the deceased's favorite food was placed on the grave. Placing such items on the grave was another African tradition.

Decorating graves with such items marked a grave of a relative. The items also were gifts that Gullah people believed could be of use in the life beyond the grave. Ancestors were thought to "retain their normal human passions and appetites, which had to be gratified in death as they had been in life." They "felt hunger and thirst." In Africa some people put out food so that the deceased "would eat the food and bless those who placed it there."[11]

In keeping with the tradition of fulfilling a just-before-death desire, one of my great-aunts placed a dish of stewed fish on her husband's grave. This act could be considered a variant of the tradition of decorating the grave with favorite items of the deceased. Grave decorations were a common practice until the late 1950s on Hilton Head Island. —*Emory S. Campbell*

Down there at the cemetery, people had a lot of china in the headstones. When they did, they put plates—just what they got—there. And when people came on the island . . . they go and pick them up. Take 'em off. They had it in the paper that ghosts [were] down there. After dar, they not sup-posed to go down there 'cause a lotta ghosts down there. This kind scare the people, so they wouldn't go to the cemetery.—*Laura Mae Campbell*

A formal ceremony eulogizing a deacon was held up to six months after the burial. The exterior church columns were wrapped in black paper, and a black bow was put on the deacon's seat. This second ceremony was held in part to assure the spirit that his or her family members and friends still cared. It also allowed time for family members who were away from the island to make plans to be present at the formal funeral. The family of the deceased always wore black. The women wore a black dress, stockings, hats, and shoes, and the men wore a black suit. The deceased was eulogized as though he or she was lying at the altar. Many times, this ceremony was as emotional as the first.

Of two cousins on the Murray family of Hilton Head, [one] was back from New York for the funeral of her father. She had been two years in New York employed as a candy-girl at Huyley's, Fifth Avenue. —*Elsie Clews Parsons (Parsons, a folklorist, visited Hilton Head in 1919.)*

My granddaddy, Jackie Lawyer, he was a deacon and they preach his sermon six months after. They raise so much sand in that church and say that ain't preach Jack's sermon right. They raise some sand in that church.—*Corrine Lawyer Brown*

They [the women] wore black for a year or two. If it was your mother or husband you did. For your aunt it was six months.— *Laura Mae Walters Holmes*

In 1953, a state-operated car ferry began from Buckingham to Jenkins Island. The Farmers Club arranged for a new service—that of transporting the body of a Hilton Head Gullah native back to the island for burial. Then the Farmers Club opened a funeral home on Hilton Head. A club member, Charles Frazier, Sr., was the funeral director of records and a licensed operator. Club secretary Thomas S. Barnwell, Sr., was chief operator of the funeral home. The funeral home worked closely with the Wright-Donaldson Funeral Home in Beaufort. In addition, well-known Gullah men, Ben White, Sr., and Alex Patterson, Sr., began selling caskets through a new business venture, White-Patterson.

Naomi Frazier, who grew up with the old ways, began selling artificial flowers in her home. Flowers had not been used on graves before. Hilton Head's Gullah people blended new ideas into their creolized culture.

CRIME

They didn't carry nobody to no law. If anything happen, the church would take that.— *Isabel Brown*

The people would go to the deacons with a problem. They used to call you up in the church. They would put you the back seat and you would have to explain yourself to the people.— *Julia Grant Bryant*

In the 1920s the Beaufort County sheriff remarked that Gullah people were law-abiding "because the Negro fears the Lord more than he fears the law."

Certainly, Hilton Head was known as a peaceful island where few crimes occurred. But fearing the Lord was only one part of the reason few crimes of any sort were committed on the island and taken to the mainland to resolve.

Gullah people on Hilton Head settled their disputes at their community praise house whenever possible. The praise house functioned as a religious court and was considered to administer the "just law."

The "just law" was a concept that existed during slavery and gained new importance during disenfranchisement and segregation. The "unjust law" was off-island in the county courts of law. It was much safer to trust one's fellow praise-house member to settle a dispute. Under the "just law," praise-house members were required to take a problem which occurred in the community to church leaders "for review and an opportunity to mediate" before resorting to a governmental court. And as few offenses involved violent crime, the praise house was quite capable of handling disputes.

"If you had a quarrel with your neighbor, for instance, the praise house would mediate it," Emory S. Campbell remembers. Regular meetings of the praise houses were Sunday, Tuesday, and Thursday evenings, and meetings to settle arguments often were held on Saturday or Sunday afternoon.

"If somebody's horse ate up all your beans, for instance, and they didn't want to make amends . . . the issue would land before the praise-house elders," Campbell said. (For Gullah farmers who relied on their crops to feed their families and to sell at market, the loss of a crop would be a serious matter.)

Each praise house usually had three leaders. People looked up to the leaders and especially to the praise-house head.

In the example of a horse eating a neighbor's beans, the praise-house system worked like this:

One man went to see the other.

"Your horse got loose last night and ate my beans."

If the other man ignored the victim, then the victim brought the dispute to the praise house in a special evening meeting. Witnesses were heard. Just punishments for a member who had violated community rules were debated as if the praise house was a court. It was a religious court and taken quite seriously. Justice was meted out. Maybe the man whose horse ate the beans had to replace the beans or give the victim potatoes or something else to replace the crop that was eaten.

The man whose horse ate the beans regained his community standing once he had made restitution. Before that time, he was consigned to sit on the back bench, reserved for those in bad grace or for young people who were not yet praise-house members.[12]

Within Hilton Head's tight-knit communities, the praise-house justice system worked because few members wanted to face community censure.

Ironically, the most notorious crime to occur on Hilton Head took place in the same decade the Beaufort County sheriff stated that islanders were law-abiding because they feared the Lord. A well-regarded white store owner and his wife were murdered one Saturday evening in 1923. W. D. "Willie" Brown, a northerner, had opened the largest general store on Hilton Head following the Civil War, bought land, became a postmaster, and frequently testified on behalf of black Union veterans in their pension case applications.

Two black men came in shortly before closing, robbed Brown, killed Brown and his wife, and set the store afire. The county law was called in, and for a brief time Gullah people feared suspicion would fall on them.

The two men turned out to be strangers to the island. They later were caught off-island and executed. Life on Hilton Head resumed its peaceful pace, but Gullah residents mourned the Browns and remembered them through the decades.

On the rare occasions when the law was called in, island magistrate Ben Hudson contacted the county. In the 1930s and 1940s, a Gullah man, Moses Milton (also spelled Middleton), was a deputy sheriff and escorted people accused of a crime to Beaufort.

WORK SONGS, SPIRITUALS, SHOUTS, AND HYMNS

Work songs, spirituals, shouts, and hymns punctuated everyday life on Hilton Head. "Michael Row the Boat Ashore," a song known around the globe, is thought to have originated in the islands around Hilton Head. The song was heard there in 1861 by northerners who had arrived to help formerly enslaved people learn to read and write. This song, among others heard on the Union-held sea islands, was published in the 1867 book *Slave Songs of the United States.*

"Michael Row" fits into the category of "work songs," the songs workers sang in unison to make their work go faster and easier. Northerners heard "Michael Row" used as a rowing song. It was a lively song, sung "when the load was heavy or the tide was against us."[13]

People on Hilton Head had their own version of the song. Although some northerners tried to reproduce Gullah pronunciation, the Hilton Head version of "Michael Row" was written in proper English. Perhaps Gullah people on Hilton Head were more in a hurry to get where they were going than people on other islands, as they did not ask the archangel Michael to row the boat. They asked him to *haul* it:

Michael haul the boat ashore.
Then you'll hear the horn they blow.

Then you'll hear the trumpet sound.
Trumpet sound the world around.
Trumpet sound for rich and poor.
Trumpet sound the jubilee.[14]

The work song most linked with Hilton Head was said to have been improvised by bondsmen building earthenware forts for their masters' use in fending off the Union's expected invasion of the island. Gullah islanders followed their masters' commands, but their voices lifted in song spoke to how eagerly they awaited the arrival of the Union.

No more peck of corn for me, no more, no more
No more pint of salt
No more driver's lash
No more mistress call, no more, no more[15]

The song spread throughout the South under the name of its last line, "Many thousands go." It later was sung in churches on Hilton Head.

Spirituals—to one missionary's ear pronounced as "sperichils"[16]—were plentiful on Hilton Head and other sea islands. While Negro spirituals were sung in other parts of the country, the missionaries had not heard several sung elsewhere before, including "Rock O' Jubilee," "No Man Can Hinder Me," and "O' Jerusalem,

Early in de Morning." Still others, such as "Cross Jordan" and "O Lord Remember Me," were already in Methodist hymnals, but northerners found Gullah renditions so different—in tone, wording, and style—that they seemed altogether new.

Spirituals were sung in both the small praise houses where Gullah people met several nights a week and later in Gullah churches as they became established. Many spirituals were also sung as work songs.

Throughout slavery and freedom Hilton Head Gullah worshippers constantly sang work songs, spirituals, and secular songs, and many women hummed as they worked throughout the day.

For decades on Hilton Head, lively shouts rang from small praise houses where community members gathered to give praise to God. A praise house served as a place where community residents could worship through the week. While shouts could be either religious or secular, praise-house shouts were sacred songs, often spirituals. In what is usually called a "ring shout," shouters moved counterclockwise in a circle in shuffling steps to avoid crossing their feet or lifting them off the floor. Otherwise, it was considered secular dancing.

The rhythm was set by hand clapping and foot stomping or tapping a stick on the wooden floor (that may have replaced drums outlawed by slaveholders). The shouters progressed slowly at first, sometimes

silently, with "a jerking, hitching motion which agitates the entire shoulder," an observer wrote in 1867, adding, "The song and dancers alike are extremely energetic." The singing, hand clapping, foot stamping, and stick tapping often grew until it almost shook the house.

The dance movements and rhythm form a cultural tie to West Africa, where similar forms of devotion have been found. Many Civil War missionaries were appalled at the shouts, as they did not resemble any religious ceremony in their experience. Laura Towne, a founder of the Penn School on Saint Helena Island, first thought the shouts savage. Eventually, though, she lived in the sea islands long enough to record in her diary, "attended a fine shout today."

Some of the old spirituals disappeared over time, replaced by newer hymns. Many of the newer ones did not originate on the island. But both new and old songs and spirituals helped Gullah worshippers capture the spirit to praise God.

Among the many songs sung on Hilton Head from the 1930s through the 1950s were "Amazing Grace," "Come By Here, My Lord" ("Cum By Ya"), "Down By the Riverside," "Father I Stretch My Hands to Thee," "Blessed Be the Tie," "I Am Bound for the Promised Land," "I Am Going Home on the Morning Train," "Get Right with God," "Give Me that Old Time Religion," and "Glory, Glory Hallelujah." Others from the same time period included "I Am Leaning on the Lord," "I'll Fly Away," "Jesus on the Main Line," "Traveling Shoes," "Just a Closer Walk with Thee," "Precious Lord," "Satan, Your Kingdom Must Come Down," "Wade in the Water," "Walk in Jerusalem Just Like John," "We Are Climbing Jacob's Ladder," "When We All Get to Heaven," "When the Saints Go Marching In," and "Wings Over Jordan."

EDUCATION

They had good schools here in my time. I had a teacher to teach me come here from Parris Island. It was Reverend Saul Campbell. It was Earlene Frazier's daddy. Her mother and father were graduate college students. They had these schoolhouses. Some of them had two rooms. Some didn't have but one. You had to go off [the island] to go to the high school at that time. They would attend school in Beaufort. These people really did struggle to send their children off for education. Yeah, but they did it. Some children had to work their way through. Some could pay.— *Naomi Frazier*

Teaching slaves to read and write had been illegal under South Carolina law, so when the Port Royal Experiment got underway during the Civil War, contrabands were eager to taste these forbidden fruits. The first school on Hilton Head began just two months after the Union invasion. In January 1862, Bostonian Barnard K. Lee became the first teacher on the island. Then missionaries arrived in the spring, expanding educational opportunities.

Four teachers, sponsored by freedmen aid societies in the North, began setting up rough schools wherever they could find a place to do so on Hilton Head. They set up temporary classrooms in everything from praise houses to cotton barns and sometimes held lessons under the trees.

The first school building on Hilton Head was built in the freedmen's village of Mitchelville in 1863. Near the end of the war in 1865, students in Mitchelville could hear battle raging twelve miles away. By the time the war ended, Mitchelville had adopted the first compulsory education law in the state. None had previously existed for either whites or blacks.

During the height of Reconstruction, seventeen teachers taught on Hilton Head. Most were sponsored by the American Missionary Association (AMA). Money from northern donors to the AMA and similar societies then declined.

The work of the freedmen aid societies had shown the country that newly freed people indeed could learn and that the seeds of education had been sown in Hilton Head's sandy soil. The 1874 catalogue of Hampton Normal Institute bore witness to that. One Jacob Brown of Hilton Head was listed as a junior that year. Brown presumably was preparing for a teaching career. Where

Brown went next is not known. But that a young Hilton Head man had made it to the leading normal and industrial school in the country slightly less than ten years after the end of the Civil War was extraordinary.

Following Reconstruction, disenfranchisement, and the passage of Jim Crow laws, public funding for education for black children shrank, compared to funding for white students. Gullah families on Hilton Head took extra steps to educate their young.

Schooling on Hilton Head at first consisted of three months per year, from November to February—after the harvesting of crops and before the planting of crops began in March. A person was considered to have done well if he or she completed three years of education.

Parents then started coming up with the money to pay teachers for an extra month so the schools could stay open longer. They continued this practice as the number of publicly funded months increased.

In some communities, the one-room praise house doubled as a school. Children and their families might attend prayer services in the praise house three nights a week, and children would attend classes there daily. In the Chaplin area, the Grand Army Hall, used by veterans, became a school during the daytime, attended by students from the communities of Chaplin, Marshland, and Gardner.

Several schools were styled after Rosenwald Schools. Julius Rosenwald of Sears & Roebuck fame became interested in funding black rural schools after getting to

Cherry Hill School, built ca. 1937, was a one-room schoolhouse that was used for classes until 1950. *Courtesy of the Coastal Discovery Museum*

know black educator Booker T. Washington. At least five hundred schools were built in South Carolina. None were built on Hilton Head, possibly because Washington had tried an agricultural experiment on the island from 1906 to 1912. It failed due to misunderstandings between the islanders and those running the agricultural colony, but the colony included a school that encouraged several students to pursue further studies.

The lack of a formal Rosenwald School did not stop islanders from using the architectural plans for Rosenwald Schools to build their own. One was in Squire Pope. Another was built in Cherry Hill on land donated by a Gullah islander. Another was built in Chaplin. The schools built in Chaplin and Honey Horn were the two

Cherry Hill School has been preserved by St. James Baptist Church and is listed on the National Register of Historic Places. *Photo by Will Warasila*

largest, having been built during the Washington experiment. The others were one-room schools. All were simple frame buildings but represented an improvement over the school buildings previously used.

At the Spanish Wells School, grades eventually went through the sixth grade. Then they dropped back to the fifth grade as Robinson Middle School opened in the late 1940s or early 1950s, offering grades six through eight. The school was named after William Robinson, a white man from Gastonia, North Carolina, who used to hunt on Hilton Head. The school had three classrooms, each with a little porch attached, and three teachers. It was painted gray and had a nice architectural style but lacked indoor plumbing. It was located off Beach City Road.

Robinson Middle School students, ca. 1950, with teacher Rosalie Barnwell (left front) and Diogenese Singleton (right front), head teacher/principal. *Collection of Nell Barnwell Hay, daughter of Rosalie Barnwell*

The county opened a consolidated elementary school in 1954, replacing the island's long history of community schools. Gullah families saw the school as an advantage, but also recognized that the school was built to forestall integration.

EARLY TEACHERS

As early as the 1870s, the Penn School on Saint Helena began training and sending out teachers to the surrounding sea islands. Hilton Head no doubt benefited from this.

The first Gullah teacher born and reared on Hilton Head Island is believed to be Solomon Campbell, the grandson of "Walla," an enslaved man living on Hilton Head at the time the Union captured Hilton Head in 1861. To family members, Walla is known as Wallace, and there is some thought that he may have arrived on the island from Edisto in the 1820s.

Born in 1874, Solomon Campbell was educated at South Carolina State College. He taught at the Honey Horn School and on Long Island (now Calibogue Cay). Julia Aiken Campbell, born on Saint Helena in 1878, was married to Solomon and also taught at Hilton Head schools. Both Solomon and Julia were highly regarded teachers. (See Solomon Campbell's photo in chapter 20.)

ADVANCED DEGREES

Having obtained college degrees in education, Gullah women Lucinda Patterson and Ruth Jones were among the many excellent teachers Hilton Head was fortunate to have.

One of the students at the "failed" Booker T. Washington school on Hilton Head Island had excelled beyond anything Washington expected from the students. Born in 1904, Thomas Robinson, the son of Chamberlin and Florence Robinson, attended the Penn School after going as far as he could on Hilton Head. He went on to Hampton Institute next, where he got a high-school diploma in 1928.

After Hampton, Robinson received a master's degree of education in industrial administration and administration from Pennsylvania State University. Years later he also received a doctor's degree in education administration from Penn State.

In between, he headed the Industrial Arts Department at Alabama State University, then became principal of the Alabama State Laboratory School, and later served as professor of education at Alabama State University. He kept pursuing his doctoral degree and received it in 1954—two years before the bridge connected Hilton Head to the outside world.

Robinson was the first—but not the last—Hilton Head Gullah person to receive a PhD. The early dreams of education, and the hard pursuit of learning by many Gullah people, came to fruition when Robinson received his long-awaited doctorate degree.

BOARDING SCHOOLS

Parents had to make arrangements for children to attend schools off-island after completing the schooling available on Hilton Head if the student was to further his or her education. Some families were determined that their children should receive additional education and saved and sacrificed in order that they might. For the few families that could afford to send their children off-island, there were educational choices available.

The Penn School on Saint Helena, founded in April of 1862 by white northern missionaries Laura M. Towne and Ellen Murray, was the first school for freed blacks in the sea islands. In 1901, it became the Penn Normal and Industrial School under the leadership of a board of trustees that managed to maintain support for the school for almost fifty years. Students from Hilton Head could board there for approximately ten dollars a month in the early years. The school was highly respected by Sea Islanders and it educated both girls and boys, some of whom participated in work programs to offset their boarding costs. The school originally carried students through the seventh grade. Later, the curriculum expanded to award high-school diplomas.

The Mather School in Beaufort was also started by a white missionary. Rachel Crane Mather of Boston began the school in the late 1860s to educate the island's black girls and young women.

The school first operated in partnership with the American Missionary Association and then, from 1882–1968, with the support of the Women's American Baptist Home Missionary Society. In the 1950s, it began admitting men.

By that time, students also could attend a black school in Bluffton, the Michael C. Riley Elementary School. Some Hilton Head Gullah students also attended Beach High School in Savannah and Savannah State College.

My grandmother told me that some of the slaves could read. And they would hide, you know . . . they would go into the houses [slave cabins] at night and teach each other.—Naomi Frazier (Frazier's grandmother was a slave on Hilton Head when the

Union captured the island during the
Civil War.)

I remember when there wasn't no teacher on this island, not one. And the first ones was Solomon Campbell and Edward Campbell. They gone to school together and they gone to college together.—*Isabel Brown (Brown's daughter, Frances Jones, grew up to be a teacher on neighboring Daufuskie Island. Her retirement created the vacancy filled by author Pat Conroy, who wrote the well-known book* The Water Is Wide, *based on his experiences on Daufuskie.)*

William and Laura Mae Holmes, natives of Hilton Head, lived in and raised their family in the Squire Pope community. *Photo Courtesy of Jessie M. Henderson*

Well, I couldn't leave Henry Bennett [her husband]. He could read. His granddaddy would make him go to school. . . . The old man tell him to get the light and light 'um, and you'll going to see to read tonight.

I ain't get none [education] myself. But now why I didn't get none, 'cause my parents sent me to school, but I would go and fall down in the water and thing' and don't want to learn nothing. So the other day, I said, well, God, I sure done a fool thing. I could have get a little, cause I know children [who] been to school . . . but their parents were strict on them and make them go. Make them read in the dark in the night time, throw water in their eye . . . and tell them they got to read. But you see we parents [her

parents] didn't have nothing hardly. They didn't [get] strict on we to do nothing.—*Regina Bennett*

I went far as fourth grade in the school been on Chaplin. They called the place "Grand Army Hall." To tell you the truth, I could go to school 'cause it wasn't but one child my mother had, and she try to do everything to make me be better and know more. But I didn't. After she gone to New York, I stopped. I gone to Savannah and been working. —*Nancy Ferguson*

I gone to second grade. Promoted for third grade. I had to stop because my mother wasn't making nothing.—*Thomas Holmes (born 1915, Squire Pope Community)*

I went to Pope School. You go three months for free, and my granddaddy pay for the rest. I think I went to sixth grade. After that I didn't see nowhere else to go, unless you go off, and I didn't go off. —*Laura Mae Walters Holmes*

Our parents didn't have no education. They could figure. . . . They could count money, but they didn't have too much of that in those days. —*Julia Grant Bryant*

Everybody more or less could count money, you know.—*James Bryant (birth year unknown, Squire Pope Community)*

When my mother an' them come up here [to Braddock's Point], there was school; but when we come up [grow up], there was no school at Braddock's Point at all. We didn't get to school until I was up in age. They have to send a teacher (from Spanish Wells) over to Braddock's Point. Then they was teaching our school over there at a place they call Long Island [between Braddock's Point and Lawton Plantation] in a big house.

    I quit when the school leave from Long Island. [Later] I went to adult school at night. . . . I get my little bit o' learnin' from dem.—*Laura Mae Campbell*

Hannah Barnwell teach me; Olivia Wright teach me; Miss Julia Campbell the only one get some

sense into me, 'cause [with] all them other teachers I was playing. But when I got down to Miss Julia, I wasn't playing. Julia Campbell was strict, and she make you learn.—*Ben White, Jr.*

I didn't get to go to school the first year because my mother told me it was too far for me to walk. It was at least three miles. And I stand up on the porch and watch all them fellas going to school. Boy, I hated that. But it's a funny thing, it was fun. People had fun going to school—look forward to going to school.

    They must of had two kinds of primers, beginner and advanced, because you used the same book must be about two or three years and then you get another book. And then we got to the place where we had two and three books. Oh, we thought we were big wheel then.—*Charlie Simmons, Jr.*

Mother was the cook at the school. They built a separate kitchen on the outside. It was a one-room flat top, you know, not expensive, more like a little trailer. I believe that all the schools worked like that at that time. You had to pay five cent a day for lunch. Whoever couldn't afford it, they would bring lunch. There was a lot of time a lot of children didn't bring lunch, but their friends would share that peanut butter and jelly sandwich, you know. The county would furnish most of the food. We had rice some day. We didn't have no grits now; bread, soup, and sandwich. We had, you know, like can milk. We had fruits—prunes and apples . . .

We start school at nine o'clock. In the beginning you sing a song, and everybody had to say a Bible verse. Then we had a prayer, then we go back to class. And the teacher would start with primary, first grades, then they had a study period. She would give 'em work to do, then she move to second grade. She would give second grade a study period and move back to first grade. We were loaded with books. The first grade, I think had a writing book and this little primary book and a little spelling book. And these were no hand-me-down books. These books were ordered from Louisiana, R. L. Bryan Company I think it was called.

The county sent a booklist out and the parent had a special meeting they go and pick these books for us. Our parents ordered the books, you know. We had the best books. They had parent-teacher meetings and that night that school be loaded. Yeah, they really work with the teacher, the teacher work with parents.—*Henry Ford*

When I was going into the first grade from Pope School for one year, the next year they sent us to Honey Horn School. So now instead of me going into the second grade, I went into the first grade again. They did that automatically—they didn't test you or try to find out anything. I went back to first grade. And then they sent us back to Pope School and back again. That made me two years behind in grades, so anybody who was born in 1925, those are the people that I was in grades with because of that going back and forth.

I'd finished the seventh grade here that May, went to New York, and school started in September. I had my report card, went into the eighth grade and right away what the counselor wanted to know was why you so far behind in years and grades. So they said okay, you stay in the eighth grade until December. In January we will test you and [see] if you meet the requirement for the ninth grade. So I took the test in January, passed the test, went into the ninth grade. Now came June when it was time for graduation, I graduated from the ninth grade to the tenth grade. So then I completed high school.—*Ruth Germany*

When I reach third grade, I could not add, I could not subtract, I could not divide. I could not do nothing and it look like . . . I was not interested in school. My brother was smart, so they say if William can do it, you can do it. One night my mom told me before I left school that day—she say we got along night ahead of us. I didn't know what she was talkin' about.

Bear in mind now we had to go home, and we

had to get the firewood . . . we had to cut the wood up for the chimney and for the woodstove. We had a old wood stove to cook on. . . . We had to feed the cows; we had to feed the horses. And we had to bring that bucket of water in every night. Just before dark all that have to be done. When it get dark you would have to be in the house under that lamplight getting your lessons. That would be right after supper.

But this particular night my mom said, "You gonna learn your lesson this night 'cause we are not goin' bed [until you do]." Everything went fine except when we got down to the math part. I could not add fifteen and fifteen. I couldn't get that you have to carry. My mom say, "You have to carry the one over, so it will come out right." . . . We worked on that thing about two hours, and it's getting late. I say, "I don't know [how]. I can't. . . ." About 11 o'clock she got my attention and she was maulin' me in the head, and, oh man, my head start getting sore. . . . Sleep in your eye and you're crying and everything, and she say, "Henry, look at this . . . fifteen plus fifteen. Five plus five equal ten. Put [carry] that one over here. Now where you goin' put that one at?" It was right there and so, oh, about twelve o'clock, man, I was singin' that thing.

I went to school that next day and Miss Wright, she said, "Who wants to go to the blackboard?" I used to sorta duck from goin' to the board to put our lesson up, but that day I was ready. My hand went up. I went on up to the blackboard. I got my lesson that day.—*Henry Ford*

School was a two-room schoolhouse. There was one in Squire Pope, and Jonesville, Baygall, and one in Chaplin. And it was a two-room schoolhouse what they called multiple grades. My teachers were my mother, Mrs. Olivia J. Wright, and Hannah Barnwell. They were good—they were better than good. My mother, I think she went to Savannah State for a while.

It wasn't like you did something at school and your parents didn't know nothing about it. In my case, my parent was there, so she knew. But in those days, you know, if you do something in school, they'd send a note or tell your parents, and when you get home you got it again. . . .

Back then, teachers were respected. I know a year after my mother retired, before she died, students from years past would come by and say Miss Wright was my teacher.

For subjects we had your traditional "Dick and Jane" and then we have a little history and a little science. Tom Barnwell, Sr., had a big truck, and we used to ride to school with him in the truck, and then later on, I don't know whether Mr. Charlie Simmons had a contract with the county or what, but he used to take us back and forth in the later years. . . .

[When I came along] we went to school nine months out of the year. . . . The environment . . . was good and during recess time you knew everybody there, and we would play games, mostly baseball with a stick or an old can. We had enough students to have two baseball teams, so I figure maybe thirty or forty children.—*Caesar Wright*

I went to Chaplin School. Reverend (Solomon) Campbell was the teacher, and he had this switch. You had to have your hand out when you do somethin' bad, then he come up and whack! So what we did, as he come down to you, you bring your hand up to meet the switch.

I got sent home for something. I don't know, I did something, so a teacher name Rosalie Badger give me this letter to take home. I was scared to death. I gave the letter to my mother. My father didn't touch the note, but the next morning we got up before daylight and loaded two wagons with plows and some rakes.

We went down there by the Wileys, [where my father had] about ten acres of property. We plowed from the time we got there until he looked up and decided it was twelve o'clock. We ate and drank some water, he had three or four quarts of water with him, but there was no ice. We stayed out there until it was dark and the next day was a repeat the same thing.

When I went back to school, I was the best kid in school. He didn't say a word about the note. Instead, he taught me a valuable lesson. You either gonna make it a little easier for yourself and do some studying, or you're gonna stay down and be doing the drudgery work all your life.—*Charlie White*

I went to Penn School in 1943, and in 1949 in the twelfth grade, that's where I met Rosa [his wife]. I don't remember exactly how much it cost to go to Penn, but we went on the *Cleveland* [a steamboat]. We caught the *Cleveland* and went to Beaufort. I think somebody from Penn must have picked us up from the *Cleveland*.

When you got there and enrolled or registered, they didn't allow you to come back home until Christmas. You come back for the Christmas holidays and you go back and you don't come back again 'til school close. The only way they let you come, there must be a real, real good reason for leaving because they were very, very strict on that.

After Penn, I went to South Carolina State. I graduated from Penn in 1949, and I was lucky enough to have gotten into State the same school term, September. Then of course, the Korean conflict was going on. I started my sophomore year in October of 1950, and I got drafted. I spent my basic training out in Fort Hood, Texas. I stayed to Texas, and left Texas and went to Germany. I think

I stayed in two years. I got my degree in business administration in 1956.—*Charlie Simmons, Jr.*

LIVELIHOOD

I used to go fishing, in a rowboat by myself. Go all day and take the bateau and the oars, throw the anchor out. When I done throw the anchor, [I] put my boat up in a place, a creek like. A little water be around. That tide coming up then. It would come and rise with the tide. I cast that net and get my shrimps.

When I done get my shrimps, I pull my anchor up, and I throw it out and go in the deep like. Throw my anchor out there. I had my line and hook. You used to rig that yourself, and you throw that out in the water down in the deep you know like. Fish catch right on to that hook. And you know when it catch it. You just pull them in. Pull them in until you get them in that boat.—*Nancy Ferguson*

For Gullah people to muster enough resources to feed their family and allow their children to get at least some schooling took hard physical work and ingenuity.

The land and the sea was all they had. As Elijah Jones, Jr., born in 1925, put it, "[W]e had to work out of the field and creek—catch fish and crab and such and go in the field."

Most Gullah families on Hilton Head farmed at least a small plot of land but pieced together their livelihood from both the land and the sea. They farmed from spring to late fall and then, especially during the 1920s into the 1940s, often worked at one of the oyster factories on Hilton Head and surrounding islands during the winter months.

Besides the major categories of farming and catching or harvesting seafood, some islanders owned small community stores, built boats, or piloted large boats that shipped fish and produce to Savannah. Some women picked a plant called "musk" to supplement their income. Other Gullah people gained employment by filling the needs of well-to-do hunters who visited the island to shoot wild game. A smaller number of Gullah people taught school or were midwives on the island.

Still others worked off-island, at least periodically, in order to earn more money than they could on the island. Often the men worked as longshoremen and women provided domestic help for white families in Savannah or other locations, and returned to Hilton Head on the weekends.

BY LAND

Farming was critical to people's daily lives, not only to put food on the table but also for cash crops to sell off-island. Planting began in March and continued through April and beyond, but preparing the fields began much earlier. The islanders tilled the soil and fertilized the fields, often using mud from the marsh, and prepared furrows for the seed.

Row boats in Skull Creek.
Photo by Will Warasila

By the time the bridge to the mainland ended Hilton Head's isolation, a few farmers had tractors. Most Gullah families farmed on a smaller scale, however, and relied on horses or mules. If they lacked seasoned work animals, they had to tame and train a horse (a wild marsh tacky from the beach) or train a mule.

Both horses and mules had to be taught certain commands. "Gee" meant go right, "haw" meant go left, "whoa" meant stop, "get up" meant go, "alright" meant turn around and go from one furrow to the next. Back up commands also were used if a point in the row had been skipped.

Common crops included beans (both low-growing and high bush beans grown on a pole), corn, early June peas, sweet potatoes, Irish potatoes, cabbage, greens, cucumber, squash, and cotton. Cotton usually was harvested in September or October. Corn was harvested in October or November.

To harvest corn, a horse- or mule-pulled wagon proceeded down the middle row of a corn field and field workers would break the corn off the stalk. When the wagon was full, it was driven to the barn and unloaded.

Some corn was taken to market in Savannah, but the corn was too important to a family's survival for all of it to be sold. Corn was ground into grits or cornmeal, staples the family needed year-round. Corn also was fed to horses, chickens, turkeys, pigs, and other animals during the winter. Corn shucks were used to start cooking fires in woodstoves, make pillows for the beds, or make nests in the chicken coops.

Traditional Gullah foods included some that were domesticated in Africa and introduced to the New World through the slave trade. Okra, benne seed (sesame), sorghum, and yams fell into this category. Peanuts and lima beans, although originally grown in other countries, probably were brought from Africa during the slave trade.

Other traditional Gullah crops, including cow peas (a form of field pea or black-eyed pea) and watermelon, had been introduced to Africa by the Spanish and then brought to the United States in the hulls of ships along with slaves.

Some species of cotton closely related to the luxurious long-staple cotton grown in the sea islands and surrounding areas were first domesticated in Africa and had long grown there. Indigo was cultivated in Africa for many years. Rice had been grown in Africa. Because they knew how to cultivate these crops, many enslaved people were brought to Hilton Head and other sea islands for this purpose.

In addition, corn and tobacco, although domesticated in the Americas, were also cultivated in Africa. Cow peas and watermelon fall into the same category. Many Africans arriving on Hilton Head likely already knew how to grow all of these crops. Gullah islanders drew from a body of passed-down knowledge in planting and tending their crops.

Families that did not own land often rented it from others. Almost no official sharecropping existed on Hilton Head. Gullah people resisted the practice. In a few cases, when a white landowner wanted a family to farm on shares, that family moved rather than submit to what usually turned out to be an unfair practice.

Likewise, a number of families moved to Hilton Head from nearby Pinckney Island after a new owner introduced sharecropping there. Gullah people were determined to preserve their independence.

In my great-grandfather's time, [at] Braddock's Point, they planted peas, beans, corn, rice, benne (sesame), peanuts, and vegetables. Green vegetables would be all in the summer. We would can them. [We] dried peas and you raised hogs, . . . and cured it for the summer. . . . The only thing you selled was your cotton, and you would sell pigs. But these beans and peas, you would dry and have for your own use.— *Isabel Brown*

They cut it, the green marsh; and then after it dry, then they sprinkle it in the fields. . . . My dad had everything on the farm. Had everything you can name. Dey had a cow, they had horse, they had chicken, they had hog. And they plant everything on the farm: okra, peas, butter beans, onion, cabbage, collard greens, corn, everything. . . . See, we were livin'. We had no money, but we had plenty to eat. Ooh, had plenty to eat — *Laura Mae Campbell (Campbell said that they took the horse to the marsh, loaded the fresh mud in a wagon, and hauled the green marsh back home to dry.)*

My mother and father were born on this island and lived at Joe Pope [also known as Leamington]. They used to rent, and they pay their rent [to a white landowner]. How much they paid now, I don't know. They [her parents] worked for themselves. They worked on the white man property . . . but they worked for themselves. What they had was their own. They work for what they need. They didn't take [shares] you know. . . . No [they were not] sharecroppers.— *Nancy Ferguson*

When I came here these people had a lot of beans and vegetables of every kind. They had fruit trees. They had a big freeze here one year and [it] kill a lot of the orange trees.

I don't think there are many homes you could go in there, and they didn't have plum trees and peach trees, and fig trees. Some had banana trees. They had everything. They didn't have to worry about anything. People used to raise a lot of turkey and chicken. . . . And watermelons, those folks use to make some watermelon that was so big. I remember a man who is dead now, Mr. Wiley, Gene Wiley's daddy, gave us some Stone Mountain watermelon one night when we came here. He was cutting it with a saw. It was just that big.— *Naomi Frazier*

I guess they would start sometime as early as March planting things, but they knew what to plant when, even when it came down to sweet potatoes. They would plant the sweet potatoes, which would be the actual sweet potatoes, little pieces, you know, they would put in the ground. When that came up and it got vines, then about June or July, they're gonna cut the vines and then they're make another field and they're gonna do what they call "stickin' the potato vine." That where you're gonna get your new potatoes from. We used to call the ones that you originally put in the ground the "big mommas," because they used some big ones. But the new potatoes would be from the ones where you "stuck" the vine.

My brothers and my father, they would do the plowing of the field and then when it comes to planting process, like my mother would help, because again, our family was small as I came along. Say if my mother was digging the hole because she didn't want us to put it in too deep, she would tell me how many of the seeds to drop in, and you had to bend your back when you put it in there, and then my brother would come along and he would cover the hole. And so that's the way we would do the planting.—*Ruth Germany*

Now once it came up, I would help, but my mother used to say I used to cut too many of her stuff down.

So I didn't get to hoe very much. Usually it was her and my brother and my older brother did that. And then when it comes time for harvesting, I would help to pick the beans, pick the peas, you know, I would go in the field and cut the okras and pick tomatoes, stuff like that. I would help to do that.

When it comes time to harvest the potatoes now, which would be sometime in October, November, I would have to help again with taking the hoe. They would cut down the rows and then you take the hoe and you just turn it over so that the potatoes come, and then I would go along and have to pick up the potatoes, and you make piles as you go along.
—*Regina Bennett*

We used to plant anything for farm market, something for our children, yourself and your children—corn, peas, potatoes, butter beans, cotton, Irish potatoes. Older people used to do the same thing and we come behind them and we do the same thing, too. Somebody carry you to Savannah, you get ten cents a peck for butter beans. And when you get there and you couldn't sell them, you bring them back and destroy them. You couldn't eat them then because they get soft.—*Nancy Ferguson*

A lot of people left Pinckney Island and moved to Hilton Head 'cause we couldn't stand the pressure that they put [on us]. When you plant things you had to give them some [a share—sharecropping], and so we just move. . . . 'Cause our father make our things, and they [the landowner] want so much every time. So we all move over here.

—*Corrine Lawyer Brown (Brown was born on Hilton Head Island. Early in her life, relatives took her to Pinckney Island to be raised. Her grandfather, Abraham Jones, had a large farm there.)*

About the mid part of February or the early part of March, I would come here and spend that time just to help the old man [his father, Ben White, Sr.] with some work because I loved to farm. I would get absence from my job about twice a year, between February and March, and again 'round about the last of October or the early part of November. I would take that time and help the old man. There wasn't a tractor on Hilton Head in those days. Different people began getting mules. They figure the plow been too heavy for the horse, and they could get something that was a little more stronger with a mule. The old man got a mule. Mr. Chris Green used to work for the old man for $40 a month. He used to work from January to January. . . . I would ask the old man— I was a young man in those days—how can he work for forty dollars a month, and take care of his wife and children? "Ben, you ask a good question, but you know you don't cross the bridge until you get to it."—*Ben White, Jr. (born 1925)*

Oh, my God, we came from a mighty long ways, the hard way. Boy, the first time I hit the lucky number on the farm was in 1943. It was after the 1940 storm put the tide over that land. I gone and plant a field of watermelon down by the salt-water bridge, right down there on this side of the Fort. There was a creek call Coggin Creek.

Three rows of corn and four rows of watermelon. That watermelon grow unusual. And boy, we never could gather all them watermelon. Ollie and Little Mack, they tried to pick up each end of a watermelon, and they couldn't do it. And that watermelon, the first trip I made to walk the row, you would pick up about three hundred. Go over to Savannah on Charlie Simmons's boat with them.

I pray to God from Charlie' boat on to Savannah. I said Lord, if we was to get three and a half, not over five dollars a hundred. I say Lord, I am going to see if I can get seven dollars a hundred for my watermelon today. I prayed to God all the way. I didn't enjoy myself at all on the boat.

When Charlie' boat docked, a man I had never seen nor heard of was standing on the dock. Ben Givins, he was a wholesale buyer. The man step on board of Charlie Simmons's boat and said, "How do you do, Mr. White?"

"I'm feel pretty good, how are you sir?"

He said, "How many have you got?"

I said, "About three hundred."

He said, "The Old Man [Ben White, Sr.] and I agreed for twenty-five dollars a hundred. He is supposed to be back in here around about Tuesday." He said, "I think I better take your melons."

When that man paid me that seventy-five dollars, I said, "That man must be crazy. Get away from that market, Doc. Something wrong with that man."

Before God, when we quit shipping, in '43, I had nine hundred dollars put aside in the Citizens and Southern Bank from the field. And keep a hundred dollars in the house in case of sickness or anything happen. We *had* a good start.— *Johnny White (born 1909, Grassland Community)*

Man plowing with his horse. *Courtesy of the Coastal Discovery Museum*

Making a living on the island? You either did things on land or you did things in the water — either you did farming or you did the creek for oyster, clams, fishing.

So he [Ben White, Sr., the biggest farmer on Hilton Head] chose to be a land-based operator. He was very ambitious, and you know, for a person that only went to school to the third grade, his ideas were far-reaching for the time and would probably be far-reaching even at this time because his thinking would have changed. He always looked to have bigger and better things.

As I understand it, at one time they used to grow cotton, but the boll weevil wiped that out. But the watermelon, butterbeans, okra — truck farming really was the thing.— *Charlie White*

At one point he [our father] also had beets in there because that's why I don't like beets. Since it's a root type plant, you can pull it up, clean it off, and you can eat it raw, and I used to eat it raw, you know. I guess it very nutritious, but by the time I became an adult, I had no desire to eat beets at all. — *David White (born 1940, Grassland Community)*

Big Hill was the first land purchase he [our father] made, and then he kept adding to it, and I reckon now there's thirty-two point something acres. Of course, at that time it could've been listed as thirty-five or thirty-six because people used to step things off, you know, and when they did the later survey, they had the instrument and what used to be this much was shrunk some because of the instrument. That's why most of the old deed read "ten acres more or less" or twenty whatever.

In the 1940s, we had acres and acres of crops on what is now Port Royal—we called the Old Fort down there. It was mainly watermelon and corn. We didn't own that, just rented it. Union Cemetery Road used to go straight down to the Old Fort, and that's the road we used to go down there and we used to plant both sides. We just about had that whole area planted. Then we planted a place call Capers Landing. I would say we had a good twenty acres we used to plant there. We also planted on Dillon Road, mostly corn there. Cotton Hope—we used to plant down there, where the Wileys are now. We had a lot of watermelon there. We also planted down in Jonesville, planted butterbeans and stuff back there. And then where Oak Grove Church is, at the end of the marsh in Broad Creek, we planted corn there.

It wasn't cost effective to sell to people on the island. He dealt in volume, and if someone came to him and they wanted some butterbeans to eat or some watermelon to eat, he'd give it to them.—*Charlie White*

One of the things that I can recall from being at the market at Savannah is the notion of volume sales. For example, if you had say two hundred watermelon and a potential purchaser came by and said he wanted a hundred, then our dad would negotiate a price based on volume to sell, you know, to sell that amount to him versus someone who only wanted ten or twenty-five.

I think one of the things he figured out was how to constantly have crop that he could take to market, and I guess all that was tied in with the idea of being visionary in a sense, to figure out when to do this and what volume to plant so you can get a certain yield. And I guess you could also take that further and say you could really project what that would bring in terms of dollars.—*David White*

You know in terms of taking crops to market, there was nothing but dirt roads at the time, so you use the horse and wagons, the mule and wagons. The wagons had four wheels, a box type of arrangement, sides at least thirty-six inches to forty-eight inches high. If it's watermelon, you stack them from the front to the back and then you, you see, you load in the field, from the field to the wagon, from the wagon to the boat because that was the only way to get off. You go to Savannah, then you have to offload it onto a truck, then you take it to the city market, then you unload it off the truck onto the ground of the market. During the watermelon season, there was a constant movement. Dad would be gone to the market, and we would just keep the crop going to him by whatever transportation we had. The sailboats looked like bateaux. They had a cabin so when the weather was inclement, you could be out of the weather. That's where they cooked. The rest of the boat was pretty open, and the crops were stacked. We used [to] put the butterbeans in these burlap bags about three feet wide and four feet deep.

He [Ben White, Sr.] had a series of people working with him. Nathan Rivers, Sr., was one of his foremen, and we had Herbert Chaplin and Dennis Sheppard. They were sort of the staple, and then you hire people to do things like planting season or harvesting. He paid them on the basis how many bushels, and what he paid 'em I don't recall, but I assure you it wasn't much. Mostly women did the harvesting of the butterbeans and stuff. Men handled the watermelon.

When we harvest the sweet potato, that calls for a lot of hoe work, so you wouldn't destroy the potato. You take the plow and you get it as close to the center of the row as you can, and then you use the hoe, then you rake it out, and people gather them up by size, and you put them in these bushel baskets. Women did most of the sorting and putting into the baskets.

There was one guy there in Savannah, a guy called Nappy, that he'd send stuff to if the season was winding down. He was the wheeler-dealer on the market, and they say people used to send things to him and he sold it for I guess a percentage of whatever he collected, like a broker. We used to write on the bag using this blue ink "from Ben White to Nappy" and put it on Simmons's truck or somebody's boat and you know, off it goes. And then he would send the money back with somebody.
—*Charlie White*

Folks tended to work on the honor system. I don't think it was a lot skepticism about if I send this product over to you that, you know, you're gonna rip me off or anything like that. It was pretty much an honor system kinda thing. . . . There were a few suppliers in terms of seed, fertilizer in Savannah, Leon Grocery, and I think it was Alexander's.
—*David White*

"Musk"—a plant also known as deer tongue because its long narrow leaves remind some of the tongue of a deer—flourished in the woods on the north end of Hilton Head. The leaves of the plant grew from spring to late fall.

Gullah women, and sometimes men and children, slung burlap bags over their shoulders, picked the leaves, and sold them to musk dealers. Some took their harvest directly to Bluffton by sailboat. The leaves were processed there in a warehouse, wrapped in burlap, tied with wire, and shipped to Virginia. Musk was a common additive to pipe tobacco and cigarettes until the 1960s.

Musk-picking provided a seasonal income in July, August, and September. After picking the leaves of the plant, the women stuffed them in their bags and took them home to dry in their yards, as the price for musk increased slightly for dried leaves versus green ones. Then the women sold the dried brown leaves for approximately twenty cents a pound.

Picking musk held dangers though. The plant thrived in the deep woods among palmettos and the thick underbrush where rattlesnakes thrived. The women had to contend with mosquitoes and guard against poisonous snakes. As they picked the leaves, which clustered near the bottom of the plant, their hands shared the habitat claimed by snakes.

When crushed, the leaves had a scent some compared to vanilla.

We made a good living with mus' and put it in the closet to make the clothes smell good.— *Georgianna Bryan (born 1900, Squire Pope Community)*

My mother come home with a sack of musk on her head. When she threw the sack down a rattlesnake came out the sack. I don't know how that happened, but the snake must have gone in the bag. It didn't bite her, but she been in the woods and was picking musk.— *Thomas Holmes*

A number of Gullah men on Hilton Head were distillers, turning out quantities of well-made corn liquor popularly called "moonshine." Making moonshine was an additional—and valuable—source of family income, and the men took pride in their craft. More than one distiller claimed the title of the "best" distiller on Hilton Head. They did not publicize their distilling off-island, as making moonshine was illegal. But their whiskey was well known by those who wanted it.

The quality of the moonshine produced by one of the largest moonshine operators on Hilton Head was so good that it is said that Thorne and Loomis, the northern owners of Honey Horn Plantation (from the 1930s through the 1950s) always purchased a large quantity whenever they were on the island.

The same distiller also had loyal customers on nearby Port Royal Island and in Savannah. He shipped his moonshine to the mainland by boat in five-gallon jugs placed in croaker (burlap) sacks.

Some of the whisky stills on Hilton Head were quite sophisticated. The Internal Revenue Service periodically swooped in to destroy the stills, but moonshine was made until the bridge to the mainland was built.

I know when I was twelve how to make moonshine. That was the only way a lot of 'em could really get something to drink that help 'em, you know, but back in them days, we used to cook moonshine with pride. Knowing how to do it and do it clean because, you know, like once you set your barrel up, we used to tie a bag around it to keep insects from falling in it. Then when you cook the liquor you take your time. And if you rush it, you'll scorch it, and when you scorch it, everybody can tell it's bad liquor. And I had to be careful 'cause if I didn't [I'd] get a good behind-cuttin'. The low wine, that's the last pot coming out. So you take that to cut the real moonshine to the strength you want it to be. The old man [his uncle, Willie Kellerson, who raised him] before he had a truck, he used to put it on that horse, carry it to Squire Pope, Baygall, and all over town to sell it. Everyone knew it was the best.

I remember when it was eight dollars a gallon, then it went up to ten dollars, then it went up to twelve dollars, then it went up to fifteen dollars, eighteen dollars. The last time I heard it was like twenty-five dollars or twenty-nine dollars for one gallon. I don't know when they stopped making it. I leave home in '56 and the old man still had a barrel, so I guess it must be '56.—*Abraham "Abe" Grant, Sr., (born 1937, Chaplin Community)*

Fred Owens had a store with kerosene and gas and *plenty* corn liquor.—*Ben Miller*

You know, from what I was told Dad was the best in the county in terms of the moonshine. —*Charlie White*

Gullah midwives existed on Hilton Head from the time of slavery until after the bridge connected the island to the mainland. When the Union captured Hilton Head Island in 1861, a young enslaved girl named Nancy lived at Fish Haul Plantation. She would grow up to become Nancy Christopher, a legendary midwife whose name would go down in island history.

Midwives were held in high esteem. They were the ones with knowledge to deliver babies. Their skill was critical, as Hilton Head lacked doctors.

The midwife, or "granny" as she often was called, would visit a woman when she was expecting a child and tell her when the baby was coming and prepare her in other ways. Then when the family saw the woman was in pain, they knew it was time to get the midwife.

Most people on Hilton Head remembered who their midwife had been, and midwives usually remembered the names of those they helped birth. Thus, midwives sometimes performed an additional role as memory keepers on Hilton Head.

Nancy Christopher was a particularly good memory keeper. In a 1924 pension application for the widow of James Drayton Grant, Christopher testified that she then was about sixty-seven years of age and had "been acquainted with the soldier James Drayton [Grant] ever since I had sense. I can remember him just before he went into the army."

Whether James Drayton Grant's children were still minors was an important issue in the pension application.

Children of a former Civil War soldier who were minors were entitled to a military pension until they came of age, if it could be proven that they were underage.

"I acted as midwife when the claimant's two children William and Julia were born," Christopher swore. "I have kept a record of their birth which I now show to you." (Here the special examiner noted that she exhibited "an old Bible with the following entry on the last sheet thereof, William Drayton, born October, 10, 1918; Julia Drayton, born Oct. 28, 1913. The book shows sign of age, and the writing seems to be original without any erasures.")

"I know these children were born on the dates given in the Bible," Christopher said, "because at the time of their birth I wrote the date therein. I am a licensed midwife, and in the recent years I have kept a record of births."

Other famous midwives on Hilton Head included Rhina Lawyer, Amelia White, Tina Young, Tina McKnight, Alice Capis (or Caphus), Mary Jones, Susan (Sookie) Williams, Hannah Barnwell, and Adrianna Ford.

Midwife training at first consisted of knowledge gleaned from older women. Then for many years, the Penn School on Saint Helena Island offered training in midwifery. Later, the South Carolina State Board of Health, Division of Maternal and Child Health provided training. Hannah Barnwell, for one, kept among her possessions a book on midwifery revised by the state in 1956.

Payments to midwives often were $5.00 in the 1930s. In later years payments went up to $15.00. Many times, however, people did not have money to pay. In such cases, they often paid the midwife with seafood or poultry.

Adrianna Ford was among the last active midwives on Hilton Head. She lived in Stoney, but when necessary, she would walk hours to reach the home of a woman about to give birth. She delivered scores of babies between the 1930s and early 1960s.

"She said she dreamed about talking to elders, leaders in the community. . . . They asked her to become the island's midwife," her granddaughter Gardenia White recalled. The same dream came to her several times until she knew she had to act on it. She felt she was called to midwifery.

"Miz' Adrianna," a widow raising her children, sought out a public health nurse who came to Hilton Head once a month. The nurse trained and supplied her with medicine. It was common to see Miz' Adrianna walking along the road in her proper white uniform that was always "just so."

Her "little black bag" contained conventional medicines and roots and leaves for home remedies passed down on the island. Her granddaughter remembered hurting her ankle playing when she was a child and how she could not walk. Miz' Adrianna brought her some clay wrapped in leaves. "She had me put it on my ankle and hold it there for the night. The next day, I could walk fine, and I went to school."

Laura Mae Walters Holmes and William Holmes married in 1938 and had six children, all born at home. Adrianna Ford was the midwife for all six.

Laura Mae Walters Holmes (LMWH): Well, she would come by check see how I was doing, what I'm eatin' . . . if I was eating the right food, [and] if I needed help. . . . Then [when] I start havin' pain, [I say] *get in the wagon—pick her up.*

William Holmes, Sr. (WHS): Yeah, I went [in the wagon and picked up the midwife]. That was my job in the middle of the night.

LMWH: How much it cost? I don't know how much it was. How you gon' tell me it wasn't nothin'? [Laughter]

WHS: [It] was five dollars. [Laughter.]

LMWH: Well, money was scarce . . . money was scarce.

WHS: It [there] wasn't no money, you know.

LMWH: They had the bag I know. They had the bag [of medicine and instruments]. . . . I can't tell you what all they had in it. But they had their own medicine. They get the medicine out the woods. . . . I guess they get the knowledge from the older people—or the older one, Nancy Christopher. I think she was the first one.

Hilton Head midwives had good skills and childbirth usually went well. There were exceptions, however. If the baby's feet came first, for instance, "That's a hard birth," Laura Mae Campbell said. She had several mid-wives in her time: Nancy Christopher delivered her first child, although Campbell's grandmothers—Susan (Sookie) Williams and Hannah Chisolm—were present, too. Adrianna Ford delivered her last child.

Campbell's first child, a son, died shortly after childbirth. The women took him from her and buried him. He was so young that he did not have a name yet.

Well, he died with fever. See these old people didn't know what to do then. [They used plants to bring a fever down, but if] the fever was so high, they died from that.—*Laura Mae Campbell*

A doctor in Savannah told Campbell that she would not be able to have another child. But fifteen years later she did. It was 1950, and she had planned to go to a hospital in Savannah, but the baby came earlier than expected.

Then I . . . get the pain. . . . I say, "Oh Lord!" So I had to stay here [on Hilton Head] and take it and let that baby [be] born. [I] had a lotta pain. I holler for Mamma. Mamma was right there. "All right, Mamma." Mamma say, "Be quiet! Be quiet!" That was a time. Oh boy!

The baby just come on out. They tell ya how to do. How to prop the leg up, and when the baby come out, "Okay, it's comin'! It's comin'. The head comin' first." Mama was right there. Ain't nothin' to do without Mom. Mamma didn't put [the baby] there but [I] sure was callin' for Mamma. Yes sir, Mamma was there.

They cut [the naval cord] with scissors. They knew just what to do.—*Laura Mae Campbell (Campbell's second son went on to live a good life.)*

Hunting was divided into two types: the hunting Gullah men did to feed their families and to get game or hides to sell in Savannah, and the hunting outsiders did during the winter months on Hilton Head. The latter provided jobs for some Gullah people.

Gullah men hunted for rabbits, raccoons, deer, wild turkey, wild hogs (boars), squirrels, possums, ducks, and sometimes doves. Hunting techniques varied depending on the animal.

Rabbits, for instance, were hunted with sticks and dogs. Dogs chased a rabbit to its hole and when it ran out the other end, the hunter hit it with a stick.

Dogs would "tree" a raccoon, and the hunter would throw bricks up into the tree to force the raccoon down.

Some Gullah men also used homemade iron or metal traps, which were later outlawed. Others used guns, ranging from hand guns to rifles, shotguns, and pistols.

Gullah men also caught alligators and mink and then dried and stretched their hides to sell in Savannah. A far easier type of hunting was gathering, or digging, turtle eggs on the beach.

Well-to-do visitors, from both the North and the South, were drawn to Hilton Head. Every need was attended to by Gullah people, giving the visitors the chance to bask in the natural beauty of the island, to relish the chance to hunt wild birds and other game, and to enjoy the time spent in each other's company.

Hunters began coming to Hilton Head shortly after the end of the Civil War. The island had grown quieter when the soldiers departed, and soon flocks of birds reappeared and wild game grew abundant. Wealthy white northern landowners—from Roy Rainey to W. P. Clyde and William L. Hurley, to Landon K. Thorne and Alfred A. Loomis—invited their friends to Hilton Head to hunt.

Thorne and Loomis bought Honey Horn in the early 1930s. They would arrive for spring and fall hunting seasons. Ben Jones was a chef at Honey Horn then, and Rosa Miller Bryant cooked for "Old Man Lawrence." Annie Driessen and Laura Cohen cooked there, too.

Jim Cohen of Jonesville was largely responsible for training the hunting dogs. Cohen would get the dogs to hunt for birds and make them fly up from the grass and bushes so the hunters could shoot them. He also raised some birds in cages and imported other birds. Prior to a hunt, he would "plant" the birds so that the hunters had plenty to shoot at. Cohen also trained the horses not to flinch or move when a gun was fired. He took care of the animals during the hunt and retrieved the dogs when the hunt was over.

Richard Chisolm of Spanish Wells drove the hunters to the point where the hunt would begin. He also loaded and transported the dogs in cages on the back of a truck to where the hunt would take place. With a saddlebag on each horse, the hunters had a gun, shells, and a pouch for carrying the kill.

Jim Cohen used to ride the horses while [the hunters] kill the birds. Jim Cohen and my brother John [Miller] take 'em where they can kill them quail. . . .
    Chamberlin Robinson used to take care of all the horses, the garden, and the cattle. Old Man Chamberlin.— *Ben Miller (Robinson was the father of Thomas Robinson, the first Hilton Head Gullah islander to earn a PhD.)*

I used to pump the water for to wash. You all pump the water. And if you pump two tub of water, and if anything happen every bit of that water have to throw out. Mrs. Lawrence [at Honey Horn] would not let her clothes wash in that water—say it's sour. — *Georgianna Barnwell*

A hunt club, officially organized as the Hilton Head Agricultural Society, also operated on Hilton Head. Started by well-to-do North Carolina cotton-mill owner Freno Dilling in 1917, the club lasted until 1967.
    "Camp Dilling," a rustic hunt camp with cabins and bunks, was located in the Leamington area on 1,770 acres of land. Men from North Carolina, South Carolina, and Tennessee joined the club. Most islanders referred to it as the Dillon Hunting Club.

Gullah residents Jake Brown and his wife, Eliza, lived in a wooden house with a brick chimney on club property. A lean, strong man, he was the "go-to" man on hunting days. Wearing a vest slotted with gun shells and trousers tucked into high boots, he guided the men to game. His sons, Walter, Sam, and Luther, also acted as drivers on the deer hunts.
    Charlie Wright, a Gullah man, was among the club cooks. At one dinner, Wright prepared what the hunters considered a "feast fit for a king"—venison, squirrel, wild boar, and raccoon.
    In 1955, "Brown cracked his skull and died when thrown from the passenger seat of a speeding Jeep on a sandy logging road." He had been the "master of hounds for at least 28 years and perhaps for the entire history of the hunt club" and acted as a liaison between the hunt club and Gullah people. Brown's death was considered the end of an era at Camp Dilling.[17]

BY SEA

Sometimes the women lifted their voices in song as they picked up a razor-sharp oyster shell, banged its mouth against a metal post, popped the shell open with a knife, and slid the shiny gray oyster into a large stainless-steel pan.
    The work was muscle-cramping and repetitive. A spiritual or a work song that punctuated every step in the process made the job go faster. Lilting voices turned

shucking "ohysters" into a unified stream of movements for hours on end.

Oysters were a major source of food and income on Hilton Head, Daufuskie, and nearby islands for decades. Their importance increased in the 1920s after the boll weevil had destroyed cotton crops. Many Gullah people worked in the oyster factories in the winter and went back to farming in the spring.

Steamed oysters, canned and shipped to the Midwest and other areas where fresh oysters were not available, came first. Raw shucking came later after refrigeration improved. Some oyster factories eventually did both.

One particular brand became quite popular — "Daufuskie" oysters, immediately recognizable because the can bore an image of an Indian head on a bright red label. Oysters from both Daufuskie and Hilton Head waters filled those cans.

The men harvested the oysters at low tide, and the women, and a few men, shucked them in oyster "factories." Many Hilton Head Gullah people worked for a large raw oyster factory on Jenkins Island, operated by L. P. Maggioni Company of Lady's Island. Jenkins Island also had several smaller independent raw oyster operations and a steam oyster plant.

Another large oyster factory was in the Squire Pope community, in a section called Bull Point. J. B. Hudson operated this factory, along with a smaller one just off Marshland Road. Still another, in the Stoney community, was owned and operated by S. V. Toomer.

The oyster factory owners were white, and most, though not all, of the workers were Gullah people. The South Carolina Health Department oversaw the industry.

During the winter and early spring months — months with an "r" in their name — men from Hilton Head went out in small wooden rowboats (called bateaux), anchored their boats, and picked oysters from oyster banks.

While most men took their oysters directly to an oyster factory, a few shoveled them aboard waiting sailboats. L. P. Maggioni & Co. owned several sailboats, which would carry the oysters from Hilton Head to Lady's Island. The sailboats had permanent crews of Gullah men.

Harvesting oysters depended on low tide — morning, midday, or late afternoon. Occasionally, there would be two tides during daylight hours.

The women who worked in the oyster factories usually walked miles to and from work. Women from Baygall would walk all the way to the factory on Jenkins Island (considered part of Hilton Head) and back home again at night.

Before going to bed, they would prepare a lunch to take to work the next day. There were no stores close by for the workers to buy lunch, and factories usually sold the women soft drinks.

"I work in them factories and shuck oysters," said Regina Bennett, who was born in 1902. "I walk all the way from Braddock's Point. We left home around six in the morning and walked all the way from there and go down to them factories and shuck oysters the whole day until about seven o'clock."

Oyster houses usually had concrete floors with very high tables, long enough to accommodate perhaps fifteen women on each side. The women stood on a wooden bench twelve to eighteen inches high, so they weren't on the floor. The edge of the table was about hip-high for the women when they stood on the benches. There was a hole cut in the table at each worker's position for throwing the empty shells, and posts embedded in the concrete.

The factories generally had one or two fifty-five-gallon drums in the center of the floor for heating the area and for heating lunches. But as oyster factories lacked insulation, the shuckers often were cold.

Men called shell rollers would bring in wheelbarrows full of oysters and dump them beside the shuckers. The shucker would pick up an oyster, bang its mouth against the metal post, and pop it open with her knife. The meat went into stainless-steel pails, and the oyster shells went down the hole in the bench and onto the floor. As the shells piled up, a shell roller would come in with an empty wheelbarrow, shovel them up, and take them out.

To protect their hands, the women wore gloves, and they had to buy their own—often from the company. Workers used what was referred to as an "outdoor

toilet." There was no running water, so they had to wash their hands at a pump located nearby.

Oystering provided seasonal employment, however meager, to people in the coastal islands. Pay ranged from a low of about six cents per gallon of meat up to fifty cents in the 1930s and '40s. Even though most shuckers were women, some men also shucked oysters.

"When we get home from school wasn't nothing to eat," recalled William Holmes, Sr. "So I tell Harris [his brother], say I'll let you go finish [school], and I'll go and shuck oysters.

A group of workers, including children, shucking oysters in Bluffton, across the sound from Hilton Head, in February 1913. *Lewis Wickes Hine, Photographer. Library of Congress*

"It was in the '20s when I started. I went to the oyster factory on Jenkins Island. Say, I can learn to shuck. I had to shuck 'em when they come in, you see. Steam 'em first, then I would shuck 'em.

"Then I came down here to Toomer's and they used to have them raw," he said. Holmes said he made ten cents for every gallon of steamed oyster meat, "and if I shucked four cans, then forty cents a day."

But that was "according to how your oyster is," he said. "Some of the oysters were small, and some big, and sometimes nothin' be in the shell."

Holmes said the season usually ended "the last of April. Then I used to go and farm my cousin's farm. . . . People used to make fun of me. They could smell 'em on me—'All right, you been around that old oyster factory.'"

William Holmes, Sr., didn't make a career out of oysters. World War II intervened, and in his own words he said, "When I got back from the army [Civilian Conservation Corps], I didn't care nothing about shuckin'."

Thomas Holmes said the pay was better for raw oysters. Harvesting oysters for steaming, he said, brought six cents a bushel, "and the woman open it for ten cents."

But for raw oysters, he said, it was fifty-fifty. "If the oyster is two dollars a gallon, the woman would get one dollar and the man get one dollar."

The bateaux the harvesters used ranged in length from eight to fourteen feet, with a very shallow draft. They were propelled by a pair of oars—usually hand-made—and harvesters always had a shovel at hand for bailing out of a boggy area.

The men anchored their bateaux and often got out of the boats to pick oysters from the oyster bed. They had buckets to carry the harvest to the bateaux, wore heavy gloves and hip boots, and used iron oyster grabs. Usually, a man would take along a gallon or so of water to drink, and in later years, when they became available, a flashlight for working after dark.

Harvesters watched the weather closely. To harvest the oysters, men had to watch the tides of the Intracoastal Waterway and creeks. If the tide was low in the morning, men would go out very early to harvest oysters. If the tide was late in the evenings, they would then go out late that evening. Or if there was a midday tide, the men would work then. Occasionally, if the tides ran just right, there would be two tides that the men could work.

But squalls can come up with little warning in the coastal islands. At least two men had drowned harvesting oysters.

Mary Lawyer Green's father was one of them. He drowned in 1947, when she was nine years old.

"They would go out and pick oysters, and my mother and them would shuck the oysters," she said. "His boat just capsized, and he drowned. He was by himself."

She said her mother came home from the factory, and "when he didn't come home, they were like lookin' to see what happened to him."

It was early the next day, she said, when his body was found. "They came and got her; and they took her down there," she said. The children waited outside their home, and "I heard her scream from down there," a mile and a half away.

The island at the time, she said, was so quiet "you could hear people from one end of the island to the next. Like they used to ring bells when somebody died, and you could hear that bell. When you hear that all over the island, someone is gone.

"We didn't know why, but then we realized our daddy was gone and he wouldn't come back."

Fishing was essential to Gullah life. It was of two kinds: fishing to put food on the family table and fishing commercially. There was no such thing as recreational fishing.

Each community had a serious commercial fisherman. He fished daily, supplied the community with fish, and shipped fish by boat to the Savannah market for sale. Each fisherman knew spots where he could cast his net for mullet at the right tide and come up with fish, even in the winter.

Fishermen would "bunch" the catch in strips of palmetto fronds, six to nine inches long and one-half inch wide. Two palmetto strips would be tied together to hold ten to twelve fish per bunch. Each bunch contained small mullet and larger mullet with roe (considered a delicacy similar to caviar from sturgeon). Mullet often were fried or smoked. If not to be eaten right away, the fish was washed and cleaned, salted, and hung out to dry for preservation.

Catfish was the most common fish Gullah people cooked. Stewed with gravy, catfish provided many a meal. Whiting, another common fish, was covered with cornmeal and fried.

Flounders were gigged. Men with a light and a spear called a gig went out at night into the Intracoastal Waterway. They could spot the fish with the light and then spear the flat (but meaty) fish.

Sheephead, identified by black stripes against a white body, were caught on the banks of the Intracoastal Waterway. Small fiddler crabs were used as bait.

Two larger fish also were caught in Hilton Head waters—drum and shark. Drum, named for a sound the fish makes underwater, often ran more than a hundred pounds.

For shark fishing, a dead fish was put on a hook with a long line attached to a corked gallon jug floating on the water. When the jug went underwater, the fisherman knew something large had taken the bait. Sharks ranged in size from ten to fifty pounds. The head of the shark was immediately cut off, and the shark would be skinned and salted to begin preserving.

And then they fished at night, and next morning in the day time they be working—they don't have time. They would go fishing at night, and when they come home in the morning, and I remember good, they had tubs and tubs of fish.

Well, now before they go to bed, they are going to cook. So I would stay in the bed until they cooked. They wouldn't let me clean the fish, not the boys. I was the only girl left in the house. I was small.

They would send my aunt and my sister pans and pans of fish. Then, if they want more, they would give them a bunch or two bunches, and they would take those fish and they would corn it, let it dry. It is very good that way.—*Emma Graham*

Mussels lived buried in the soft mud. They were dug with a clam pick or a similar tool. A bushel held about six hundred mussels and brought the digger anywhere from thirty cents to a dollar, depending on market prices. The best diggers dug as many as sixteen bushels during a single low tide.

Clamming was a relatively small industry on Hilton Head. A wholesaler sold the clams to the public for seventy-five cents to one dollar a bushel. The clams mainly came from beach areas. Both mussels and clams grew in Baygall and were dug and put in burlap "croaker" bags and shipped to Savannah to sell.

Crabbing was part of survival for Gullah people. Some people bogged for them by going through the marsh mud with a stick until they found one, picked it up, and put it in a sack. Crabs caught in this manner were often used as part of a family's food.

A second method, often used for commercial crabbing, was to lay baited lines along the shore of a creek. Crab boats from Port Royal Island sold line, bait (hamskin and bull-nose), and barrels to Gullah people. The buyer was a big company out of the Beaufort Blue Channel, which operated up until the 1960s.

The line along the shore would remain there until a crab snagged at it, pulling it under. Crabbers then rowed bateaux along the line, grabbing the crab with a small hand net and dropping it into a barrel. This was done repeatedly for perhaps six hours until the tides changed. The crabbing season lasted from March until October, when the water temperatures dropped and the crabs stopped biting. Gullah people on Hilton Head and Daufuskie and other parts of Beaufort County did commercial crabbing.

Well, we row from here all the way to Daufuskie Beach for crabbing. You used to get about one cent, and sometimes you go up to three cents for them.
—*Arthur Orage (born 1923, Squire Pope Community)*

I used to crab with them too. Them crabs was heavy then. We get a line from here to that wall back there, and boy, from the time we drop them lines 'til time to come back for them, we pick up five and six crab everywhere.

You ever work for that guy named Sam the crab man? Boy, that man cuss more that anyone I ever seen.

— Ben Miller

"Gone casting," Gullah people would say as they headed to a salt-water "crick" (creek). Broad Creek, Old House, and Skull Creek, all fairly shallow but navigable waters, were popular places on Hilton Head for flinging a cast net, usually from a bateau. They often got good-sized prawns if the shrimp were running.

Many Gullah people took home the makings for shrimp and gravy over rice for dinner. Leftover shrimp often ended up on breakfast plates, served over grits. (This began as a poor people's dish and in recent years has hit mainstream acclaim.)

Several Gullah people shrimped commercially, some as far south as Key West, Florida. The older shrimp boats were forty to fifty feet long and had wooden hulls and a diesel engine. Many boats were single-rigged with only one net, but by the 1950s, newer shrimp boats were double rigged and pulled two nets. The nets had a tickler chain on the bottom to stir up the shrimp so they would rise up to the net. A bag at the back of the net trapped the shrimp.

Shrimpers would put out a small net called a "try net" and trawl for ten minutes, then pull the net up. "If you have five to fifteen shrimp . . . you have hit the area where the shrimp are running, then you put out your

Arthur Orage, a Hilton Head native, was one of Hilton Head's most skilled fishermen and shrimpers. *Photo Courtesy of Lawrence Orage*

larger nets. If you're catching more [shrimp], then you know you're really hitting it," Eugene Orage recalled. It was time to put out the larger net, drag it for up to two hours, and then pull it up.

Anyone who wanted to get into shrimping usually started off as a "striker," to learn the business.

[The striker] empty the bag when it comes in, prepare it to go out, lower the outrigger as you're getting out to the fishing grounds. Learn how to do these things. It's a big job when the shrimp is on the deck and captain is in the pilot house driving the boat. The striker separates shrimp from the crabs and other fish, decides whether to head shrimp . . . or the captain decides—if it's very hot and [you got] a large catch, best to get the shrimp on ice down in the hold as soon as possible.—*Eugene Orage*

WORKING OFF-ISLAND

Gullah people had a long history of traveling back and forth between Hilton Head and nearby islands, Savannah, and other locations. So it was natural that when some determined to search for higher-paying jobs than were available on Hilton Head, many turned to Savannah. Some men worked as longshoremen, both men and women worked in industry or hotels, and many women worked as domestics.

Some Hilton Head Gullah people lived off-island for several years and then returned home, while others traveled to Savannah on the steamer and returned each weekend to Hilton Head.

A few traveled farther, choosing to live in New York City for a while, join the military, or, on occasion, move to Florida.

> I used to work in Savannah to a bag factory.
> —*Magree Reed Green (born 1907, Baygall Community)*

My father was nicknamed "Massey" Jones. He was in World War I. When he came out of the service, he was able to go to New York and work a few years. He sacrificed, and he would save his money because he wanted to go back home. He was born and raised on Pinckney Island. When he got back to Hilton Head, then he bought his place on Hilton Head.—*Elijah Jones, Jr.*

When I was working in Savannah, I would come to Hilton Head about every year and stay for about a week, most of the time twice a year.
—*Ben White, Jr.*

My pa used to run on a ship. And when Pa come 'shore, he buy for this one. He buy for that one. He buy and I remember good.

He say, after he done, he going back, the man used to run with on the place say son, say I ain't got grits. [So he helped him.] A woman stop, say he stop. Pa say he had one fifty cent in his pocket, one fifty cent, and he say he take the fifty cent and he gave it to the old woman she drop on her knees.

They done send for him 'cause he been here so long, and it is time for the ship to go back. And Pa say the old woman was there, just pray. Say when I look back, the old devil say he da pray for me. And Pa say when they gone and make the voyage round and come round say he had to hold his hat for put the money in what they pay him. When he come here, he buy people clothes and cloth and thing you could get for ten cent a yard. Buy dress for them, yes sir. My daddy.—*Georgianna Barnwell*

I finished the seventh grade in May, my mother died in July. I was fourteen almost fifteen and they sent me to New York to live. My sisters there wrote a letter to my father and told him to send me back with our cousin named Geneva. He agreed with them because it was just me and him and Leo over here in the house. That's how that happened. I had no say so in it whatsoever.

I didn't like New York. I was always a book person but did not like New York. It was just too big a city. It was kinda hard, but I found enough things to do that kept me out of trouble, and we had some elderly cousins in New York who had a business where people could go and get jobs from them. So they would always look out for a babysitting job for me on the weekends. So I did that while I was going to school until I got old enough to get [a] working permit, and you know, I just studied and I guess did what I had to do. When I was in the twelfth grade, a air force recruiter came from Mitchell Air Force Base to the school.—*Ruth E. Germany (Germany served in the U.S. Air Force for several years and later returned to Hilton Head.)*

I went to Saint Petersburg [Florida] when I was seventeen, got a construction job, was a cement dispatcher at that plant for about eight years. I decided that I wasn't cut out for that type of work, and I was forcing myself to go there. That job become just like

the school was. I can do better, so I went and fill out a application to work for National Service Industrial. They had different divisions, but I went in the textile division. I was plant porter. Cleaned the laundry, swept the floor, took the trash out. It was "Henry, we have a spill over here." Sometimes you have to take the low road before you take the high road. You have to learn, you have to think before you react.

I went a long way, in 1986 promoted to Production Man, had five supervisors working under me. I retired in 1993. They wanted me back, kept me as a consultant, went from one plant to another, Tampa, Sarasota, Orlando, Clearwater. We had seventy textile plants throughout the country, rented linen, industrial uniforms.

And all that was riding on Hilton Head. Hilton Head had it going. You had to move from where you at, but you have to remember where you come from then. If you pull the foundation out, then you don't have nothing.—*Henry Ford*

TRADITIONAL CRAFTS

Gullah people were resourceful and made utilitarian crafts for everyday use. The crafts they produced were similar to ones found in Africa and their skill in making them has become renowned.

Gullah islanders are noted for their skill in making

Sweetgrass baskets made by basket maker Beaulah Grant Kellerson. Her son, Solomon, gathered bulrush grasses from the creek that flowed near their home for his mother to use in making her baskets. *Collection of Carolyn Grant*

some islands the baskets have evolved into a decorative art form. On Hilton Head, the baskets were made to be sturdy and used for practical purposes rather than decorative ones.

One well-known type of basket is called a "fanner." A large shallow basket, fanners were used to fan the rice in the air and let the breeze carry away the chaff. First used during the days of enslavement, fanners likely continued to be used as long as islanders grew rice on the island. Laura Mae Campbell remembers her parents growing rice on their farm when she grew up.

Other baskets were used for carrying butter beans, corn, and similar domestic tasks. Women often toted baskets full of food or other items on their heads.

Caesar Johnson, perhaps the best-known basket maker on the island, was born seven ("seb'n") years after "de big shoot"—the day the Union captured Hilton Head Island (November 7, 1861). He learned to make baskets from older men on the island, including his grandfather, who was born in Combahee, South Carolina. Among the baskets Johnson made was a large oval one used to carry heavy fireplace logs.

Johnson made baskets into his eighties. While he tried to teach other people how to make them, he thought most lacked the patience to spend the time to turn out a good quality basket.

Beaulah Grant Kellerson was among the last of the basket makers on Hilton Head and was very skilled at the craft. She sold her baskets from a roadside store in

handsome coiled baskets similar to ones still found in West Africa. Many are made of sweetgrass, a sweet-smelling grass that grows near the ocean. The coils of grass are woven together with thinly sliced strips of palmetto, row after row until they form a basket. On the Chaplin community into the 1950s and beyond. Her son had a roadside stand, as well, where she sold baskets. People visiting the island bought baskets from Mrs. Kellerson. (Miss Beaulah raised her nephew, Abraham "Abe" Grant, who, with his wife, Charliemae, ran a much-loved restaurant featuring Gullah food on Hilton Head. Abe considered Miss Beaulah his mother, and his daughter, Carolyn Grant, considered Miss Beaulah her grandmother.)

The Grant family still has some of her baskets and counts them as family treasures—relics of their long heritage on the island. One of the baskets the family has "is round and deep and may have been made to carry on your head," Carolyn Grant said.

Her son, Solomon Grant, would go and gather the grass she needed. She used the bull rush, which was thicker [and harder on the hands to work with], and palmetto strips. When I was maybe ten or twelve years old, I was sitting at her feet passing her the grass bundles she needed. She had them laid out on the porch. I never learned how to make them but wish I had. I think an older person's style of teaching was, "I am going to do this, and you watch me do it."—*Carolyn Grant (born 1963, Chaplin Community)*

My great-grandfather used to make baskets. I see him make it, but I never did make it. . . . He would make it to use, [and] he would make it if different

Casting nets. *Courtesy of the Coastal Discovery Museum*

ones want it. . . . He would make peck basket, half a bushel and bushel baskets. Oh yeah.—*Isabel Brown*

Without cast nets (a type of fishing net), life would have just about come to a standstill on Hilton Head. The cast nets were that important. Seafood was a staple

Casting nets off the dock on Skull Creek, 2019. *Photo by Will Warasila*

in Gullah peoples' diet. The cast nets allowed people to pull in fish and shrimp from saltwater creeks to eat with their rice.

Skilled net-makers "knitted" large nets of cotton twine similar to those Africans had long made. The nets formed a wide circle at the bottom, ringed with weights.

Just as it took a skilled person to make a good net, it took an agile person to cast the net just right, so that it would widen into a circle as it flew over the water and sink down quickly to cover any fish below it, and then pull it up before the fish could escape.

Three kinds of nets were made on Hilton Head: the

mesh on the first was sized large enough to catch mullet (a common fish on the coast); the second was more tightly knit in order to catch shrimp; and the third was a "poor man's net," a tight mesh that could catch both mullet and shrimp.

Wintertime brought a damp, penetrating cold to Hilton Head Island. Quilts were a necessity on the island. Gullah women saved every usable piece of cloth they could to make quilts for their families. Quilt-making was an art form pleasing to the eye. But their warmth was just as important, as the fireplace was damped during the night. Quilt-making began during slavery when some plantation owners gave each slave a new blanket about every three years. Some Gullah women sometimes adopted traditional white-European quilt patterns but usually liked brighter colors more in keeping with African textiles. At least one Gullah woman remembers her mother using brightly colored fabric in her quilts.

> Most time my mother would buy material enough to make a dress for herself and a dress for me. She would use the scraps that was left over for quilting. Other times she might put pieces together and make even a cover for the bureau. Quilts were blue, yellow, red, light green . . . No dark colors, no black. Black was not something that was readily used as a part making a quilt . . . it was all colorful colors.
> —*Ruth Germany*

Where we used to live, it wasn't too many young people. So I just amused myself in the house. We used to make a lot of quilts. People could make the prettiest log cabin quilts, cotton, wool, silk, or anything. They was so industrious they would never throw away their husband pants, shirt, or nothing. They would cut it up and make it over.
—*Naomi Frazier*

TRANSPORTATION

Gullah persons who were employed by an oyster house, worked at Honey Horn plantation, or searched the woods to gather musk walked miles to their jobs. And a lot of people walked to church carrying their shoes with them so they could put them on clean once they got there. Those who were fortunate enough to have a horse went on horseback or hitched their horse to a cart. And it progressed from there until by the early 1950s, a few men had cars and used them to transport their families and just about everyone in their community. Thomas C. Barnwell, Sr., had one called "the Carryall" because that is what it did.

> We had a horse cart with two wheels. And then from that [we got] a wagon and then from that [came] the buggy time. Horse and buggy. Oh the man that had a horse and buggy was all right. Then you would go to church much better. My mother

said that several times she walked from Braddock's Point, where Harbour Town is, to Mitchellville to the church because it wasn't but one church then.— *Isabel Brown (The walk Brown's mother took was about eleven miles.)*

I know my granddaddy tied his shoes together and throw them over his shoulder and walk right from there to the Methodist Church. They walk and go back. We didn't leave the island too much. We always was homely.— *Nancy Ferguson*

Well, we went by horse and wagon and buggy and walked. We did a lot of walking.— *Emma Graham*

We had a cart, you know, with two wheels, and we had a horse. Some people had wagons, some had carts.— *Albertha Ruby Jones*

Men would ride horseback. We'd take a horse and buggy to go to church. Oak Grove, that was my church. Sometimes, I would ride horseback to church. I would ride side saddle.— *Minnie Holmes*

We used a horse and wagon.— *James Bryant*

Anything [bad] happen, one person get on horseback and ride from here must be to Baygall and spread the news. . . . I don't know who was the first black person to have an automobile. . . . I remember a time when we didn't have but a few. We didn't have that many cars—about five or six maybe, at the most.

My first truck, I remember, was 1926 T-Model Ford. Bought it from Shacklin and Russell in Savannah in 1926. Ford dealer. I guess it cost around eight hundred or nine hundred dollars. Got it over here by the *Cleveland* boat.— *Charlie Simmons, Sr. (born 1906, Spanish Wells Community)*

We had an old '29 Chevrolet truck. [Nathan] Rivers usually was in charge of that. Basically he was the foreman, the chief transportation officer and mechanic. He used it more as a bus. The people in Baygall used to call it the Grassland Bus because he used to pick people up and transport them around on the island.— *Charlie White*

The interesting thing about our dad [Ben White, Sr.], he never to my knowledge drove a vehicle, but he would, you know, always get either one of his kids or someone would in a sense be the chauffeur. — *David White*

You know, as I'm thinking, I think he tried his hand at it, but he was never good at it.— *Charlie White*

Boats and Gullah people went together naturally. Africans had boated coastal waterways and inland rivers for centuries. Freshly arrived Africans with boating skills had plenty of ways to use them on Hilton Head.

During slavery, plantation owners needed boats for

travel to the mainland and to other islands, for recreation and fishing, and for taking crops to market. Enslaved Africans rowed the boats and helped build them.

In colonial times, Skull Creek on the west side of the island was a center of boat building. On occasion, ships were built on Skull Creek. The largest ship built in colonial South Carolina was built on Hilton Head in 1773 by a Savannah shipwright. It displaced four hundred and twenty tons and was used in the Jamaican sugar trade. Enslaved Africans helping build the ship learned additional skills.

When the Union's Department of the South was headquartered on Hilton Head, the Union depended on contrabands' (slaves freed by the Union presence and by Lincoln's Emancipation Proclamation) knowledge of the maze of waterways winding through the sea islands. Hilton Head contrabands guided army boats, went on spy missions behind Confederate lines, and offloaded Union and merchant vessels arriving on Hilton Head. Enterprising contrabands trafficked among the islands, delivering fresh fish and produce to military tables.

Following the Civil War, when Gullah people were on their own and could travel as they pleased, they relied on small homemade boats more than ever. Boats were the only way on or off the island—to take crops to market, to go to Bluffton on the mainland to buy items not readily available on Hilton Head, or to work at jobs off-island.

Steamboats regularly traveled from Charleston to Beaufort to Savannah in this era and in the coming decades. The steamboats stopped at Jenkins Island, about four hundred feet from Hilton Head; Gullah people then rowed themselves or travelers the rest of the way to the island in homemade bateaux (small flat-bottom boats built by Gullah men for fishing and for other purposes).

Gullah men usually used sailboats to take crops to market in Savannah, a distance of twenty-five miles across the waters. This way of life lasted for generations.

The first major change was in 1928, just prior to the Great Depression, when Hilton Head Gullah businessman Charlie Simmons, Sr., acquired the *Edgar Hurst*, a large passenger ferryboat. The *Edgar Hurst* was the first privately owned gas engine–powered boat on the island. With it, Simmons transported people from Hilton Head to Savannah and back, making a stop on Daufuskie Island to pick up passengers.

The *Edgar Hurst* made two overnight trips weekly to Savannah. By riding it, islanders were able to get their crops to market in Savannah by early afternoon of the same day and return to Hilton Head the next afternoon. The *Edgar Hurst* operated into the 1940s, leaving from Harrison Landing (later renamed Simmons Fish Camp).

After that, other island men began to get boat motors, making transportation easier. But Simmons continued to lead the way. He bought a ferry, *Alligator*, that made a daily run in the 1940s and early 1950s between a public dock on Jenkins Island and one in Buckingham. In addition, Simmons would take shopping lists from islanders and fill those lists in Savannah. Then he would bring back the groceries in cardboard boxes, tie them with string, mark each box with the customer's name, and charge each customer twenty-five cents for his service.

Later, he bought a forty-ton barge that served the needs of the U.S. Coast Guard, the State of South Carolina, and the County of Beaufort. He transported everything from dump trucks to asphalt to maintenance crews. Charlie Simmons, with the *Alligator* and his barge, became the go-to man on Hilton Head.

I know that in slavery time they had a boat, seem like a bateau, sixteen places on each side and one man to an oar. My great-grandfather said that they used to go from Jekyll Island down some way or other to Charleston and they would race. Just like a horse race or something. That's the way colored people had to do. One man to an oar, and you better row.— *Isabel Brown*

[M]y husband and seven companions were drowned while coming home from Savannah . . . on a small sailboat [in 1873]. My husband's body was washed ashore on Daufuskie Island . . . and was buried there. . . . [He] was drowned on Saturday night, and his body was not found, and I did not see it until the second Sunday afterwards.—*Harriet Kirk (widow of Abel Kirk, veteran of the 21st Regiment, USCT)*

You couldn't get from this island without a boat. I don't say everybody had their own boat, you know. A crowd would get together, sometimes a crowd get together and that's the way we lived.
— *Nancy Ferguson*

They would cut a tree, what you would call a pine tree, any tree that was large enough for them to use. They would hew that out and make a boat out of that.

I never see them make one, but they would cut the tree down, they would shape the bow and what we call the stern, the back they would saw that off and give it a little shape. That was something that come from the Indians. The tools that they used in those days were call draw ax. Some were a double ax.

They take that pine gum and make what they call a pitch. And they pour that pitch there and in a few day it get hard and the water can't go into it. What they would do is pull that boat up on dry land and give at least about two day. They can't be up there too long because the heat would split it, the heat would split the boat. That's drying enough, and they would take that same pitch and after they fix it, they put it back in the water it swell. Those boats would not leak a quart in a month. The boats went about ten or fifteen miles an hour. They don't hardly use no ash oars. They made their oars. Some were eight feet, some were nine feet, and ten feet was the longest that oar could be. They would take two pieces of a two by four. They would nail pieces on this side and pieces on that side. That what they would make the oar out.

Sometimes they would make four or five seats into that tree. They would call it a double spoiler. They would go from here to Savannah on Saturday, leave here before day clean and get their produce and bring it back. They would have to do that. You had to work by night.— *Elijah Jones, Sr. (born 1895, Pinckney Island)*

When I was twelve years old, they had the steamer go from Beaufort to Savannah, and you could catch it down Spanish Wells landing. But most of the early time you would go in the sailboats.
— *Isabel Brown*

People went by rowboat, sailboat, and they also had steamlines from Savannah to Beaufort. They had several boat lines, these big old ship boats that you can't even explain them. They had the *Planter,* and that was a big ship boat. And they had the *Cleveland* and the *Cannonball* and the *Hildebrand.* And all these boats went to Beaufort. They used to stop out in the river, and they had a ferry boat meet them out there and you could get off and on. And the folks would enjoy it too.

They would stop there to Spanish Wells, and I

would get on and off. I was kind of scary when I first started, but I would get used to it.
— *Naomi Frazier*

You know when no wind blow, that's the only way the sailboat go . . . they go to the long way — on the ocean — and you git more wind [on the outside of the Atlantic ocean].— *Laura Mae Campbell*

[My father] and the other men would take baked potatoes and a little meat in the boat with them and row out over the sound to get to Port Royal Island.— *Georgianna Barnwell (Barnwell's father, John Miller, then a longshoreman, commuted to Savannah by steamer and to Port Royal Island by rowboat to work.)*

On the sailboat, when you leave home — like today is Wednesday, left home this evening, we would get to Savannah Thursday night. If you don't have no wind, you would get a long pole and pole your way out. Pole your way, no wind. That's the way you had to get to Savannah at that time. When you get to Savannah, your shrimps, your fish done gone bad. All day and all night to get to Savannah. If you get in the ship channel and some of them have mercy on you and pull you in, that's the only way you would make it like that.
— *Thomas Holmes*

Hannah Barnwell (center), along with her granddaughter Paulette Barnwell (L) and her mother-in-law, Georgianna Barnwell (R), who was one of Hilton Head's midwives. *Collection of Thomas C. Barnwell, Jr.*

They would go this morning [on sailboat], and then they don't get back home until here days a time. I ain't never gone on a sailboat. I scare of the sailboat. We had a tough way to go . . . but we come through the tough.— *Regina Bennett*

Elijah Jones had a sailboat. They [the men] used to take turns. One go the first of the week. Some got round here Tuesday and some of 'em would go Thursday. They got a mast on 'em, a sail go up on it. The big one had cabin, so the boys sleep in 'em and cook in there and everything.
— *William Holmes, Sr.*

Mingo Green was the top boat man at Broad Creek. Most all had boats, but I'm talking about the top man. He had a boat named the *Waldorf.* It was a little one. My daddy was a farmer. Mingo Green's boat could carry five or six hundred watermelons. So my daddy came up with the idea—he wasn't no boat man, but he got the idea. See, like you doing something and you need money to develop the thing, somebody to back you up. So the old man [Ben White, Sr.] stand up to back Mingo Green up. Armond Frazier build the boat, named the *Roam,* and put it in Broad Creek. And when time to ship, we didn't have to make five or six trips. You could carry about seventeen or eighteen hundred, maybe near two thousand watermelon like that. That *Roam* was built around about 1932.

Georgianna Barnwell, the grandmother of author Thomas C. Barnwell, Jr., in front of her home on Hilton Head. *Collection of Thomas C. Barnwell, Jr.*

George Murray's daddy, Eddie Murray, he was about second to Mingo when it come down to boats. His boat was named *Two Brothers*, 'cause he had two sons. . . . And Eddie Murray could out-sail anybody in Broad Creek.

Another one was Willie Williams. He was a first-class blacksmith and wheelwright. He was Hilton Head's top blacksmith. His daddy, PaPa, was a old slavery-time blacksmith. . . . Those boats were built right here on Hilton Head.

All of them old time fellows, most of them were boatmen. The main thing about it, they used to pick oyster. You go on to Spanish Wells, Jake Brown, he was the king bird. He the one start a motor boat from Hilton Head to Savannah. The first one was Johnny Garvin, but that didn't go but so far. He didn't last. . . . He was a man that leave Hilton Head and come back with the idea of putting a motor boat in Broad Creek. He started, but he didn't go but so far and went down.

[When] Eddie Bryan was a boy, he was on a boat going with a load of watermelon for us. He pump and bail the boat all night going to Savannah. And when day break, Eddie went out and told his old man Steven Bryan, say, "OK, Papa you go ahead and rest yourself and let me take over." He was just a boy. And I come back home and tell Papa, say that that boy is going to be a boatman one day.
—*Johnny White*

We used to take the boat to Savannah; we would have to go by the wind and the tide. It gonna take you good ten to twelve hours to get to Savannah. That's when we had good wind and tide. Bad weather? You'd have to work with that. Those boats had a cabin, and they would have a bunk on each side, two men could sleep at a time, and two men could be wide awake. And it had a little wood stove, you gon' take your food with you if you could cook. Yeah, we used to enjoy it.—*Ben White, Jr.*

My father worked on Hilton Head with my uncle, Rueben Gadson. He had a sailboat and a motorboat combined. Then he was able to get his own sailboat, *Wish Away.* Then on that, he was able to buy a launch boat called the *Hildegarde.* Then he had run the ride from Hilton Head to carry people, freight, and stuff to Savannah. He bought the launch boat from a man on Daufuskie, and he had the sailboat built from scratch. Watson Gooding built it. He built, must have been two or three of them. My daddy had the *Wish Away* registered out of Charleston.
—*Elijah Jones, Jr.*

I started with a boat I bought from Manville Oliver [in 1927] . . . he was chief engineer at Dred Morgan. Luke Graham helped me get the boat, and the boat was about 30 feet . . . and had a fifteen-horse Parma engine in it. That boat was named *Lola.* It was real sharp—dynamite boat. It run fast too. Used it for transport from Hilton Head to Savannah, Monday, Wednesday, and Friday.

Then I got another boat named *Elzie Mae,* used that in the place of the *Lola.* I take the *Lola* and make a shrimp boat out of it. After that I got another boat, named the *GSI,* and used it for passengers. It would carry fifteen or twenty. We left from Harrison Landing in Broad Creek same three days a week. This was around 1935 up to '40. It's where Brown's Point is now.

In 1940 the storm [hurricane] tore down the dock and carry the boat over on the other side near by Possum Point there, and then the storm shift and carry it cross Calibogue. . . . That boat was the *Edgar Hurst.* Bought it from the government. It was a rum runner, and it had been confiscated. The storm caught us in the first dock and carry the boat over on the other side near by Possum Point there, and then the storm shift and carry 'em cross Calibogue over into Bull Island.
—*Charlie Simmons, Sr.*

Arthur Frazier first start carrying stuff from here to Buckingham and then from Buckingham to Savannah. I first start with Frazier. I used to row that boat from Hilton Head, Buckingham, Jenkins Island, or from Bull Point, wherever we go. Cross over here and unload all them stuff. And he had a big raggedy truck he had bought to take them stuff to Savannah. I load the truck up, and after I carry the boat over there, I would leave. Then he would leave me to Old Man Lemon Frazier brother. That's where I learned to drive at. He would leave that '36 truck there, and that truck look like it was brand new. And then when he gone, I would take that truck and ride around all through Bluffton and put it on one or two wheels.—*Ben Miller*

I had a commercial license to operate the boats. Got it from the Customs House in Savannah. They give you all the rules and regulations to go by. You had to have a Coast Guard inspection every ninety days. I had a crew of three. We went [from] Hilton Head and stop to Daufuskie and right on through to Savannah. Did this about fifteen years or more.

I don't remember which one of the boats it was, but they [crew members] went swimming and they hit a bank—ran up on the bank, and it was rough, and I mean it broke the boat into pieces. They were out there all night that night floating on pieces of the boat and think they finally wound up on Daufuskie.

By that time, the road had gotten to be pretty popular, and rather than going all the way to Savannah by water, they [people] started going [by boat] from here to Buckingham [on the mainland] and by truck from Buckingham to Savannah.
—*Charlie Simmons, Sr.*

RECREATION AND HOLIDAYS

Did it ever snow when I was a little girl? Yeah, we walking from school, and your shoes just bogging down, and you so happy you just up and spinning around and walk to the factory and shuck oyster and come back and just jumping up.—*Regina Bennett*

Gullah life on Hilton Head included daily fun. Sunny skies and subtropical weather made it easy for children to entertain themselves after they finished their chores. Girls often played with grass dolls they made, and young boys rolled a string of empty cans linked together like cars in a train. The island's rare snowfalls also brought delight to many young people. Listening to a good storyteller was another treat. Whether a parent, relative, or community elder, Hilton Head storytellers brought laughter to daily life and passed on to each generation a heritage of animal tales, stories created about "rebel" times (a term some used to describe all of antebellum days), and other topics. Storytellers also preserved Gullah phrasing and language and African rhythm as they raised and lowered their voices, quickened their pace, and gave their stories twists and turns.

In addition, children grew up watching parents sing songs and perform shouts. They soon learned to imitate their elders, whether the shout was one that was performed in the praise house or a secular one, like the one below:

Mamma trim the cor-en
Yea corn
Big enough to hold you
Yea corn
Take me back to Mamma
Take me back to Ma.

That used to be like a shoutin' song. . . . We would have certain days to do that clap. And then, the people would shout. But the ones that were clappin',

they didn't do the shouting at that particular time.
— *Mary Lawyer Green*

It was just something so special about the shout. When Mama would leave to go to a meeting, my cousin and I, we would get together, and we would practice that clap . . . that's how I know how to do it.

My folks did the Buzzard Lope. That one I didn't learn too much because that let them know we were really lookin', and we weren't suppose to be.

[The Buzzard Lope was performed by adults, for adults. It told the tale of a head buzzard determining whether the carrion was safe to eat. To some it also referred to harsh slave conditions, when a field worker might die in the field and be left there until sundown when enslaved people could stop to bury the body.]

It would be my daddy and his sisters doin' it, and one would have a towel, and they would be snatchin' that towel around just like the buzzard. Now this lead buzzard be the buzzard that test the meat to see whether it was poison or not. They would move on the floor, it just had a sound. Their feet would be movin' on the linoleum . . . and then they would say, "Tis it fat, tis it pork; tis it fat, tis it pork?" And I can do just the little bit of it that I strained my eyes to see.

My folks also did "Tell Aunt Tina Tie That Dog." . . . I got that one down really good. Now when I talk to some of the [older] people [on the island] . . . they know what I'm talkin' about . . .

Oh tell Aunt Tina tie that dog.
Old dog'll bite, oh tell Aunt Tina tie that dog,
  old dog gon' bite.
Oh Aunt Tina got a mean dog, old dog gon' bite.
Oh Aunt Tina got a mean dog. Old dog gon' bite.

That's settin' the song. [There] usually be somebody to sing it and somebody to set it. The singer and the setter could be the same person but then that person would take a seat. Sing and set the song and the other people would shout.

They got Stickman. Stickman is keepin' the beat on a pallet of wood. . . . And then you find the other guy up there singin' and then those ladies doin' the shout. A lot of times I try to sing it, clap it, shout it, and all that.

Some people call it the Gullah Dance. It's a shout. If you dancing, you crossin' the feet, but [with] the shout you don't. It's a shuffle. You go all the way around this circle. Your feet is movin', and they [the ladies] move their body too. . . . They put their hand on they hip, and they move they hip, you know, so it's just a part of the shout.— *Louise Cohen*

From the early days of freedom into the mid-1900s, Gullah people on Hilton Head had their own social clubs. The social clubs sustained club members in times of need and enlivened life on the island.

The Mothers' Union was the largest organization for women on the island, and the Farmer's Club, which may have dated back to the 1800s, also was very prominent. Those two, along with the Brownsville Society, were mutual aid and burial societies.

Among other social clubs active on the island at various times were: the Boys of Pleasure, the Girls of Pleasure, the Brother's Club, the Charity Sisters (in the Pope Community), the Brother's Club, the Sons and Daughters' Auxiliary, the Friendly Sisters, the Friendly Brothers, the Harden Club (a women's club), and Rose of Sharon (predominantly a women's club although some men may have joined).

The Odd Fellows, a national organization similar to the Masons, came to the island later. It had a lodge on Hilton Head in the Baygall vicinity, close to Queen Chapel Church.

Another club active on the island later was the Progressive Club. This club existed throughout South Carolina and was part of a larger network that included several other states. The Progressive Club worked to help register voters in the 1940s and 1950s.

Many of the social clubs held regular meetings. Some held events commemorating special occasions or provided entertainment and recreation.

The Mothers' Union was well-known for its spectacular Mothers' Day program. This program was held each year on a rotating basis, at one of the Gullah churches. On this day, all women throughout the island dressed in white—white dresses, white shoes, white stockings, and white hats—for the church service.

On the evening of the Day in White service, the Mothers' Union held a program which the club members organized. Young people gave speeches, followed by a break and a dinner of fried chicken, cake, red rice, and other popular foods. The program then resumed with speeches from the women and solos and group songs. On the day of their annual turnout, the women were recognized for their importance to island life.

> I was a member of the Mothers' Union. Sometime in the summer you had to turn out in your white and have a program. It go 'round from church to church. If you a member, you wear white. There were [also] the Friendly Sisters and Girls of Pleasure. They had a Friendly Brothers, too.
> —*Corrine Lawyer Brown*

The social club best known for its flair for fun was the Boys of Pleasure. The club was located in the Pope community but included members from other communities. Club celebrations included the Fourth of July, Decoration Day Christmas, and New Year's.

New Year's was the Boys of Pleasure's biggest event. People from different communities would participate in horse racing in the Chaplin community. (Chaplin is in the area now known as Matthew's Drive, where

Matthew's Drive intersects with Marshland Road in the Gardner section.) The horse races began at a point called Meeting House Bridge. The race course ran down Marshland Road to Legg O' Mutton Road. The winning horse reached Legg O' Mutton Road first.

The horse that always seemed to win was a male horse owned by Ruben Green. His brother, Walter Green, also always had a horse in the race. The horses were island marsh tackies that the men had tamed and trained.

Members of the Boys of Pleasure also formed a musical band that was highly popular on the island. For many years, Gullah native Jamesy Reid, a guitar player and one-man band, played regularly on Saturday nights at either the Stoney or the Chaplin social hall. The crowd danced as Reid played his guitar, wash board, and mouth organ (harmonica). He also used an upside-down tub to make a washtub base.

Gatherings, parties, and dances were held at the social halls year-round. In the Joe Pope (Leamington) community, people from all over the island went to "Sugar" Brown's juke joint on Saturday nights. In later years, the Beach Club nightclub operated in the Cherry Hill/Mitchelville. Dances and parties were held in the Squire Pope social hall. The Gumtree Social Hall, on Gumtree Road, also hosted frequent dances and parties.

Other forms of recreation included sailboat racing in the summer and swimming. Gullah people swam at high tide off of a dock at Hudson's Oystery Factory in the Squire Pope community.

The Jonesville/Jarvis community had a baseball field for many years, with people in the communities playing against each other. This summer sport ended after the Church of Christ—a sanctified church—was organized in the early 1940s in Jonesville. From then on, Jonesville focused on business and church.

Winter sports included wrestling and horse racing.

At Christmas time they [the men] would have their horse races. . . . They use to get a lot of kick out of that. And Old Man Harry Burke and the old men use to wrestle. If they meet to your house they would say let's tie a fall.—*Naomi Frazier*

We used to have some good dances. . . . Let me call the names in the band. You had Abraham Johnson in the band; you had Herbert Chaplin; you had John Patterson, Rueben Green, George Murray, Samuel Christopher, and Whitaker Chisolm. He blow the horn. Then you had Dennis Chaplin, who we used to call Eagle Eye. And then we had "Son" Chaplin, he used to play with them too. I don't know where he connected. . . . Cleveland Jones used to play to those bands on Saturday night. Cleveland and Jamsie Reid. Jamsie Reid cock that little eye way up in the air there.

Those boys was the Hilton Head band. You

remember Jamsie used to play the "Flat Foot Susie" and "When My Dreamboat Come Home." John Blake and his brother Dolphus used to play accordion. "Boy" Miller, same thing. They was good too. —*Ben Miller*

A man by the name of "Tuna" lived in Savannah and would come to Hilton Head Island to play the piano at the Boys of Pleasure Hall.—*Arthur Orage*

We had accordion, oh boy, when I was little and dry legged, but I could jump too. They had a brass band on the Island. . . . That's the way they enjoyed themselves.—*Isabel Brown*

They had guitar, and they had horns, they play horns and beat the drum and all. We had an annual dance thing. The piccolo come to us on Hilton Head long in the '30s or the '40s. —*Albertha Ruby Jones*

The only thing I can recall from the beach was that we used to go down to Burke's Beach on weekends. Bradley Beach, Singleton Beach, it was a kinda like the hangout for teenagers, and it was a kind of a weekly occurrence, but I don't recall us really hanging out that much on the beach itself. The pavilion was kinda off from the water a bit, and we used to hang out in the pavilion but not actually spending that much time, you know, going down to the beach and dipping in the water.—*David White*

We used to go to school functions, and then they had the little round where you could go. There was one in Chaplin that became a little sort of a club. Then there was that old hall right across from Oak Grove Church, and that used to be a place where people can dance. Later on, I guess the Fishing Camp became a place to go. You know places like Burke Beach and those, they wasn't not even heard of then. There were some things up in Spanish Wells as I recall. There were some in Stoney. I'm sure they used to sell beer. I don't remember them selling any hard liquor.

And then the piccolo [jukebox] was available then. You put the money in the thing, yeah. I think most of the music was played by, you remember, James Dupree and those guys. He used to play the mouth organ and jazz horn. And it seem like somebody had an accordion. If this is all you've ever heard, it sound good to you, you know. —*Charlie White*

Gullah people on Hilton Head Island annually celebrated the signing of the Emancipation Proclamation until after the bridge to the mainland was built. Crowds of excited Hilton Head contrabands and black soldiers had attended the original 1862 New Year's Eve celebration held in anticipation of President Abraham Lincoln signing the Emancipation Proclamation the next day.

Lincoln's signing of the historic document on January 1, 1863, at last made the freeing of the slaves an official purpose of the Civil War in addition to reuniting the nation. It also bestowed freedom on all slaves within the rebellious states, though Lincoln lacked power to enforce that edict without a military victor.

Yet for former slaves within the Union-held sea islands, freedom was instantaneous. As soon as Lincoln put pen to paper, their status changed from that of contrabands (or "spoils of war") to freedmen. The glorious occasion was never forgotten in the sea islands. When the first anniversary of the proclamation's signing came around, people in the sea islands gathered again to celebrate the wondrous day.

January 1, 1864, was cold with a piercing wind, according to Thomas Wentworth Higginson, commander of the First South Carolina Volunteers. Yet the bleakness of the day did not dampen the ardor of those attending what General Rufus Saxton told freedmen was "the birth-day of your liberties." Hilton Head islanders played a major role in the celebration.

A grand civic and military procession led to Camp Shaw, the base of the First South Carolina Volunteers. The procession included white friends of the freedmen, wounded and disabled soldiers, the First South Carolina Volunteers, detachments from other colored regiments, colored laborers and mechanics in the quartermaster's department at Hilton Head, colored sailors of the navy, general superintendents of labor and instruction, missionaries and pastors of churches, and freedmen of the various islands including Hilton Head.

When the procession reached the platform where the ceremonies were to be held, "the exercises were commenced with a prayer by Rev. Abraham Murchison, the [N]egro preacher on Hilton Head Island. Next, school children sang a hymn and then the president's Proclamation of Emancipation was read by Gilbert Pillsbury, superintendent at Hilton Head."

"From 1863 on it seems that people commemorated that day in the low country, at least in these islands," Emory S. Campbell said, looking back at life on Hilton Head. "People were jubilant because they knew this was the day. . . . The message, almost one hundred years later, was how important it is to be free."

The celebration took place at church and was like a church service except that it was centered around the Emancipation Proclamation. Sometimes teachers spearheaded the commemoration. From his own middle-school days in the early 1950s, Campbell particularly remembers one teacher who put the program together: Mrs. Ruth Jones. Mrs. Jones, an attractive woman who had taught in New York, seemed very worldly to the students. She was a stickler on students doing things just right.

School children were the main attendees, but some adults attended, too. Campbell remembers his father attending.

People would arrive there by noontime for the program, dressed in their Sunday best. "In those particular days," Campbell said, "you iron and starch your pants, starch your shirt, put on a jacket, and your shoes were polished, and your hair was combed and groomed, neat and clipped."

The program opened with a scripture that was like an invocation. Then the congregation sang an opening song. "There was clapping and stomping because we didn't have a piano. . . . Everybody participated because they had to provide the beat."[18]

A student choir whose members were picked by the teachers sang other songs, and students recited poems and selections such as the Gettysburg Address. "When Malindy Sings," a poem by the African-American poet Paul Laurence Dunbar, was often recited at the program. In the poem, Malindy, a black girl whose singing rings, "F'om de kitchen to be big woods," so outshines Miss Lucy, a white girl, that Miss Lucy is told she might as well put away her music book because if she practices till she's gray, she never can match Malindy.

"There was lots of pride. We were prideful whenever we talked about black history, black heroes, emancipation, and slaves. We were proud of black citizens. There was a sense of accomplishment," Campbell said.

The program always included "My Country, 'Tis of Thee" and "America the Beautiful." "We still lived the lessons of Emancipation Day," Campbell said. (The celebration of Emancipation Day continued to be celebrated after the bridge. This event endured nearly into contemporary times.)[19]

Decoration Day is a special holiday in late May, when Gullah people pay homage to veterans of American wars—particularly those who died in the Civil War. Decoration Day later became known as Memorial Day.

The first Decoration Day took place in Charleston, South Carolina, shortly after the Union capture of Charleston and the end of the Civil War. It was held on May 1, 1865, on the grounds of the planters' horse track, the Washington Race Course and Jockey Club. In the last year of the war, the Confederates had turned it into an outdoor prison for Union soldiers.

The soldiers were kept in the interior of the track under poor conditions. More than two hundred and fifty "died of exposure and disease and were hastily buried in a mass grave behind the grandstand. Some twenty-eight black workmen went to the site, re-buried the Union dead properly, and built a high fence around the cemetery. They whitewashed the fence and built an archway over an entrance on which they inscribed the words, 'Martyrs of the Race Course.'

"Then, black Charlestonians in cooperation with

white missionaries and teachers staged a parade of ten thousand people on the slaveholders' race course."[20]

A white northerner, Ester Hawks, MD, who had taught school on Hilton Head, recorded in her diary that the area surrounding the clubhouse of the racecourse was "thronged with vehicles of every description and pedestrians of all ages, from the baby in arms to the white hairs of bent old age. All faces wore the sweetest smiles and nearly every hand bore bunches or baskets laden with beautiful flowers."

At 10:00 a.m., a procession formed with school children in the front. They passed under the flag stretched across the street, which led to the soldiers' graves, singing as they went, "My Country, 'Tis of Thee."

The procession arrived at what Hawks called the "bleak spot," an enclosure where the Union soldiers were buried in long trenches. As procession members "entered the enclosure where our poor soldiers lay, every voice was hushed, and with quiet reverent steps they marched around the yard depositing their floral offers on the new made graves. . . . It was one of the most touching sights I ever witnessed!" Hawks said. "The ceremonies in the yard consisted in singing . . . hymns by the Baptist Church—prayer by a colored clergyman—and reading of appropriate passages of scripture, none but colored people officiating. . . . By 2:00 p.m. the speaking and eating were over, thus ending the impressive ceremonies of the first Decoration Days."[21]

Three years later, in 1868, the commander of the Grand Army of the Republic (GAR), a national politically active national veteran's organization, officially sanctioned Decoration Day as a day set aside to honor both the Union and Confederate Civil War dead and to console their grieving widows, children, and other relatives. As had occurred at Charleston, the GAR commander recommended "strewing with flowers, or otherwise decorating the graves of comrades who died in defense of their country."

In 1878, South Carolina's Reconstruction Governor David Henry Chamberlain expressed hope that Decoration Day would promote reconciliation rather than feelings of hatred or hostility between the former foes. Governor Chamberlin noted, however, that "we must pronounce secession and slavery wrong, if we would duly honor the memory of the martyrs of the Union and freedom."

Putting the heated atmosphere of the times behind proved impossible at that time. Instead, South Carolina and other southern states instituted a separate memorial day known as Confederate Memorial Day. In the sea islands of South Carolina, Decoration Day became regarded as a black holiday. This did not detract from the holiday's deep importance to Gullah people.

In the sea islands, President Lincoln had planned ahead and set aside land on a former plantation in Beaufort to become a national cemetery for the war dead. The cemetery sits on a twenty-nine–acre land tract the federal government purchased for $75.00 in a federal tax sale in 1863.

The remains of the Union dead on Hilton Head were among the first soldiers after the war to be removed and placed in the Beaufort National Cemetery. Also at this time, soldiers and sailors who died on islands surrounding Beaufort and Hilton Head and those initially buried in Charleston, Morris Island, Savannah, and East Florida were interred in the National Cemetery. Although most of Hilton Head's black Union dead were moved to Beaufort, the gravesites of some black Civil War veterans are still on Hilton Head Island today.

The memories of Union soldiers and sailors were vivid on Hilton Head where the soldiers—white and black—had ushered in freedom. Gullah people made an annual trip to Beaufort to pay homage to the war dead, celebrate their deliverance from slavery, and decorate the graves of Civil War veterans.

Early ceremonies included parades and marches of memorial groups and military organizations, invocations by ministers, and speakers. Speakers often included a representative of the GAR.

Hilton Head Island had its own Grand Army post, the Abraham Lincoln Brigade. It met at the Grand Army Hall in the Chaplin community, had officers, and even had its own stationery in the 1890s. Representatives of the Abraham Lincoln Brigade no doubt marched in the parade in memory of their Civil War comrades. Some brigade officers, including Matt Jones

of the Stoney community, owned a GAR uniform and likely wore it on Decoration Days.

The trip to Beaufort from the north end of Hilton Head was seven miles by boat. Islander Isabel Brown, born in 1884, remembered going to Decoration Day as a child in the 1890s. In those days little children didn't get to go everywhere, she said, but Decoration Day was an exception.

When she went with her parents, "We used to go from here on sail boat. And sometimes after you getting [on in age]—I was twelve years old—they had the steamer go from Beaufort to Savannah and back, and you could catch it down [at the] Spanish Wells landing. . . . But most of the time, you would go in the sail boats. . . . You would leave here on the 29th—you would have to leave that night to be there by morning."

As the decades passed, the immediate sense of mourning faded. A festive air arose. Steamboats like the *Cleveland* would leave Savannah and stop along the way to pick up passengers at Daufuskie Island, Hilton Head Island, and Pinckney Island before reaching Beaufort. A band played music on the boat. Vendors along the riverside in Beaufort sold hot dogs, cake, candy, sodas, deviled crabs, and other foods, and even set up a small fair for people to attend. In addition, people would throw flowers in the river in memory of the soldiers. When Decoration Day ended and night came, the boat left from Beaufort and returned people safely to their islands.

Gullah native Arthur Orage recalled the time when

he was living in Savannah in the late 1940s and decided to catch the Decoration Day steamboat over to Hilton Head to visit. When he got to Hilton Head he meant to get off, "but the music was so good I keep going" on to Beaufort.

"The fare was no more than thirty-five cents to ride from Savannah to Hilton Head—seventy cents round trip. I remember that," Orage said.

In later times, women dressed in uniforms and caps marched on this day, and the water was strewn with flowers.

People would say, "Are you going to the 29th?" Meaning that they left here on the 29th—the evening of—and got to Beaufort the next day. Behind the celebration there was real fundamental thought about celebrating freedom and those soldiers. I used to take my children there every year.
—*Emory S. Campbell*

Decoration Day, now Memorial Day, is still celebrated today at the Beaufort National Cemetery. The day includes a parade and a program. Women in the parade wear uniforms and caps. Since the 1970s, the parade has included both black and white citizens who come to honor those who died in many wars.

In addition to picnics and a band that performed in the Marshland community, Hilton Head Gullah farmers got together on July 4th and rode their horses out to inspect the crops. The ride allowed farmers to gauge whether the crops would provide people with adequate food in the coming seasons and whether the cash crops (such as watermelon, cotton, and others) also would bring prosperity. It fostered people's sense of self-sufficiency and independence on a remote island.[22]

Thanksgiving was celebrated, but to a lesser extent than Christmas. Services were held at the praise house. Most food crops had been harvested by then.

Thanksgiving—a lot to be thankful for? Oh yeah, we had plenty to eat. One dress to wear to school.
—*Nancy Ferguson*

Around Thanksgiving time, we used to be out of food. . . . Everybody had a hog and chicken and cows. We sold the cows. We didn't eat too much meat.
—*Henry Ford*

Christmas, while a religious holiday, also was a highly enjoyed social occasion on Hilton Head. For many Gullah people, getting ready for Christmas included preparing the house: white-washing the fence, raking the yard, and sketching curtains.

In order to get Christmas money, islanders took the turkeys they had raised all year to Savannah to sell. Everybody would come back with gifts for Christmas day—"some long boxes," Naomi Frazier, born 1905, recalled.

Islanders also formed Christmas Clubs in which every family contributed money and the funds would be dispersed before Christmas. This allowed families to make sure they would have money available for gifts for their children. By the 1940s some fortunate youths received a bicycle. Earlier, much simpler gifts were given.

Even in antebellum days Christmas was a big occasion. White planters in the Beaufort District (including Hilton Head Island, Port Royal, and several other surrounding islands) gave bondsmen and -women three to four days off. Many planters gave gifts to enslaved people, ranging from tobacco and pipes to molasses or salt, all of which were rare items in slave life. Enslaved people on Hilton Head were allowed to visit friends and relatives on other plantations on the island.

After freedom, Gullah people continued the tradition of visiting each other, adapted it, and made the holiday their own. On Christmas Day friends and neighbors of the different communities visited from house to house, where festive foods awaited them at each stop.

Much baking and cooking occurred before the big day: pies, cakes, chicken, raccoon, deer, possum, pork, gravy, corn bread, and fried cracklings. Even homemade wine and moonshine was available for adult guests. Women vied to make the best sweet potato pie or other tasty treat. Visitors usually knew just which dish they wanted to sample when they arrived at a particular house.

Adding to the fun, men and women would go around in separate groups or clubs and sing shouts—some of which were secular and some religious. Visiting did not end on Christmas Day. People kept visiting for days until they had been to everyone's house.

Among the clubs that made rounds were the Harden Club and the Mothers' Union. Ladies of the Mother's Union went to each other's houses. They began the day after Christmas and took the whole week up to New Year's.

And you know what we used to plaster the walls with? Paper. Newspaper or magazine. Go to the white people, yeah, and they give you a magazine, and you bring 'em home. All that pretty picture you come on, [like the] Christmas time girl? The whole house pretty, done with all them pictures. Beautiful. — *Laura Mae Campbell*

Older people would sit up all night at Christmas Eve and cook chicken and turkey and potato pone. Kids help with the grating . . . we had fun doing it. We didn't buy potatoes, they were potatoes off our farm.— *Henry Ford*

Christmas was the biggest [holiday]. What did we do? Go from home to home and shout and eat. — *Julia Grant Bryant*

A crowd would get in a bunch together and go from house to house. A lot of people don't even cook on Christmas Day. They just be serving 'cause they do

it all that night [before]. If they don't finish [their rounds] they would go until they finish . . . until they would go to everybody's house.
—*Emma Graham*

We used to go round in a club. Harden Club. . . . Yeah. We used to go 'round in that club.
—*Corrine Lawyer Brown*

Children would start [coming] around maybe noon time. . . . Everyone got something, a orange or a half of orange and a slice of cake. . . . But the older people [men], you have some start coming around for a little toddy — they come early . . . around eight o'clock. And that was moonshine now; they wanted to make as many houses as they could.
—*Henry Ford*

From house to house. From house to house. Talking and dancing and having their fun. . . . It wasn't much drinking as far as I know, now. Unless it been in different areas.—*Thomas Holmes*

Christmas Eve night our daddy and mother been to the [praise house]. People sing and pray all night long, then we not gonna sleep. . . . My brother Johnny and I . . . sit up there and sit up there. When Santa Claus come, we gone try and catch him so we can take some toys off him. . . . We stay up ever so late, been almost time for day, can see the break of day . . . we never could catch Santa Claus. Santa

Claus must be come in there when he know we went to sleep, 'cause after being up all night, you had to sleep a hour.—*Ben White, Jr.*

In elementary school we used to write letters to Santa Claus and send them in to the radio. They would read some [on the air] and some just call the names. The teacher had a special day to mail them to WTOC radio in Savannah. We would rush home [to hear]. My name was called every year in the forties.
—*Henry Ford*

New Year's Eve was celebrated at the praise house in a service known as Watch Night. People began arriving at the praise house about nine o'clock on New Year's Eve. The service continued until midnight when the New Year came in.

Songs, religious shouts, and spirituals filled the overflowing small community praise houses. Praise-house members testified as to the blessings they had received in the departing year, expressed each other good wishes for the coming year, and watched for its arrival.

The praise houses usually did not have clocks or bells to ring, so an appointed "watchman" stationed outside the praise house would watch the moon to tell when midnight arrived. The praise-house leader would ask the watchman how much time remained in the old year, and the watchman would yell out in count-down fashion intervals such as "thirty minutes," "fifteen minutes," "five minutes." When the watchman announced the arrival of the New

Year, such spirited shouting erupted in the praise house that everyone in the community could hear it.

People then would go home and eat Hoppin' John—peas (usually field peas) cooked with salt pork or ham hocks and served over rice. Field (or cow) peas were among the foods brought from Africa in the holds of slave ships as food for African slaves. Black-eyed peas, a variety of field peas, were seen in the Carolina colonies before the early 1700s. Hoppin' John became a traditional dish in the Low Country. You had to eat Hoppin' John on New Year's to make sure you would have good luck in the coming year, and greens to bring in money in the coming year.

> Back at home, your mom and dad would have a big pot of Hoppin' John and rice and greens cooked on the stove.—*Henry Ford*

New Year's Day also had plenty of recreation. People from various communities would come to participate in the horse racing down in Chaplin.

> The horse races began at a point called Meeting House Bridge. The racecourse ran down Marshland Road to Legg O' Mutton Road. The winning horse reached Legg O' Mutton Road first, and the horse that always seemed to win was a male horse owned by Ruben Green. His brother, Walter Green, always had a horse that would be in the race as well.—*Thomas C. Barnwell, Jr.*

While many adults would be watching the race, schoolchildren and a few parents would be attending the annual Emancipation Day celebration once again. The New Year came in as the old New Year had. At the first anniversary of Emancipation Day in 1863, Union General Rufus Saxton told the freedmen that that they had advanced further in a very short time than he ever had anticipated they could. "Onward, ever onward," Saxton urged the freedmen. That spirit continued in the annual Emancipation Day celebration.

REFLECTIONS ON GROWING UP AFTER THE BRIDGE

by Carolyn Grant

I grew up Gullah, but it wasn't until later in life that I learned how the Gullah culture enriched and shaped me. As my history was revealed through stories from relatives and other Gullah descendants of Hilton Head Island, I knew it was a story I wanted to capture in a book. I made writing that story a life goal. So too did Thomas C. Barnwell, Jr., and Emory S. Campbell, who along with my father Abraham "Abe" Grant, Sr., were born and raised on Hilton Head in an era before developers moved in and introduced the island as paradise to the rest of the world. For many years, Mr. Barnwell, Mr. Campbell, and I collected historical information, conducted interviews, searched for publishers, connected with a writer/researcher, who helped us create a more powerful narrative, and spent many evenings together sharing conversations and memories. Those conversations were partly my lessons about a culture that was present all my life yet was struggling to remain alive. Gullah history and culture were not taught in the public schools I attended on Hilton Head or Bluffton. It wasn't a language spoken in schools. But signs of the culture were all around us in many other ways.

My home and family life were filled with Gullah influences—language, food, farming, fishing, oystering, religion, basket weaving, land, beaches, family, history, community, education, all ways of life on Hilton Head. While these traditions existed, they weren't commonly referred to as Gullah. You just knew them as a way of life. My father, who operated a roadside convenience store, recalled that a group of white customers had stopped by his store in the late 1950s and inquired about the dialect of the island's black people. They used the term *Geechee*, he said, and wanted to know why black people on the island talked so funny and fast that you couldn't understand them. When I was growing up, Geechee was used to describe poorly spoken English. But unbeknownst to me, there really was some legitimacy to the way black people on the island spoke. I later learned it was the Gullah language, a dialect that evolved from the merger of English with West African phrases and words my enslaved ancestors brought to this country.

My great-aunt Beaulah Grant Kellerson, who raised my father Abe as her son (his biological mother was her younger sister Bell Grant), was a colorful storyteller who shared vivid details of her life growing up on Hilton Head, picking crops, shucking oysters, and making sweetgrass baskets. She had given birth to one son, Solomon Grant, and was married to William "Willie" Kellerson, who farmed land and picked oysters for a living. The 1900 census listed her birth year as March 1898, but she emphatically declared that she was born March 10, 1900, as the eldest of eight children to Abraham Grant and his second wife, Peggy. Family history shared by relatives trace Peggy's roots back to the historic Mitchelville, the first freedmen's village in the United States. What is known about the elder Abraham is that he, like many other enslaved persons escaping slaveholders, heard of a place called Hilton Head where they could be free.

Sometime in the late 1800s, a formerly enslaved man named Backus Drayton fled from Jacksonboro, South Carolina, to find his way to Hilton Head. Jacksonboro is a small community north of the state's Combahee River in Colleton County. In 1863, Harriet Tubman, abolitionist and leader of the Underground Railroad, used information she gathered from slaves to help Union soldiers navigate their ships through mine-filled waters of the Combahee River; once ashore, they rescued more than seven hundred enslaved men, women, and children from a nearby plantation and helped them on their journey to freedom.

On his journey, Backus met and was joined by a young man named Abraham, who family members said had come from an area around Georgetown, South Carolina, a city about 165 miles from Hilton Head. The two men traveled together to Hilton Head, the place where they hoped to begin their new lives in freedom. It's likely that they and many others heading to Hilton Head traveled by foot until they reached the end of their mainland journeys and could see in the short distance the island they yearned to step foot on. Fearing they would be captured, both Backus and Abraham changed the surnames their slaveholders had given to them. Backus adopted the name of Ferguson. Abraham's slave-given surname is unknown, but he took the name of Grant. Once they arrived and settled on Hilton Head, Backus and Abraham produced two of Hilton Head's large, prominent families—the Ferguson family, which established their family compound in the Big Hill community of Hilton Head Island, and the Grants, a family of farmers that settled initially in the Joe Pope Plantation area of the island and later in Chaplin. In the early 1890s, they were living on and farming property owned by the North Carolina Hunting Club and providing other services such as cooking, cleaning, yard care, and taking care of horses and dogs.[23] Through the years, the Grants worked hard, acquired property, and farmed their land. Eventually, two of my uncles opened roadside stands to sell their fruits and vegetables.

As a young girl, Beaulah had learned how to weave baskets from her mother, Peggy. She made large baskets with covers, fanners, small trays, and other forms and sizes for a variety of uses. For many years before, she and her husband carried her baskets to the market in Savannah to sell along with their locally caught fish and homegrown vegetables.[24] In the 1950s and 1960s, she was selling large sweetgrass baskets for $5.00 from her son's roadside stand until her nephew Abe encouraged her to raise the price. Although this art wasn't maintained by her grandchildren, nieces, and nephews, including me and my siblings, we did watch and learn about the making of sweetgrass baskets at the feet of our great-aunt, who we affectionately called Annie (our way of saying "auntie"). We would gather on the porch that wrapped around her home, where we would bundle grass to pass to her to weave into the baskets and listen to her hum spirituals and tell stories. She was among the last of Hilton Head's old-time basket makers.

As a young boy, Abe helped his Aunt Beaulah and Uncle Willie on their farm, but farming wasn't his favorite task. He admired the Gullah men in his community who owned community stores and desired to open one himself. "My uncle was working at one of the saw mills on the island, and he told me to come to the mill to get some slab," my father recalled. So he hitched his marsh tacky horse to his wagon, headed to the saw mill, and loaded up the wood for his uncle, who wanted Abe to build a horse stable. Instead, Abe used the wood to build a small store on the ocean side of the road in

Solomon Grant.
Collection of Abraham and Charliemae Grant

and John Patterson, transporters who traveled back and forth by boat and road to Savannah after a road system connected Buckingham Landing to Bluffton and beyond. Boats took people and freight from Jenkins Island to Buckingham where they boarded trucks and cars for the trip to Savannah via road. Before then — in the mid- to late 1940s — Charlie Simmons, Sr., was the main transporter to Savannah from Hilton Head, all the way by boat. Abe's store, called Kellerson's at the time, became a main stop for visitors and newcomers making the island their home. At the same time that Abe was operating his small store, workers were building a bridge to connect Hilton Head to the mainland. The bridge ultimately would become Abe's ticket to a whole new world and lead him to experiences he would use later to fulfill his dreams.

The bridge opened under much fanfare in 1956. Soon after, Abe packed some of his belongings, left his store in the capable hands of his aunt, and hoped he could make a life and living beyond Hilton Head. He got a ride to Savannah and boarded a shrimp boat bound for Key West, Florida, with his biological father, James C. Frazier, known to be one of the most skilled shrimpers between Hilton Head Island and Florida. He took Abe under his wing to teach him shrimping and navigational skills that many Gullah men had mastered to support their families. Shrimping didn't work out well for Abe. He left Key West and headed to Miami, where found work at a Sealtest dairy and in a restaurant. There he

Chaplin. "That's where I began," he said. Too young to get a permit to operate the store, Abe convinced his aunt to apply on his behalf, and at sixteen years old he became one of Hilton Head's youngest store owners.

He would send his order for honey buns, sweet rolls, soda, coffee, and other merchandise from Savannah markets with Charlie Simmons, Sr., Arthur Frazier, learned tricks and trades of what would become his future business.

In 1961, when his aunt was no longer able to manage the store, Abe returned to Hilton Head to run his business. Upon his return, another young man, Harold Smalls, who came to work on Hilton Head from a small town in Hampton County, South Carolina, introduced Abe to his sister, Charliemae, who had been living and working in Savannah, Georgia. The two soon married. They bought land on the opposite side of the highway and built a larger store, where they grew a business enterprise that included Abe's Grocery Store, Abe's Driftwood Lounge (which started out as a members-only club and featured bands and disc jockeys from around the Low Country), Abe's Motel and Rentals, and Abe's Restaurant, later renamed Abe's Native Shrimp House. The lounge and restaurant featured a large chimney that was a conversation among restaurant customers. "Some of the bricks had the fingerprint of slaves during the time when they were making bricks. They would pick them up before they hard and their fingerprint was in it," my father recalled.

Abe's would become famous worldwide for serving unique Gullah dishes that he and his wife enjoyed while growing up. Food was part of the Gullah tradition, as Gullah islanders grew or caught almost everything they ate. Both of my uncles who lived near us, James Grant, Sr., and Solomon Grant, Sr., farmed their small acres of land and taught their children how to grow and harvest

Abraham Grant, Sr., and his wife, Charliemae, owned Abe's Native Shrimp House Restaurant and other businesses. They were in business for nearly fifty years before retiring in 2001. *Collection of Abraham and Charliemae Grant*

Abraham and Charliemae Grant in their store, ca. 1970s.
Collection of Abraham and Charliemae Grant

crops. My siblings and I often helped in the fields picking tomatoes, beans, corn, and other crops that would
be sold at their small roadside stands. Sometimes we
would join our cousins to sell fruits and vegetables to
people who had moved to the island or were visiting.

Rather than surviving off of farming, shrimping, and
picking oysters, Abe incorporated what he learned from
these Gullah traditions by preparing and serving home-
cooked Gullah dishes. Visitors and workers arriving on
the island were in search of places to enjoy meals and
drinks. They would find their way to Abe's for hot sandwiches, fried fish and chicken, shrimp, oysters, crab, lima

Abraham and Charliemae Grant in their restaurant, 1987.
Collection of Abraham and Charliemae Grant

beans with smoked neckbones, collard greens, gumbo,
corn bread, and more. In the mid-1970s, Abe's became
a full-service restaurant—also the first on the island
to offer a full buffet. Buffet prices started at $2.50 and
customers lined up to get their full share. A Charleston

writer noted that Abe's, he believed, was the first restaurant to serve shrimp and grits: "Cruising past the marinas, condos, and hotels, I float back to the 1960s, when my college roommate drove us out from Savannah to Hilton Head for a night of beer drinking and live music at Abe's Driftwood Lounge. A ramshackle roadhouse and pool hall, it was run by Abe Grant, an African-American entrepreneur who later opened Abe's Shrimp House—like the Driftwood, long gone—which was possibly the first restaurant in America to offer the now ubiquitous dish of shrimp-and-grits."[25] That dish, along with others, became specialty Gullah meals that we served through the history of the restaurant. Shrimp was a part of most dishes. Popular among customers were shrimp and okra, shrimp gumbo, fried shrimp, flounder, catfish, boiled crab, liver and onions, red rice, corn bread, and more. My siblings and I learned our work ethics and Gullah cooking by working alongside our parents in their businesses.

As youngsters, we stocked store shelves with goods. Through the week, we had to dust shelves and make sure all the merchandise was lined up, neat and orderly. We learned to operate the cash register, bag groceries, clean the store, pool hall, and lounge, and clean motel rooms before the next group of renters arrived. We also learned to head and peel shrimp, greet and serve customers, set up food on the buffet line, and prepare food. There were always chores to be done.

Our family home and business were both located in

Abe's Restaurant and Motel.
Collection of Abraham and Charliemae Grant

the Chaplin community of Hilton Head. It was one of several close-knit Gullah communities on the island and a popular destination because of the stretch of beaches. Several families started operating businesses in Chaplin before and after the bridge—Henry Driessen, whose grandfather had a store, had continued the operation selling an array of snack foods, merchandise, and Gulf gas. His wife, Pheobe, my first-grade teacher, helped at the store. Diogenes Singleton, who also was an educator, operated a convenience store and an Amoco gas station. Other members of the Singleton family and the Burke family opened and operated juke joints on the beaches that became well known among residents and visitors—Singleton Beach (also home to Collier's

Beach), Burke's Beach (home to Burke's Hideaway), and Bradley Beach.

Black families from off-island also invested in beach property and built a scattering of homes for their enjoyment. Between Easter and Labor Day, the beach spots attracted hundreds of blacks, many who came from the mainland. For years black Savannah residents had been banned from the beach at Tybee Island, Georgia. Despite numerous "wade-ins" at Tybee Island beach in the 1950s and 1960s and other protests, Savannah's black citizens still could not use the beach. "At that time blacks had to go to Hilton Head Island in South Carolina to use a beach."[26] You could see cars lined along the road from the main highway leading to the Hilton Head beaches, where people would eat boiled crab and shrimp and fried fish or chicken sandwiches, dance, drink, go swimming and fishing, or just hang out on the wide, sandy beaches. With its beaches and businesses, Chaplin was a vibrant Gullah community. Late at night, when the crowds had dispersed, you could hear the ocean waves rolling back and forth on the beach. Years later, that sound slipped away as more and more developments encroached on beaches.

By the time I started attending elementary school, the one-room schools where many island residents before me learned had consolidated into one school—Hilton Head Elementary School. It was located in the Stoney community and opened in 1954, two years before the bridge. Some of my teachers were strong Gullah women, many of whom had been born and raised on Hilton Head. After their own education in the island's one- or two-room community schools, their parents had sent them to Penn School or Mather School to finish their education. From there, they obtained college degrees and eventually returned to Hilton Head. They taught me and other students how to speak well and lose the rich Gullah dialect, before it was even fully developed. While the teachers didn't dwell on Gullah history, they did stress learning, manners, good behavior, hard work, respect for your elders, and other virtues influenced by Gullah traditions.

The one-room schools disappeared, but churches remained as anchor institutions in the communities. Praise houses no longer existed and neither did the tradition of seeking, a process many people had to go through in the past in order to become members of a church. Up until the late 1970s, we attended a different church each Sunday, where you could see families you hadn't seen all week or in several weeks. Sunday services were rotated among the churches. Choir members, ushers, and deacons—no matter which church you were a member of—served every church. That cohesiveness was part of the Gullah way of life on the island.

Most members of the Grant family joined Queen Chapel African Methodist Episcopal Church, which holds the distinction of being the oldest A.M.E. church in South Carolina. My siblings and I attended Sunday school and other services at Queen Chapel. I followed

The Grant family in front of their store: Abraham and Charliemae Grant and their children, author Carolyn Grant and her brother, Anthony "Tony" Grant, ca. 1965. *Collection of Abraham and Charliemae Grant*

Author Carolyn Grant on her family's former homesite in the Chaplin Community, where the Grant family has lived since the late 1800s. *Photo by Lisa Staff*

suit and joined the family of Grants who were members of the church. Later, I became a member of Mount Calvary Baptist Church and was baptized the traditional Gullah way in Skull Creek. Dressed in a white robe and with a white cloth wrapped around my head, I, with other baptismal candidates, strolled from the church to Skull Creek as members sang in unison, "Take me to the water to be baptized."

When I left Hilton Head in the early 1980s to attend Spelman College in Atlanta, Georgia, I encountered some students who thought there were no black fami-

lies on Hilton Head and that it was just a resort that attracted seasonal visitors. Along with that, they were unfamiliar with the Gullah culture overshadowed by the development activity that was bringing hundreds of new residents and visitors to Hilton Head. When I brought college roommates home during breaks, they could barely understand my parents, who still sometimes spoke in the quick dialect that characterized Gullah speech. I often had to clarify words and phrases for my roommates.

After finishing college and working in a few newspaper reporting positions, I returned home to work at the *Island Packet* newspaper and my parents' restaurant. Both gave me the opportunity to begin preserving and sharing Gullah culture by writing about it. It became evident that more and more people wanted to learn about this culture I was privileged to be part of while growing up on Hilton Head. But there was more to the culture than the food we prepared and served at Abe's and the people and traditions I wrote about. The stories shared in this book gives insight into a way of life and traditions that were passed down through generations of ancestors who worked as enslaved people on plantations on Hilton Head and across South Carolina and fought for freedom. It also documents the history of how people survived on an island accessible only by boat before the bridge connected it to the mainland, and how people acquired the land they passed down to their descendants. We certainly hope this account of Gullah life helps readers not only understand how our lives evolved on Hilton Head, but also how the culture evolved and survived. This history is the foundation on which I and other blacks, born and raised on Hilton Head, have built our lives. And, it is the foundation on which we hope future generations will build their lives and keep the Gullah culture alive.

Notes

PART I

Chapter 1

1. WPA Federal Writers' Project, Vol. XIV, Part III, Slave Narrative Collection, "Account of Sam Mitchell," 202–203.

2. William Frances Allen, Charles Pickard Ware, and Lucy McKim Garrison, eds., *Slave Songs of the United States*, "Many Thousand Go" (New York: Dover Publications, 1995), 48 (originally published by A. Simpson & Co. [New York: 1867]).

3. *New York Times*, "News from the Great Fleet," November 6, 1861.

4. South Carolina Historical Society (SCHS), *Claims vs. U.S. by South Carolina Citizens for Losses*, 1861–62, Vol. 2. (Losses of at least thirteen major planters on Hilton Head Island are shown.)

5. *The War of the Rebellion: A Compilation of the Official Records of the Union and Confederate Armies*, Series 1, Vol. 6, Part 1 (Washington, DC: Government Printing Office), November 24, 1861, "Report of Brig. Gen. Thomas F. Drayton," 8.

6. Lawrence S. Rowland, Alexander Moore, and George C. Rogers, Jr., *The History of Beaufort County, South Carolina, Volume 1, 1514–1861* (Columbia: University of South Carolina Press, 1996), 451.

7. *Harper's Weekly*, "The Capture of Beaufort, South Carolina," November 30, 1861.

8. SCHS, Pope Family Papers, Folder 11/550/5.

9. *Harper's*, "The Capture of Beaufort."

10. *Harper's*, "The Capture of Beaufort." Rowland, Moore, and Rogers, *The History of Beaufort County*, 455.

11. National Archives and Records Administration (NARA), pension file of James Drayton, pension certificate 69194. (NARA has pension files of black Union soldiers. These files have recorded the words of these soldiers in standard English rather than in the Gullah tongue.)

12. William S. Pollitzer, *The Gullah People and Their African Heritage* (Athens: University of Georgia Press, 1999), 68.

13. NARA, pension file of Adam Jenkins, pension certificate 720739. Thomas F. Drayton may have bought Adam's father, Charles, on behalf of Mary B. Pope and her estate, from the Jenkins family. Drayton increased the acreage of Fish Haul by buying the adjacent Pineland Tract from a member of the Jenkins family.

14. NARA, pension file of Jacob Jenkins, pension certificate 1060194.

15. Richard Dwight Porcher, and Sarah Fick, *The Story of Sea Island Cotton* (Charleston, SC: Wyrick & Company, 2005), 455.

16. Description is based on an 1862 photograph of slaves at General Drayton's plantation by Henry Moore.

17. *Harper's*, "The Capture of Beaufort."

Chapter 2

1. "Chronology of Hilton Head Island," https://heritagelib.org/chronology-of-hilton-head.

2. Ibid.

3. Lawrence S. Rowland, Alexander Moore, and George C. Rogers, Jr., *The History of Beaufort County, South Carolina,*

Vol. 1, 1514–1861 (Columbia: University of South Carolina Press, 1994), 452–54.

4. *The War of the Rebellion: A Compilation of the Official Records of the Union and Confederate Armies* (hereafter cited as *Official Records*), Series 1, Vol. 6, Part 1 (Washington, DC: Government Printing Office), November 8, 1861, "Report by Q. A. Gillmore," 30.

5. Robert E. H. Peeples, *An Index to Hilton Head Island Names (Before the Contemporary Development)*, 13. Cited by Heritage Library, https://heritagelib.org/myrtle-bank-elliott-plantation.

6. Virginia Holmgren, *Hilton Head: A Sea Island Chronicle* (Hilton Head, SC: Hilton Head Island Publishing Co., 1959), 114.

7. Stephen M. Weld, *War Diary and Letters of Stephen Minot Weld, 1861–1865* (Cambridge, MA: Riverside Press, 1912), 43.

8. Holmgren, *Hilton Head*.

9. National Archives and Records Administration (hereafter cited as NARA), Martha Fields, pension certificate 385493.

10. Michael Trinkley, *Archaeological Excavations at 38BU96, A Portion of Cotton Hope Plantation, Hilton Head Island, Beaufort County, South Carolina* (Columbia, SC: Chicora Foundation, 1990).

11. NARA, Matthew Jones, pension certificate 599714.

12. South Carolina State Auditor Claim Books, 1861–1862 (34/309–311), Vol. 2, George Stoney, 32.

13. Holmgren, *Hilton Head*.

14. NARA, Simon Grant, pension certificate 644690.

15. NARA, Maria Grant, pension certificate 820844.

16. Holmgren, *Hilton Head*.

17. NARA, Mary Brown, pension certificate 679582.

18. *Official Records*, Report by Brigadier General Thomas F. Drayton, Series 1, Vol. 6, Part 1, November 8, 1861.

19. NARA, Renty Miller, pension certificate 700299.

20. Ibid.

21. South Carolina Historical Society, List of chattel, Estate of Mrs. Mary B. Pope, Thomas F. Drayton, administrator. Accessed at Heritage Library, Hilton Head.

22. Weld, *War Diary and Letters*, 42.

Chapter 3

1. Willie Lee Rose, *Rehearsal for Reconstruction: The Port Royal Experiment* (New York: Oxford University Press, 1964), 108.

2. Ibid.

3. NARA, Renty Greaves, pension certificate 823054. Greaves states that he and his family reached Hilton Head on November 9, 1861. He does not, however, say how long the trip took. The overnight journey seems reasonable, based on the accounts of other escaping slaves.

4. The copy of the quartermaster's December payroll (for work in November) available to the authors is incomplete (accessed at the Robert W. Woodruff Library, Emory University, Atlanta, GA).

5. Charles Nordhoff, *The Freedmen of South Carolina: Some Account of Their Appearance, Character, Condition, and Peculiar Customs* (New York: Charles T. Evans, 1863).

6. Rose, *Rehearsal for Reconstruction*, 22–23.

7. *The Negroes at Port Royal, S.C., Report of the Government Agent* [written by Edward L. Pierce] February 3, 1862, 302–315.

8. *First Annual Report of the Port Royal Relief Committee, March 26, 1863* (Philadelphia: Merrithew & Thompson, 1863), 4–13.

Chapter 4

1. "From Gen. Hunter's Department," *New York Times* (hereafter cited as *NYT*), April 19, 1862.

2. South Carolina Historical Society (SCHS), *Claims vs. U.S. by South Carolina Citizens for Losses, 1861–62*, Vol. 2.

3. "A Negro Conventicle—The Rev. Abraham Murchison—Trip to Seabrook—The Drayton Plantation—The Elliott Plantation—Rose and Her Family—A Negro Bayoneted—

The Contrabands at Seabrook—A Human Phenomenon—Cotton Planting—The Bombardment of Fort Pulaski to Commence," *NYT*, April 7, 1862, 2.

4. Edward A. Miller, Jr., *Lincoln's Abolitionist General: The Biography of David Hunter* (Columbia: University of South Carolina Press, 1997), 67; cited in Catherine Clinton, *Harriet Tubman: The Road to Freedom* (New York: Little, Brown and Company, 2004), 154.

5. *The War of the Rebellion: A Compilation of the Official Records of the Union and Confederate Armies*, Series I, Book 6, Part 1, 263–264. Hunter to Stanton April 3, 1862 (hereafter cited as *Official Records*).

6. Ibid.

7. "From Gen. Hunter's Department," *NYT*, April 19, 1862.

8. Ibid.

9. Ibid.

10. Willie Lee Rose, *Rehearsal for Reconstruction: The Port Royal Experiment* (New York: Oxford University Press, 1964), 147. Hunter's regiment is referred to as "the first nucleus of a black regiment."

11. Rose, *Rehearsal for Reconstruction*, 145.

12. *Official Records*, Series I, xiv, 342.

13. *Official Records*, Brigadier General Isaac I. Stevens, commanding post at Beaufort, Port Royal, May 11, 1862, (Washington, DC: Government Printing Office, 1898), 48.

14. *Official Records*, Series III, 53–53. Pierce to S.P. Chase, May 12, 1862.

15. Abraham Lincoln, "Proclamation Revoking General Hunter's Order of Military Emancipation, May 19, 1862, and Indorsement Relating to General David Hunter's Order of Military Emancipation," May 17, 1862.

16. Benjamin Quarles, *The Negro in the Civil War* (New York: Da Capo Press, 1989), 112–13.

17. *The New South*, "Departure of General Hunter," September 8, 1862.

18. Rose, *Rehearsal for Reconstruction*, 191.

19. Joel Williamson, *After Slavery: The Negro in South Carolina During Reconstruction, 1861–1877* (Chapel Hill: University of North Carolina Press, 1965), 14–16.

20. Thomas Wentworth Higginson, *Army Life in a Black Regiment* (New York: Firework Press, 2015), 21

21. Ibid.

22. Family story, as told by Louise Cohen, granddaughter of Mariah.

Chapter 5

1. *Frank Leslie's Illustrated Newspaper*, July 19, 1862, 289.

2. Ibid.

3. *New York Times* (hereafter cited as *NYT*), October 8, 1862.

4. James McPherson, *The Negro's Civil War: How American Blacks Felt and Acted During the War for the Union* (New York: Ballantine Books, 1991), 152.

5. *The War of the Rebellion: A Compilation of the Official Records of the Union and Confederate Armies* (hereafter cited as *Official Records*), Chapter XXVI, Mitchel to Edward M. Stanton, Secretary of War, Washington, D.C., September 20, 1862, 384–85.

6. *Official Records*, General Orders No. 27, Hilton Head, August 17, 1862, 376.

7. Charles Carleton Coffin, Four Years of Fighting (Boston: Estes and Lauriat, 1866), 244.

8. "The Negroes," *The New South*, August 30, 1862.

9. "Important from Port Royal," *NYT*, October 19, 1862.

10 "Dedication of the Negro Church," *The New South*, October 18, 1862.

11. Ibid.

12. *Official Records*, Chapter XXVI, General O. M. Mitchel to Major-General Halleck, September 20, 1862, 383, and C. H. Crane, medical director, Department of the South, to Major W. P. Prentice, September 18, 1862, 384.

13. Charles Nordhoff, *The Freedmen of South Carolina: Some*

Account of Their Appearance, Character, Condition and Peculiar Customs (New York: Charles T. Evans, 1863). Accessed at Emory University, Special Collection, Atlanta, Georgia.

14. Charles Carleton Coffin, *The Boys of '61*, http://www.gutenberg.org/files/34843/34843-h/34843-h.htm#page224.

15. Coffin, *Four Years of Fighting*, 225–27.

16. *Official Records*, Abram Murcherson to Major General J. G. Foster, 12 Aug. 1864, M-268 1864, Letters Received, ser. 4109, Department of the South, RG 393, Pt. 1 [C-1327], http://www.freedmen.umd.edu/Mercherson.html.

17. Ibid.

18. "From Gen. Hunter's Department," *NYT*, April 19, 1862.

19. Nordhoff, *Freedmen of South Carolina*, https://play.google.com/books/reader?id=joV61U91lqgC&hl=en&pg=GBS.PA1, 18.

20. Nordhoff, *The Freedmen of South Carolina*, 18.

21. *The New South*, May 6, 1865, http://digital.tcl.sc.edu/cdm/fullbrowser/collection/NSN/id/268/rv/compoundobject/cpd/272/rec/16.

22. Willie Lee Rose, *Rehearsal for Reconstruction: The Port Royal Experiment* (New York: Oxford University Press, 1964), 227.

Chapter 6

1. National Archives and Records Administration (hereafter cited as NARA), Simon Grant, pension certificate 644690.

2. NARA, Samuel Christopher, pension certificate 933856.

3. Catherine Clinton, *Harriet Tubman: The Road to Freedom* (New York: Little, Brown and Company, 2004), 164–68.

4. "The Expedition up the Cohambee," *The New South*, June 6, 1863.

5. Sarah H. Bradford, *Harriet: The Moses of Her People* (New York: George R. Lockwood and Son, 1886), 40–41.

6. Ibid., 41–42.

7. Clinton, *Harriet Tubman*, 167.

8. NARA, Renty Greaves, pension certificate 823054.

9. NARA, Simon Christopher, pension certificate 933856.

10. Nancy Burke, Patricia Burke, and Susie Marquis, eds., *They Served: Stories of the United States Colored Troops from Hilton Head Island, South Carolina* (Hilton Head Island, SC: Heritage Library Foundation).

11. Gerald Schwartz, ed., *A Woman Doctor's Civil War: Esther Hill Hawks' Diary* (Columbia: University of South Carolina Press, 1984), 87.

Chapter 7

1. Robert J. Zalimas, Jr., "A Disturbance in the City: Black and White Soldiers in Postwar Charleston," in *Black Soldiers in Blue: African American Troops in the Civil War Era*, ed. John David Smith, (Chapel Hill: University of North Carolina Press, 2002), 362–64.

2. Frank. A. Rollin, *Life and Public Services of Martin R. Delaney* (New York: Kraus Reprint Co., 1969), 199. The account does not mention a specific regiment, but it well could have been the 21st, as that regiment entered first, in the afternoon.

3. Zalimas, "Disturbance in the City," 361–62.

4. *Charleston Daily Courier*, February 20, 1865, in Zalimas, "Disturbance in the City," 362.

5. Zalimas, "Disturbance in the City," 362.

6. Ibid.

7. William S. Pollitzer, *The Gullah People and Their African Heritage* (Athens: University of Georgia Press, 1999), 7.

8. Zalimas, "Disturbance in the City," 365–66.

9. Ibid., 366.

10. Ibid., 366–67.

11. "From South Carolina," *New York Daily Tribune*, April 4, 1865.

12. The *New York Herald Tribune* account did not name the black societies participating in the parade. Black societies in general, in places such as Hilton Head, existed as helping organizations set up and run by blacks to help in times of illness, death, and other needs.

13. "From South Carolina."

14. Akiko Ochiai, *Harvesting Freedom: African American Agrarianism in Civil War Era South Carolina* (Westport, CT: Praeger, 2004), 148.

15. Wendell Phillips Garrison et al., *William Lloyd Garrison, 1805–1879; The Story of His Life as Told by His Children.* (New York: The Century Co., 1885), 141. Digitalized by the University of Michigan, 2005.

16. Ibid., 139–41.

17. Ibid., 147. Garrison made this comment at the freedmen's celebration at Zion Church in Charleston, April 15, 1865, but it can be considered as also applying to the people of Mitchelville.

18. Garrison, *William Lloyd Garrison*, 141.

19. Ochiai, *Harvesting Freedom*, 133.

20. Laura M. Towne, *Letters and Diary of Laura M. Towne: Written from the Sea Islands of South Carolina, 1862–1884*, Rupert Sargent Holland, ed. (Cambridge, MA: Riverside Press, 1912; reprint, Salem, MA: Higginson Book Company, 2007), 160–61.

21. Willie Lee Rose, *Rehearsal for Reconstruction: The Port Royal Experiment* (New York: Oxford University Press, 1964), 343. Towne to "S," April 23, 1865.

22. Ibid.

23. Gerald Schwartz, ed., *A Woman Doctor's Civil War: Esther Hill Hawks' Diary* (Columbia: University of South Carolina Press, 1984), 131.

24. Rollin, *Life and Public Services*, 195–96.

25. Elizabeth Hyde Botume, *First Days amongst the Contrabands* (Boston: Lee and Shepard, 1890), 176.

Chapter 8

1. National Archives and Records Administration (hereafter cited as NARA), James Drayton Grant, pension certificate 933856.

2. Butler Seabrook does not appear in the 1870 Census, suggesting that he had died.

3. Eric Foner, *Reconstruction: America's Unfinished Revolution, 1863–1877* (New York: Harper & Rowe, 1988), 70.

4. Ibid.

5. W. T. Sherman, Order by the Commander of the Military Division of the Mississippi, In the Field, Savannah, Ga., January 16, 1865, http://www.freedmen.umd.edu/sf015.htm.

6. Josephine W. Martin, ed., *"Dear Sister": Letters Written on Hilton Head Island, 1867* (Beaufort, SC: Beaufort Book Co., 1977), 86–87.

7. Ibid.

8. Interview of Naomi Frazier by Annie Green and Polly Talsid, November 10, 1977.

9. NARA, monthly land reports issued by Martin Delaney of the Freedmen's Bureau.

10. Martin, *Dear Sister.*

11. NARA, Monthly land reports.

12. Ibid.

13. Ibid.

14. 1868 Voter List for Hilton Head and Bluffton Electoral Districts. Heritage Library, Hilton Head, SC.

15. 1868 Federal Agricultural Census, Hilton Head Island. Available at Heritage Library, Hilton Head, https://heritagelib .org.

Chapter 9

1. South Carolina Historical Society (hereafter cited as SCHS), Letter from Thomas F. Drayton to Messrs. Rutledge & Young, March 8, 1873, (T) 308.01.

2. Interview of Naomi Frazier by Annie Green and Polly Talsid, November 10, 1977.

3. SCHS, Valuation of Property on Drayton Track, Hilton Head Island, Thomas F. Drayton Case records, (T) 308.01, 01–02.

4. Silas B. Wright, collector in the Beaufort, SC, office of the United States Bureau of Internal Revenue.

5. SCHS, Drayton Case records.

Chapter 10

1. House of Representatives, Misc. Papers, Nov. 9, 1877, Vol. 3, No. 11, Papers in the case of Tillman vs. Smalls, 5th District South Carolina, 1–694. All information in this chapter is from these papers.

Chapter 11

1. Thomas Holt, *Black over White: Negro Political Leadership in South Carolina during Reconstruction* (Champaign: University of Illinois Press, 1977), 173.

2. *Charleston News and Courier*, April 12, 1877, cited in Holt, *Black over White*, 173.

3. George Brown Tindall, *South Carolina Negroes, 1877-1900* (Columbia: University of South Carolina Press, 1952), 15.

4. Ibid.

5. *Charleston News and Courier*, May 10, 1877, cited in Tindall, *South Carolina Negroes*, 15.

6. *Beaufort Tribune*, October 30, 1878.

7. Ibid.

8. Joel Williamson, *After Slavery: The Negro in South Carolina during Reconstruction, 1861–1877* (Chapel Hill: University of North Carolina Press, 1965), 401–11.

9. Laura Towne, *Letters and Diary of Laura M. Towne: Written from the Sea Islands of South Carolina, 1862–1884* (Cambridge, MA: Riverside Press, 1912; reprint, Salem, MA: Higginson Book Company, 2007), 287. Entry of November 6, 1878. She had attended a meeting where Smalls spoke of the incident. In addition, a newspaper, which went unnamed in her account, apparently covered the event.

10. Ibid.

11. Ibid., 291.

12. Ibid.

13. Holt, *Black over White*, 211.

14. Towne, *Letters and Diary*, 120.

15. Ibid., 292.

16. Ibid.

Chapter 12

1. Interview with Laura Campbell by Carolyn Grant and Emory Campbell, June 30, 2001, when Laura Campbell was in her nineties.

2. Interview with Joseph Walters by Carolyn Grant and Thomas Barnwell, 1975.

3. Clara Barton, *A Story of the Red Cross: Glimpses of Field Work* (D. Appleton and Company, 1928), 43.

4. Clara Barton, *The Red Cross in Peace and War* (Washington, DC: American National Red Cross, 1906), 77, 212. Field report of John MacDonald, Manuscripts Division, the American Red Cross.

5. Barton, *Peace and War*, 214.

6. William Marscher and Fran Marscher, *The Great Sea Island Storm of 1893* (Macon, GA: Mercer University Press, 2004), 59.

7. Barton, *Peace and War*, 214.

8. Ibid., 216.

9. Ibid., 218. Sewing circles were set up in each district of the Sea Island Relief project.

10. George Brown Tindall, *South Carolina Negroes, 1877–1900* (Baton Rouge: Louisiana State University, 1966), 69.

11. Ibid.

12. Ibid., 86–87. Citation quotes the *Columbia Daily Register*, November 2, 1885.

13. Ibid.

14. Leon F. Litwack, *Trouble in Mind* (New York: Vintage, 1999), 206.

Chapter 13

1. Neil Christensen, Jr., *Southern Workman*, "The Negroes of Beaufort County, S.C.," October 1903, 481–86.

2. National Archives and Records Administration (here-

after cited as NARA), pension case of Renty Cruel, alias Renty Greaves, pension certificate 823054.

3. *Beaufort Gazette* obituary places the funeral at the First African Baptist Church.

4. NARA, widow's pension application, Elizabeth Greaves.

5. The oral history of the White family records that Benjamin White, Sr., was the son of Renty F. Greaves and Hanna White and that the Chisolm family raised Benjamin White following his mother's death.

6. *Selected Land Deeds in Gullah Communities on Hilton Head Island, Beaufort County, S.C.*, commissioned by Thomas Barnwell, Jr., 2007.

7. Beaufort County Deed Books, 1902.

8. NARA, pension case of Caesar Jones, pension certificate 912315.

9. Anthony Dimock, *Wall Street and the Wilds* (New York: Outing Publishing Company, 1915), 144.

10. Virginia C. Holmgren, *Hilton Head: A Sea Island Chronicle* (Hilton Head Island, SC: Hilton Head Publishing Co., 1959), 128.

11. *Selected Land Deeds.*

12. Thomas L. Johnson and Nina J. Root, eds., *Camera Man's Journey* (Athens: University of Georgia Press, 2002). Julian Dimock's photographs, described in the text of this chapter, are shown in *Camera Man's Journey.*

Chapter 14

1. Letter from Booker T. Washington to the Birmingham, AL, *Age Herald*, November 13, 1898, in *Booker T. Washington Papers, Vol. 4*, Stuart B. Kaufman, Barbara S. Kraft, and Raymond W. Smock, eds. (Urbana: University of Illinois Press, 1975), 509.

2. Letter from Booker T. Washington to Robert C. Bedford, March 21, 1905, in *Booker T. Washington Papers, Vol. 8*, Louis R. Harlan, Raymond W. Smock, and Geraldine McTigue, eds. (Urbana: University of Illinois Press, 1979), 221.

3. Louis R. Harlan, *Booker T. Washington: The Wizard of Tuskegee, 1901–1915* (New York: Oxford University Press, 1983), 214.

4. Library of Congress, Frederick Douglass Correspondence, Clyde to Douglass, February 3, 1890.

5. *Selected Land Deeds in Gullah Communities on Hilton Head Island, Beaufort County, S.C.*, commissioned by Thomas Barnwell, Jr., 2007.

6. Georgianna Barnwell interview by Susan Barnwell, April 28, 1976.

7. Interview of islander Thomas Holmes, September 30, 2003.

8. Harlan, *Wizard*, Booker T. Washington to J. R. E. Lee, March 28, 1908, 215.

9. Harlan, *Wizard*, Lee to Washington, May 9, 1908, 216.

10. Ibid. (G. Barnwell identified the date as the first Sunday after Decoration Day, in her 1976 interview).

11. Ibid.

12. Washington to Clyde, in *Booker T. Washington Papers, Vol. 9*, Louis R. Harlan and Raymond W. Smock, eds. (Urbana: University of Illinois Press, 1980), 553.

13. Oral history relayed by islander Frederick Orage to Emory S. Campbell, March 22, 2006.

14. Harlan, *Wizard*, 216.

15. Ibid.

16. Ibid., 217.

17. Ibid.

18. Ibid.

19. Ibid.

20. Island history gathered by authors Emory S. Campbell and Thomas C. Barnwell, Jr.

Chapter 15

1. Beaufort County (SC) Court of Common Pleas. All information in this chapter is from the *Tillman v. Smalls* case.

Chapter 16

1. National Archives and Records Administration (hereafter cited as NARA), pension records, Matthew Jones, pension certificate number 696947.

2. Ibid.

3. NARA, Moses Brown pension file, pension certificate number 610226.

4. NARA, Matthew Jones.

5. Ibid.

6. NARA, Pension records, Flora Jones, pension certificate number 944999.

7. NARA, Pension records, James Drayton Grant, pension certificate number 933856.

8. Ibid.

9. NARA, Pension records, Renty Miller, pension certificate number 700299.

10. Ibid.

11. Ibid.

Chapter 17

1. Interview of Emory Campbell by Christena Bledsoe, September 11, 2014.

2. Campbell interview.

3. Thomas C. Barnwell, Jr., from his knowledge of island history and culture.

4. Ambrose E. Gonzales, *The Black Border: Gullah Stories of the South Carolina Coast* (Gretna, LA: Pelican Publishing Co., 1999), 10.

5. Ibid., 277.

6. Margaret Wade-Lewis, *Lorenzo Dow Turner: Father of Gullah Studies (Columbia: University of South Carolina Press, 2007),* 73–74.

7. Lorenzo Dow Turner tapes, copies provided by Thomas Klein, West Georgia College, Carrollton, Georgia.

8. Turner tapes.

9. Lorenzo Dow Turner, *Africanisms in the Gullah Dialect* (Ann Arbor: University of Michigan Press, 1974), 43.

10. Naomi Frazier interview by Annie Green and Polly Talsid, November 10, 1977.

11. Thomas Holmes interview by Thomas C. Barnwell, Jr., September 10, 2001.

12. Naomi Frazier interview.

13. Isabel Brown interview by Eula Chisolm and Dick Caldwell, June 23, 1977.

Chapter 18

1. The term "Old Man Depression" was used by a North Carolina Civilian Conservation Corps (CCC) publication: Alfred Emile Cornebise, *The CCC Chronicles: Camp Newspapers of the Civilian Conservation Corps* (Jefferson, NC: McFarland & Company, 2004), 234.

2. The Junior League of Charleston, *Charleston Receipts* (Charleston, SC: Walker Evans & Cogeswell Co., 1950; reprint Memphis, TN: Wimmer Brothers, 1993), 171. Gullah men and women used distinctive rhythms while hawking their produce to housewives.

3. Interview of Fuskie Simmons by Caroline Grant and Thomas C. Barnwell, Jr., September 1995.

4. Interview of Arthur Orage and Ben Miller by Thomas C. Barnwell, Jr., October 16, 2003. Orage was born April 15, 1923; Miller was born October 15, 1925.

5. "Still More Lights for Old Huntington," *Huntington* (NY) *Long Islander*, December 5, 1930, 16.6. Emory Campbell heard this story from islander Henry Driessen. Whether or not the story is embellished is not known to the authors, ut it does follow the form of traditional tales where the Gullah men and women slipped one over on the white man in power.

6. Interview with Arthur Orage and Ben Miller by Thomas C. Barnwell, Jr., and Carolyn Grant, October 16, 2003.

8. As told to Emory Campbell.

9. Interview with Isabel Brownby Eula Chisolm and Dick Caldwell, June 23, 1977. Mrs. Brown turned 93 that year.

10. Beaufort National Cemetery, Beaufort, SC, https://www.beaufort-sc.com/beaufort-national-cemetery.html. Potter, who cared for soldiers in Beaufort's military hospitals, erected the monument in 1870. Potter was also the force behind the construction of an 1870 marble and brick box monument honoring 175 civil war soldiers from 18 states.

11. *Columbia State*, June 2, 1897, cited in George Brown Tindall, *South Carolina Negroes* (Columbia: University of South Carolina Press, 2002), 289.

Chapter 19

1. Thomas C. Barnwell, Jr., private papers: "Selected Land Deeds in Gullah Communities on Hilton Head Island, Beaufort County, S.C." Commissioned by Barnwell and conducted by Cherese Chisolm of Heritage Title Abstracting Services, Beaufort, SC, August 9, 2007. Stephen Hamilton purchased eleven acres from Clyde in 1902. Paul Brown bought 10 acres in 1903. Minus Graham is said to have bought a somewhat larger parcel from Clyde in 1902; however, 1945 deeds state that Minus Graham "died intestate on or about the year 1895, leaving as his only heirs his son, Luke Graham, and a daughter, Catherine Johnson." The 1902 deeds were recorded in the Beaufort County Deed Book 24 at page 358. An explanation for the date of the 1902 sale (after Minus Graham is deceased) is not known by the authors. Clyde's part-time vacation retreat, Honey Horn, had been under construction by two Graham brothers—white planters from Grahamville on the mainland—when the Union invaded. As Minus Graham came to Spanish Wells from Honey Horn, it raises the question of whether his family had been enslaved on this plantation before the Civil War.

2. This and all other quotes following without indicated sources come from Emory. S. Campbell, family history.

3. Lorenzo Dow Turner, *Africanisms in the Gullah Dialect* (Columbia: University of South Carolina Press, 2002), 176–77.

"Wala" was used as a feminine name in several West African languages. (In Yoruba, it meant "a board used by Mohammedan in writing." In Bambara, *wala* had a similar meaning—"the small board of Mohammedan students." In yet another language, it meant "to scrape, to carve in wood." The masculine form of the word, according to Turner, was *wali*. It too had several meanings. One of several Bambara uses of *wali* was "an official position and title." William S. Pollitzer, in *The Gullah People and Their African Heritage* (Athens, GA: University of Georgia Press, 1999, 56) links the name "Wally" to Gambia.

4. Emory Campbell, "A Sense of Self and Place," in *African American Life in the Georgia Lowcountry: The Atlantic World and the Gullah Geechee*, Phillip Morgan, ed. (Athens: University of Georgia Press, 2010), 182.

Chapter 20

1. Interview of Emory Campbell by Christena Bledsoe, 2013.

2. *New Georgia Encyclopedia*, https://www.georgiaencyclopedia.org/articles/history-archaeology/world-war-ii-georgia.

3. Interview of Elijah Jones, Jr., and Viola Holmes by Thomas Barnwell, Jr., and Carolyn Grant, October 3, 2003.

4. Ibid.

5. Ibid.

6. Thomas C. Barnwell, Jr., from his extensive general knowledge of Hilton Head history.

7. Island history provided by authors Thomas C. Barnwell, Jr., and Emory Campbell.

8. NAACP Voting Rights Microfilm Reels, Introduction, x–xi. (John H. Bracey, Jr., University of Massachusetts–Amherst).

9. *Elmore v. Rice*, Civil Action RICE Civil Action No. 1702. 72 F. Supp. 516 (1947).

10. George Tindall, *South Carolina Negroes* (Columbia: University of South Carolina Press, 2003), 303.

11. NAACP Legal Defense Found, *Smith v. Allwright*, June 6, 1944. Argued November 10 and 12, 1943, reargued January 12, 1944, decided April 3, 1944.

12. https://constitution.findlaw.com/amendment15.html.

13. *Smith v. Allwright*

14. *Elmore v. Rice*

15. Ibid.

16. Ibid.

17. "Civil Rights site recognized, then razed," http://south carolina1670.wordpress.com/2012/07/31/civil-rights-site -recognized-then-razed/.

18. Tinsley F. Yarbrough, *A Passion for Justice: J. Waties Waring and Civil Rights* (New York: Oxford University Press, 1987), 64.

19. *Brown v. Baskin*, 78 F. Supp. 993 (1948).

20. Ibid.

21. *Time*, "South Carolina: The Man They Love to Hate," August 23, 1948.

22. United States Department of Labor, Bureau of Labor Statistics CPI Inflation Calculator, http://www.bls.gov/data /inflation_calculator.htm.

23. Beaufort County, SC, county auditor. The duplicate of the 1949 tax list, provided to Thomas C. Barnwell, Jr., in February 2013 by the county, included Hilton Head Island and Daufuskie, excluding nonresidents.

24. Ibid.

Chapter 21

1. Interview of Charles Simmons, Sr., and Charles Simmons, Jr., by Carolyn Grant and Thomas Barnwell, July 23, 1995.

2. Michael N. Danielson, *Profits and Politics in Paradise: The Development of Hilton Head Island* (Columbia: University of South Carolina Press, 1995), 13.

3. Interview of Charles "Fuskie" Simmons by Carolyn Grant and Thomas Barnwell, Jr., August 12, 1995.

4. Interview of Charles Simmons, Sr., and Charles Simmons, Sr.

5. Danielson, *Profits and Politics*, 6. *The Islander*, Hilton Head, South Carolina, March 1970, is cited.

6. Danielson, *Profits and Politics*, 14.

7. Interview of Thomas C. Barnwell, Jr., by Christena Bledsoe, October 10, 2014.

8. Interview of Emory Campbell by Christena Bledsoe, February 2, 2012.

9. Danielson, *Profits and Politics*.

10. Interview of Deacon Thomas Holmes and Laura Holmes by Carolyn Grant and Thomas Barnwell, Jr., July 23, 1995.

11. Barnwell interview.

12. Ibid.

13. Campbell interview.

14. Ibid.

15. https://www.sciway.net/hist/governors/byrnes.html.

16. Campbell interview.

17. South Carolina Highway Department photograph, March 9, 1955.

Chapter 22

1. Michael N. Danielson, *Profits and Politics in Paradise: The Development of Hilton Head Island* (Columbia: University of South Carolina Press, 1995), 168.

2. Interview of Emory Campbell by Christena Bledsoe, September 12, 2008.

3. Ibid.

4. Ibid.

5. *Journal of the House of Representatives of the First Session of the 91st General Assembly of the State of South Carolina*, printed under the direction of the State Budget and Control Board, 1955.

6. Campbell interview.

7. W. D. Workman, Jr., "Byrnes Crossing Opened to Public," *Charleston News and Courier*, May 20, 1956.

8. Ibid.

9. "Man of the Year," Time, January 6, 1947.

10. Workman, "Byrnes Crossing Opened to Public."

11. Emory S. Campbell, personal observations.

12. "James F. Byrnes Crossing to Hilton Head Dedicated," *Evening Post*, May 20, 1956.

13. Interview of Mary Lawyer Green by Christena Bledsoe and Carolyn Grant, September 2007.

14. Danielson, *Profits and Politics in Paradise*, 16.

PART II

1. Sarah H. Bradford,, *Scenes in the Life of Harriet Tubman* (New York: Classics of Liberty Library, 1995), 43; originally printed by W. J. Moses, 1869.

2. Margaret Washington Creel, *A Peculiar People: Slave Religion and Community—Culture among the Gullahs* (New York: New York University Press, 1988), 194.

3. Joseph A. Opala, *The Gullah: Rice, Slavery, and the Sierra Leone–American Connection* (Freetown, Sierra Leone: United States Information Service, 1987), 15.

4. Ibid.

5. William S. Pollitzer, *The Gullah People and Their African Heritage* (Athens: University of Georgia Press, 1999), 109.

6. Gullah Geechee Cultural Heritage Corridor Commission, "Language and Oral Traditions," in *Gullah Geechee Cultural Heritage Corridor Management Plan* (Denver, CO: National Park Service, U.S. Department of the Interior, 2012), 62.

7. Elsie Clews Parsons, *Folk-Lore of the Sea Islands, South Carolina* (Cambridge, MA: The American Folk-Lore Society, 1923), xiv, 93.

8. Moses Grant, *Looking Back: Reminiscences of a Black Family Heritage on Hilton Head Island* (Orangeburg, SC: Williams Associates, 1988), 14–15.

9. Creel, *A Peculiar People*, 288.

10. Bradford, *Scenes in the Life of Harriet Tubman*, 44.

11. Creel, *A Peculiar People*, 116.

12. As recounted by Emory Campbell.

13. William Frances Allen, Charles Pickard Ware, and Lucy McKim Garrison, eds., *Slave Songs of the United States* (New York: Dover Publications, 1995), 48 (originally published by A. Simpson & Co. [New York: 1867]), xvi.

14. Ibid.

15. Ibid., 48.

16. Ibid., ii.

17. Richard Rankin, *A New South Hunt Club: An Illustrated History of the Hilton Head Agricultural Society, 1917–1967* (Winston-Salem, NC: John F. Blair, 2006).

18. As recounted by Emory Campbell.

19. Ibid.

20. David N. Blight, "The First Decoration Day," *Newark Star Ledger*, April 27, 2015.

21. Gerald Schwartz, ed., *A Woman Doctor's Civil War: Ester Hill Hawks' Diary* (Columbia: University of South Carolina Press, 1989), 138.

22. Island history provided by Thomas C. Barnwell.

23. Grant, *Looking Back*, 12.

24. Dale Rosengarten, *Row Upon Row: Sea Grass Baskets of the South Carolina Lowcountry* (McKissick Museum, University of South Carolina, 1986), 28.

25. John Huey, "The Ultimate Boat Trip Through South Carolina's Undiscovered Lowcountry," retrieved from https://www.msn.com/en-us/travel/tripideas/the-ultimate-boat-trip-through-south-carolinas-undiscovered-lowcountry/ar-BBVy0A7.

26. Charles Lwanga Hoskins, "African Americans on Tybee Island," *Savannah Herald*, Dec. 17, 2014.

Acknowledgments

Tank ya, plenty plenty.

Or, Tank ya. We 'preciate oona help.

(Gullah translation: Thank you. We appreciate your help.)

TELLING THE UNTOLD STORY of generations of Hilton Head Island natives—who are Gullah Geechee descendants of slaves brought from West Africa to the South Carolina Low Country—has been one of our greatest desires. We came together as a team to share our treasured history, which we hope will broaden the understanding of Gullah culture worldwide. We owe immense gratitude to many individuals and organizations who shared their stories, provided a wealth of information and resources, and accommodated our many requests. Among those we wish to thank for their assistance and support are the many Hilton Head Island Gullah families and individuals who cooperated with interviews and provided invaluable information about life on Hilton Head Island before the bridge connected the island to the mainland in 1956; members of the former Hilton Head Island Human Relations Council, who conducted some of the earliest interviews with Gullah Islanders; Tiffany Garvin, who transcribed tapes and organized notes and interviews; Grace Cordial of the Beaufort County Library; Natalie Hefter at the Coastal Discovery Museum; Priscilla Pomozol at the Hilton Head Island Branch of the Beaufort County Library; the staff of the Hilton Head Island Heritage Library, especially John Griffith and Linda Piekut; the South Carolina Historical Society; and many other persons. We posthumously thank the late Cornelia Bailey, whose referral led us to Christena Bledsoe. We extend our deepest appreciation to Ms. Bledsoe, who, with her professional writing talent and expert research, helped us bring our story to life, and to Nancy Matoba for her detailed review and professional editorial support. We thank God for the seed he planted in our minds and hearts to write this book and for placing people in our lives to bring this book to fruition.

Thomas C. Barnwell, Jr.: It has been an amazing journey working on this book project, and I am deeply appreciative to all who helped to make it possible. I especially want to thank the special people in my life who journeyed with me: my wife, Susan, who showed great patience with me as I worked on this project, hosted many guests in our home, and handled numerous other tasks for me; my parents, the late Thomas and Hannah Barnwell; my grandmother, the late Georgianna Miller Barnwell; my teachers; my adopted family, Benjamin and Wilhelmina Barnwell of the Eustice Community on St. Helena Island, SC; and my cousins, Ruth Jones and Cora Jones. I also thank my children and grandchildren for their support and hope this book helps them sustain our heritage. I appreciate my co-authors and friends, Emory S. Campbell and Carolyn Grant, for coming together in partnership to tell the story of our community.

Emory S. Campbell: Behind every great book are great people with great stories. When we began to consider book covers, I was honored to have a photo of my maternal grandfather and grandmother, Perry and Rosa Williams, chosen for this special placement. I give thanks to them for helping to raise me and my siblings to appreciate and embrace our culture. I thank my siblings and first cousins for allowing this photo to be shared. With inspiration and support from family, I was honored to be a part of the team to write and share the history of Gullah people. I especially thank my wife, Emma, for her long-standing support, love, and hospitality, and my children and grandchild, for whom this body of work is a lasting legacy of their heritage. I owe much gratitude to Thomas C. Barnwell, Jr., and Carolyn Grant, my co-authors. We envisioned a book that would fill the gap in Gullah history, and I'm grateful to have worked with them to get our story written.

Carolyn Grant, PhD: My Gullah heritage was passed on to me from my great-aunt, Beaulah Grant Kellerson, and my parents, Abraham and Charliemae Grant. They inspired me through their vivid life stories and experiences, and I am proud to have documented their amazing lives and contributions. I thank both of my parents for participating in interviews; my mother for preparing delicious Gullah meals; my sisters and brothers Anthony, Lillian, Terry, and Abraham Jr. for their support (together we shared the Gullah experience in our family home and community); and my nieces and nephews, especially Sonya and Jaala, who have endured listening to me as I shared our family's Gullah history and who will keep our culture alive. I am forever grateful to my mentors and co-authors, Thomas C. Barnwell, Jr., and Emory Campbell, for all of the knowledge and wisdom they have shared with me as we worked on this project.

About the Authors

Emory Shaw Campbell is president of the Gullah Heritage Consulting Service, a Hilton Head Island–based firm. He manages the Gullah Heritage Trail Tours as well as offers lectures and courses related to Gullah Geechee culture.

Before his current position, he was the executive director of the Penn Center on St. Helena Island, SC, for twenty-two years. The center was established in 1862 as the first school for formerly enslaved citizens and is currently the leading repository of Gullah cultural heritage.

Campbell was the valedictorian of the Michael C. Riley High School Class of 1960. In 1965 he earned his undergraduate degree in biology at Savannah State College (now Savannah State University) and continued his studies in environmental engineering at Tufts University in Boston, MA, where he earned a Master of Science degree in 1971.

Campbell served as the first chairman of the Gullah Geechee Cultural Corridor Commission established by the U.S. Congress in 2006 to preserve Gullah Geechee cultural heritage. He has received numerous honors for his cultural and environmental preservation work including an honorary Doctor of Humane Letters degree from Bank Street College, New York City, and the University of South Carolina–Beaufort. He resides on Hilton Head Island in the neighborhood of his birth.

Thomas Curtis Barnwell, Jr., was born in 1935 on Hilton Head Island, SC, and is a fourth-generation islander who is considered one of the Gullah elders of the island. Barnwell grew up on Hilton Head Island when the only transportation on and off the island was by boat. Like his fellow islanders, he attended the small community schools on Hilton Head through sixth grade then had to leave the island to attend middle school, high school, and college.

Barnwell's work and professional career was primarily in Beaufort County, SC, and included community organizing, community development in healthcare as founding director of Beaufort-Jasper Comprehensive Health Services, affordable housing and cooperatives, and development of family land.

Barnwell testified before the U.S. Senate Committee on Hunger and Malnutrition and Human Needs in February 1969 and before the House Committee on Banking, Currency and Housing relating to the National Consumer Cooperative Bank Act in June 1976.

Carolyn Grant is a former staff writer for the *Island Packet* and the *Greenville News*. She earned a Bachelor of Arts degree in English from Spelman College, a Master of Science degree in journalism from Northwestern University, and a Doctor of Philosophy degree in public health from Walden University. In addition to writing for newspapers, Grant currently works in the healthcare marketing and public relations field. She serves on the board of directors for numerous organizations and is a freelance writer. Although now closed, Grant worked with her family's restaurant business, Abe's Native Shrimp House, which preserved Gullah culture and history through the preparation of Gullah cuisine. Grant is a member of Mt. Calvary Missionary Baptist Church, which is 103 years old.

Christena Bledsoe, a writer and former reporter at the *Atlanta Journal Constitution*, cowrote *God, Dr. Buzzard, and the Bolito Man* by Cornelia Walker Bailey, which received starred reviews from *Kirkus* and *Publishers Weekly*.